D0048997

THE RACE
UNDERGROUND

THE RACE UNDERGROUND

BOSTON, NEW YORK, AND THE
INCREDIBLE RIVALRY THAT BUILT
AMERICA'S FIRST SUBWAY

DOUG MOST

ST. MARTIN'S PRESS

NEW YORK

THE RACE UNDERGROUND. Copyright © 2014 by Doug Most. All rights reserved.
Printed in the United States of America. For information, address St. Martin's Press,
175 Fifth Avenue, New York, N.Y. 10010.

www.stmartins.com

Library of Congress Cataloging-in-Publication Data

Most, Doug.
    The race underground: Boston, New York, and the incredible rivalry that built America's first subway / Doug Most.—First edition.
        pages cm
    Includes bibliographical references and index.
    ISBN: 978-0-312-59132-8 (hardcover)
    ISBN: 978-1-4668-4200-7 (e-book)
    1. Subways—Massachusetts—Boston—History.   2. Subways—New York (State)—New York—History.   3. Boston (Mass.)—History—19th century.   4. New York (N.Y.)—History—19th century.   5. Whitney, Henry Melville, 1839–1923.   6. Whitney, William C. (William Collins), 1841–1904.   7. Subways—United States—History.   8. Subways—United States—Design and construction—Case studies.   9. Urban transportation—United States—Case studies.   10. Competition—United States—Case studies.   I. Title.
    HE4491.B782M67 2014
    388.4'20974446109034—dc23   2013030525

St. Martin's Press books may be purchased for educational, business, or promotional use. For information on bulk purchases, please contact Macmillan Corporate and Premium Sales Department at 1-800-221-7945, extention 5442, or write specialmarkets@macmillan.com.

First Edition: February 2014

10   9   8   7   6   5   4   3   2   1

For
Mimi,
Julia,
and Ben

CONTENTS

Constructing the tunnel will be simple,
just like cellar digging.

—JOHN B. MCDONALD, THE FIRST CONTRACTOR HIRED TO BUILD
THE NEW YORK CITY SUBWAY, JANUARY 18, 1900

Introduction

TWO CITIES, ONE CRISIS

IN THE SECOND HALF OF the nineteenth century, the horse-pulled streetcar, clip-clopping along at five miles per hour and filled with an unbearable stench, slowly began to cripple two great American cities. In Boston and New York, there were too many people and no safe, fast, reliable way for them to move from one neighborhood to the next. In the summer heat, carriages inched forward until the animals reared up their legs in frustration, and police had to come out swinging their clubs to restore peace. During the winter it was no better. Horses struggled to get their footing in the snow and ice and were driven to exhaustion or sometimes death. When a solution to the problem finally emerged—a subway—it was rejected time and again, either by corrupt politicians, selfish businessmen, or terrified citizens. "A menace to the health of the public," a man of the times said. A newspaper article went even further, describing a subway ride like "living in a tomb."

This is a story about fabulously wealthy Gilded Age industrialists and dirt-poor immigrants during a period when Fifth Avenue mansions and Beacon Hill brownstones stood blocks from sheet-covered shanties and rat-infested tenements. But it's also about an age of innovation, an exhilarating time after the Civil War when the telephone, lightbulb, typewriter, cash register, dishwasher, sewing machine, electric motor, and even dynamite were born of a need to make life simpler.

As the pressure mounted on Boston and New York in the final decade of the nineteenth century to reduce the congestion on their streets and expand their livable boundaries, it was an unlikely pair of brothers from a tiny town in central Massachusetts who rose up to help. They were powerful men. Respected, ambitious, and rich, they were willing to bribe whomever they needed and able to buy whatever they wanted. Two years and two hundred miles apart, they would lean on each other, learn from each other, love each other, and, in one particular moment of desperation, they would even share their most important employee, a brilliant young engineer, with each other. But they could not have been more different.

The older brother was a late bloomer who lived near Boston. He was short, stocky, nearly deaf after a childhood bout with scarlet fever, and walked with a stoop. He might have amounted to nothing if not for his father's help. The younger brother, living in New York City, was the family star. Athletic and lean, he attended Yale and Harvard, married into a fortune, rescued the United States Navy, and was recruited to run for president. Together they came from a long line of Puritans, a family that over four centuries would claim ties to the Revolutionary War, the cotton gin, the color motion picture, a world-famous museum, and even a baseball team called the Mets. Of their family's many achievements, these brothers would notch the most significant one of all. They helped launch the birth of the subway in America and, with it, a new era of rapid urban transit.

This is as much a tale of American ingenuity and the perseverance of man as it is about two powerful siblings and two rival cities. Boston and New York, in their pursuit to move their people faster, safer, and farther, would each experience death and destruction, breakthroughs and breakdowns, thrilling firsts and embarrassing failures, all while keeping a close eye on the other's progress. The stories of their two subways would captivate and galvanize their citizens and drag out for decades, straddling the end of one century and the start of another. In one of these cities, the race underground actually started twenty-five years before it did in the other, on a mild fall afternoon not long after the final shot of the Civil War had been fired.

That was the day an odd-looking, churchgoing, opera-loving skinny young inventor looked out onto his city's streets and decided he could no longer tolerate the mayhem.

Part One

THE VISIONARIES

I

A SECRET SUBWAY

THEY CAME ON FOOT, AND BY CARRIAGE, and from the city and around the country. On September 12, 1867, thousands of people lined up outside the Fourteenth Street armory, a hulking gray building in downtown New York, to see what the future held for them. The women wore hoop skirts and their finest bonnets, the men came in their dark suits and perfectly knotted ties. The American Institute Fair was more than an event. It was a monument to the times, the place to come and see the latest crazy ideas that the inventors of the day had dreamed up and to get a glimpse of the fantastic future. This year one particular innovation, which a reporter for *The New York Times* had seen during a sneak preview and raved about in an article, was turning the thirty-seventh year of the fair into a spectacle before it even opened.

The American Institute Fair, started in 1829 as a way to encourage innovation in the country, showcased a collection of novelties, some practical, some bizarre. For a number of years the fair had no permanent home, until it grew so big that organizers decided it deserved its own space. A group of financiers, including August Belmont and William Cullen Bryant, two of New York's richest men, imagined a warehouse-sized building more grand than London's glittering Crystal Palace. And on Forty-second Street and Sixth Avenue, in the same place where George

Washington's troops had once been chased across a field by redcoats, that's what they built. Their own Crystal Palace was shaped like a Greek cross and topped by an enormous 123-foot-high dome, the tallest in America. With eighteen hundred tons of iron and fifteen thousand panes of clear enameled glass, there was nothing else like it. When it opened on July 14, 1853, President Franklin Pierce was there to welcome in a new era when dazzling advances in technology and science would define the country's direction.

One year later at the fair, a clever mechanic named Elisha Graves Otis showed how climbing hundreds of stairs no longer had to be an obstacle for cities to grow upward. His elevator, a new invention that was pulled up by ropes, was not only safe but heralded the age of buildings much taller than eight, ten, or twelve stories. With a crowd standing around his elevator, Otis rode it to its highest level and, for the riveted audience below, reached out and cut the elevator's only rope. Instead of plummeting down, he fell only a few inches and then stopped, showing everybody how the safety catch he had installed worked.

A few years after that, in 1856, another promising inventor and entrepreneur brought a typewriter he'd been tinkering with to the fair. A short and skinny thirty-year-old man with slicked-back black hair and a razor-thin mustache, Alfred Beach was a devoted churchgoer and opera lover who rose early and went to bed early. When he was awake, he was in perpetual motion, exercising regularly and working with one thing or another. He despised vacations. Any spare time that he had, he spent toying with wires, cables, or any contraption he could get his hands on, always with the hope of understanding how it worked and how it could be improved.

In 1848, after Beach had spent almost an entire year exploring the inner workings of the typewriter, he discovered that by having the keys strike both sides of the paper rather than one side, embossed, or raised, letters would be created that could be felt. He knew that if the letters could be felt with the fingertips, then the blind would be able to read. The device worked, and it won him praise from fellow inventors and affirmed in his own mind a desire to do something even greater. It took him years to refine his idea enough to where he was comfortable showing it to the world. And when he finally brought it to the American Institute Fair in 1856, it was a hit. It was recognized as the most advanced typewriting machine yet and won first prize and a gold medal.

Those were the sorts of inventions that drew people, sometimes more than five thousand a day, to the fair every year. And Crystal Palace was as much of an attraction as the inventions inside. The palace was described as "beautiful beyond description." It was also thought to be indestructible thanks to its cast-iron beams. But on October 5, 1858, with two thousand people roaming the exhibitions, one of the storage rooms caught on fire. In minutes the flames had shot through the wood flooring and began melting the walls and roof. As the crowd raced outside to safety, Crystal Palace was swallowed up by sparks, smoke, and flames until it collapsed into a heap. Days later, just five years after its celebrated opening, it was nothing but a pile of rubble. Scavengers came to sift through the remains in hopes of finding a souvenir from the building that was supposed to signal America's new dawn of invention.

Erecting a new permanent home for the fair was out of the question. In 1867, its home was the Fourteenth Street armory, between Sixth and Seventh avenues, a building as plain as Crystal Palace was extravagant. Inside, there were tables and booths showing off the dreams of hundreds of inventors: medical instruments, pianos, sewing machines, steam engines, wagons, sleighs, electric telegraphs, boots, hats, gloves, kitchen utensils, furniture, artificial limbs, wigs, fishing tackle, pocket knives, umbrellas, and toys. There were inventions that rolled along the floor and others that lined the walls. But it was the latest idea from Beach, this one suspended from the ceiling, that crowds flocked to see.

ALFRED ELY BEACH WAS BORN into a prestigious family on September 1, 1826, in Springfield, Massachusetts, an hour west of Boston. His father, Moses Yale Beach, owned *The New York Sun,* a popular daily newspaper that sold for a penny, mostly to the city's working class. He sent his boy to Monson Academy, one of the very best private schools, near

Springfield. Alfred Beach learned from his father at an early age that it was fine to dream big but more important to respect an honest day's work. His first taste of labor was as a newsboy, hawking *The Sun* on the streets of New York. From there he moved on to work in the press room, where he set type and left each day covered in ink and sweat. And after that he moved up to the newsroom, first to do menial accounting work, and then to work as a reporter.

He loved working with his father. But he dreamed of striking out on his own. In 1845, another young man from Massachusetts named Rufus Porter presented him with that chance. Porter had just published the very first issue of a weekly magazine he created, called *Scientific American*. Four pages long, it sold for a subscription rate of two dollars a year. The first edition included a note from Porter explaining how useful he believed his publication could be. "As a family newspaper," Porter wrote, "it will convey more useful intelligence to children and young people, than five times its cost in school instruction."

Scientific American was published every Thursday morning and was filled with original engravings of new inventions, improvements, or ideas, along with scientific essays, poems, and even things completely unrelated to science, like moral and religious musings. But Porter saw himself as more than an inventor or editor. He was also an artist who enjoyed painting portraits. Not surprisingly, he quickly lost interest in a magazine devoted to science, and, barely ten months after he founded *Scientific American*, Porter went looking for a buyer.

Beach was twenty years old and because of his father's newspaper saw the value of the printed word. But he didn't have the money to go it alone. He needed a partner. Thinking back to his days at his private school in Massachusetts, he reached out to a good friend that he thought might make the perfect business partner. Orson Desaix Munn moved to New York, and in July 1846 the two of them paid $800 for the tiny, obscure technical magazine and its subscription list of two hundred names. It marked the beginning of a friendship and partnership that would last nearly fifty years.

Scientific American had only a few hundred subscribers under Rufus

Porter. But as Alfred Beach and Orson Munn learned once they took it over, inventors of the day saw real value in the magazine. The inventors wanted help from like-minded dreamers who saw the potential in their ideas. Beach and Munn had barely settled into their offices in 1846 when they were besieged with letters from inventors, or sometimes with unannounced visits. The requests were always the same: Help me apply for a patent and secure it, and I'll pay whatever it takes. Beach and Munn realized that *Scientific American* was more than a magazine. It was a trusted brand.

Late in 1846, the two launched a new business. If an inventor had an idea, the owners of the Scientific American Patent Agency would happily take their money, help them write the perfect patent application, and track the progress of it once it reached the U.S. Patent Office in Washington. There was no other business like it in the country, and before long Beach was traveling to Washington every two weeks to monitor the hundreds of patents he or Munn helped write. Eventually the business was filing three thousand patents a year and Beach was forced to split his time between New York and a branch office in Washington, directly across the street from the patent office. The patent business earned Beach a fortune and some measure of fame. He became a pied piper of sorts for the American inventor, the one they all sought out for advice, opinions, or help with a patent. Thomas Edison walked in one day to show Beach a device he called the phonograph. Beach turned a crank on Edison's small machine and a voice piped up, "Good morning, sir. How are you? How do you like the talking box?" He liked it, and he helped Edison file a patent. He also would help Alexander Graham Bell, Samuel F. B. Morse, and thousands more.

But it was *Scientific American* that gave Beach the platform he craved to promote his own personal interests and inventions. Beach and Munn were able to quickly resurrect the magazine by focusing its content less on the highly technical science stories and more on what they knew best: curious inventions and practical, interesting patents. Simply by printing a weekly list of patents given to them directly from the U.S. Patent Office, Beach and Munn increased the number of subscriptions to *Scientific*

American, and it took off: by 1848, not even two years after they bought it, the circulation exceeded ten thousand readers.

Beach was becoming a man of real importance. When his father decided in 1848 to hand over management of his newspaper to his two sons, Moses and Alfred, Alfred's prominence reached even greater heights. He owned the most respected and lucrative science magazine in the country. He had the attention of every serious and not-so-serious inventor across the land. And now he was running a daily newspaper with more than fifty thousand readers in the nation's largest city. He had a vast and growing audience riveted on his every opinion. And he was only twenty-two years old.

THE MID–NINETEENTH CENTURY WAS a magical time for anybody who loved to tinker and had good ideas and good hands. Inventors were changing the way people lived their lives and ran their businesses. Elias Howe, not yet thirty years old, introduced his sewing machine in 1846, and within a few years the garment-making industry was revolutionized and clothes became more affordable. In 1847, a middle-aged inventor from Charlestown, Massachusetts, named Samuel Morse, who had been working for more than a decade to perfect his idea of speeding up long-distance, person-to-person communications, received a patent for an invention called the telegraph. A year later, a blacksmith from New Bedford, Massachusetts, changed the whaling industry with a new type of harpoon. And farming was in the midst of huge change. The American economy relied heavily on the success of the farmer, who might spend an entire day doing backbreaking work in the fields to plow or harvest only a single acre. But as 1850 approached, each passing year brought farmers more relief. A grain elevator invented in Buffalo dramatically sped up the hoisting of grain from ships into bins. The production of artificial manure to help crops grow began to take off, and the artificial-fertilizer industry was born. New inventions allowed farmers who were previously able to manage only a dozen acres to handle a hundred or more. Amid all this upheaval, no industry underwent more dramatic change than the transportation industry.

In 1825, most commuters who lived in cities got to work the same way. They walked. Only the rich could afford to own or hire a private carriage, and the idea of multiple people riding together in the same vehicle seemed farfetched. New York City had nearly two hundred thousand residents, most of whom were crowded into a small portion of the island. Only as more immigrants arrived and the population grew did the footprint of the livable parts of New York expand. That's when Abraham Brower saw an opportunity.

Brower asked the coach-making business of Wade & Leverich in 1827 to design and build for him a vehicle that could hold twelve people. The vehicle, which he called *Accommodation*, had large wooden wheels with spokes, open sides, and two compartments inside, each with a forward-facing and backward-facing seat for three people. Steps on the side made getting in and out easy, and for a flat fare of one shilling, passengers could be whisked almost two miles up and down Broadway. In bad weather, the driver would sometimes go slightly out of his way to get a passenger closer to home.

Emboldened by the success of *Accommodation,* Brower added a second vehicle with some improvements. The door was in the back, with iron stairs, and inside the seats ran lengthwise instead of across. The new design made the ride more social for passengers, thus the name *Sociable* was painted on its side. Boston, in the same year, had seen a similar service introduced, which ran on a regular schedule. For twelve cents, passengers could ride between South Boston and the downtown area. But no other American city jumped on the experiment, and for a short period Boston and New York alone had these precursors to urban mass transit systems.

While Americans were just getting used to the idea of riding with others, Brower began to hear of an even bigger, more lumbering vehicle taking over the streets of Paris and London. It was called an omnibus, and on a spring day in 1831, he introduced it to the streets of New York. The sight of the driver sitting on a raised seat and a small boy standing on the rear steps to collect the fare of twelve and a half cents was jarring for New Yorkers at first. But before long more than a hundred decorated omnibuses were crowding the streets of the city, with names painted on the sides, from *George Washington* to *Lady Washington* to *Benjamin Franklin*. They were popular. And they caused complete chaos.

For the individual owners of the omnibuses, nothing mattered more than the paying passenger. Drivers whipped their horses repeatedly to speed them past a competitor to the next potential fare, even if it meant a harrowing few seconds for those already on board. Grazing a lamppost to cut a corner or to cut in front of a rival was fair game, and pedestrians not paying attention could get maimed by a cornering horse or the trailing carriage. Nobody benefited more from the crowded, jostling cars than the pickpocket. The omnibus, which had started out with such promise, quickly lost favor with the people. "Bedlam on wheels," is how *The New York Herald* described it. The bedlam would not last, and it would give way to something better.

ON A BITING MORNING IN late 1832, Walter Bowne, a former state senator entering his third term as New York mayor, joined a sidewalk crowd of high-society gentlemen in top hats and ladies in satin dresses standing in the Bowery district. They came to see where street transit systems were headed. A year earlier, Bowne had signed an ordinance allowing the New York & Harlem Railroad Company to build a railroad between the Harlem River and Twenty-third Street. It was promised to the city that a transportation system on rails would be a dramatic upgrade for passengers, a smoother and faster ride than wooden wheels on cobblestone streets, and much easier for the horses. It took months for a route to be agreed upon, and on November 26, 1832, shouting spectators lined the downtown streets to come see what they had been told was the future of transportation.

Flat iron strips had been fastened to blocks of stone embedded in the ground, and steel wheels were designed with grooves to ride directly on the rails. The new carriages, on the outside, looked no different than omnibuses except they were bigger, able to carry up to thirty people. But the three compartments each had their own entrance door, and the seats and sides were lined with a fine, plush cloth.

When the signal was given, the horses trotted off and the first carriage filled with city officials zipped away behind them at a speed the spectators had never seen. It even caused some to gasp, with a mixture of fear and excitement. A second car followed right behind, carrying the top men of the New York & Harlem Railroad Company. As the vehicles pulled away, the railroad officials knew that for their experiment to succeed financially, passengers would have to feel safe riding on rails rather than on the solid street they had grown accustomed to. They would need to prove that starting and, more important, stopping were as simple as applying the brake designed to grind the wheels to a halt. The two carriages had gone only a few blocks when John Lozier, the vice president of the company, stood at the corner of Bond Street. As the trotting horses neared, he raised one arm. The driver of the first car quickly brought his vehicle to a stop. But the driver of the second, thinking he was still steering an omnibus, pulled on the reigns of the horses rather than applying the brake, as he'd been taught. The horses neighed and slowed, but they couldn't stop in time, and they collided into the first car. The passengers emerged unscathed, and the damage to the cars was minimal. Other than a few snickers from the spectators, what perhaps was the first street railway accident in the United States could do nothing to dampen the excitement of the ride that preceded it.

"This event will go down in the history of our country as the greatest achievement of man," Mayor Bowne said afterward.

The Courier & Inquirer, one of New York's leading papers of the day, gushed over the event. "Those who made violent objections to laying down these tracks and fancied a thousand dangers to the passing traveler, now look at the work with pleasure and surprise," the paper wrote the next day.

By the 1840s the omnibus was not even a decade old on the streets of New York, Boston, Baltimore, Philadelphia, Pittsburgh, Albany, and Cincinnati. But already it was dying. A respected doctor and author named Asa Greene had made the routine challenge of crossing Broadway sound like a modern-day video game. "You must button your coat tight about you, see that your shoes are secure at the heels, settle your hat firmly on your head, look up street and down street, at the self-same moment, to see what carts and carriages are upon you, and then run for your life."

The street railway car carried more passengers, rode faster, and provided a quieter, smoother ride than the omnibus, and any fears that people had of its safety vanished once they climbed on board. The "age of the omnibus" that the newspapers had been so quick to herald only a few years earlier was over. The age of the street railway was here.

ON NOVEMBER 3, 1849, Alfred Beach could see clear down to the Hudson River from his top-floor office in downtown New York. That morning, *Scientific American* had published an article he wrote suggesting just about the craziest idea that New Yorkers had ever heard. It would be laughed at, mocked, and, ultimately, ignored. Nobody took it seriously in the days and weeks after it appeared, except for the young man who wrote it.

Looking out from his window at the corner of Fulton and Nassau streets in one of the city's tallest buildings, Beach could look up and see the next tall building being built, or he could look out to the water and see the parade of boats floating past in the New York harbor. The waters used to be filled mostly with tugboats, fishing boats, sloops, and the occasional mammoth steamship pulling in from Europe after the long crossing. But more recently, Beach was seeing a new type of boat dominate the harbor: Ferry boats, operated by more than twenty competing lines, were whisking an increasing tide of passengers out of Manhattan and taking them to the nearby shores of New Jersey, Staten Island, or Brooklyn. The suburbs were calling, luring city residents with open land, affordable rents, and a peacefulness that made New York feel increasingly less appealing. But there was also another, more troubling, reason that the big city no longer held the allure it once did.

On the chopped-up streets, garbage and debris were mixing with the perfume of horse-drawn carriages and piles of dung to create an odor that was almost unbearable to breathe in. And the packed sidewalks and overcrowded streets were grinding New York to an angry standstill. On some mornings, the carriages would be forced to stand motionless for half an hour or longer. When they finally moved at all, it was inches or feet at a time. One horse would lurch forward, then another, and just when it seemed as if the congestion was about to ease, it wouldn't. All day long, drivers jostled with other drivers, whipping their own horses or the one next to them, competing for passengers. The horses didn't like it any more than the well-dressed passengers inside the carriages they were pulling. The animals neighed at each other and sometimes raised up their front legs, causing fear and pandemonium. Pedestrians who tried to cross the street knew the risk they were taking carried deadly consequences with one misstep.

"We can travel from New York half-way to Philadelphia in less time than the length of Broadway," *The New York Tribune* wrote. Beach didn't see a problem in this clutter. From high above the city streets, he saw opportunity.

In 1849, Beach, by now sporting the skinny mustache that would become his trademark feature, lived a walkable distance from his office. And yet dodging the horses, the carriages, and the throngs of people each day turned his short walk from his office near City Hall to his house over on West Twentieth Street into a treacherous hour-long commute. After three years of listening to a parade of inventors promote their dreams to him, Beach decided it was time to share his own dream for his city, in an essay he published in *Scientific American*.

"Nothing less than a railway underneath, instead of one above," he wrote. "Railway life down stairs, instead of railway life up stairs. The idea is at least original, but anything except feasible, that is so far as the expense is concerned, for there would lie no difficulty in executing the work. To tunnel Broadway through the whole length, with openings and stairways at every corner. This subterranean passage is to be laid down with double track, with a road for foot passengers on either side—the whole to be brilliantly lighted with gas. The cars, which are to be drawn by horses, will stop ten seconds at every corner—thus performing the trip up and down, including stops, in about an hour."

Beach's proposal went nowhere. The newspapers ridiculed him and New Yorkers sneered. Who would risk going down there under the streets and sidewalks? That's where you go when you're dead. It was ludicrous. "It's better to wait for the Devil than to make roads down into hell," one critic said of the idea of subways. Only somebody who worked at a science magazine would believe something so outrageous could actually work. On and on the criticism went. Reluctantly, Beach took the hint and moved on.

ON MARCH 4, 1861, IGNORING the advice of those who feared for his safety, the president-elect, Abraham Lincoln, decided to travel through the streets of Washington to his inauguration with President James Buchanan. Together, in a horse-drawn carriage, they rode from the Willard Hotel to the steps of the Capitol Building. In the two months leading up to the inauguration, Texas, Georgia, Alabama, and South Carolina had seceded from the Union, and a civil war appeared unavoidable. Yet in his speech Lincoln promised peace unless an attack on his people left him no choice.

"There needs to be no bloodshed or violence," Lincoln said, "and there shall be none unless it be forced upon the national authority." Five weeks later it was, with the first shots fired at Fort Sumter. Not even the Civil War, however, would slow the transportation revolution under way. On January 9, 1863, nine days after Lincoln ended slavery by signing the Emancipation Proclamation, workers in London achieved one of mankind's greatest industrial breakthroughs. After four years of digging through mostly thick clay and rock, London opened the world's first subway.

But while London's subway, which came to be called the Underground, proved that a long tunnel could be built beneath a city to carry trains and move millions of passengers, it had numerous fundamental flaws. Those trains were powered by steam, and from the very first day the tunnels were filled with dark soot, black smoke, and showers of sparks that made for an altogether miserable traveling experience. Even the chief inspector of railways in Great Britain, Captain Douglas Galton, cautioned other cities from following London's lead. "An underground road is enormously expensive to construct," he said. "It greatly interferes with street traffic during construction, from the large quantities of material to be removed and brought to the surface; it can never be wholesome or free of deleterious gases, and in foggy weather it is always full of thick atmosphere, which increases the liability to accident and is very disagreeable to passengers." A rousing endorsement to a historical achievement it was not.

Beach believed the air in a subway had to feel no different than the air above ground, and just like he had taken apart the typewriter and made it better, he set to work to improve upon London's breakthrough. Five weeks after the underground Metropolitan Railway opened (and introduced "the metro" into the lexicon of transportation), Beach found his inspiration.

WHILE LONDONERS WERE STILL BUZZING over their new subway, another invention in the same city caught Beach's eye. The British postal service had approved a charter for a British engineer named T. W. Rammell and his partner, J. Latimer Clark. The two men had designed an underground, airtight tube that could carry mail and packages the short distance between a London post office and nearby suburb. Distributing the mail throughout the world's largest city was an immense and time-consuming task, and Rammell and Clark promised to make it easier. Their tube was only four feet in diameter, hardly big enough to carry people, but what excited Beach, and impressed British postal officials, was how the mail was moved inside Rammell's tube.

With a thirty-horsepower steam engine, Rammell produced compressed air that could blow a five-foot-long canister through the tube. The tube could carry 120 mailbags a day, blowing them the one-quarter mile in fifty-five seconds, a huge improvement over the ten minutes it took workers to push mail carts the same distance. It was so efficient that the post office gave Rammell a contract to build a maze of forty-eight tubes under

London's streets. When Beach heard how well this pneumatic-propulsion system worked, and that a couple of curious daredevils had even managed to climb aboard it for a short joyride, he was more certain than ever. It was clean. It was smooth. And when *Mechanics' Magazine* wrote of Rammell's invention, "We feel tolerably certain that the day is not very distant when metropolitan railway traffic can be conducted on this principle with so much success," Beach was convinced.

In 1865, he did for himself what he had done thousands of times for other inventors. He began the application process for a patent and set his eyes on the 1867 American Institute Fair.

"LADIES AND GENTLEMEN: IN THIS metropolis of the commerce of the new world, the American Institute uplifts the banner of labor and of creative art," Horace Greeley, the president of the institute and long-time editor of *The New York Tribune,* told the thousands gathered on the armory's floor in his opening address on September 12, 1867. He spoke about America's ability to create tools for farming that were far superior to anything seen in Great Britain. "No nation on earth can make them as good in quality or as cheap in price as we can make them here." His speech ended with loud applause, and the doors to the fair were thrown open.

Alfred Beach was there. And instead of one invention, he came with two. One was a small tube, twenty-four feet long and two feet wide, which was built to move letters and small packages through it with air blown by a fan. But most visitors barely stopped to study it.

His second idea was suspended from the ceiling by strong cables, and it stretched across the vast room, to all four corners. There was a long plywood tube, and fitted snugly inside of it, with only an inch to spare on the sides, was a cylindrical car with an open top that was big enough to hold ten people. The car rested on four wheels, and a steam engine positioned at one end of the tube powered a large fan that blew the car on its rails. When the fan was reversed, it acted like a vacuum and sucked the car back to its starting point. Throngs of people would stand for hours beneath the tube, lining up to ride it or simply to watch the car go back and forth. Beach himself made sure everybody at the fair, in the city, and beyond knew about the excitement surrounding his creation.

In an article in *Scientific American* published just before the fair opened, Beach wrote that he had developed a transportation system that was as "swift as Aeolus (god of breezes) and silent as Somnus (god of sleep and dreams)."

Halfway through the fair, on October 19, another article on Beach's pneumatic tube appeared in *Scientific American*. At the time that his article appeared, more than twenty-five thousand people had already ridden the tube and a new line was forming every day. Beach wanted to make sure the crowds kept coming.

"The most novel and attractive feature of the exhibition is by general consent conceded to be the pneumatic railway, erected by Mr. A. E. Beach," the article began. It spared no words of self-praise. "The car fits the tube like a piston and travels both ways with the utmost regularity and steadiness. Nothing can be more gentle and pleasant than the start and stoppage; no jerking or wrenching of any kind is observable."

The article focused on the railway's details, but in one line, it planted the notion that perhaps the pneumatic railway was the future of transportation. "It is probable that a pneumatic railway of considerable length for regular traffic will soon be laid down near New York."

Of the hundreds of inventions that filled the floor of the armory for six weeks, Beach's pneumatic tube was the sensation that could not be ignored. Everybody wanted to ride on it, and by the time the fair closed in November, more than seventy-five thousand people had. Beach wanted everyone to remember what they had witnessed, so that he could begin to push the idea with New York's lawmakers. He published a pamphlet in which he described in the simplest terms how his pneumatic railway worked.

"A tube, a car, a revolving fan!" he wrote. "Little more is required. The ponderous locomotive, with its various appurtenances, is dispensed with, and the light aerial fluid that we breathe is the substituted motor."

New Yorkers believed.

"Passengers by a through city tube could be carried from City Hall to Madison Square in five minutes, to Harlem and Manhattanville in fourteen minutes, to Washington Heights in twenty minutes, and by sub-river to Jersey City or Hoboken in five minutes," *The Times* wrote after the fair had ended.

Beach was jubilant. Just as it had in 1856 for his typewriter, the American Institute Fair once again awarded him its top prize, and New Yorkers were buzzing with talk about this sleek, quiet, smooth-riding train and how Alfred Beach had struck upon a solution to the overcrowding that everybody was clamoring for. Everybody, that is, except for the one person who really mattered, a three-hundred-pound state senator who also happened to be the crime boss ruling New York City.

WILLIAM MAGEAR "BOSS" TWEED JR. ran the most corrupt political machine in the country, Tammany Hall, and it was tied closely to the city's omnibus system. Tweed, with his blue eyes and long mess of a gray beard, stood six feet tall and was grotesquely overweight. Nothing happened in his city without his approval.

Born into a Scottish-American family in 1823, he joined his father's business making chairs as a boy, and in his early twenties he showed his outgoing spirit by convincing some seventy-five friends and strangers to join a fire company he was starting up. It came to be known as "Big Six," and it was the first sign of the power of persuasion that Tweed could have over people. His men wore red shirts, and they elected their husky leader as foreman; soon he was wearing a white fire coat while leading Americus Engine Company Number 6 in fighting fires. It proved to be a short-lived career for him when the city's chief fire engineer booted him out for fighting with other fire companies, but all that did was raise Tweed's profile in a city where Democrats were hungry for leaders. They drafted him to run for assistant alderman as a twenty-seven-year-old in 1850, and he lost. But a year later he was back, and this time his victory marked the beginning of what would be two decades of ruling the city by whatever means necessary.

Using kickbacks, violence, and bribery, Tweed became the third largest landowner in the city and one of its richest men (a point he took great
pride in, by flaunting his giant mansions, private cars, yachts, and a diamond pin that he wore every day on his shirt). For years, as New York's
deputy street commissioner and later as public works commissioner, he
extorted a nickel out of every omnibus fare in the city. And with twenty-
nine bus lines and fourteen horse-pulled lines carrying more than one
hundred million passengers a year in New York, Tweed had become a very
wealthy man. Boss Tweed, determined to maintain his stranglehold on
the city's street transit system, blocked any attempt that came along that
might threaten his empire, with a whisper, a nudge, a payoff, a threat, or a
promise. He instructed those in power, all the way up to the governor's
office, to reject what he said to reject and approve what he said to approve.
And they did. Most men who ran up against Boss Tweed eventually
backed down, knowing it was a fight they could never win. One did not.

TWEED REFUSED TO GIVE BEACH a penny for his project or to grant
him the charter that he needed. In 1868, Tweed was at his most powerful,
after the candidates he owned had won city and statewide offices. If he
didn't want something done, it didn't get done. But Beach was a foe unlike any Tweed had encountered. Beach believed that his pneumatic subway was going to change the city, maybe even the world. That attitude
drove him in the same year that he unveiled his subway to donate a large
sum of money to open what eventually became the Beach Institute in
Savannah, Georgia, a school for freed slaves that was staffed with white
teachers from the North. With his school, as with his subway, Beach
was determined to build a proud legacy. And nobody, not even the man
who ruthlessly reigned over the city, was going to stop him.

Beach knew he couldn't outmuscle Tweed. And he was far too proud
to be bribed and pay Tweed a cut of his subway fares. He would have to
outsmart him. In 1869, he applied to the New York State legislature for a
charter to build not the giant, people-moving tube he had shown at the
fair, but the much smaller one to carry mail. He proposed building an

underground mail line near Broadway that would run between Cedar and Warren streets, connect to the main post office at Liberty Street, and provide even faster mail service than the telegraph. Tweed studied Beach's proposal carefully. The tubes Beach was proposing to build each had a diameter of just four and a half feet, far too small to carry a train car that could hold people. Satisfied that Beach's idea posed no threat to him, Tweed and the rest of the state lawmakers granted Beach his fifty-year charter to build mail tubes under the city.

But Beach's deception had only begun. A few weeks later, he sheepishly returned to the state legislature with a minor request. He asked the lawmakers to amend his charter so he could build one large tube for much less money than it would take to build two smaller ones. Tweed, by then, had moved on to other concerns and nobody questioned Beach's request. It passed.

That tweak gave Beach the proper paperwork he needed to carry out the most daring project New Yorkers had ever seen. He had no intention or desire to speed up mail service in New York. He was going to build a subway in secret. And he would do it almost directly across from City Hall and Boss Tweed's minions.

DEVLIN'S CLOTHING STORE WAS A five-story, thriving commercial success. Brothers Daniel and Jeremiah Devlin opened their business in 1843 a few blocks away from City Hall, but when business took off they needed more space for their endless racks of ready-made frocks, suits, umbrellas, underwear, ties, and trousers. One of the reasons the new space near the corner of Warren Street and Broadway worked so well was the gigantic basement, which went two levels deep underground.

Alfred Beach needed just such a space for his own new business, the Beach Pneumatic Transit Company. After scouting for real estate all along Broadway, when he saw the basement of Devlin's and noticed that it could be accessed from the sidewalk of Warren Street, he negotiated a deal with the brothers. For $4,000 dollars a year, starting on December 1, 1868, he leased their entire basement for a period of five years.

Beach spent the next year focused on the single piece of machinery he would need to dig his tunnel. The device he came up with was ingenious. It resembled a hollowed-out barrel and used a water pump to exert pressure and a sharp digging mechanism that could loosen sixteen inches of soil with each push forward. He also designed a metal hood over the edge of the shield that would protect his workers from falling debris, or in the catastrophic event of a collapse.

But before he could start digging, a different kind of catastrophe nearly derailed Beach's project in the fall of 1869. A pair of Boss Tweed cronies schemed to drive up the price of gold by buying it in bulk. By late September the price of gold had risen to an astronomical $137 per ounce, and by the morning of Friday, September 24, it had risen to $150. Frenzy enveloped Wall Street, and riots nearly broke out. The National Guard was put on notice. And yet gold kept rising, to $160, as lunchtime passed. Brokers' lives were destroyed, and one even shot himself at home before the day was over. By the time the government intervened in the afternoon and sold $4 million in gold, it was too late. Wall Street's first "Black Friday" exposed how two men, acting alone, could bring the country to the brink of financial ruin.

Black Friday touched everybody, including Beach, who lost a fortune. But he was too far invested in his subway to stop, and three months after Black Friday, he was ready to start tunneling. In late December of 1869, Beach; his son, Frederick, whom he tapped to be the foreman of the project; and a small group of men started arriving at Devlin's after the store had closed for the night. They brought down picks, shovels, covered wagons, bricks, lanterns, and other tools. Following Beach's instructions to tunnel south directly under Broadway from Warren Street and then curve slightly to just below Murray Street, the laborers worked quietly to avoid rousing suspicion on the streets above. Night after night, six men would stand inside the shield while another half dozen would perform the more tedious tasks to polish the tunnel. Some carried out the dirt in the covered wagons, others laid the bricks to line the tunnel, and still others laid the tracks to carry a single car. The walls were painted white, iron rods were installed through the tunnel's roof up to the pavement, and gaslights and oxygen lamps were hung. It was an efficient operation. But it was also scary work, too claustrophobic for some workers, who simply walked off the job. The rumbling from a street railway's wheels overhead created a terrifying roar that made the late-night work nerve-racking. Still, thanks to surprisingly soft soil and the efficient tunneling shield, the digging went quickly. On a good night, one crew would dig forward eight feet.

Beach was relieved at how smoothly the work progressed until one night when the shield buckled and the ground shook. The soft dirt had come to an abrupt end, and the workers stared at a stone wall in front of them. It was an old Dutch fort from before the Revolutionary War. Beach faced a dilemma. Either the wall had to come down or the project was over. And nobody knew if removing the wall would cause Broadway to buckle or collapse from above. Beach told his men to carefully chip away at it and take it down, stone by stone. It took several nights, and Beach stood by as every stone was removed and passed from worker to worker and carted out into the night. But the ceiling held, the wall came down, and the digging resumed.

As hard as Beach tried to keep the work a secret from the world above, it was impossible. The operation required wooden scaffolding and iron tubes and occasional pieces of enormous machinery that would arrive at the corner of Broadway and Warren, where it would sit for hours or days before mysteriously disappearing down the steps, never to be seen again.

New York's mayor, Abraham Hall, one of Boss Tweed's loyalists, grew increasingly suspicious of what the Beach Pneumatic Transit Company was up to, and when a section of Broadway near Warren Street sunk ever so slightly, the mayor acted. On January 3, 1870, he sent an aide over to the construction site with a written order, demanding to be let in so he could inspect the work. He got nowhere. Beach's men had strict orders to let nobody in and to remind anyone who tried that they were granted a charter by the state to complete their tunnel. As for whether his work was responsible for that minor sinking of Broadway, the response from Beach was simple: Nonsense! The New York Times reported the flap the next day and suggested that Hall was not going to back away.

"As the street in which the company have commenced operations is partially blocked up with wooden scaffolding and iron tubes, it is likely the mayor will at least counsel them to remove these," the paper wrote.

But Beach was equally stubborn. On January 8, he released a statement: "In reference to the ridiculous stories that have been circulated about our men being sworn to secrecy, and the doors being closed to all persons, there is no truth to them." The company promised to make any repairs to the surface roads and begged for four more weeks of patience.

Mayor Hall backed off, and Beach bought himself time. And one month later, fifty-eight days after the digging began, the tunnel was finished. It was a perfect cylinder of 312 feet. All that was needed now were the two most important pieces, the subway car and the fan to blow the car down the tracks.

The design for the car was unlike anything people were riding on the streets above. It was much smaller than the horsecars, and upholstered seats lined the sides so that it felt like a comfortable lounge inside, with bright lighting and plenty of room to hold twenty-two people. The sliding doors closed with a whoosh.

As for the fan, Beach knew that he needed one so powerful it could easily blow a car 120 feet long and fourteen feet wide down the tracks. He found it in Connersville, Indiana, where the P. H. & F. M. Roots Company had built a powerful fan to ventilate mines. The Roots Patent Force Rotary Blower, nicknamed the Western Tornado, was the critical piece to Beach's pneumatic subway. At fifty tons, it was so big it took a train with five platform cars to deliver it from Indiana. It was discretely placed at the Warren Street end of the tunnel, and testing of it began.

The air for the fan came through a shaft and grate near Murray Street, inside City Hall Park, and when the fan was working it would occasionally blow the hats off unsuspecting pedestrians passing over the grate. Down below, it worked just as Beach hoped. Vacuum-tight doors in both stations controlled the air pressure so that the passengers barely noticed the breeze from the fan. When it was in "blowing" mode, the car gently but swiftly flew down the tracks at about six miles per hour, until it tripped a wire that caused a bell to ring back at Warren Street. That was the trigger for the engineer to pull a rope that reversed the fan, putting it into "sucking" mode. And then the car would return in an equally smooth ride.

The pneumatic subway worked. But Beach didn't just want to impress the visitors he was planning to invite down. He wanted to dazzle them, not to mention distract them from any fears they might have of being underground with vermin and demons. He remembered the stories about how dark and miserable the London subway was. And he knew he had only one chance to convince New York that his subway was the future of transportation. He spared no expense, using more than $70,000 of his own savings to make sure the station was a place where people would actually enjoy waiting. The waiting room was enormous, more than 120 feet long, and it was lavish, with chandeliers, mirrors, a towering grandfather clock, a fountain with a basin stocked with goldfish, paintings, settees, and a grand piano.

News that the tunnel was finished leaked out on February 19, 1870, after a reporter for *The Tribune* disguised himself as a worker and snuck in. His story the next day provided a detailed description of the tunnel and the stations, but it was the accompanying editorial attacking the subway as useless and not worth any further attention that galled Beach. A week later, he decided it was time to let his work be judged. On February 26, 1870, Beach invited lawmakers, reporters, and dignitaries from the science community to step down into the basement of Devlin's.

THE FINAL TOUCHES PAID OFF. Not a single criticism was heard. The tubular train worked beautifully, whisking the visitors one block, from Warren Street to Murray Street, and then sucking them back. The reviews the next day were glowing.

"The problem of tunneling Broadway has been solved," wrote *The Evening Mail.*

"Certainly the most novel, if not the most successful, enterprise that New York has seen for many a day is the pneumatic tunnel under Broadway," *The New York Times* gushed. "A myth, or a humbug, it has hitherto been called by everybody who has been excluded from its interior; but hereafter the incredulous public can have the opportunity of examining the undertaking and judging of its merits. Yesterday the tunnel was thrown open to the inspection of visitors for the first time and it must be said that every one of them came away surprised and gratified. Such as expected to find a dismal cavernous retreat under Broadway, opened their eyes at the elegant reception room, the light, airy tunnel, and the general appearance of taste and comfort in all the apartments; and those who entered to pick out some scientific flaw in the project, were silenced by the completeness of the machinery, the solidity of the work, and the safety of the running apparatus."

Beach reacted swiftly, and two days later, on March 1, he threw open his tunnel to the public. Come and ride my subway, he crowed, for just twenty-five cents. And to prove that he, unlike his nemesis Tweed, was not motivated by money, Beach promised to donate all the money raised to the Union House for the Orphans of Soldiers and Sailors.

Come they did, by the thousands. They had read about the tunnel and the enormous fan, and they sat down in the car leery that it would blow them right out of their seats. Instead, the breeze was barely noticeable and many of them enjoyed the ride so much they stayed on for multiple trips, going back and forth between Murray and Warren for twenty minutes or more. One woman later described her ride as "most delightful" and called Beach's invention "one of the greatest improvements of the day."

"We took our seats in the pretty car, the gayest company of twenty that ever entered a vehicle," she wrote. "The conductor touched a telegraph wire on the wall of the tunnel and before we knew it, so gentle was the start, we were in motion, moving from Warren Street down Broadway. In a few moments the conductor opened the door and called out, Murray Street with a business-like air that made us all shout with laughter. The car came to rest in the gentlest possible style and immediately began to move back to Warren Street where it had no sooner arrived, than in the same gentle and mysterious manner it moved back again to Murray Street."

This, Beach told his visitors, was only the beginning. He proudly told them the days of riding in a dusty horsecar on crowded streets were coming to an end and that no snowstorm would ever again cripple their city. Daily trips to work that used to take an hour might only take a few minutes, he promised.

"We propose to run the line to Central Park, about five miles in all," Beach said. "When completed, we should be able to carry twenty thousand passengers a day at speeds up to a mile a minute."

There was only one obstacle. Boss Tweed was enraged. Not only had Beach snuck around him to complete his subway, he had done it directly across the street from him.

"New York needs a subway," Beach said after learning of Tweed's reaction.

Tweed was unmoved. The two men were poised to go to battle. It would not be a fair fight.

IN LESS THAN A YEAR of operating, more than four hundred thousand passengers rode Beach's one-block train for the sheer novelty of it. That emboldened Beach even more. Imagine, he argued, if it actually took them places! State legislators saw the public's enthusiasm for the subway and wasted no time taking up Beach's request to extend his line up to Central Park and to raise the $5 million he needed from private investors. But at the same time, Tweed was drafting his own bill. He called his the Viaduct Plan, and he made sure that it landed on the desk of Governor John Hoffman, a man he helped get elected, at the same time as Beach's proposal.

BOSS TWEED'S VIADUCT PLAN was absurd. It called for forty-foot stone arches to be built throughout the city to carry elevated railroad lines. And the astronomical $80 million tab would not only be footed by New York taxpayers, but Tweed arranged the financing in such a way that he personally stood to reap a fortune from it.

Both bills passed easily, and they landed in Governor Hoffman's hands in early 1871. New Yorkers anxiously waited for him to decide between a clever subway that would relieve their city once and for all of the unbearable congestion or one more attempt by their corrupt state senator to hold them hostage. What nobody knew at the time was that three years earlier, in 1868, when Hoffman was running for governor, Tweed had sidled up to him one afternoon at a campaign stop and whispered in his ear that if the governor stuck by his side, he'd be the Democratic nominee for president in 1872.

It's likely that promise was still echoing in Hoffman's ears in March 1871 as he considered both Beach's bill and Tweed's proposal. Beach's bill came first, and he swiftly vetoed it. Legislators tried to override Hoffman's veto, but Tweed's influence, along with the opposition of the city's chief public works engineer, were too much to overcome and the override failed by one vote. To no one's surprise, Hoffman then signed Tweed's Viaduct Plan into law.

It was a devastating blow for Beach. He had stuck to his honest roots. He had persevered. He had succeeded in building a tunnel like nothing anybody had seen before, a subway that people wanted to ride. And he had still lost. Unable to extend his one-block tunnel any further, as each day passed the curiosity around it wore off and the crowds thinned. New ideas were gaining greater interest, like the one Tweed had proposed, only more refined. After all, why tear up the town to bury tracks underground when you can build tracks overhead on pillars with much less disruption and still reduce congestion on the streets? Maybe the elevated rail really was the future, after all.

As for Beach, he had a subway to nowhere. And he could not keep pouring his own money into it just to keep it going for the sheer novelty. He needed one last break to keep his dream alive, and New Yorkers were pulling for him. At a humdrum town meeting on congestion, a lawyer and respected judge named Sanford E. Church summed up the feelings of the masses. "Next to the air we breathe, or the food we eat," he said, "no one thing in city life touches so vitally the comfort and interest of every citizen, of every condition, in every calling, every day, as this question of city transit."

• • •

ONE DAY EARLY IN July 1871, a young man walked into the offices of George Jones, the publisher of *The New York Times*. He said his name was Matthew O'Rourke, that he used to work as a bookkeeper in the city's comptroller office, and that he had tried to tell his story to other newspapers, but none of them seemed interested. He also used to be a former military reporter, which is why when he saw some odd claims that had been filed under "Armories and Drill Rooms" for half a million dollars, he didn't ignore them. And when he left his job a few months earlier, he copied a few dozen of the suspicious entries. Jones, whose newspaper had spent almost a year looking into Tweed's Tammany Hall ring, was almost giddy with excitement when he heard O'Rourke's story.

The paper's first story corroborating O'Rourke's details ran on July 8, under the headline: MORE RING VILLAINY: GIGANTIC FRAUDS IN THE RENTAL OF ARMORIES. And in its coverage, *The Times* asked the same question New Yorkers were asking: "Who is responsible for these frauds?"

Of course it was Tweed. Beach had his opening.

It took him a year and a half to scrape together one last effort to get his subway bill back before lawmakers. It was the same plan as before, except for one dramatic change. After two years of operating his tunnel, Beach finally conceded that pneumatic propulsion was not the future, after all. Blowing such a huge volume of air required tremendous energy that was too costly to sustain, and too hard to control over great distances. Moving packages was one thing. Moving people was another. Reluctantly, Beach embraced the idea he had loathed at the start, and he proposed steam power for his tunnel. The smoke, steam, and sparks London was dealing with were all surmountable with engineering changes, he believed, and he couldn't deny that steam was a proven power source.

On April 9, 1873, legislators passed Beach's subway bill again. But it was too late. He didn't have investors lined up, and when the economy collapsed on September 18, 1873, triggering the country's worst depression, far worse than Black Friday in 1869, Beach was done for good. Banks folded. Businesses went under. Millions lost their jobs and all their money in the panic of 1873. And New York, the nation's financial and cultural capital, became a city full of the homeless and hungry, with more than a quarter of its people suddenly out of work. Even Boss Tweed finally was brought down. After his arrest in 1871, it took almost two years for prosecutors to convict him, but they did, and on November 19, 1873, he was sentenced to twelve years in prison.

By then, Tweed's most stubborn foe was bankrupt and exhausted. After operating his one-car, one-station subway for almost three years, Alfred Ely Beach, still only forty-eight years old, abandoned the dream he had pursued for a quarter century and began to rent out his tunnel to anyone who would pay him. It was a pathetic end to what was once a promising vision. The pneumatic subway tunnel was converted into a shooting gallery and then eventually into a vault to store wines. Unable to continue affording the upkeep of his tunnel, Beach sealed it up for good in 1874 and returned to his roots as the editor of *Scientific American*.

YEARS LATER, A SOLITARY FIGURE with white hair, sitting on a wine crate, could sometimes be seen staring off into the darkness. He had failed in his promise to deliver New Yorkers a subway. But that would not be Alfred Beach's legacy. Until he came along, the idea of walking down a staircase beneath their streets, standing on a concrete platform, and waiting for a train to whisk them away through a dark and mysterious tunnel sounded like some sort of fantastical science fiction tale to New Yorkers. Now, when you peel back the modern layer of any big American city and look beneath its skin, below the steel and glass skyscrapers, below the cars, trucks, taxis, bikes, and pedestrians, that's where Alfred Beach's legacy endures. In the subway tunnels beneath the streets.

Embracing that world underground did not come easily for man.

2

WHERE SPIRITS, THE DEVIL, AND THE DEAD LIVE

FEAR OF THE UNDERGROUND HAD BEEN INGRAINED in humans for thousands of years. Long before Beach published his dream on the pages of *Scientific American,* the underground was seen as an underworld, a terrifying place inhabited by Lucifer himself, deadly spirits, and any number of angry, evil devils. That belief began to weaken with the age of the great explorers in the fifteenth, sixteenth, and seventeenth centuries, but people remained uneasy with the mystery of what might be down there, living or dead. And literary novels of the times provided little comfort. They were crafted in such a way as to be so eerily close to what peoples' forebears had believed that the public struggled to separate truth from fiction. In 1787, the English author William Beckford published a popular gothic work called *Vathek,* in which a powerful heroic figure strikes a pact with the oriental Satan and enters a subterranean palace by way of a secret opening in a rock. Deep inside the earth, Caliph Vathek encounters a pale species with glimmering eyes and burning hearts. He is consumed by their evil and filled with hatred. This, the Argentine essayist Jorge Luis Borges, would write years later, was "the first truly atrocious Hell in literature." Vathek's journey influenced not only the reading public but also future writers, including Keats, Byron, and Edgar Allan Poe, who took a particular interest in the idea of a world underground. In 1838 Poe wrote about a young stowaway on a whaling ship in *The Narrative of Arthur Gordon Pym*. Though it was a work of fiction, Poe drew his plot from credible theories that the earth was as hollow as a balloon and that deep inside its core breathed any number of undiscovered civilizations. Only as scientists learned more about the earth and technology got better did people begin to finally accept that the hidden worlds and sea creatures described by Poe and later by nineteenth-century science fiction writers like Jules Verne in *Journey to the Center of the Earth* and H. G. Wells in *The War of the Worlds* really were fiction.

STICKS, ROCKS, PICKS, SHOVELS, even fingers. These were the first tools of tunnel digging. Tunneling is older than Rome and the Egyptian pyramids. The earliest tunnels were typically the work of slaves, whose only choice to avoid torture and beatings was to descend into the underground and to dig for their lives. Freezing water seeping out of the ground numbed their feet and helped them work since they could no longer feel the cuts the jagged edges were inflicting on their soles. There were no helmets to protect their skulls or gloves to protect their skin. There were no wheelbarrows to cart out the rocks and dirt they loosened. They carried out backbreaking loads in sacks made of animal skin. Catastrophes struck without warning, from floods to cave-ins to rickety ladders collapsing. And with no explosives to blast through the earth, the workers lit huge fires right up against the face of the tunnel. Once the rock was glowing hot, they splashed it with cold water, sometimes mixed with vinegar. The primitive combination of heat and then a cold chemical reaction helped crack and chip the rock. Not surprisingly, death by scalding was common. But even worse, the fires sucked up what little oxygen there was underground, suffocating the slaves. If the fire didn't work, another method used was to spin metal tubes into a rock until a hole was just big enough to drive a wooden wedge into it. The wedge was drenched with water, which caused it to expand and split the rock and push the tunnel forward. Both methods were crude and dangerous and slow. It was only because human life had such little value that hundreds of deaths in a single mishap could be dismissed so lightly.

Monte Salviano was tunneling in its infancy. It took thirty thousand Roman laborers thirteen years, from 54 B.C. to 41 B.C., to build the three-mile rock tunnel for moving water through the Italian peak. A long and narrow tunnel runs near Jerusalem, between the Pool of the Virgins and the Pool of Siloam, which is believed to have been dug before Christ's birth to carry water into Jerusalem in the event of an attack by the Assyrians. Aztecs built tunnels to mine for gold, silver, and copper; the Incas dug them to drain large lakes; and the Babylonians dug a tunnel to divert the Euphrates River. War was another primary reason for building the earliest tunnels, allowing fighters to sneak up on their enemy and attack with no warning, burning their tunnel behind them as they stormed forward so nobody could escape.

The English led the modern tunneling revolution, digging underground not because they had to, but because they dared to. In 1766, work began on the Harecastle canal tunnel in Staffordshire, England. It was a mile and a half long, nine feet wide, and twelve feet high, just large enough to allow a seven-foot barge to pass through. But so tight was the fit that the only way to propel the boat forward was for the crewmen to lie flat on the deck on their backs and stretch out their legs to touch the roof and sides of the tunnel to push the barge along. It must have been a terrifying experience for these leggers, as they were called. Their barge would slide into blackness, with no light to see up, down, behind, or ahead. Reaching out with a hand or leg would find the wall, but it also might encounter a sharp rock jutting out. The sounds of rippling water, the creaking barge, the heavy breathing of the men next to you, or maybe screeching bats echoing loudly in the tunnel all enhanced the fears. Those fears persisted for decades as more tunnels were built. At the Saint-Quentin Canal in France in the early 1800s, barges stacked up at the entrance with no captain willing to go first. Authorities had to offer free canal trips for life before the first man would finally agree to take his boat through and break up the logjam.

Americans were determined to prove that they were no less bold than the Europeans. Between 1818 and 1821, the men who owned the Schuylkill and Susquehanna Canal in Pennsylvania went out of their way to create a right angle through a hill in the path of their canal, just to show that it could be done. The Auburn Tunnel was the first transportation tunnel built in the United States, used to move coal down the Schuylkill. But at just 450 feet it was a novelty more than a practicality, and it was soon shortened and eliminated.

Canal tunnels were an efficient way for commercial transportation to go through hills and mountains, since laborers did not have to rely on horses and donkeys to trudge slowly over and around them. There was no greater proof of the value of a well-placed canal than the opening of the Erie Canal. New York in 1825 was a city of 170,000 residents, an insignificant blip on the world's map when Tokyo, London, and Paris had all surpassed one million people. Nearly all of those New Yorkers were squeezed into the southernmost portion of Manhattan, getting around mostly by horseback or on foot. Only the wealthy had the means to venture north if they desired, traveling by horse up the narrow, unpaved Post Road to explore brooks and ponds, see deer and rabbits, and even pick wildflowers and tulips in the largely desolate northern half of the island. If someone really wanted countryside, they could take Post Road all the way through the village of Harlem and ride a ferry at Kingsbridge across the Harlem River.

But when the Erie Canal opened for business on October 25, 1825, all of that began to change. It connected New York's Hudson Valley to the Great Lakes region, reducing the time to move freight from the city to the upper Mississippi Valley from twenty-six days to six days and transforming Gotham into the hub of the nation's imports and exports. Between 1820 and 1870, three out of every four immigrants who came into the United States entered through New York, and by 1880 New York City's population had exploded to 1.2 million. The canal also drove an emotional wedge between New York City and Boston, at the time the first and fourth largest cities in the country. When Massachusetts decided that instead of following New York's lead in building waterways, it would focus on building railroads, it was like the small brother telling the big brother it was time they went their separate ways. And the big brother built up some resentment. When Massachusetts invited New York's governor to the opening of yet another railroad in 1851, the invitation was declined in a threatening tone. "We have seen you invading our soil, filling our valleys, boring our mountains at some points, leveling them at others, and turning your steam engines loose upon us to run up and down, roaming at large throughout our borders," New York's governor wrote back. "I must warn you to pause and take breath before making fresh tracks upon our territory." Massachusetts and its capital city would not listen. And decades later, when it came time to resolve their urban congestion woes, Boston would again follow its own instincts rather than mimic what New York had done.

Meanwhile, with each new wave of immigrants arriving in the second half of the nineteenth century, squeezing everyone into the fingernail of the island of Manhattan became impossible, and the city's newest arrivals pushed their way north. Walking was soon no longer an option to get everywhere. The horses would feel the strain, too. And those rivers and bays that surrounded Manhattan, separating it from New Jersey, Brooklyn, and the bucolic Hudson Valley, were suddenly obstacles that needed to be bypassed so the growth could continue. Ferries were too slow. Suspension bridges were just beginning to be built. New Yorkers were about to learn that there was only one direction to look to ease their city's congestion. Down.

IT HAD TO BE the strangest dinner party ever thrown. Beneath the streets of London on Saturday evening, November 10, 1827, crimson velvet drapes covered the brick arches; two long tables covered in white tablecloths filled the floor space; large, handsome candelabras lighted with portable gas provided the light; and the British army's uniformed Band of the Coldstream Guards supplied the music, playing their favorite sounds from the romantic German opera *Der Freischütz*. More than a hundred men came together for a banquet beneath the streets of London, not so they could celebrate the unusual tunnel they were digging, but to try to reassure the skeptical public that it would be safe to come down there once it was finished. At one of the tables sat British royalty. At the other table sat a hundred anonymous bricklayers and miners, or navvies as they were known. They were not the bottom of the working class, but rather the top of it, honest, independent, well-compensated men who wore tall and sturdy laced boots and kerchiefs in their shirts. They were also not ones to miss an opportunity to get drunk at someone else's expense, and so on this night they bent their sore and bandaged fingers around glasses of warm beer mixed with gin and allowed themselves a rare evening of merriment away from the daily grind and grime. When the festivities wound down, the workers raised a special pickax and spade, along with their glasses, and shouted out a toast to the man who had dared to construct the tunnel.

ALMOST FROM THE DAY he was born in 1769 in Normandy, Marc Isambard Brunel's life was one adventure after another, filled with rebellion, bankruptcy, jail, and inventions. When his father pushed him to become a priest, Brunel refused and spent his teens sketching and earning a measly living painting. After just three lessons in trigonometry as a teenager, Brunel astonished his teacher by vowing to determine the height of the church spire in their town. His mind worked faster than others', and he began to show the same prodigy-like qualities as a European peer of his born a decade earlier. Sadly, their lives and accomplishments did not overlap for long. Wolfgang Amadeus Mozart died at age thirty-five, leaving the world to wonder how much more he might have achieved in a full life. Perhaps he would have found the same success in his later years as Brunel did. Brunel drifted from Paris north to the city of Rouen in his twenties, and then one summer's day in 1793 he hurried to catch an American ship bound for New York, only to discover on board that he had lost his passport. No matter, for when the authorities asked for his papers, his calligraphy and architectural skills saved him. "Having borrowed a passport from one of his fellow passengers," Brunel's biographer wrote, "he soon produced a copy, so admirably executed in every minute detail, even to the seal, that it was deemed proof against all scrutiny." His forged passport worked, and Brunel soon found work in upstate New York as a land surveyor. It was there that he had the fortune to meet the recently resigned U.S. treasury secretary Alexander Hamilton. Brunel flourished with Hamilton's assistance, and before long he had been hired as the chief engineer for New York City. During this time he designed a two-thousand-seat playhouse on Chatham Street in New York and he very nearly designed one of the most important buildings in American history. Brunel's drawings for a new capitol building to be constructed in Washington impressed the judges of a $500 prize offered by Thomas Jefferson, but his design was deemed too expensive to build and the winner was a late entry by a little-known physician, painter, and amateur architect. Brunel stayed on as New York's chief engineer until he felt the pull of home, and on January 20, 1799, he set sail for England.

Brunel began to tinker, first on a writing and drawing machine, and then on a contraption that measured out pieces of thread and wound them into small balls of cotton. The cotton balls were soft and elegant, although exactly what purpose they might serve was not entirely clear. Had Brunel patented his machine, there is no telling the fortune that might have come his way. Instead, he failed to act, and the machine was widely adopted and used, and he received not a penny for his contribution. One bad business break after another eventually landed him in serious debt, and in 1821, Brunel, with a wife and three young children at home, was jailed at King's Bench Debtors Prison. It was a humbling and humiliating experience.

Just before his imprisonment, Brunel, by now fifty years old, had sketched out in detail an enormous, cast-iron, circular device. He called it a shield, and in his patent application he described it as a machine for "forming tunnels or drift-ways underground." There was nothing else like it. With hydraulic presses rotating it and propelling it, this shield could push forward underground, excavating dirt and rock while supporting the ground above the hole that it dug. The shield, Brunel believed, was the future of tunneling, but from behind bars there was little he could do with it.

In a letter that he wrote to authorities, Brunel begged for his release. He explained that he had refused offers in prior years to leave England to help another country with an engineering crisis, because his loyalty to his new homeland mattered most to him. "If I see honourable and personal employment here," he wrote, "you may be assured that I shall not be wanting in zeal, but shall devote my future services and talents for the benefit of this country." Every day he remained imprisoned he grew more dejected about the time away from his family. He wrote an emotional letter to his close friend, Lord Spencer: "My affectionate wife and myself are sinking under it. We have neither rest by day nor night. Were my enemies at work to effect the ruin of mind and body, they could not do so more effectually."

As Brunel's depression deepened, the Duke of Wellington finally recognized the good that Brunel could do for their country. The duke ordered that the five thousand pounds Brunel owed be taken from the Treasury and used to free Brunel of his liabilities. In a gracious letter of thanks, Brunel wrote to the duke on August 21, 1821, and promised that the only way he could express his gratitude was in "preparing plans for the service of the British government." As it so happened, the duke had just the project for him.

On February 18, 1824, a group of men gathered at the City of London Tavern in the Bishopsgate neighborhood. With its low ceilings, flagstone floors, roaring fires, and cavernous dining room that could seat 350 people, it was one of London's most popular restaurants. It was also an appropriate place to make history. That evening, after a long round of toasts, the Thames Tunnel Company was created. Its mission: to build the world's first tunnel for vehicular traffic and to do it directly beneath the Thames River.

TRAFFIC IN LONDON WAS AT a standstill, particularly across London Bridge. Thousands of people were crossing the Thames River daily either on the bridge or by ferry, but the waits became interminable, and the merchants downtown were helpless as they lost business to the round-the-clock congestion. The city needed a thoroughfare to connect the two banks of the Thames, for pedestrians and for a steady line of carriages, too. A bridge was the obvious solution, but London already had those. Brunel proposed something bolder. Using his patented shield, Brunel suggested that he and his nineteen-year-old son, Isambard Kingdom Brunel, would burrow a tunnel under the bed of the Thames. Until then, whenever workers had bored underground, the edge of a river had always marked the end of the line. It was a river, after all. Where else was there to go? Brunel dismissed that defeatist attitude. *You go under the river, that's where you go.*

THE FATHER PUT THE SON in charge, and in 1826 their work began. Isambard Brunel was just twenty years old, a heavy smoker and Napoleon-like in stature, but his father entrusted him with the role of chief engineer on the project. The Brunel shield was an amazing machine, twelve linked frames made of cast iron, each twenty-two feet tall and three feet wide. Three compartments stacked on top of each other were able to hold and protect workers from falling debris. The compartments were fenced in on the sides and open in front, where the workers could stand and reach out their arms to work. A large screw on the shield's bottom was turned to push it forward, and as it inched ahead, workers in the compartments efficiently bricked up the tunnel wall. Wheelbarrows carried the excavated mud to a long string of buckets that were lifted up a shaft. The process was smooth, but slow. On a good day, the shield pushed forward twelve inches at most, and each one was nerve-racking for the workers. The roof of the tunnel was just sixteen feet beneath the riverbed of the Thames, and that meant that water leaked and even flooded daily.

On May 18, 1827, around five o'clock in the morning, Richard Beamish, a twenty-nine-year-old Irishman working as an assistant civil engineer on the Thames Tunnel, noticed that as the tide rose, the ground in the tunnel seemed to come alive. Occasional bursts of diluted silt leaked in, but that was not unusual. The workers that arrived at six in the morning were reluctant to enter the tunnel, but the day passed uneventfully. As night arrived, Beamish anticipated trouble, and he removed his polished Wellington shoes for a pair of greased mud boots and shed his holiday coat for a waterproof one. It was well into the evening when Beamish heard one of his most powerful men cry out for help, and he sent an equally strong worker to find him. A rush of water suddenly burst into the tunnel and lifted the men up, and quickly the water level began to rise up their legs and reach their waists. Beamish feared for the men working on the shield, but they managed to scurry down and to reach the bottom of the shaft, where they could climb a staircase to safety. That's when Beamish looked down the tunnel and saw a sight he would never forget.

"The water came on in a great wave," he recalled. "A loud crash was heard. A small office, which had been erected under the arch, about a hundred feet from the frames, burst. The pent air rushed out; the lights were suddenly extinguished." The men climbed the staircase in darkness, and as they reached the surface, they heard a hundred voices shouting. "A rope! A rope! Save him! Save him!"

Below, one old worker had been caught by the wave and was hanging on for his life. Without hesitating, young Isambard Brunel, whose father was out having dinner at the time and thus had no idea of the near catastrophe he was missing, grabbed a rope, slid down an iron pole in the shaft, helped tie the rope around his worker's waist, and called for him to be hoisted up. Once he was up, the men conducted a roll call. "To our unspeakable joy," Beamish wrote years later, "every man answered to his name."

SUCH GOOD FORTUNE WOULD NOT last. On the morning of January 12, 1828, Beamish arrived around six and waited with the next shift while they downed some warm beer. Suddenly, a watchman rushed over to them. "The water is in! The tunnel is full!" Beamish grabbed a crowbar and broke down a locked door to a staircase that descended into the shaft. He had only gone down a few steps when Isambard Brunel, hurled up from the tunnel by the massive wave, landed in Beamish's arms. "Ball! Ball! Collins! Collins!" Brunel muttered the names of men he had been with just seconds earlier, and now they were gone, along with four others who perished in the flooded tunnel. More than four thousand bags of clay and gravel were needed to plug the hole in the riverbed that had caused the disaster, but it almost did not matter. Calls for the tunnel to be sealed up poured in to Marc Brunel. The risk, the public cried, was not worth more deaths. But even though his own son was nearly killed and required months of recuperation from both a knee injury and internal wounds, Brunel insisted the work continue. "The ground was always made to the plan," he said. "Not the plan to the ground." But until more money could be raised, and the public reassured, Brunel and the Thames Tunnel would have to wait. A brick wall was erected in the tunnel, and it was turned into a tourist attraction for a small fee so that the tunnel company could at least recoup some of its costs. "The Great Bore," as journalists derisively called the tunnel, was presumed dead.

ON MARCH 24, 1841, Marc Isambard Brunel was knighted. And nearly two years to the day after that, on March 25, 1843, the Thames Tunnel opened. What Brunel had predicted at the start would take three years to build had taken eighteen. "Another wonder has been added to the many of which London can boast," the London *Times* wrote. "Another triumph been achieved by British enterprize, genius and perseverance." The tunnel would not have been built had the Duke of Wellington not freed Brunel, who used a government loan in 1837 to restart the tunneling. A new and improved shield also helped, this one weighing 140 tons. It replaced Brunel's original one and proved to be stronger, faster, and safer.

For the opening ceremony, a "tunnel waltz" was composed, flags were raised, bells rang out, and, at four in the afternoon, a signal gun fired and a procession began moving down a spiral staircase into the western archway of the tunnel. Marc Brunel, who had suffered a stroke a year earlier that left him mostly paralyzed on his right side, insisted on attending the celebration and was greeted with cheers as he walked through the tunnel. The throng of thousands burst into song, and the words of "See the Conquering Hero Comes" echoed off the walls. More than a hundred burners atop lamp posts placed in the arches provided the light. The first day the tunnel was opened, fifty thousand people walked the entire length. But there were others who could not bring themselves to join them.

Marc and Isambard Brunel had dug a tunnel beneath the Thames River wide enough to serve as a road for vehicles. They had proved that the underground could be safely conquered and that man no longer had to stop digging when a river stood in the way. But what the father and his son could not do, the London *Times* reported on the day of the Thames Tunnel's opening, was wipe away centuries of man's fears overnight.

> The majority of the visitors went the whole distance, 1200 feet; many, however, proceeded only a little way, pausing and looking about with an air of suspicion every four or five yards, while some would not venture into the tunnel at all, but remained in the shaft or on the staircase, yet amongst the majority there was a perceptible anxiety, and notwithstanding the brilliance of the lights, the singular reverberations of the music, the shouting of the admirers of the undertaking, and all the means that were taken to give éclat to the event, and encouragement to the spectators, notwithstanding also the physical heat that oppressed them, it was evident that there was a lurking, chilling fear in the breasts of many.

3

A FAMILY FOR THE AGES

ON MAY 6, 1635, JOHN WHITNEY and his wife, Elinor, gathered up
their five sons, boarded the small wooden ship *Elizabeth and Ann* from
England, and crossed the rough seas of the North Atlantic to start a
new life. Some time later, their ship, carrying 120 passengers, pulled into
Massachusetts Bay, and they quickly settled into a sixteen-acre farm-
house in Watertown, the second largest settlement in Massachusetts next
to Boston. Two months after arriving, on July 5, Elinor Whitney delivered their sixth son, Joshua, the first Whitney to be born in America, and
two more boys would soon follow, making eight total. Though Elinor
died before she turned sixty, her older husband had plenty of life left in
him. Four months after his wife's death, John Whitney married Judith
Clement. However, like his first wife, she also died before he did. When
John Whitney finally died on June 1, 1673, at the age of eighty-five, he left
behind him a collection of boys who scattered across Massachusetts to
raise their own families. None took more pleasure in this, apparently,
than General Josiah Whitney, who, when he wasn't busy defending Boston
Harbor during the Revolutionary War, was busy in other ways, fathering
sixteen children with his first wife, and then nine more with his second.
Of all of the general's descendants that would follow, it was a grandson of
Josiah Whitney who began the family's ascendance to greatness.

James Scollay Whitney was born on May 19, 1811, in the Western Massachusetts town of South Deerfield. His father owned a country store in town, and when James wasn't attending class, he was working beside his father at the store. By the time he was twenty-one, he had inherited the store from his father and faced an important moment in his young life. He could choose to settle in South Deerfield and live a respectable life defined by his father's business. Or he could set out for bigger things.

Three years later, James Whitney made his decision. A superb horseman, he had always been interested in military affairs, and in 1835 he was commissioned as a brigadier general in the state militia. For the rest of his life, anybody who knew him closely didn't call him by his name, but simply General.

In 1836, Whitney married into one of the state's most prominent families. His bride, Laurinda Collins, was a descendant of Governor William Bradford, a man who was so popular that he was elected to his office thirty times in the 1600s and who helped settle Plymouth Colony and drafted the Mayflower Compact. Not even a year after they married, their first child was born. On September 16, 1837, a girl they named Mary Ann arrived. Two years later, Henry was born, on October 22, 1839; and two years after that, on July 5, 1841, William arrived. Two more children, Susan and Henrietta, would follow (Henrietta's twin died unnamed just three days after being born).

With a growing family, the couple was eager to start their own life, and so they left South Deerfield for nearby Conway, a hilly town cut through by two pretty streams, the South and the Bear, and not far from the shadows of Mount Tom and Mount Holyoke. In Conway James Whitney built a long white two-story home. His family lived in the back, and in the front he opened a country store with his brother-in-law, Anson Shepard. Shepard & Whitney established itself in Conway as the place to come and talk. The giant elm tree out front and the old stove in the center of the store became popular spots for people to gather around and to talk not only about local gossip but also about more important affairs affecting their town, their state, and their country. James Whitney could talk politics with anyone, and in just three years he established himself as one of

Conway's most astute political and financial leaders, comfortable swap-
ping opinions on business and the military with anyone in earshot. Over
the course of his sixty-seven years, until the day he died on a cold Boston
street, it would remain one of James Whitney's most endearing traits, the
ability to befriend people no matter their politics, wealth, cultural interests, or personal agenda. It was a quality his sons took to heart at an early
age, even as they went their separate ways.

HENRY

The boy was not even ten years old when the old gentleman who ran a
country store in Conway decided to teach his young employee a game.
This wasn't the boy's first job. Living in the small town of about fourteen
hundred people, Henry Melville Whitney used to help a local farmer drive
a cow out to pasture in return for twelve cents a month and one egg. But
one Sunday, while hurrying home from church, Henry took a shortcut
and snagged the velveteen pants his aunt had sewn for him on a fence,
and thus he needed to earn some more money. Which is how Henry
found himself stocking shelves at a country store.

On his first day, after the owner had outlined his duties there, the boy
had a question.

"Where do I sleep?" he asked, knowing that he'd be working long days
and would need some place to rest.

The two grew close, until one day the storekeeper pulled out his chess
set. It wasn't an easy game to teach such an active boy, since it involved
patience and strategy. It was made even more difficult because Henry
could hardly hear his instructions, the result of a near-fatal bout with
scarlet fever when he was little. As he grew up Henry learned from his
mother, Laurinda, that if he stuck a finger into a glass of water and then
into his ears, it helped just enough to make hearing easier. It was one of
many lessons the Whitney children learned from their mother. She ran a
tidy house, writing proper letters to her extended family on a regular basis and making sure the children never neglected their studies or chores.
She had a favorite outfit that she wore nearly every day, a simple black
dress and a crisp, fully starched white hat with streamers. Her prim look

did not do her outgoing personality justice. She was as talented a horseman as her militia-trained husband, maybe even better, able to control a four-horse team with ease and grace. It was a feat that always impressed her children.

Her skill and competitiveness rubbed off on Henry, as the storekeeper would learn. He had figured that playing chess would be a fun way for him and his young worker to fill the long days and evenings. And he enjoyed Henry's eagerness to try new challenges. Over the course of several weeks and months, he taught Henry the rules of chess. And each day Henry soaked up a little more strategy and acquired a little more skill, until one day he beat his teacher. And then the next day, he did it again. This was not what the storekeeper had in mind when they had started playing, but he had clearly underestimated the boy's thirst for knowledge and competitiveness. They continued playing every day, until the pupil became the better player and the teacher grew frustrated about losing all the time; eventually their games stopped.

WILLIAM

Henry was not exceptionally close with his younger brother, William Collins Whitney, while growing up, even though they were only two years apart. But over the course of the second half of the nineteenth century, as they traded occasional letters; mourned the losses of parents, siblings, and even children; married and raised their own families; loaned each other money; and rose up to become powerful businessmen in New York and Boston, no two siblings would change the course of life in the American city more than the Whitney brothers. They did not compete with each other so much as they observed and learned from each other. But it wasn't always that way. Only one of them, it could be said, was driven to succeed from his youngest days.

Where studies were of little interest to Henry, William was called Deacon for his habit of reading the Bible for hours beneath the shady trees by the river near their home. In 1856, the two boys attended Williston Seminary, a new boarding school in nearby Easthampton. Their school was chosen for good reason, especially given that its tuition, nine dollars a year, was not inexpensive for the times. It was founded by a long-ago uncle of the boys.

At Williston Academy, nobody was allowed to coast, which is perhaps why only one of the Whitney brothers managed to sustain the grades and level of interest the private school demanded of its students. Will was the serious one who studied Homer and Virgil, algebra, and geography. He focused especially hard on the headmaster's Bible study course. After graduating Williston, Will Whitney wanted to attend West Point and to follow the path of his father by joining the military. With his education and James Whitney's connections, gaining acceptance to the academy would not have been a problem. The problem was that his father did not want that for his son. The idea of Will in the army depressed his father so much that Laurinda finally had to go visit Will and make him an alternative proposal. She begged him to choose Harvard, Yale, or Williams, and he relented, enrolling in 1859 at Yale, where the tuition of $216, while unaffordable to most families, was well within reason for the comfortable Whitneys. Will excelled in one area that fascinated him. Debate. He also made some of his best and lifelong friends, including a rich and equally ambitious young man from Cleveland, Ohio, named Oliver Hazard Payne, an economist named William Graham Sumner, and Henry Dimock, who would join Will Whitney not only in a Wall Street law practice but also in family, when he married Whitney's sister Susan. While some of Whitney's classmates left school in 1861 to join the fight as the Civil War began, he did not. Instead, Whitney enjoyed his time at Yale, rowing on the crew team, joining Skull and Bones, and excelling in English composition. The law in particular called to him, and as graduation neared and he was presented the opportunity to make a commencement speech, he seized the moment.

On July 30, 1863, speaking to his graduation class and with the esteemed Yale faculty members seated behind him, he railed against Republicans, against the Civil War, and against immigration, and he took particular umbrage at what he perceived as a shortage of bright and ambitious men seeking public office. As with every previous Yale address, Whitney, wearing a slim-fitting suit and high waistcoat, spoke from memory, at least at the start. The expectation of the school's elders was that the student should be so honored to speak that they would stand in front of a mirror for hours rehearsing their speech until it was just so. "The Drama closes when the nation, sick at heart and worn out by faction and misrule, sinks out of sight in history, or yields itself a willing victim to some ambitious and able usurper," Whitney said. His classmates gasped at his words, but there was greater shock when he paused, reached into his pocket, and calmly pulled out the rest of his speech and continued to read it, thinking nothing of the sacred tradition he was breaking.

Afterward, when his good friend Sumner asked him why he did not follow the rule of reciting his speech by memory, Whitney seemed nonchalant about his brazen act. "It was too much bother to memorize so many words," he answered.

He moved back home after Yale so that he could attend Harvard Law School with his friend Henry Dimock. But Will's patience with schooling was fading. Though Harvard Law School at the time claimed some of the great legal minds in the country, they could not hold the attention of the two chummy Yalies. Barely one year after enrolling, Whitney and Dimock left Harvard, convinced they could just as easily pass the bar requirements and become lawyers by clerking in a law office as they could by sitting in a boring classroom on the Charles River. And they were not interested in clerking in Boston. Nowhere was the legal field more cutthroat than in New York, and competitor that he was, Will Whitney was drawn to it. He arrived in Manhattan in the fall of 1864 with grand ambitions, and the streets and social scene of Gotham would never be the same.

HENRY

By the time he was well into his thirties, Henry Whitney had collected a range of business experiences, most of them in banking and shipping, running the Metropolitan Steamship Company his father had launched. But he had no career to speak of or family to surround himself with. After leaving Williston early, Henry had never attempted college. Any real jobs he'd held he owed to his father, not to his own hard work or entrepreneurial spirit. He worked in his father's store, he clerked in his father's bank. As he was approaching forty years old, Henry had even followed his parents and moved into a house right near them in Brook-line, a large home on Pleasant Street in the neighborhood known as Coolidge Corner. The only reason he was financially sound was because his father's businesses had done well. Henry owned more than half the shares of the Metropolitan Steamship Company. But even Henry knew that he was still lost, and it bothered him.

"My dear Bill," Henry wrote in a letter on May 10, 1865, while in Alabama. "I have but a moment in which to write and will therefore be brief. The weather is now oppressingly warm and I have thus far enjoyed the trip." His letter told of a man who ran a cotton mill and who was quite the inventor, but needed help securing a patent. "I have told him that you would probably call," Henry said. A month later, Henry wrote to his brother again, this time to say he was considering leaving the north for good and settling down south. "If there was anything in New York that I might turn my hand to," he wrote, "that would suffice to procure me daily bread, and some of the entrées and dessert, I would not think of leaving at all. And it must be that there is plenty to do if one is only willing, patient and persevering."

Henry was neither willing nor patient nor persevering. But he couldn't change. Life had become one adventure after another, and as he bounced from Mobile, Alabama, to Pensacola, Florida, to New Orleans, his name was a commodity only because of his bloodline.

"His own means don't amount to much," one newspaper story said of Henry. "Operates in connection with his father and not supposed to have much personal responsibility."

It was a perception he was determined to change. The second half of the nineteenth century was an exhilarating time to be a dreamer in Boston. The city was a magnet for men with great personal ambitions but no stable business to speak of. Henry Whitney would fit right in. But not everyone found comfort so easily in Boston.

In March 1868, a scraggly dressed drifter from Ohio with nothing in his pockets arrived in the city looking for a job. It didn't take him long to find work at a local Western Union branch. His coworkers were more educated than he; most of them were college graduates, while he had not even finished high school. But none of them were as curious or as well read or as skilled in telegraphy as their newest colleague, Thomas Edison.

Edison befriended an inventor whose small shop at 109 Court Street in Boston's Scollay Square had for twenty years been a place where an assortment of bells, batteries, alarms, and other gadgets had been born. The walls were covered in soot and dirt, and the ceiling beams overhead were caked in dust. Not an inch of floor space was left unused. There were pulleys whirring, leather belts racing, racks of steel and castings scattered about the floor. A loud steam engine helped keep the place warm. Edison was at home working here, and it wasn't long before he got a patent for his first invention, an automatic vote-counting machine, and he proudly took it down to Washington to show the politicians there how much easier voting could be. In the nation's capital, Edison got a lesson in politics. It turned out that politicians didn't want it to be easier to cast a vote. They liked their traditional way of shouting out yay or nay because it provided a way to stall a bill if they were opposed to it. If they said nothing, nothing happened. But a voting machine would make stalling impossible, and they sent Edison back to Boston.

After a few more months on Court Street, and a few more promising inventions that went nowhere, including a stock ticker, Edison decided he was not going to be able to achieve what he wanted in Boston. Still broke, he left his equipment and headed south in 1869, just one year after arriving. Edison's year in Boston may not have been his most fruitful, but it sparked in him the desire to do something special. His time would come. When it did, Henry Whitney would be there.

WILLIAM

The heart of New York in the late 1860s was lower Manhattan, and there was very little development north of Thirty-fourth Street. Broadway, Fifth Avenue, and Park Avenue were all swarmed with horse-pulled coaches and wagons, to the point where it became a parlor game to see how many vehicles would pass by a single spot in an hour, morning, or full day. One curious businessman stood at the corner of Broadway and Chambers Street for thirteen hours one day in 1852 and counted an average of 470 vehicles passing by in both directions every hour. The gap between one car and the next was usually thirteen seconds. Fifteen years later, in 1867, a reporter for *The New York Tribune*, wondering how much things had changed, conducted the same experiment for the same period of time. In thirteen hours, he counted 13,391 vehicles in total, or 1,030 every hour, the absurd equivalent of 17 every minute.

The conditions were perfect for entrepreneurs like Alfred Beach to develop solutions. But as Beach learned, and as Will Whitney would soon discover, dirty politics in New York always won out over the public's clamor for improved services.

As his law practice with Dimock grew, Whitney saw that culture was one way to establish his place in the city. He learned to love opera, gained membership to the Century Club, and found himself shoulder to shoulder with the city's elite, from John Jay to Edwin Godkin to J. P. Morgan. And when the American Museum of Natural History opened, he took an immediate interest that helped him become a trustee there. As Whitney's stature grew, he began to think about the state of his city and ways to make it more livable. You cannot ride in New York City, Mark Twain would write, "unless you are willing to go in a packed omnibus that labors and plunges and struggles along at the rate of three miles in four hours and a half." As miserable as sitting was, standing was worse. "They are so crowded," Twain wrote, "you will have to hang on by your eye-lashes and your toe-nails."

In 1867, sensing the power that Whitney might one day hold, a Michigan railroad man named Hugh B. Willson, who had witnessed the opening of the London subway four years earlier, mailed Whitney an outline for his own plans to build a similar project in New York. He had designed a subway tunnel to be constructed under Broadway and powered by steam. And he even suggested a brilliant idea to make it profitable: use the tracks for freight trains between midnight and six in the morning. Willson hoped to get a man like Whitney to purchase stock in his company and even act as its director, which would give it credibility. But Whitney wasn't yet sold on London's subway.

"I am entirely satisfied that the time has come when some kind of steam railroad must be built on the island of New York in order to transport the passengers," Whitney wrote to Willson. "If no other mode were practicable, I should advocate the construction of the underground railroad, not only as a necessity but as a paying investment. But the result of my observation in London leads me to prefer greatly the elevated railway, and believing it to be entirely feasible and not more expensive than the underground system, I cannot act as a Director in your company and do not wish to take any stock. In all my conclusions I may be mistaken, but I think it is better to state them frankly."

By 1867, with his practice stable and one of his biggest clients the Metropolitan Steamship Company run by his father and brother, Will Whitney had reconnected with his college friend Oliver Payne. Payne, unlike Whitney, had fought with the Union Army during the war and survived battle injuries, and when he returned home to Cleveland, his father, a wealthy businessman and popular Democratic congressman, handed him $20,000 and sent him out into the world to grow the family fortune in oil and iron. His first destination was New York, where about 1,500 families earned more than half of the city's wealth. The few dozen millionaires who lived in the city at the start of the Civil War in 1860 now numbered several hundred, including some worth more than $20 million. That was the sort of company the Paynes were used to keeping, and in the winter of 1868 Oliver Payne paid a visit to New York and to Whitney. He came with a guest.

FLORA PAYNE WAS A hell-raiser. Six months younger than Will Whitney and the sister of his college roommate, she was not beautiful and had a square face and almost masculine jawline. But her outward confidence made her appealing to men who could match her self-assuredness. She had been properly schooled as a young lady, first in Cleveland and then in New York. But she hated etiquette lessons and often fled school and flaunted any punishment thrown her way. Her father hoped a more strict school in Cambridge, Massachusetts, might fix her, but her Midwestern blood was not a good match for the uptight, puritanical Boston bluebloods, and she couldn't retreat home fast enough.

During a visit to the Fifth Avenue Hotel to see her brother in February

1868, Flora was introduced to Will Whitney by Oliver. He suspected they might be a match. The handsome, slim, brainy, six-foot-tall lawyer and the brown-haired, graceful, well-traveled Midwestern daughter of a rich senator were smitten. Years later, Oliver would admit that he was sure if the two ever met "they would fall in love with each other." So sure was he that he arranged for them to meet not just at the hotel, but in the romantic, top-floor dining room overlooking New York City.

In a letter he wrote to Flora years later, Whitney described that first meeting and admitted to being flustered by her brashness. "How you looked I plainly recall in your blue dress and with the blue and gold book in your hand when you threw down the gauntlet for a flirtation. 'So you are the Will Whitney that I have had held up to me for so many years?' I must have been a little blundering at picking it up I imagine, for the attack was unexpected and bold . . . You asked me to order for you and then criticized and complimented until my time to go."

They went to dinner together, saw the opera, sipped tea late into the night, and flirted openly. And when she returned home to Cleveland, they began to fall in love through an almost daily flow of intimate letters back and forth, until finally she invited him out to meet her parents. He was prepared to propose to her on that trip, but, unsure of her willingness to commit, he hesitated. He almost scared her off, in fact, with a letter in which he wrote of having six young ladies that he loved with all his heart. "Henry and I won't ever marry," Whitney wrote. But it was merely his way to draw her closer, and on her next visit to New York, in December 1868, he decided the time was right. Flora got them tickets to the opera, and he arranged for a carriage, but she, in her typical sarcastic wit, wrote him a few days before to say the ride was unnecessary. "The carriage would undoubtedly be a vast ornament to us," she wrote, "but as I am in good health I would suggest we walk the three steps that lie between the hotel and the Opera House." Whitney was hooked. He adored the way she spoke her mind, and after he proposed and she accepted, they raced back to Cleveland to share the news and get her father's approval. Of course he approved, and while Whitney returned to his job in New York, Flora stayed behind to start planning their wedding, and their life.

They married at Cleveland's First Presbyterian Church on October 13, 1869, and the groomsmen included Whitney's best friends, William Sumner and Oliver Payne, and his brother from Boston, Henry. They honeymooned in Niagara Falls before stopping in Canada and then Brookline to see Whitney's family. It was the first time Flora had met Whitney's mother, and Laurinda was quite impressed with her new daughter-in-law.

"You have got a sweet, good wife, William," she told him before they left, and she made him promise that he would love and respect her even when times got rough.

Flora's father gave the couple money to start their life in grand style, by building a brownstone in the fashionable Murray Hill neighborhood on Park Avenue. They had two servants and a cook. And within five years they also had three children, Harry, Pauline, and William Payne Whitney. A fourth, Olive, would come later.

HENRY

In October 1868, Henry's impatience began to resurface. He had bought two parcels of land in Brookline, almost seventy thousand square feet, on a hunch that the land would be valuable one day. It paid off quicker than he could have imagined. Three and a half years after buying the tracts, in 1872, he sold the land for more than twice what he had paid. The deal marked the beginning of Henry's transition ashore, from a maritime shipping magnate running the Metropolitan Steamship Company to a businessman who saw even greater potential in real estate and in the role that it could play in the growing world of street railways.

It was Whitney's good fortune that in the second half of the nineteenth century Brookline, Massachusetts, was the perfect place to be dreaming big dreams. In 1871, the street railways of Boston carried 34 million passengers. Ten years later, that number would double to 68 million. There was nowhere else to build tracks unless the boundaries of Boston expanded, which put anybody who owned significant chunks of land on the outskirts of Boston in a most enviable position. In the wealthy enclave of Brookline, only a few miles from the congested downtown business district, Henry Whitney was the biggest landowner of them all.

In the fall of 1878, Henry finally took another big step. His parents lived on Pleasant Street in Brookline, and one of their neighbors was the retired U.S. navy admiral Joseph F. Green. In 1878, Green's youngest daughter, Margaret Green, was twenty years old. She was bright and beautiful and, to James Whitney's oldest son, irresistible. She had short and curly brown hair pulled back from her pretty face. Though she had little formal education and came from a modest household, Margaret was bright and opinionated. She had never lived anywhere but Brookline. Henry, on the other hand, was wealthy, thanks to a portfolio full of shipping-company stock, and ambitious. And he had traveled all over the country. They were a handsome, if oddly matched, couple, but they fell in love after dating only a few months, and despite his being almost twice her age, on October 3, they married.

Whitney and his bride settled into a red brick, ivy-covered mansion on Warren Street in Brookline's Coolidge Corner very close to where his parents lived. For him, it was a natural transition into a large, meticulously maintained home like the ones he was raised in. But for Margaret, it was a bigger adjustment. She decorated the home with the assistance of designing experts and an almost unlimited budget. Leather-bound copies of all the classics, along with encyclopedias, were chosen to stock the library in the house. A Steinway grand piano was brought in, and beautiful oriental rugs were placed in every room. The walls were covered with artwork, etchings by Whistler, watercolors by Winslow Homer. Giant plaster replicas of the marble Parthenon frieze lined the winding staircase. The house was warm and inviting and appropriately New England, with heirlooms at every turn and a fireplace crackling. The home was cavernous for two people, and only the sound of children would change that.

WILLIAM

William C. Whitney was thirty-four years old when, in 1875, he took over the office of corporation counsel to the city of New York, at an impressive salary of $15,000 a year. The job was vital to the city. Whitney replaced a Tweed crony who had ignored the crime ring and thus made it even stronger and more difficult to take down. Not only did Whitney immediately fire anyone in his office with the slimmest connections to Tweed or Tammany Hall, but he replaced them with some of the most distinguished, well-respected, and brilliant lawyers in the city, men who would go on to be Supreme Court justices and U.S. circuit court judges. Their task was clear: clean up nearly four thousand pending suits against the city that were seeking in excess of $20 million, most of them from contractors hired by the Tweed ring that was now being dismantled piece by piece.

In two years, Whitney reorganized the department and saved the city millions by exposing hundreds of frauds. More important, the job immersed him in city, state, and even national politics and helped him forge relationships with powerful men, like Governor Tilden, and a little-known mayor from Buffalo named Grover Cleveland.

As corporation counsel, Whitney gained some unique insight into the operations of the city's transportation systems. He took a particular interest in the two dozen or so independent street railway franchises clogging New York's streets. The cars were filthy and uncomfortable, and the railways were constantly breaking down. Their owners paid virtually nothing to the city, and yet they had licenses that seemingly allowed them to go wherever they wanted, whenever they wanted, for as long as they were in business, with little regard for what was best for the city or for passengers. The railway companies cared only about how many fares they collected each day. And because crossing through the city often required the use of two or three different lines, if someone wanted to step off one car and transfer to another, well, that was more money in the pockets of the railway magnates. A free transfer was unheard of. Just as Alfred Beach almost three decades earlier, New York's young and ambitious corporation counsel saw how these railway franchises held the people of New York hostage. In the horrendous clutter of New York's streets, Whitney, too, perceived that there was a vast fortune just waiting to be made, if the right solution could be found.

HENRY

Henry Whitney's marriage, followed by the sudden death of his father just three weeks later, made him a better man. Three children born in three years starting in 1879—Ruth, Elinor, and Laura—also helped him. Their last two children, James and Josephine, would come later. Henry accepted his new responsibilities and displayed an energy and focus that those close to him had never seen before. A close observer of Henry Whitney's said that in managing his company's affairs, "he exhibited for the first time, in a broad and striking manner, indomitable energy and resource." In only a few years, between the steamship business and the water company that he also inherited, he rose to be the successful businessman his father had always hoped he'd become. His personal wealth soon approached half a million dollars, double what it had been around the time of his father's death.

The Massachusetts Board of Railroad Commissioners was supposed to bring order to Boston's streets, but it granted charters to more than twenty companies to pick up passengers in downtown Boston. Instead of cheaper fares, organized routes, and controlled congestion, Boston had no fare system at all (fares ranged from five to ten cents), and there were overlapping routes in some areas, while others got no streetcar service at all. The competition created mayhem. Fast, slow, race, brake, the streetcars showed no regard for the passengers on board or those waiting to be picked up. "The car that was left behind would then fall back and go as slowly as possible in order to get passengers from the car in the rear," one president of a rail company said. "All this led to blockades, accidents, and other serious injury to the service." The more Whitney rode these lines, the more he believed he could fix them.

Whitney was not yet in the streetcar business, but he was in the development business. And he was beginning to realize how much the two were intertwined. Without a fast and reliable transit system, there could be very little development. With each new piece of land in Brookline he bought up, Whitney's prominence grew and it became obvious to observers that he had great intentions for all of that property. He was on his way toward investing more than $800,000, and he would soon own almost four million square feet of land in Brookline and neighboring Brighton, most of it along the main thoroughfare, Beacon Street. He also had his eyes on more properties that would give him another million square feet. He was lining up some of his closest friends, including Eben D. Jordan, a Maine merchant and the founder of a giant department store in Boston, and W. W. Clapp, the editor of a local newspaper, and together they set out to change the way the people of Boston moved through downtown and out to the growing suburbs.

Whitney knew that Brookline was closer to the business district than many of the other communities Boston had swallowed. He traveled into Boston most days in a private carriage, a trip that took about an hour. Whitney took an easy route east from Coolidge Corner, down Beacon Street, through Kenmore Square, and right into the business district. For most of the way, the street was more than fifty feet wide, a straight thoroughfare unlike most of the narrow, twisting streets of Boston. And its width allowed a steady stream of horses to travel back and forth between Brookline and Boston without getting jammed up too tightly.

On August 9, 1886, a petition signed by a hundred residents of Brookline was presented to the town selectmen. They wanted Brookline to take control of Beacon Street and convert it to what was called a townway. The selectmen approved it, and the land along Beacon Street immediately became more valuable for anybody who owned there, putting Henry Whitney in an enviable position. One of the first things Brookline did was hire the same architect who had designed a necklace of connecting Boston parks a decade earlier. They asked Frederick Law Olmsted to landscape the wide boulevard of Beacon Street into Boston and make it into one of the prettiest streets in all of the country. As a Brookline park commissioner, Whitney knew Olmsted's work. In hiring him for his own plan, he described Olmsted as "a man who stands second to none in this land for laying out avenues of this kind, whose fame extends from Maine to Mexico." Whitney's vision was to see Beacon Street, now dotted by only a few scattered mansions, become a busy thoroughfare not only lined with apartments, homes, and stores but also formed of two roads, not one. One would handle the personal vehicles of the wealthy residents. The

other would be strictly for commercial vehicles coming in and out of
Coolidge Corner. The boulevard would be two hundred feet wide, flanked
on both sides by bicycle and bridle paths, and lined in the middle by
American elm trees.

But that wasn't all. The signature piece of his plan was in between the
rows of elms. There, Whitney wanted a street railway track, slightly hidden
by the trees so that the cars would feel less intrusive to the community.
Whitney knew that in 1884, one of Boston's biggest streetcar companies,
Metropolitan Railroad, had tried to build a streetcar line from Brookline
to Boston, but was denied by the state legislature.

Three years later, he was determined to avoid the same fate. At a hearing in January 1887 before Brookline's Committee on Roads and Bridges,
Whitney admitted that, yes, his plan, if successful, would most likely
bring him great riches. But he pointed out that others would benefit, too,
and that proved key to convincing other landowners along Beacon Street
to give their land to the project. The only objectors to his scheme feared
higher taxes and argued that the widening would benefit the richest the
most. These were points nobody could argue with, but there was not enough
opposition, and shortly after Brookline's committee approved Whitney's
plan, the state legislature did as well.

Whitney next set out to create a subsidiary of his land company, called
the West End Street Railway Company, to build and manage a street railroad along the beautiful new boulevard and connect Boston's downtown
with the blossoming and affluent suburb of Brookline. And he made an
offer Brookline could not refuse. He gave the town 630,000 square feet of
his own land, which was just over 10 percent of his total land holdings.
But it was almost half the total needed to complete the widening of Beacon Street. And he also agreed to donate $100,000 to the project if Brook-
line gave the remainder, which put his share of the total cost around
one-third. Both of these offers were generous and shrewd. Travel by rail
was quickly becoming popular in America. In 1880, the country's railroads and street railways had carried 59 million people. By 1885, the figure
was up to 80 million. And by 1887, it was more than 90 million and
climbing.

By convincing the town to widen the boulevard and build approximately eight miles of suburban tracks, Henry Whitney guaranteed that his remaining properties would skyrocket in value. And with his actions, real estate was no longer his biggest enterprise. Henry Whitney was now in the transit business. His brother would soon join him.

WILLIAM

In 1878, after very little debate, New York City had opened its first elevated, steam-powered train line, the Sixth Avenue elevated, and soon Els were running along Second, Third, and Ninth avenues. The city was no longer bursting at its Forty-second Street seams, and with the Els came rapid development into the Fifties, Sixties, Seventies, and even as high as Eighty-third Street. New York had the first legitimate rapid transit system of any kind in the country and the first network of elevated railway lines in the world. It was from this growth that New York's newest fashionable neighborhood emerged, Fifth Avenue, through the East Fifties.

William and Flora Whitney had been content in their home at 74 Park Avenue near Fortieth Street. They had lived there since marrying and had seen three children born there. Only a few months after James Whitney's death, they were not particularly in the mood to uproot. But when Oliver Payne, Flora's brother and William's classmate from Yale, learned that one of the city's most historic homes, the red brick Frederick W. Stevens mansion at 2 West Fifty-seventh Street at the corner of Fifth Avenue, was for sale at a price between $600,000 and $700,000, he had to buy it for his sister. Oliver was a bachelor, and as the one who introduced them, he had taken it upon himself to play sort of a paternal figure for the couple.

It filled four city lots and was blocked at the front by iron-grille doors. The winding central staircase carved out of dark wood was spectacular, and the library on the ground floor covered almost half the length of the home. As beautiful as it was, the Whitneys had to go shopping to fill it, and Flora did so with great enthusiasm. She covered the floors with rich oriental rugs and the walls with bright tapestries and works by the French painter François Boucher, whom Whitney had a special affection for. The Whitneys may have left behind the neighborhood of the Morgans, but in their new home, they were trading up to live across the street from Cornelius Vanderbilt II, whose daughter Gertrude would in a few years marry Will Whitney's oldest son, Harry. It was that marriage that assured the Whitney family's legacy would thrive into the twentieth century and beyond. Gertrude Vanderbilt Whitney became a prominent sculptor and art collector, and after she established the Whitney Studio in Greenwich Village in 1914 and accumulated more than five hundred works of art, she offered them with an endowment to the Metropolitan Museum of Art. When the Met rejected her, she founded her own museum, the Whitney Museum of American Art, on West Eighth Street, for young artists. It would become one of the great enduring legacies of the Whitney family.

Whitney's four-year term as New York City's corporation counsel ended in 1880, and he briefly considered leaving and returning to private practice. But he accepted a second term, and he began to weigh his next move. As for Flora, she threw herself into entertaining. It was a role she relished—and that her husband despised. But Whitney was nothing if not savvy. He recognized that his wife could help him make his own fortune and chart his own course. And so Flora Payne Whitney became New York's grande dame of elegant dinner parties. And William Collins Whitney, already an important man in New York who had horses, yachts, museum-worthy paintings, and an entire library of books at his disposal, set his sights on leaving the law and turning to politics.

ON A FEBRUARY MORNING in 1882, William Whitney was driving his carriage through the north stretch of Central Park. Riding his horses provided him with a rare moment of solitude away from his four children, the dizzying social calendar that his wife kept for them, and his tedious legal work. He enjoyed riding despite how harried the streets could be at certain hours. Only the wealthiest New York residents had private carriages, and because Whitney's parents, both skilled riders, had taught him well as a boy, he insisted on driving his own horses whenever he could.

On this winter day, the forty-one-year-old Whitney was ready to head for home when he pulled up behind a pair of chestnuts trotting through the park more slowly than he preferred. Impatient, he steered his animals out of the park onto Fifth Avenue heading south and pushed them to pick up the pace. He had gone only two blocks when he saw a large wagon heading in his direction. Just as they neared, a handcart pushed by a boy veered out from behind the wagon. Whitney's horses dashed across the avenue, still in his control, until they came upon another wagon. He tried desperately to straighten them out, but instead he lost the reins. In an instant, Whitney was flying through the air. His carriage had struck a curb and tossed him clear into a telegraph pole, while his horses ran ahead without him down to Eighty-third Street. One of them broke a leg and caused the other to stop. The injured horse was shot dead on the street by a police officer, while a battered Whitney was taken home. His doctors were called to his mansion, and they told him that while he was a lucky man, he had fractured his left ankle, bruised his left knee, and sprained his left wrist. Bed rest, they ordered. Whitney had hoped that a leisurely ride might clear his head so he could think about the next chapter in his career. Instead, it had landed him on crutches. Telling him to sit still proved fruitless, since only a few days later, still bandaged in splints, he got himself back into his carriage for another ride. But that only set his recovery back further, while providing endless amusement for the city's papers like *The Tribune*. "Tammany may as well take warning," the paper wrote. "There's no use trying to upset or break down this man. He doesn't know when he's smashed up and keeps right on as usual!"

That was certainly true. But after a decade bogged down in the minutiae of city politics, Whitney was ready for his next challenge. He had no idea how much his life was about to change.

ON MONDAY, NOVEMBER 6, 1882, eight months after his riding accident, Whitney sent his letter of resignation to New York's newest mayor, Democrat William R. Grace.

Whitney chose the day before the election to step down because he had put hundreds of hours into backing the campaign of the Democratic candidate for governor and wanted to enjoy the election without worrying about any implications on his job. He also wanted to return to private practice. He had collected a wealth of expertise in finance, taxation, and franchises, and along with his past experience in banking, real estate, and transportation, he hoped to build a thriving practice and finally make his own fortune. His resignation letter summarized what he had told a reporter a few weeks earlier, when he said, "I am exceedingly anxious to get out of the office." Unanimously, the newspapers praised his seven years of service as corporation counsel, and some predicted that the Democratic party would be wise to find a powerful place for him.

Even if he had no interest in running for elected office again, after a disastrous run for district attorney early in his career, Whitney still loved the game of politics. When Buffalo's mayor, Grover Cleveland, considered a run for governor early in 1882 and sent an aide down to the city to collect the advice of a few trusted and respected political leaders, Whitney was blunt with the aide. Go back upstate, he said. Build a stable of delegates who will support Cleveland no matter what, and then we'll talk. Privately, Whitney was sure Cleveland had no chance, even though he did like and respect him for the way he ignored anyone with ties to the Tammany Hall machine.

"Frankly I think there is no more chance of his being nominated for governor than there is in his being struck by lightning," Whitney said.

But lightning did strike after Cleveland's aide took Whitney's advice back to Buffalo, and on November 7, the day after Whitney had resigned his counsel job, Grover Cleveland swept into the governor's office by a huge margin.

Whitney was exhausted. It had been an emotional year, between his riding accident, Cleveland's campaign, his resignation, and Cleveland's election. He retreated into private life and work, and he spent time with his family. While Whitney had been busy building his career, his wife had come to love the New York society scene, throwing parties and making sure they did not miss any. They certainly didn't miss the party that came to define the Gilded Age, when Mrs. William K. Vanderbilt threw an extravagant ball on the evening of March 26, 1883. The Vanderbilt mansion at the corner of Fifty-second Street and Fifth Avenue was ablaze in light and the sidewalk outside pulsed with a crowd that watched as mounted police struggled to keep order while more than a thousand costumed guests paraded inside.

AS THE SPRING OF 1883 arrived, Flora Whitney was eager to take the children on a vacation. It was an exciting time in New York, as construction on the Brooklyn Bridge, expected to open by the summertime, was finishing up. But Flora's mind was elsewhere. Anytime she would see one of the massive British White Star steamers pull into New York harbor, she desperately wanted to board one and sail away. William Whitney was simply too busy with his practice to go, but he wanted his wife to enjoy herself and encouraged her summer getaway. He promised to write her frequently, just as he had during their courtship. She packed up their four children and, on May 23, the day before the Brooklyn Bridge opened to the public, hugged her husband a tearful good-bye, and the five of them boarded a ship for Europe. She was eager for her children to see the museums and the opera, to hear another language, and to broaden their education. As the boat pulled out, eleven-year-old Harry kept his father in sight as long as he could by running the length of the ship.

Four days after his family left, Whitney mailed off the first of his many letters. "There is nothing prettier in the world than your relation to your children," he wrote his wife.

But he grew worried a few weeks later, when she didn't reply to his question about how the children were. Instead, uncharacteristically, she had sent a very brief letter with few details. In another letter, however, that arrived June 5, he received his answer. Harry and Willie were deathly sick, and six-year-old Olive, their youngest, had just died of diphtheria while they were in Paris. Whitney was crushed and immediately arranged the seven-day voyage to meet up with his family, even as he fretted that more of his children might die before he got there. The day before he sailed, he sent Flora one last cable. "Bear up, My Dear, we must. You must for me and I will for you. It is true that nothing could have taken so much from us as this but it is passed and cannot be recalled. I must see her face once more, remember this in making arrangements."

He arrived to find that Harry and Willie had recovered, and Pauline never caught the illness. But Whitney's heart was broken all over when he saw Olive's face through a glass-covered coffin and read the diary Flora had kept about Olive's last hours.

"The only time [Olive] spoke when I could not understand her was about twenty minutes before she died. 'Mama, hold my hand,' rang in my ears. I went away and when I returned to see her she had on her steamer dress, a crown on her head of white rosebuds, garden pinks and white flowers at her feet, with a bunch of pinks in her clasped hands." Flora wrote how she went down to see Harry, and when she returned to Olive, she was gone. "The eyes sunken, the sweet mouth and nostrils black; but the head and the little ears charming and the expression as though she was dreaming in a soft still way."

Before Whitney sent her body back to New York for burial, he clipped a lock of Olive's blond hair. He placed it inside an envelope and would hold on to it for the rest of his life.

HENRY

Boston was bursting, and Henry Whitney was poised to capitalize on the city's growth and its expansion. On March 4, 1887, he stood before the general court of Massachusetts to present two ideas. He had recently toured Berlin's popular tramway system, and when he came to speak he was armed with maps, schedules, and even sample tickets from the company that operated Berlin's system. Because he was addressing a government body that had oversight over Boston and the entire state of Massachusetts, he came in prepared to emphasize that his plan would benefit not only the eight hundred thousand people in the metropolitan district but also those as far out as Lynn, Salem, Lowell, Lawrence, and other cities.

Whenever he made an important presentation, several habits of Henry Whitney's surfaced. His dark blue suit, perfectly tailored to fit his stout frame, was his choice of business wear, along with a plain white shirt and light blue tie with white dots. He also tended to drum his fingers in a nervous, impatient sort of way. And, as he learned at a young age, a moistened finger in his ear did a little something to help his defective hearing. His hair was also meticulously combed, dark in the back and on top, but graying above the ears. Only his thick blond mustache hinted at his more youthful side.

In Whitney's mind, if he controlled Beacon Street, he controlled Brookline. And if he controlled Brookline, he controlled the one wealthy community that Boston's leaders and thriving streetcar companies had so desperately wanted for years. The suburbs, he had been telling people, were the key to unlocking Boston's gridlock. If more people moved farther out of the city, it would encourage the street railway companies to follow them out there. And if those streetcar companies in Boston wanted to capture the growing business coming from Brookline, they would need tracks to connect them there. Tracks need land, and that was something Whitney owned in abundance.

He had just one problem. Starting up his West End Street Railway Company was proving more challenging than he anticipated. *The Boston Globe,* in 1887, showed just how busy Tremont Street was downtown when it counted 303 cars passing by the Park Street Church at rush hour, a staggering number. A *Globe* writer said traffic moved at "a mile an hour pace." There simply were too many people and not enough trains.

Riders may not have been happy. But the railway companies were getting richer by the minute, and they would fight to keep any new competitors away from their passengers. Whitney had to convince lawmakers that he had a solution to make the streetcars less crowded, and the streets of Boston, too. His speech showed the confidence of a man no longer living in the shadow of his father, or even his more successful brother in New York.

"That the streets of Boston are and have for a long time been overcrowded with cars and vehicles," Henry Whitney said, "and that to remove or diminish the difficulties arising therefrom, and to furnish such further accommodation as the public requires, it has become necessary to construct tunnels under Boston Common and under Beacon Hill, so-called, in said City of Boston, running to some central point near Tremont and Park Streets, and diverging in various directions to different portions of said city." He said the tunnel he was proposing was "somewhat similar in construction to the Greathead system," a reference to British engineer James Henry Greathead, whose tunneling shield that dug the London Underground was a vast improvement over the one Marc Brunel had designed for the Thames Tunnel. Whitney even outlined the path of the tunnel. "Our proposed tunnel follows the edge of the Common on Tremont Street, then across Park Street under the Park Street Church, and under the Granary Burying Ground, through Tremont place."

It was the first time anybody had proposed to tunnel underneath the streets and parks of Boston. But he was not done. He also asked for what he described as "uniformity of practice" in how street and other railways were overseen, to eliminate the varied fares being charged, the overlapping routes, and the dangerous braking and racing that went on to pick up passengers. It was his way of saying the city needed to consolidate its transit system from half a dozen smaller competing companies into one giant operation.

"Your petitioner," he said, "further represents that it believes that improvements have recently been made in the use of electricity as a motor which render it practicable to use the same in the operating of street railways."

That statement was even more bold than his tunnel proposal. Boston's population had exploded by 400 percent in Whitney's lifetime, from 171,030 in 1840 to 848,740 in 1890, and the city's boundaries had expanded because of all the towns it had annexed. Horses could no longer power a regional transportation network. The electric streetcar could not arrive soon enough.

The other railway companies fought back against Whitney, to no avail. The oldest ones, the Cambridge and the Metropolitan, merged their powerful systems into one. But Whitney used his financial capital and his political muscle to start buying up stock in the Cambridge, Metropolitan, South Boston, and Middlesex lines, sparking fears that he was moving toward creating a monopoly. The financial capital of his company would grow from $80,000 to $7 million if he got his way, and after weeks of negotiations, he did.

In the fall of 1887 at a meeting of his new corporation, Whitney spoke not only about his vision for the West End Street Railway, but about his style of management, which he expected his employees to follow.

"I believe that this company is destined to play a very important part in the lives of this whole community," he told his employees. "I am myself deeply sensible of the responsibility which this organization holds in this community."

One of his first acts was to make sure that not only did he keep his friends close, but he kept his enemies closer. Calvin Richards, head of the Metropolitan line, was the first to exchange his shares of Metropolitan for preferred shares of West End stock and was put in charge of the West End's daily operations as general manager. Another onetime competitor, Prentiss Cummings, president of the Cambridge Railroad Company, became vice president of the West End Street Railway.

"Into whose hands will all this pass?" Richards said in explaining his decision. "What kind of men are they? It will pass into the hands, not of a set of speculators, whose headquarters are in a different city, and who long tried to obtain this control, but into the possession of Boston men; will be owned by Boston capital and managed by Boston experience. At the head of it will be a man who has done more to build up our city, both in its real estate and its commercial interests, than any other man of his age; a man who believes, evidently, in the importance of Boston's citizens to own, run and build the street railways of their own city."

On June 15, 1887, three months after Whitney's impassioned speech, the general court of Massachusetts passed an act that gave Whitney all that he asked for: consolidation and permission to "locate, construct and maintain one or more tunnels between convenient points in said city, in one or more directions under the squares, streets, ways and places, and under public and private lands, estates and premises in said city."

With one fell swoop Henry Whitney, a man who had spent the first half of his life squandering opportunities and searching for a purpose, had taken a confusing, expensive mess of a transportation network in

Boston and consolidated it into one company. Whitney's action had, in an instant, handed him control of 3,700 employees, 1,700 street railway cars, 8,400 horses, and 200 miles of track. Those were numbers that made him the sole owner of the single largest street railway system in the world, bigger than anything in London, Chicago, or New York, cities whose populations dwarfed Boston's.

To better organize the business operations, the West End Street Railway Company was split into eight divisions with distinct territories to cover, and each one was responsible for managing their own passengers, employees, horses, and cars. Routes were identified by different colored signs, and signs were placed on cars to tell passengers the final destination. A final change was made that showed the impressive clarity that Whitney had in mind for his system. Instead of continuing to charge riders fares based on how far they traveled, from a few pennies up to ten cents, he implemented a flat, nickel fare for all rides and even allowed free transfers at certain stops. The flat fare was criticized by the small number of riders who rode only a few stops, but they were far outnumbered by the cheers from the increasing number of passengers coming to Boston from the suburbs, who were used to paying the most expensive fare.

WILLIAM

When he returned home to New York in the summer of 1883, William Whitney focused on his grieving wife. Flora comforted herself the only way she knew how, in a world of ball gowns, operas, and extravagant parties. Whitney was content to let her be, knowing the joy she took from entertaining. When his father-in-law ran for the U.S. Senate in Ohio, Whitney was there to help him. And when New York Democrats came looking for a name to run for the presidency, Whitney threw out the name of the man he had already helped get elected once. "If our delegation will present the name of Mr. Cleveland with any degree of unanimity, he will, in my opinion, be nominated," Whitney said.

He was right again. Cleveland won the Democratic nomination. And on November 4, 1884, when the electoral college votes were counted, Cleveland had 219 to Republican James G. Blaine's 182. No state decided the election more than New York. Cleveland had won Whitney's home state by 1,149 votes. That meant if a mere 575 votes for Cleveland had instead gone to Blaine, New York's electoral votes would have gone to Blaine, and he would have won the White House. Only a few people could reasonably claim that they had personally helped convince at least 575 New York voters which way to go in the election, and therefore could argue they had a direct role in electing the president. Surely one of them was Joseph Pulitzer, whose *World* newspaper had aggressively hammered Blaine for months and lampooned him as the candidate for the rich. Another was William C. Whitney. Grover Cleveland was the next president of the United States, and there was no way he was going to Washington without the man who landed him there.

ON A FRIDAY EVENING late in 1884, Whitney sat down in his palatial home on West Fifty-seventh Street, took out several sheets of small stationery, and began to pen a letter to his good friend, the president-elect of the United States.

"Governor—Pay no attention to newspaper or other advocacy of me," Whitney wrote. "You owe me nothing and I should feel really hurt if I thought you would have any feeling of obligation to me. What I have is from sense of duty to our party and our country—It was right (the result has proved it) and that's enough—I want you to succeed and you will. If for reasons personal and sound you should desire me that's one thing— but I hope you believe this of me—that if you shouldn't it would not make the slightest difference in our relations nor in my feelings nor in what I would do for you—I must free my mind by saying this." The letter went on for four pages and was serious and business-like, and it ended with Whitney promising to visit Cleveland in upstate New York in the next few weeks.

It must have been a difficult note to write. Grover Cleveland was Whitney's close friend and political ally, a man he helped get elected governor of New York and then president of the United States. The two men owed each other enormous debts of gratitude. Cleveland knew that he would not be headed for the White House were it not for Whitney's wealth and power in their home state and his ability to round up votes. And thanks to Cleveland's victories, Whitney was officially a man of influence, no longer dependent solely on the fame of his wife's family.

It was as if Whitney wrote the letter hoping to convince Cleveland not to offer him a cabinet position in Washington. But Cleveland's inauguration was scheduled for March 4, 1885, and he was determined to have his full administration in place by then. With Whitney's involvement in his father's freight-carrying Metropolitan Steamship Company and his legal background, he seemed like the perfect fit for secretary of the interior. In mid-February, however, Whitney received a telegram at his home, and inside he found a different and unexpected job offer. Three weeks later, on March 7, 1885, William Collins Whitney was sworn in as secretary of the navy.

HENRY

On a summer's day on the outskirts of downtown Boston in 1887, a problem was reported on Boylston Street of the Roxbury Crossing line of the new West End Street Railway Company. Rather than dispatch one of his men to investigate, the president of the company, as he enjoyed doing from time to time, took to the matter himself. He did not want to cause any alarm among the drivers on the Roxbury line by announcing his intentions, so he merely stepped onto the front end of one of his horse-drawn cars, paid his five-cent fare, and quietly blended in with the rest of the passengers. He stood with one foot on the step and the other on the platform, holding on with both hands while looking down at the experimental conduit beneath the car. He knew his position to be against the railway regulations, but he wanted to see if he could spot the problem himself without making a fuss or attracting attention from passengers. Suddenly, he felt a tap on his shoulder.

"Excuse me, sir, please step up onto the platform," the conductor told him.

Henry Whitney turned and nodded, but he did not come all the way up as required, and so the conductor stopped the car a few seconds later and walked back over to him.

"You'll have to step up on this platform," he said. "It's against the rules of the road to ride on the step. You might fall off and get hurt and then you'd be suing the road for damages and where would I be?"

Whitney laughed at the irony in the conductor's words. If anyone sued the company, Whitney would be the one faced with the consequences. As the owner of the largest streetcar company in the world, Whitney was an immensely popular boss. He visited his car stables frequently, chatting up his workers about their personal lives, riding in the front of cars with drivers or the rear with the conductors, and, most important to them, reducing their hours and raising their wages from two dollars to two dollars and twenty-five cents a day. Even when a grievance arose, the workers were encouraged to simply go see the president, and he would hear them out and resolve the issue then and there. When he would bump into one of his men on the street, he acted as if they were friends, greeting them with a bright smile and firm handshake.

But there were always times when he believed it best to avoid interacting with his workers, and so when Whitney was asked a second time to step up onto the platform, he did so without ever identifying himself so as to avoid embarrassing his conductor. As the car rolled into Boston's congested business district, Whitney discreetly hopped off near the Arlington Street stop, stepping right into a muddy puddle that splattered his dark pants before vanishing into the sea of people. As the trolley pulled away, a passenger on board who had witnessed and overheard the exchange approached the conductor.

"Do you know who that was?" he asked.

"No, and I didn't give a damn," the conductor said.

"That's President Whitney," the passenger said, before bursting out laughing and getting off the car himself a few stops later.

A look of fear crossed the conductor's face. He had just chastised his boss without recognizing him. Was this to be his last day working for the company? Hardly. The company president never mentioned the incident, and the conductor gained a special appreciation for how genuine Henry Whitney was.

ON JANUARY 26, 1888, Whitney hired Daniel Longstreet from Providence as his new general manager. Getting Longstreet was a coup. One of Rhode Island's most respected public figures, he had joined a Rhode Island Civil War regiment when he was just fifteen and earned great respect for taking such risk so young. Three years later, he took his first job as a conductor in Providence on a Union Railway Company horsecar, and very quickly he rose up the ranks into a clerk's position and soon treasurer, which put him in charge of the finances of over six hundred men, and of fifty miles of routes. He was seen as a prince of a man, and when it was announced he was joining Whitney in Boston, the papers described it as a devastating blow for the city he was leaving. "How the company can spare the services of Mr. Longstreet is the puzzle of Providence," *The Globe* wrote when his hiring was announced.

Whitney knew what he was getting in Longstreet, an experienced manager with strong opinions. They would not always agree, and Whitney was better for it. He was no longer the impetuous, risk-taking businessman. He was thorough, patient, and smart. And he knew of some interesting trolley experiments taking place in Pennsylvania and in Richmond, Virginia, where he had already made one trip to meet with a promising young engineer. With his consolidation complete and his eyes set on tunneling under the Common, Whitney forged a new course for Boston. He told Longstreet to pack his bags. He had reached a conclusion. The experimental battery wasn't the future of transit. And neither was the cable streetcar that had gained popularity out west in San Francisco but had quickly proved to be prone to breakdown. Steam was too dirty. And the horse was too slow.

On a mild spring day in 1888, the two men boarded a steam train in Boston. A young man down south had something he wanted to show them.

4

HISTORY MADE IN RICHMOND

IN THE THIRTY YEARS AFTER the Civil War, Richmond, Virginia, was one of America's fastest-growing cities. Between 1860 and 1890, its population more than doubled, to 81,388. By the mid-1880s, some of the city streets were paved and the Richmond City Railway was running steam trains through much of the downtown, along with horsecars. Three suburban districts had been swallowed up by the city, and there was a desperate need to expand transportation out to the people in those parts. The owners of the horsecar companies, however, had no desire to go there. Too far, too expensive. Only when the Richmond city council gave its approval in March 1887 to build the Richmond Union Passenger Railway did the owners realize they could be replaced. They agreed to expand. But they were too late. The West End Ward and the Clay Ward were both too far removed from downtown, and getting to them required going over a stretch of land that was rugged, hilly, and unpaved. Horses couldn't make it. And cable would be too expensive. Richmond's city officials prepared to build a new railway to reach its outlying areas. And they wanted to operate the railway with electric power. All they needed was the right engineer for the job.

The quest to find something faster than the horse, cleaner than the steam locomotive, more reliable than cable cars, and capable of powering entire transit systems would take nearly a decade and become one of man's great pursuits of the second half of the nineteenth century. For some of the world's most brilliant engineering minds, it was an outright obsession. Their names were Charles Van Depoele, Walter Knight, Edward Bentley, Thomas Edison, Werner Siemens, Leo Daft, and, one of the last and the youngest entrants into the field, Frank Sprague. The solution was obvious to all of them: electricity. But discovering the best way to harness it, to turn it into a source of power that could move not just one but multiple trains over rolling hills at the same time, that was the real challenge. In what evolved into a fierce competition, these men followed each other's progress closely in designing an electric street railway system. Sometimes they teamed up with one another. Sometimes they sold out to one another. At other times they complained that their valuable ideas had been stolen. Yet if they shared one belief, it was that while the London Underground was an impressive achievement and the cable streetcar was a sight to behold, rolling through the streets as if it were being pulled along by some invisible magical force, neither of them were the long-term solution for cities.

IN THE SPRING OF 1882, a skinny young American naval officer with round glasses and a slight lean to his walk stepped off the *Lancaster,* a naval ship that was docking in Gibraltar near the entrance to the Mediterranean Sea. He was a long way from his hometown of Milford, Connecticut, a city on Long Island Sound about ten miles southwest of New Haven. But while he was only twenty-five years old, Frank Julian Sprague was fast on his way to becoming one of the most promising engineers in the world. After making his way north to London, he walked down a steep staircase to ride the Underground for the first time, and he made his way over to the Crystal Palace Electrical Exhibition, where the latest breakthroughs from around the world in the field of electricity were on display.

Despite his age, Sprague was already a peer of the more experienced engineers who were exhibiting inventions at Crystal Palace. He was working on a small electric motor that would one day, he hoped, be able to power elevators, printing presses, and clothing manufacturers around the world. And so his presence in London did not go unnoticed. He was offered a chance to be a member of the Jury of Awards and the secretary of the prestigious scientific group. He eagerly accepted both positions.

Sprague was born on July 25, 1857, and he was a studious boy growing up. His mother, a schoolteacher, died when he was just eight, but in those few years she left a stern impression on him about the importance of his studies. His father sent him off to New York to live with an aunt, and in school he became intensely focused, one of the smartest boys in his classes. His favorite subjects were math and science, and his high school principal thought he might excel by attending either West Point or the United States Naval Academy. Sprague's interests seemed perfectly suited for either of them. After graduating from high school, Sprague traveled to Springfield, Massachusetts, on a June morning to take the entrance examination for West Point. By accident, he found himself staring at a four-day exam for the Naval Academy. He didn't panic, and he scored the highest among the thirteen candidates. "A career afloat was far from my ambition," Sprague would say later, "but having won out I decided to at least try it."

First, he needed the money. Sprague borrowed four thousand dollars from a local contractor and a bank, and in September 1874 he left for Annapolis. He graduated four years later; after that, he spent two years out at sea followed by one year ashore that included a brief tour at the Newport, Rhode Island, torpedo station. While he was at sea, Sprague seemed amazed at the journey life had thrown him and unsure what to do with his spare time. He wrote stories that he filed for *The Boston Herald* while in Asia. And he looked for any opportunity to tinker with wires and contraptions.

Two years later, Sprague filed his first patent, on October 4, 1881. His idea was called a dynamoelectric machine, and he applied to show it at the Paris Electrical Exhibition. But when his request was denied, Sprague found himself instead on a naval ship that was departing New York to join up with the American naval fleet in the Mediterranean. When his ship was delayed, he landed in Europe in the spring of 1882, took a three-month leave, and made his way to London. It was there, while at London's Crystal Palace, that Sprague had the meeting that would change the course of his life.

Edward Hibbard Johnson had an eye for talent. He was the one who had hired Thomas Edison in the early 1870s to work for a new company called Automatic Telegraph, which its founders saw as a competitor to Western Union. Johnson and Edison worked closely over the next decade, and in fact Johnson was in London to promote Edison's progress with electricity, specifically his incandescent lightbulb. Like Sprague, Edison believed the potential uses for electricity were endless. A few years earlier, Edison had left New Jersey for a trip out west. He was already using small electric motors he'd invented to power a sewing machine and a water pump at his home, and he was beginning to wonder if that same idea could be applied to transportation. In his trip to the Great Plains, Edison saw farmers making long and costly trips just to get their produce and grains to the steam railroads. It occurred to him that if the farmers had a lighter, cheaper, narrower railroad, powered not by steam but by electricity, it could serve as a much more efficient link to the transcontinental railroad. Farmers could then spend more time harvesting their land and would be more productive. Edison returned to New Jersey and set to work, excited about the idea of applying electricity to transportation. He hired a crew to build a track one-third of a mile long and a mechanical engineer to work with him on an electric locomotive.

In 1879, before he had invested much time in electric transit, Edison was, at thirty-one years old, already one of America's most famous and prolific inventors. That year, after a brief period when he took time to finish inventing his phonograph, he was determined to perfect electric lighting. On October 21, 1879, he successfully tested the first incandescent electric light, and two months later he demonstrated it publicly to hundreds of witnesses at his research laboratory in New Jersey. He lit up his lab, the town's streets, and a few nearby homes.

Edison and Johnson employed a number of bright engineers to help with Edison's electricity experiments, and in 1882, when Johnson began talking electricity with Sprague at Crystal Palace, it became obvious to Johnson that this was a young man they should employ. In March 1883, after Sprague resigned from the navy, Johnson nudged Edison to hire him. When Edison didn't act immediately, Johnson grew frustrated because he knew Sprague was turning down other offers for the chance to work with Edison.

"I hear nothing from you as to young Sprague," Johnson wrote Edison in April 1883. "An ensign in the U.S. Navy doesn't have enough surplus pocket money to allow him to loaf long. Beside, he is not one who can endure it long. He is very anxious to get to work."

Finally, Edison wrote back. "I received your favor of the 11th this morning and at once called you 'Send Sprague.'"

Johnson, it turned out, was not the only one nudging Edison.

Electrical World, a publication that closely monitored the progress in electricity, made a boast in 1883 that seemed like a pointed attack on the wizard from Menlo Park. *Electrical World* said that while Edison's incandescent light was impressive, it was time to move on and discover other ways the power of electricity could be applied. "The electric light has long ceased to be a curiosity or even a novelty," the publication proclaimed. "It has become a common, every-day affair. To the scientist, to the electrician, it looms up even as a thing of the past. The question to which he now turns is: What shall we do next?"

SPRAGUE SPENT THREE MONTHS in London, and by the time he came home he not only understood the problem with the subway but also had begun to design a solution in his head and on paper. He looked at London's tracks and believed they could serve as one conductor of electricity. But he also came to believe that a second conductor that ran overhead along the tracks and was connected by wire to a moving train could be the missing piece. If electricity could move a single train, could it one day power an entire transit system like the Underground? After leaving the navy, Sprague took the job to work with Edison expecting to be given time to turn his track drawings into experiments. Edison had other plans for him.

When Sprague returned to America in 1883, twenty years had passed since London's subway opened. But no other city had bothered to replicate it since then. Urban transit had become the single biggest civic headache. Traffic was an outright obsession of newspapers and their readers. Day after day, the drawings in any major city newspaper showed overcrowded streets that portrayed the country as bordering on outright panic. Streets were filled with so many moving pieces, of all shapes and sizes, it was a miracle anybody got anywhere. Chairs on wheels, covered wagons, omnibuses, trolleys on tracks, and more, all of them pulled by horses, created an almost deafening wall of sound.

It remained a stubborn problem for which no city had found the perfect solution. London had come closest. It had proved not only that a tunnel could be dug safely underneath a city's streets but also that trains could be run on tracks through those tunnels. The key to the Underground was a centrally located steam engine, powered by coal. When the engine produced mechanical energy, a machine called a dynamo converted it into electric current, which was passed immediately through a rail to the street railway cars. The dynamo (the word comes from the Greek *dunamis,* which means "power") was the earliest form of what is known today as an electrical generator, and it would soon prove critical to the future of the electric railway, as well as to all industries that relied on power to make and move goods. A motor on the cars then converted the dynamo's electric current back into mechanical energy, which powered the wheels to turn and move the streetcars. It was, to say the least, quite complicated. But the complicated technology was not the only reason that no other city besides London had built a subway yet. The giant steam locomotives also scared cities away. They pumped out black smoke and pungent gas and rained down hot steam and showers of soot and sparks into the enclosed tunnels, making the experience of riding the Underground filthy, dangerous, and unpleasant.

An English journalist named Fred T. Jane captured the experience after taking a ride one summer morning aboard locomotive number 18 around the Circle Line of the Underground. For the *English Illustrated Magazine,* Jane wrote of "visions of accidents, collisions and crumbling tunnels" floating through his mind. Sarcastically titled "The Romance of Modern London," Jane's article told a riveting account of how uncomfortable a ride on the Underground could be.

"No time is wasted at stations on the Underground and a minute later the train was off, off into a black wall ahead with the shrieking of ten thousand demons rising above the thunder of the wheels," he wrote. "The sensation altogether was much like the inhalation of gas preparatory to having a tooth drawn. I would have given a good deal to have waited a minute or so longer. Visions of accidents, collisions and crumbling tunnels floated through my mind; a fierce wind took away my breath." The average speed, as Jane described it, was twenty-five miles per hour, but there were a few spots where the train reached forty miles per hour. As his train reached the Gower Street station, Jane described the air as growing more foul until he was coughing "like a boy with his first cigar." At that point, the driver turned to Jane. "It is a little unpleasant when you ain't used to it," he said. "But you ought to come on a hot summer day to get the real thing."

The author's trip lasted a little more than an hour and covered thirteen miles of track and included twenty-seven stops. When his ride was over, the engineer said to him, "This finishes our journey, unless you'd like to go round again." Jane politely declined.

MAY 24, 1883, WAS A sunny day in New York City and one of America's brightest days in history. But as Sprague, now a twenty-six-year-old former U.S. Navy ensign, stepped off his steamship in New York's harbor after journeying across from England, he paid little attention to the crowd of excited people making their way east through the city's streets. He was thinking only about the job that was waiting for him across the Hudson River in Menlo Park, New Jersey, with Thomas Edison.

There was a marching band and police escorts on horses, followed by twenty-five carriages, all moving down Fifth Avenue to Fourteenth Street, where they turned east and made their way down to City Hall. The festivities were all part of a celebration New Yorkers had been anticipating for more than a decade, much as they'd been waiting for a subway. After fourteen years of construction, and two dozen deaths, President Chester A. Arthur and New York's portly governor, Grover Cleveland, who would soon be the next president, were in town to celebrate the opening of the Brooklyn Bridge. Shortly before two in the afternoon, the long procession lined up and headed on foot for the historic march across the East River. As the president, the governor, the mayor, and other dignitaries walked across the 1,595-foot span, behind the band and soldiers from the Seventh Regiment, the sun reflecting off their bayonets, loud applause followed their every step. The promenade where they walked had been open to ticket holders for hours, who lined both sides of the bridge. An estimated 250,000 people followed in the next twenty-four hours. But it was the presence of President Arthur that *The New York Sun* could not ignore the following day in its report. It described the bridge's opening as a climax that ended fourteen years of suspense, "since the president of the United States of America had walked dry shod to Brooklyn from New York."

In speeches that day, it was hailed as "a wonder of science," a monument to "enterprise, skill, faith, endurance." To build the bridge, workers used compressed air to go deep into the river and sink two enormous granite foundations into the river bottom, forty-four feet down on the Brooklyn side, and seventy-eight feet on the Manhattan side. Any engineer could surely have appreciated the challenges overcome to build what many called the Eighth Wonder of the World. But years later Sprague recollected his thoughts that day. "I arrived home on the day the Brooklyn Bridge opened," he would write, "and promptly reported to my employer, who seemed to think that a salary of $2,500 was per year unduly munificent."

If Edison had shown even half the interest in applying electricity to transportation as he did in his work with incandescent lighting, he might have solved the street railway riddle as well. During a visit to Boston, Edison witnessed firsthand the shortcomings of relying on horses for urban transportation. He rode one of Boston's street trolleys into the city's North End, but when the horses struggled to climb a hill near the top of

Hanover Street, it seemed as if they might slide dangerously downhill. In his diary, Edison recounted the experience: "The executive department of my body was about to issue an order of ejectment when some of the passengers jumped out and stopped the car."

That should have been enough to steer Edison toward solving the problem of the electric motor. But it didn't. Motors bored him. The phonograph and the lightbulb filled most of his days. He left the worry of electric motors to others on his team, like his newest member, Sprague.

Aside from feeling underpaid by Edison, Sprague was troubled even more by his assignment. E. H. Johnson had told Edison that Sprague's interest was in electric motors and recommended Edison use Sprague to research them. But Edison's interest remained in lighting, and he wanted his newest employee to help run his construction department in the cities that were installing central stations for Edison's lighting system. Sprague had little interest in lighting, but he followed his instructions and went off to Sunbury, Pennsylvania, and then Brockton, Massachusetts, to get their plants up and running. His displeasure at the assignment was evident in his work. In Sunbury one day, he forgot to oil a new electric dynamo, causing its bearings to burn out hours before the plant was to be unveiled and leading to one very long night for himself and Edison in making the repairs. In general, however, it was only late at night that Sprague was able to focus on what he wanted: building an electric motor.

The next year only reinforced in Sprague's mind how badly he wanted to be a pioneer in designing the perfect electric motor. In April 1884, when Edison finally asked Sprague to step away from lighting and turn his attention to using electricity to create power, it was too late. Sprague had decided he no longer wanted to report to Edison or have to rely on Menlo Park's resources. He told Edison he had made such progress on his own that he wanted to be recognized for what he achieved independently, and not as an Edison apprentice.

"You will surely understand me when I say that I desire to identify myself with the successful solution to this problem," Sprague wrote to Edison on April 24, 1884. He said he wanted to pursue electric traction with the "same spirit with which you attacked the electric light, with the result of making yourself world-famous."

It was not a resignation letter, but it may as well have been. "As your subordinate, I cannot work with the same freedom as if I take the future into my own hands," Sprague wrote. In the letter Sprague told Edison that he was willing to continue working together, but only if their arrangement changed, and he said if Edison wanted him to resign, he would. If not, he asked to work on his own projects predominantly, and consult on Edison's as needed. He assumed Edison would never accept those conditions, and he was right. On the same day he received his employee's letter, Edison replied. "Sprague, as we are about to close out our construction dept.," he wrote back, "I think the best way is for you to resign on the 1st for the reason that your position would be so curious as to be untenable."

The following day, Sprague submitted his resignation letter. "Trusting that the reasons given in my letter of yester-date meet with your approval, I am, very truly yours, Frank J. Sprague."

Not even a full year after one of the world's brightest young engineers reported to work for, and to learn from, one of the world's most famously accomplished engineers, their professional relationship was over. Six months after leaving Edison's employment, at just twenty-seven years old, Sprague took his first step toward independence. He began to devise the electric motor, which was needed to give cities hope that a more enjoyable subway experience was possible than the London Underground.

IN NOVEMBER 1884, WITH A measly budget of $100,000, Sprague gave himself a salary of $2,500 and incorporated the Sprague Electric Railway & Motor Company. At the time he launched his company, Sprague was still a single man who enjoyed burying himself in his work for months, sometimes years, before taking a break. But somehow in the spring of 1885, he found the time and the desire to visit New Orleans. There, he met a younger, beautiful, dark-haired woman whose marriage had recently failed, whose father had long ago died, and whose mother was a famous doctor in the South. Twenty-one-year-old Mary Keatinge and Frank Sprague fell in love in no time, and on April 21, 1885, at Trinity Church in New Orleans, they were married. *The Daily Picayune*'s society column sounded almost mournful at the loss of a woman it described as one of the city's "loveliest and most charming girls."

She would need her charm to make new friends, because back in New York after their honeymoon, her husband once again lost himself in his work. A motor that Sprague had displayed a few months earlier at the International Electrical Exhibition in Philadelphia had been widely praised for several features that others had struggled with. It produced no sparks. And it could operate at a constant speed for long stretches, whether it was pulling twenty pounds, two hundred pounds, or more. Even Edison, who came to Philadelphia for the exhibition, was impressed. "His is the only true motor," Edison told a reporter one day. Edison believed not only that Sprague's invention could run streetcars but also that it was the future of the subway.

In January 1886, Edison gave an interview to *The Boston Daily Globe*. Only a few weeks earlier, Sprague had visited Boston to speak to the Society of Arts. In his speech, Sprague explained the blueprint for his electric streetcar system. Edison was well aware of what Sprague had said, and when *The Globe* asked him about whether an electric subway was far off, Edison said the problem was that city planners were overthinking the idea. He said it didn't require any patents, just a very simple way to dig and to place electrical wires under the ground and insulate them. That's it. "The peculiar device which ought to be adopted in New York and all other cities is a simple tunnel, or horizontal hole in the ground," Edison said. "It should be as simple as possible—a plain viaduct, in which the various companies can lay their electrical contrivances and supply the means of insulation. I suppose they are bound to hear everybody, but, having heard, they should cast aside all newfangled inventions and throw the companies on their resources; else they will be in constant trouble."

Edison's words came at the same time Sprague's electric motor was being snapped up in the United States, and across Europe, for all sorts of uses, from factory mills, where it could speed up production of clothing, to presses, where it made printing immeasurably faster, and even to the central power stations Edison needed for his lighting systems. In Boston, a furniture dealer installed an elevator powered by a Sprague motor, triggering a wave of sales in the city and across the country. Within a few months, 250 Sprague motors were being used in the States, and soon the company had a catalog listing all the various-sized motors it produced, from the biggest, one hundred horsepower, to the smallest, at half horsepower. Sales were so brisk that Sprague leased a factory space in New York for manufacturing. Quicker than even he'd imagined, he was achieving the fame that he'd hoped for by leaving Edison.

IN EARLY 1886, IN A narrow alleyway between two brick buildings near the Durant Sugar Refinery off East Twenty-fourth Street, Sprague gave New Yorkers a glimpse of their future. In the alley, there was a stretch of track two hundred feet long and barely ten feet wide and generators that could supply up to six hundred volts of electricity.

His visitor on this day was a small thin man who was increasingly powerful and well on his way to becoming one of the most loathed men in the country. Jay Gould was raised poor in upstate New York and, after moving to the city, became involved first in the leather trade and then in the stock market, where he wormed his way up through lawsuits, bribes, and lies. By the mid-1880s, Gould was, despite efforts to beat him down, a powerful player in New York thanks to his controlling interest in the Manhattan Elevated Railway Company, which helped him become one of the ten richest men in America, not to mention one of the most vilified. In the early 1880s, he had infuriated New Yorkers when he tried to convert Battery Park, valuable to the working-class Lower East Side families because it was the only nearby open space, into an elevated loop. Now, a few years later, he was exploring new ideas, which is how he came to meet with Sprague. If Gould could be convinced of the possibility of Sprague's invention, he had the fortune to pour into it.

Sprague had been tinkering for years with motors on streetcars. The biggest advantage his idea offered over steam was that electricity eliminated the need for big, expensive, and powerful locomotives because each car could have its own motor. That would allow for longer trains to carry more passengers and provide greater relief from congestion. And, with a few central stations providing all the power, electric traction would be vastly cheaper than hundreds of steam locomotives or thousands of horses that lasted only a few years. Sprague recognized the potential fortune he had in electric traction, and he knew that if he ever managed to perfect a system it would be too big an idea to go alone. There was too much demand for electric streetcars from around the world. He needed a capitalist, someone willing to gamble on the future with him, someone with a whole lot of money who was willing to take an enormous risk. After more than a year of making speeches and presentations to any gathering that would listen about the benefits of electric power, he found a group of wealthy railroad owners and potential investors, Gould among them, who were not only interested in his invention but also ready if he could prove to them it worked.

Sprague could only get a railroad flatcar, not a streetcar, to run his experiment at the sugar refinery. It was so wide that it barely fit on the tracks in the alley. But it would have to do. Underneath Sprague's flatcar was his breakthrough, a way to effectively link traction motors to the wheels in a secure fashion. The motors were mounted in what he called the wheelbarrow fashion. A part of the gear-drive motors was attached around the axle of the car, and a part was mounted with a spring onto the frame. This allowed the motor to bounce on the tracks without losing the gear it was in, a problem that plagued other innovators who'd been experimenting with the same idea. Another tweak that Sprague introduced on his flatcar was a braking system in which the motors acted as generators during braking, actually delivering electricity into the car's system even while helping it slow down.

Nervous and determined to make sure his experiment went as planned for Gould, Sprague decided to drive the car himself rather than rely on an assistant. When Gould arrived at the sugar refinery, he was at first reluctant to climb aboard the funny-looking flatcar, unsure about this new technology and wary of this young engineer he hardly knew. But Sprague convinced Gould to come up, and he positioned Gould to stand at the front. Sprague thought having Gould at the front would make the quick ride more exciting for him, and for the first few seconds everything went fine as the flatcar pulled away smoothly and the group relaxed. Then disaster.

"Desiring to make an impressive demonstration of how readily the car could be controlled and braked in the short distance available for movement, I handled the controller rather abruptly," Sprague recalled later. He tried to impress Gould with the motor's ability to accelerate the streetcar, but instead he pushed the motor too hard and caused a fuse to blow, which triggered a bright yellow flash, a loud explosion, and then a storm of sparks, right where Gould stood. It so surprised Gould that he tried to jump off the moving car in a panic and had to be restrained. Gould was more embarrassed than hurt, but it didn't matter. Sprague tried to reassure his visitor that "this young volcano was only a safety device," but Gould was having none of it. There was no way he would trust the invention after that, and he left, never to return. Sprague's golden opportunity was gone.

The Manhattan Elevated Railway Company, which controlled the Second, Third, Sixth, and Ninth Avenue elevated lines, and which was Sprague's ticket into Gotham, would not be investing in electricity anytime soon. As for Sprague, he continued to run successful, impressive, and speedy demonstrations of his invention for more than a year, moving from the sugar-refinery alley to the long, straight stretch of elevated tracks at Thirty-fourth Street. But at the end of 1886, running out of money to fund his test runs and unable to line up a contract to run his electric cars, Sprague finally picked up his life and prepared to leave New York.

SPRAGUE HAD FIRST REVEALED DETAILS about his innovation in Boston, at a meeting of the Society of Arts a few weeks before his embarrassing gaffe with Gould. In Boston he revealed that he had discovered a way to return electric current from the train to a third rail on the tracks while braking, which allowed for safer slowing and stopping, especially down hills. This mechanism also essentially turned every motor on every car into a generator that would feed power back into the system for every car to be able to use. That would save enormous amounts of money, by Sprague's calculations 71 percent on the Third Avenue elevated line of the Manhattan Elevated Railway Company. But Sprague knew that a New York example was of little interest to Bostonians and might even turn them off. And so, toward the end of his speech before the members of the Society of Arts, he addressed their city's woes and revealed just how closely he had been studying Boston, even while he was experimenting in New York.

"I have presented these facts about the present and future of the elevated roads of New York for your serious consideration," Sprague said, "not because you are particularly interested in New York, but because the problem of rapid transit in Boston has become one of the urgent needs of the present. As the elevated roads in the former city met with great opposition, so has the project of reaching the suburbs of Boston aroused a host of objectors."

He was correct. Bostonians were in the midst of a furious debate over how to extend their streetcar lines to the growing suburbs. Sprague was well aware of Boston's objections to elevated trains, mainly that the streets were too narrow and twisting to accommodate a massive network of overhead rails. But he tried to assure his audience that they should reconsider. "Such roads can be built," he said, "the structures of which will not take up as much room in the streets, will not obstruct the air and light much over one-half as much as the New York roads, and I feel confident that they can be built for less money."

And, he said, with trains powered by electricity rather than steam, the conditions plaguing New York would never be experienced in Boston. "Dust, smoke, cinders, oil and water will disappear," he said. "Power will cost less. Trains can run at shorter intervals and under more perfect control. The energy of the train will become available for the purpose of braking. Repairs of the superstructure will be less. In short, electric propulsion, more than any other thing, will make practicable for Boston what it has so long and so sadly needed, rapid transit to its suburbs. I need hardly point out to you the increase in the value of this property, which will more than pay the cost of the roads."

Frank Sprague was no fool. By talking about street railways in Boston and how they would increase property values in the suburbs, he had to know that one man in particular would be paying rapt attention. Henry Whitney owned not only the largest street railway system in the world but also valuable property in Brookline that he envisioned as an ideal stretch for electrified tracks. Sprague had successfully launched tests of his electric railway in small towns like Wilkes-Barre, Pennsylvania; Wilmington, Delaware; and St. Joseph, Missouri, but he also knew that those were tiny experiments that garnered little attention. He needed a metropolis to win the credibility that he craved. He had hoped it would be New York. But that was history now. He set off to find another investor in another city, someone who, unlike Jay Gould, didn't scare so easily.

THE CONTRACT THAT RICHMOND OFFERED Sprague to electrify twelve miles of tracks put the city at little risk but was an enormous gamble for him. They wanted him to supply the city with forty cars, each equipped with two motors. They wanted him to install an overhead system of wires to carry the electric current and a 375-horsepower generating station. Of the forty cars he supplied, thirty had to be able to operate at the same time. And there had to be a guarantee that the cars could climb a hill with an 8 percent grade, not to mention maneuver around twenty-nine curves, including half a dozen sharp ones. Those last two stipulations may have been Sprague's toughest challenges. The largest electric railway system at the time had eighteen cars and operated in Montgomery, Alabama, and the terrain those tracks covered was flat, nothing like Richmond's. Now Sprague had to design a system to move thirty cars at once, over steep hills. And, even if he managed to achieve all the demands Richmond put on him, Sprague still had to show that his system worked for sixty days, and only then would the railway pay him $110,000. The completion deadline for the entire operation was ninety days from the day that enough track work was finished so the electrical work could begin. If he didn't meet all the requirements and dates, he got nothing.

It was an absurd arrangement, but to Sprague it was a challenge. He was being asked to furnish new streetcars with nearly as many electric motors, eighty, as there were being used throughout the rest of the world. And he had only blueprints of a plan and some experimental motors to start with. But Richmond was the break he'd been looking for, and there was no way he could pass it up. He signed the contract, and on May 25, 1887, his crew went to work at the corner of Twelfth Street and Franklin Street in downtown Richmond. The paper was barely dry when a dangerously high typhoid fever lay Sprague out, flat on his back. Weeks passed before he could barely move. And the clock was ticking.

WHEN SPRAGUE FINALLY GAINED ENOUGH strength to return, nine weeks had passed and Richmond was losing patience. His first day back was October 1, 1887. Two of his chief assistants, S. Dana Greene and Oscar T. Crosby, were, like Sprague, young graduates of the military academies, and in Sprague's absence they made remarkable progress. In Richmond, Greene tackled the tracks, and in New York, Crosby worked on the motors. Sprague employed a team of a dozen bright young engineers, some from Ivy League schools, others from West Point or his own alma mater, the United States Naval Academy in Annapolis. Greene and Crosby were his stars.

The tracks that awaited Sprague in Richmond were an unexpected problem for the men. Not only were they fastened insecurely to the ground, they were joined together weakly and laid unevenly on a bed of red clay. In wet or humid weather, hardly a rare occurrence in Richmond, the clay became wet goop, the tracks sunk into the ground, and all rail travel ground to a halt. Sprague described the tracks as "laid for profit, not for permanence," and he was being kind. They were a disaster. He and his men spent weeks filling mud holes and strengthening the ground around the tracks, but that was only the beginning of their struggle. When Sprague returned from his illness, he took the time to walk along the route where his streetcars would run. Franklin Street, in particular, scared him. It was a steep hill that ran underneath a small bridge that connected two of Richmond's biggest hotels, the Exchange and the Ballard. When he saw that hill, he knew just how powerful a motor he would need. "I was for a moment doubtful of the outcome," he confessed later.

The motors that had been invented up to that point were impressive. But they were also useless to Sprague now. They were little more than experiments: unreliable, expensive, and certainly impossible to replicate on a wide scale. They were designed for onetime use only, not for any widespread application. Sprague needed a motor that was cheap to build, easy to manufacture in large quantities, reliable to run, capable of speeds that no electric motor had achieved before over any great distance, and, last, able to power a fully loaded streetcar of several thousand pounds over steep hills without causing panic among passengers that it might begin to roll backward. That motor had never been built. And now Sprague needed eighty of them. Quickly.

His first attempt failed, and it was such a frustrating experience that he could often be heard telling one of his chief employees to "go to hell" in a burst of anger. So many breakthroughs had been achieved, but the failures seemed sure to doom Sprague's team. Overhead wires for carrying the electric current were strung along the Richmond tracks with little problem. A rigid line that connected the roof of the car to the overhead wire was designed in such a way that a derailed car could return to its track without assistance. That was critical, since it eliminated the need to equip each car with a ladder, as Sprague had first done. Even finding the right lubrication to keep the motor gears grinding was a challenge that took weeks to resolve.

Once those details were worked out, two seven-horsepower motors that were mounted on several streetcars didn't work. As soon as they reached a significant hill, the car would stop cold. It happened so many times that Sprague finally ordered a handful of muscular men to stand at the rear of the car, hop off, and push as soon as the car stalled. At night, when the city slept and to spare Sprague and his men from any embarrassment, mules were sent out to pull the disabled cars home. The workers called it "playing mule."

More power was needed, and with his ninety-day deadline looming, it was obvious Sprague would never make it. The railway owners considered canceling his contract and walking away, but he convinced them to remain patient by altering his deal and saving them money. Sprague's $110,000 payment was cut to $90,000. And instead of getting all of it in cash, as the original agreement said, he would get half in cash, half in bonds of the railway company. A bad deal became worse for Sprague, but he didn't care. He contacted a machine maker in Providence, Brown and Sharp, and pleaded for them to make him new gears for his motors, capable of climbing steeper grades than he'd first expected. They agreed, and in a few weeks the new motors were mounted beneath the streetcars, and a new test run was arranged.

THE MORE PROGRESS SPRAGUE made with his system in Richmond, the more the word spread and the more Henry Whitney warmed to the idea of electrifying Boston's system. On October 10, 1887, a cloudy and brisk afternoon, an ordinary-looking streetcar rolled slowly out of a shed in Cambridgeport just across the Charles River from Boston. It was an open wooden car with rows of benches front to back and no windows. It was a curious sight, this streetcar. There was no horse in front of it and no paying passengers inside, but it was crowded nonetheless as it first started moving west down the Cambridge track. It was only an experiment involving a single streetcar, not an entire system of them, but the electric streetcar of the West End Street Railway Company was ready for its first test.

Along with reporters from Boston and Cambridge newspapers, the seats inside were filled with some of the most important railroad men involved in the project and observers from other cities who came to see if an electric trolley system could work for them. In all, forty-four people started on the trip, and six more would be picked up along the way. There was Calvin Richards, the president of the Metropolitan Railroad Company; Prentiss Cummings, president of the Cambridge Railroad Company; Henry D. Hyde, representing Whitney's West End company; C. W. Watson, of the Cleveland street railway; and a dozen other men. Manning the controls was Dana Greene, from the Sprague Electric Railway, an electrician who was also the most experienced person in dealing with the electric motor. Frank Sprague was closing in on his design, which would allow a city to convert its entire streetcar operations to electricity, and this experiment was one more effort to convince Henry Whitney how beautifully it could work.

Whitney was certainly leaning toward electrification, but he was not yet fully convinced. He was so skeptical that even as he was experimenting with electric streetcars, engineers in Boston were tinkering with designs for a cable car system.

The plan on this day was for the electric streetcar to head west toward Harvard Square and then loop back toward Boston, pass down Charles Street, along Beacon Street, and eventually to Huntington Avenue before turning around and heading back to Cambridgeport. As the car made its way toward Harvard Square, those on board could not help but notice the reaction of the horses that they passed. As the electric streetcar rolled by, horses could be seen flinching and fidgeting, pricking up their ears and tossing their heads high in the air, as if they sensed their pending demise.

The streetcar picked up speed as it moved toward the square, surpassing ten miles per hour without any hitch. It stopped and started smoothly and took the turns with a grace that no horse-pulled car could ever do. It was nothing like the herky-jerky rides that passengers had grown accustomed to. The longer it traveled, the more people seemed to line up along the road to see the curiosity, and soon it was almost like a parade route. An old woman on the side of the road, apparently unconvinced at what was really powering the vehicle, was heard muttering to her neighbor as the car passed her, "the pesky thing must be pushed along by the men inside."

The first glitch came as the car reached Harvard Square. As the streetcar went around a sharp bend at the corner of Main Street and Mount

Auburn Street, the forward wheels caught on a safety rail intended to protect against derailment and came off the track. The streetcar came to an abrupt stop. To the passengers, it was an odd experience. Streetcars pulled by horses almost never fell off the tracks because the horses on sharp turns moved outside the rails and kept the forward wheels closely pressed against the inner edge. And even when a horse-pulled car did derail, the conductor was able to stop the horses instantly so that the car veered only a few feet from the rails and could be easily righted and get back on its way. But an electric streetcar had to rely on its own agility and cornering to stay on the tracks. And there were no horses to stop it quickly and the braking system was hardly perfect. A brisk-moving electric streetcar could go as much as fifty feet off the tracks before finally coming to a stop. Making matters worse, electric streetcars were much heavier than their horse-pulled brethren, so lifting them back onto the rails would only be possible if a large number of men were on hand for the task. Finding a permanent solution to this problem would take engineers more than a year, and it involved attaching a secondary wire from the streetcar to the overhead wire to create a power source that could move the car back onto the rails.

That solution did not exist on this day, but fortunately the car strayed only a few feet from the tracks, and, with help from the passengers and the viewing crowd, the delay was brief and the streetcar was quickly on its away again, moving toward Boston. A second pause came about twenty minutes later as the car reached Charles Street in Boston. Once again it fell off the tracks, which prompted Cummings, of the Cambridge railroad, to joke aloud that they must be riding on a portion of the Metropolitan railroad track, to which Richards, of the Metropolitan, shot back, "Yes, that bad portion we bought from the Cambridge railroad." Their jovialness might also have been bolstered by the growing crowds along their journey. Many of the people watching even moved alongside the car, forming almost an escort for the second half of the trip, until the streetcar had made its way back to the shed in Cambridgeport, pulling in easily and without a single accident. The people on board applauded.

The electric car had covered the distance from Harvard Square to

Huntington Avenue, before turning around, in fifty minutes. It was almost the same amount of time a typical horse-pulled car would have taken, but that was partly due to the nine-minute delay caused by the derailment. Everybody on board agreed the ride had been much more pleasant than anything they had experienced before.

A MONTH AFTER WHITNEY'S SUCCESSFUL test of the electric trolley in Boston, a crowd was letting out of the theater in downtown Richmond on a chilly, clear November evening and spilling out into the streets atop Franklin Street. Sprague was ready to find out if any or all the improvements his crew had made in the last month actually worked, and the theatergoers, entirely unaware, were about to get an impromptu show. Sprague took a car out of the shed on Church Hill. On board was a group he had organized that included George Burt, the Richmond streetcar superintendent; Dana Greene; and a reporter from the local paper, *The Richmond Dispatch*. After months of work, Sprague needed to know if just a single one of his self-propelled streetcars could climb a significant hill in the city, because if the answer was no, then he was a long, long way from fulfilling his end of the contract.

With Sprague manning the controls, the car lurched around a sharp curve and pulled to the base of a steep hill. Burt turned to Sprague. "If you can get out of such a curve as that we just left," Burt said, "you can go up the side of a wall."

Sprague was skeptical, and he feared that even if they did climb the hill, the motors would work so hard they'd burn out and be destroyed. Yet somehow he did pull the car over several rolling hills, through a sharp turn, and eventually up to the top of Franklin Street, an especially long hill right where the excited theatergoers were milling about, not quite sure what they had just witnessed. He had done it. It was surely one of the hardest roads an electric streetcar had overcome anytime, anywhere, and Sprague might have allowed himself a smile if not for a buckling noise he heard from the overheated motors. He knew it could only mean one thing. The car, after working so hard, had stalled, directly in front of a large and enthusiastic crowd. He had raised the hopes of the city by climbing such a steep hill, and now Sprague was determined to avoid any embarrassment. He raised his voice to Greene just loud enough to be heard by passersby, and he told him there appeared to be a problem with the car's circuits and that he needed some "instruments" to fix it. As the group on board disbursed, including the *Dispatch* reporter, Greene understood Sprague's code perfectly and went off to fetch some mules. Sprague, hoping the crowd would be gone by the time Greene returned, turned off the lights inside the streetcar so it went dark and, like a child playing hide-and-seek, lay down on a seat so it appeared as if no one was there. By the time Greene came back, nobody was around. The mules, Sprague recalled later, were "the most effective aids which could be found in Richmond under the circumstances." With their help, the car was able to return to the shed.

The next day's *Dispatch* gushed with enthusiasm, unaware of the glitch at the end of the journey.

"It is a success! It is a revolution! It travels over more than two miles of track in Richmond!"

But Sprague knew the truth. Getting a single car carrying a handful of passengers to climb one steep hill was not an achievement worth celebrating. His contract demanded he build an entire system that allowed multiple cars, carrying hundreds or thousands of people, to move at the same time up and down those hills. "My own reputation and future career, as well as that of my associates, seemed blasted if failure marked the Richmond road," he wrote later. The test was nothing but a signal that they were getting close and heading in the right direction.

The next few weeks were exhausting for Sprague and his team, as they made adjustments to the motors, the wires, the tracks, all to improve on what had been a successful, if flawed, trial run. One innovation that was born during this period was a uniquely designed pole connecting the car and the overhead wire that was easily reversed when the car reached the end of its line. By January 1888, Sprague could not delay opening the line any longer. City officials and the owners of the Richmond Union Passenger Railway, which was on the brink of bankruptcy, were demanding results from him. The telephones in Richmond, only a recent addition to the city, had stopped working with so much electricity directed toward Sprague's work. Picking up a phone greeted a caller with only a hissing noise and nothing else. Sprague had to convince the city all of the troubles were worth their patience.

He achieved a greater success on January 7, 1888, when they were able to run nine cars and carry several thousand passengers around the city. And two days after that, a passenger named William A. Boswell stepped onto car number 28, which traveled along Church Hill; handed the five-cent fare to the conductor; and became the system's first paying passenger, even though it wasn't officially in operation yet. By this point, Sprague was exhausted, but he knew there could be no resting. He was bleeding cash so badly that he was forced to take out a $45,000 loan just to avoid personal bankruptcy. Worried about creditors, he ordered his bookkeepers to save dollars wherever they could and to put off paying any bills that could be delayed. "Don't pay a bill that you can help until after April 1st," he ordered. One day in mid-January, feeling particularly low, he wrote to a friend, "I am completely overwhelmed with work, so much so that I hardly know whether I stand on my head or on my heels at times."

Finally, three weeks later, on February 8, in a cold, drizzling rain, Sprague opened the Richmond line for service to the general public. The crowds flocked on board in the early days, but repeated fits and hiccups on the trolleys almost doomed the effort from the start. Cars would creep forward and then stop suddenly in the street, unable to budge. Workers would climb underneath to see if they could determine the problem, and if they could not, to avoid grinding the entire system to a standstill, they would pull the stalled car off the tracks so another could pass by. At first Sprague was convinced the problem was mechanical, something to do with the gears not being cut correctly. It was his Irish mechanic, Pat O'Shaughnessy, who discovered it was something more simple. The gears needed more oil, and by day's end the cars were running smoothly.

But then one winter morning a new problem greeted Sprague. He looked out the window of his rooming house downtown and saw that his overhead wires were coated with ice from the sleeting rain that had fallen overnight. Passengers were waiting as usual for streetcars to carry them, but no streetcars were moving, until, to Sprague's astonishment, one appeared from around the corner, and then another, and then another. At first Sprague didn't understand what had changed, until he looked more closely and saw that on the roof of the lead car, O'Shaughnessy, his trusty mechanic, was balanced precariously while swinging a broom at the overhead wires. Each whack of the broom brought down a shower of ice and snow, but it worked. It was clearly not a long-term solution, but for one day, at least, winter would not beat Sprague's electric trolley.

The next few months were not much better. A few consecutive days of consistent service would be interrupted by a few days of broken-down trolleys, burned-out motors, and worn-out gears. Passengers got used to the failures. They even assisted when needed. If a car derailed, all the passengers would step off, and the sturdiest ones would lean a shoulder into the car and hoist it back onto the rails. But when it was a problem with a motor, there was little they could do. Old motors were being shipped up to Sprague's New York factory by train, and repaired ones were returned. It may have been the only large-trolley, big-city electric railway system in the world, but it was hardly a booming success. "Greene," Sprague said one day to his trusty assistant, "this is hell." It grew so desperate that Sprague looked to save a dollar wherever he could, cutting workers and holding off making any payments that could wait.

But then, when no one seemed to notice, it wasn't hell anymore. The new motors coming back from New York worked better than the old ones. The gears stopped breaking down. The trolleys derailed less frequently. The central power plant proved capable of powering the operation. And a system that for weeks was using only ten or fifteen cars was, by the spring of 1888, using twenty. And then thirty. And then, with no fanfare at all, the magic number written into the contract, forty, was reached. Soon, Sprague's electric railroad cars were averaging eighty miles per day and forty thousand paying passengers per week. Cash was coming in, and relief was in sight. It was a good thing, too. Sprague had 140 men working for him who needed to be paid.

When the Richmond Union Passenger Railway Company told Sprague he had fulfilled his contract on Tuesday, May 15, 1888, the news, which he would later call a "supreme moment" in his life, could not be celebrated as he hoped. The railroad syndicate that hired him for the Richmond job went bankrupt. Banks took over for the syndicate, but Sprague had lost more than $75,000 making Richmond's trolley system work.

It would have been disastrous, except that Sprague, a great engineer, was equally adept at marketing. The day after receiving the news about his contract, on Wednesday, May 16, 1888, Sprague sat down and wrote a letter to Henry Whitney in Boston. Whitney and Sprague were not friends, but they were hardly strangers. Sprague's electric motors were being used in Boston more than in any city in the world, and Whitney was well aware of it. One of Boston's biggest printers, C. A. Heyer & Son, went so far as to print business cards that said they used Sprague motors and invited customers to come see them.

Sprague knew that Whitney was exploring options for his enormous streetcar system, and he wanted to be sure no decision was made before the two men talked. In two weeks, the first horsecar would ride over Whitney's new Beacon Street route in Brookline, and Whitney knew that could not last. He wanted it electrified. Sprague's letter had to give him hope. "We are ready to run commercially," Sprague wrote. "Kindly suspend order of renewal until I come there Friday."

As word of his achievement spread north and into the Midwest, Sprague was suddenly very much in demand. Cities big and small that had or were considering trolley lines sent officials to Richmond to witness what he had built and explore whether it could work on their streets. With his tracks, motors, and overhead wires, Sprague had single-handedly transformed an entire technology and at long last found a reliable replacement for the horse-pulled trolley.

When Sprague had started work in Richmond in 1887, there were fewer than ten electric railways running in the United States, all of them small systems of just a few cars operating over a couple of miles of track. By the end of the decade, more than two hundred electric railways would be operating or be under construction across the country. In New Orleans, a cry for electric trolleys rang out, and signs around the city appeared with a testament to how frustrated city residents had become. "Lincoln set the negroes free! Sprague has set the mule free! The long-eared mule no more shall adorn our streets." In truth, Frank Sprague had only set the mule free in Richmond. What he needed now was an even bigger customer to take a chance on his system and prove to the world that it worked.

HENRY WHITNEY AND SPRAGUE BY now had traded cordial letters and met in person, and each was well aware of how important they could be to each other. Sprague could make Whitney a fortune. And for Sprague, Whitney represented opportunity. If the owner of the biggest streetcar system in the world embraced and purchased his new technology, cities everywhere would line up to follow. Whitney could make Sprague a hero.

Sprague was eager to receive his visitors from the north in the summer of 1888, because he'd learned in advance that it was Longstreet, not Whitney, who would need the most convincing. Longstreet's fear, which he was repeatedly telling Whitney, was that big cities like Boston would be disastrous for electric streetcars. As soon as traffic jammed up and a long line of cars formed, Longstreet argued that it would put a huge strain on a dynamo when the cause of the traffic cleared and all the cars started up at once. Dynamos would constantly be breaking down under the burden of city traffic, at an enormous expense, in Longstreet's opinion. Longstreet argued that a cable road made the most sense for Boston. Cable-pulled cars were cheaper and cleaner than horses and easy to maintain. As further evidence, Longstreet pointed out to Whitney that New York City was investing in cable as the future of its street railways. But even as Boston began making its own plans to install cables, Whitney was skeptical. It was, he told Longstreet, too important a decision to get wrong.

Boston's streets were narrower than New York's and had far more turns, unlike New York's long and wide boulevards. Additionally, no one had figured out how to get a cable system across a drawbridge, and Boston had several of those. Would routes merely end at a bridge? That seemed wholly unfair and unrealistic to passengers on the other side. Just because New York was chasing cable didn't mean Whitney had to follow. What if they were wrong in New York about the future? Or what if cable was right for New York, but wrong for Boston?

Sprague decided the only way he could convince both men was if he set up the precise situation that Longstreet was most worried about and then proved it was a baseless concern. He knew there was risk to overtaxing his system, for if his experiment failed, surely Whitney and Longstreet would depart on the next locomotive back to Boston and turn to cable instead of electricity to power the Boston streetcars. He dreaded a repeat of what happened with Jay Gould. But Sprague believed he had no choice.

ON A WARM NIGHT in early July 1888, after service for the day had ended and Whitney and Longstreet had retired to their downtown hotel, Sprague had his men park twenty-two streetcars at the base of Church Hill, inches apart from one another, in a straight line. He told his central-station engineer to build up as much steam as the boilers could hold and to keep the fires hot. It took almost five hours for all of the preparations, and it was almost midnight when Sprague was ready.

He had one of his men rouse Whitney and Longstreet from bed. They were part of a group of a half dozen who had come down from Boston. Most of the others were members of the Boston Board of Railroad Commissioners, but two of them had financial interests in the trip. Samuel Little was the president of the Rockland Bank, and Asa Potter was a long-time friend of Whitney's and president of the Maverick Bank. All the men had ventured to Richmond for the same reason Whitney did, to see if Sprague's electric railway really worked. If it did, Whitney, a rich man in his own right, knew he would need the help of other capitalists to invest in it.

All the men were staying at the five-story Exchange Hotel, at the corner of Franklin and Fourteenth streets. Whitney was sleeping when there was a knock at his door. He was told a test run had been arranged that would surely quash Longstreet's cynicism and that it had to be seen at once. "On receiving word about midnight that we were willing to make such an experiment, he immediately arose and we were soon on our way to the eastern sheds, two miles from the station," Sprague recalled years later.

The entire group of men walked the few blocks to the central station in the dark, and then they were taken by horse-drawn carriage two miles away to Church Hill. When they arrived at the corner of Twenty-eighth and P streets, Sprague explained to his audience that he had lined up twenty-two cars in tight formation in a place normally designed to power only four cars, spaced well apart. But tonight, he said, they would see much more than that. Before his guests' arrival, he had ordered his engineer back at the central power station to raise the pressure of the maximum voltage in the system from 400 to 500 volts and to hold it there no matter how much strain was put on the system.

AT 12:20 A.M. ON July 8, 1888, with his groggy visitors from Boston looking on, Sprague waved a lantern in the air, and the motorman inside the first of the twenty-two cars started to inch his car forward, and as soon as they had room in front of them, the motormen behind followed. The system had never had to endure such a huge strain, and a few seconds after the convoy began, the lamps inside the cars dimmed almost completely out, until only a faint orange glow appeared. Back at the central power station, the engineer strained as the voltage dropped to 200 volts per car. But it didn't matter. Gradually the lights inside the trolleys brightened again, and the cars picked up momentum with every foot. No fuses blew. No motors stalled. All twenty-two cars climbed the hill successfully and soon disappeared over the hill and out of sight.

"This was an experiment that had never before been made in any part of the world," *The Richmond Daily Times* reported. "And it was perfectly successful." Whitney, Longstreet, and the rest of the Boston contingent headed for home the next day, their questions answered, and their city's future decided.

· · ·

TWO YEARS EARLIER, THE Third Avenue Street Railway Company
of New York City had been faced with a decision almost identical to the
one that Whitney had been wrestling with for Boston. The men in charge
of the New York decision had traveled north to Providence late in 1886 to
see how well an experimental electric line there was working. It was operating smoothly, and it offered great promise, but when the New Yorkers
learned that an electric railway would cost their city 25 percent more
than a cable-pulled railway, their decision was made in haste.

In making his decision, Henry Whitney did not ignore the cost. It was
clear that cable was the cheaper alternative. But now, at the age of forty-
nine, with a wife; five children; a beautiful, ivy-covered home in Brookline; a vacation estate on the South Shore in the pretty coastal town of
Cohasset; and an enormous operation in the West End Street Railway
Company, he was a changed man, a patient, mature businessman. His patience had led him to Richmond, introduced him to Sprague, and helped
him set the course for the future of Boston.

In 1888, there were six thousand miles of street railway systems across
the United States, and more than 90 percent of those miles were operated
by horses. Only eighty-six miles claimed electricity as the power source,
and the remaining miles were powered either by cable-pulled streetcars
or tiny steam locomotives. As for the streetcars themselves, 21,736 were
pulled by horses, 2,777 by cable, 258 by steam, and just 166 by electricity.
It was very much a horse-pulled world when Henry Whitney and Frank
Sprague turned Boston, and the rest of the country, in a new direction.
Boston was going to be the first major city to say good-bye to the horse
and welcome the age of the electric trolley.

IT WOULD TAKE A DISASTER unlike anything history had ever seen
in order for New York's leaders to reach the same, obvious decision. Heading into the weekend of March 10, 1888, New York City, like the rest of
the East Coast, was winding down one of the warmest winters in years.

Snow was the furthest thing from peoples' minds. If not for the events that were about to unfold, New Yorkers might have ridden cable-pulled streetcars and elevated railways well into the next century, and a subway might have been put off for another fifty years. But on that unusually mild late winter weekend, bright sunshine turned to light rain. And then it started to come down harder. And finally the wind kicked up. Hundreds of New Yorkers were about to die. And as the clock ticked past midnight and into Monday morning, their only clue that something catastrophic was unfolding was that it started to get a little colder outside.

Part Two

THE BLIZZARD AND THE BILLIONAIRES

5

THE BLIZZARD THAT CHANGED EVERYTHING

IT WAS SWALLOWING HIM UP like white quicksand. And the more that ten-year-old Sam Strong struggled to climb through the heavy snow in his new, thigh-high rubber boots, navy blue overcoat, heavy winter cap, woolen gloves, and the muffler around his neck, the more it buried him alive. "You could go to the North Pole in that outfit," his aunt had said to him only a few minutes earlier. But she went right on buttoning him up, and on the morning of Monday, March 12, 1888, she pushed him out the door as if it was just another day. "Hurry up now, so you won't be late for school."

The night before, Sam had looked out the window of their apartment on West 123rd Street near Lenox Avenue north of Central Park and amused himself by watching through the raindrops as the gas lamps on top of the wood and iron posts flickered to life. Lamplighters walked by nightly with a five-foot-long stick. They would reach up until their burning wick was safely under the glass globe, turn the gas lever to ignite the gas jet, and wait until the lamp inside was aglow before moving on to the next one. For a young boy, it was endless entertainment to see globe after globe light up on the street.

The next morning after breakfast, Sam was again looking out the window, but now the rain had stopped and the street was blanketed in white.

He watched as a grown man, at least a full hundred pounds heavier than he was, got blown right over by the howling wind. He told his aunt what he saw, but she wasn't worried. She needed him to run an errand for her before school. A dressmaker was coming to the house at seven thirty in the morning, and she gave Sam a list for the store. Whalebones, chalk for the dressmaker, and a large needle, all to help sew a new corset. When Sam went to the basement to leave, he found it blocked by a pile of snow. He turned around, came upstairs, and went out through the front door instead, floundering and slipping and sliding down the steps without actually feeling them under his feet. The snow was whirling so much it was nearly impossible to see. It felt like needles on his soft cheeks. But for a schoolboy who came from Indiana, it was also an adventure.

The streets of Harlem should have been bustling with pedestrians on their way to work, schoolchildren, and horse-pulled streetcars, and there should have been a constant rumbling overhead from the steady stream of elevated trains. Instead, as he set out on his walk, the city felt deserted. The entire transportation network was being shut down, one system at a time, first the wagons loaded with goods, the horsecars next, and ultimately the steam-powered elevated trains would be paralyzed, too. Any cars that were visible were either abandoned or barely able to move. The snow was waist deep with every step Sam took, and when he finally made it to Lenox Avenue, then Sixth Avenue, and headed north, the wind nearly blew him backward until he could go no farther. He was thrown into a tall snowdrift, and, unable to move, he cried out for help. The whipping wind drowned him out, and the barrage of flakes started to overtake his small body.

The worst natural disaster in American history was reaching its epic force, a storm that, when it was over, would force cities up and down the East Coast to reexamine everything from the way food was delivered to stores to how power lines and telephone lines sent signals into homes to the way transit systems kept passengers moving no matter how miserable the weather. It would spark the rise of one of New York's most important political advocates for the construction of a subway. But it would also claim more than four hundred lives. Sam Strong was one of the first to face the full brunt of the storm's wrath.

IF ANYBODY EVEN SAW THE brief item inside *The New York Times* on the bottom of page 13 on Friday, March 9, they probably ignored it. The four lines appeared under the headline A BLIZZARD IN MINNESOTA and described a heavy snow storm that was crippling trains in that state. Coming only a few months after the "Schoolhouse Blizzard," another storm that killed 235 people, mostly children on their way home from school, across Montana, Minnesota, Nebraska, Kansas, and Texas, this latest one was tracking a similar path. If its course held, it would strike Pennsylvania, and if it didn't fizzle out there, New York would be its next target.

In what seemed like a strange move at the time, John Meisinger, the hardware buyer for E. Ridley and Sons, a department store in Manhattan, spent $1,200 leading into the weekend to purchase three thousand wooden snow shovels. He was merely planning ahead, expecting to keep them in his basement until the following winter, but when a newspaper reporter learned of his curious purchase in such warm weather, he mocked him in an article, calling him "Snow Shovel John."

Saturday was a beautiful springlike day that caused purple and yellow crocuses to prematurely bud and brought out a long line of carriages in Central Park. On Long Island, farmers planted potatoes, and up in New Haven, picnickers lined the riverbank near Yale University, watching the rowers glide down the calm waters of the Connecticut River. In Washington, President Cleveland and his young wife took advantage of the springlike weather and left town for a vacation weekend. That night, on the ninth floor of the Equitable Building, one of the tallest buildings in the world, the army sergeant Francis Long stood in the offices of the New York City Weather Station, where he worked a desk job for the U.S. Signal Service. He looked out at the great city and saw bright stars against the dark clear sky. Down below, he saw throngs of people walking back from the three-mile-long torchlight parade celebrating the arrival of the Barnum and Bailey Circus. With spring beckoning, Walt Whitman, the staff poet at *The New York Herald*, wrote a short piece that weekend titled "The First Dandelion."

> *Simple and fresh and fair from winter's close emerging.*
> *As if no artifice of fashion, business, politics had ever been.*
> *Forth from its sunny nook of shelter'd grass—innocent, golden,*
>   *calm as the dawn,*
> *The spring's first dandelion shows its trustful face.*

It started as a gentle and mild rain during the day, hardly ominous. But it picked up Saturday evening, and the wind started to whistle through the streets, and the temperature plummeted. Only then did New Yorkers begin to suspect that this was no ordinary late-winter storm approaching. In fact, it was two storms, one coming north from the Gulf of Mexico, a second moving east from the Great Lakes. As his Saturday night shift ended, Francis Long put out to the newspapers his weather forecast for the following day. "For Maine, New Hampshire, Vermont, Massachusetts, Rhode Island, Connecticut, eastern New York, eastern Pennsylvania, and New Jersey, fresh to brisk southerly winds, slightly warmer, fair weather, followed by rain. For the District of Columbia, Maryland, Delaware, and Virginia, fresh to brisk southeasterly winds, slightly warmer, threatening weather and rain." His work done, he headed down for the streets. The weather center would close for the Sabbath at midnight, and nobody was scheduled to return until five o'clock in the afternoon the following day. During those seventeen hours, the mildly unsettling weather that Long predicted turned into a beast. Those seventeen hours would have several lasting effects. One of them was the Weather Bureau's decision years later to begin staying open on Sundays, to avoid missing any unpredictable and dramatic shifts in a weather pattern like the one that happened in the early morning hours of Sunday, March 11.

By Sunday morning, the entire East Coast was getting soaked, from Roanoke to Washington to Pittsburgh to Buffalo. In New Jersey, one minister awoke, took in the ominous sky, and tweaked his morning sermon he was about to deliver. "I had the strangest of feelings," he told his parishioners. "It was as if the unholy one himself was riding in those clouds." New England was under a dark shadow, and when a freezing gale from out over the Atlantic Ocean moved back inland and picked up the moisture coming up from the south, the rain turned to snow. Baltimore was one of the first cities to feel the impact, and by dinnertime its streets were covered with six inches, and twenty-five-mile-per-hour winds were whistling past the homes. As midnight approached, Philadelphians saw their trees coated in ice and then watched as branches snapped from the weight. By Monday morning, roofs would blow clear off houses in Philadelphia and southern and central New Jersey, powerful wind gusts of more than seventy miles per hour would shatter windows, and snowdrifts six feet tall would line the streets. The storm only got stronger as it moved north, and by the time it reached New York it was at its peak of fury. The Brooklyn Bridge, only five years old, was ordered closed, so that nobody would be blown off the side by a seventy-five-mile-per-hour gust or get stranded on the walkway and die from the cold. Like most cities, New York did not have an antilittering law, and the newspapers, stray pieces of household trash, tin cans, and shards of broken glass all swirled up into minitornadoes that made walking around treacherous. Worst of all was the stench from the wind blowing up the frozen bits of manure and urine that more than sixty thousand horses had left behind on the streets.

THE GIANT HAND REACHED OUT and pulled Sam Strong up from the drift.

"You hadn't ought to be out in this, Sonny," the policeman hollered to him. "You go straight home."

But Sam had his aunt's list to fulfill, and he continued past more abandoned streetcars on 125th Street, shocked to see a team of horses trying mightily to pull a carriage. He finally reached his destination, Brady's Notion Store, only to find that the snow was piled so high it blocked the door and the window and that it was obviously not open for business. Determined not to disappoint his aunt, even though he knew he was already late, he trekked on for another half mile in search of another store before finally giving up hope and turning around. His aunt and uncle were watching for him out the window, and when he finally appeared and slowly trudged up the front stoop, fighting with every step, they met him at the door and hustled him out of his clothes. He had lost all track of time and was bordering on delirious. The errand he had expected might require just thirty minutes had taken the entire morning.

"Although I had fought the snow for more than four hours," the boy recalled later, "I had failed in my mission. There were many tears." His aunt warmed him up and tucked him back into his sheets. "I was in bed with glass bottles filled with hot water, a big slug of raw whiskey and some food, and I was asleep, not waking until night and then only for more food and drink. I was exhausted." Sam Strong's determination that day was no fluke. Later, after studying at Columbia, he was Dr. Samuel Meredith Strong, and he went on to become the first flight surgeon in the United States Army, and, as a surgeon living in Queens and practicing in Brooklyn, he built and used the first airplane ambulance.

FOR ONE WEEK IN MARCH, bad weather brought the entire northeast to a standstill. A train that left Bridgeport, Connecticut, at 5:41 A.M. on Monday morning went two miles in an hour before it was trapped in a drift. At least it was close enough for the passengers to get off and walk back. Others were not so lucky. Steam trains from Baltimore to Montreal were buried beneath piles of snow, literally stopped in their tracks or derailed, often great distances from any population hub. Once a train stopped, it was over. The snow was falling so fast and accumulating so quickly that anything that wasn't moving was covered over in minutes. If animals were on board, there was little effort made to save them. If it was a passenger train, the best hope was that there was enough food on board to feed folks until help arrived or that they were near enough to a farmer who could supply them with enough water, milk, and food to ration among themselves. Staying warm was a different problem. Steam trains had small coal or wood stoves, and to keep the fires burning passengers stuffed into them seats, card tables, luggage, bags full of U.S. mail, and anything else flammable they could find. And because power and telephone lines all came down in the storm, the crews at the stations had no way of knowing where a train was stopped.

AS BAD AS IT WAS for the street railways, it was worse for New York's four elevated lines. In the early hours of the storm, it appeared as if the Els might be immune from the conditions. It was harder for the snow to accumulate on the narrow overhead tracks. But what quickly became apparent was that it was easier for the tracks to freeze. By Monday afternoon, icicles were hanging off the tracks and the trains were slowing down to carefully navigate the sharp curves and stop within the required boundaries of the stations.

A Third Avenue elevated train heading downtown carrying five hundred passengers struggled to climb the icy grade near the Seventy-sixth Street station and came to a stop on the slight hill. As it sat on the tracks and its crew tried to strategize a plan to keep moving forward, twenty minutes passed. Suddenly, the passengers heard the shrill of another train's whistle barreling toward them from behind. While the first train could not move, the second train could not stop, and a massive tragedy seemed all but certain. Just before his train smashed into the one ahead, the fireman on board the second engine leapt off onto the platform, where hundreds of waiting passengers were watching in horror. As he turned to watch the collision, the fireman yelled to the engineer on the first train.

"Jump, for God's sake, jump!" he screamed.

It was too late. The enormous boom and passenger screams from the collision were followed by a plume of smoke into the snowy air. The two trains slid forward a few more feet, and the tracks shook, but somehow the trains wobbled and did not fall. No car fell off the track, and what seemed like a sure disaster that would cause hundreds of deaths was, incredibly, a minor accident. Passengers smashed windows to free themselves and walked back along the track to the platform or made their way to the ladders that the quickly arriving firemen were leaning up for them.

Though the engineer on board the struck train who had not jumped survived, the engineer who had been unable to stop the second train did not. Samuel Towe was still breathing when he was yanked from the wreckage, but his bones were broken and his skin was burned, and he died before he could be taken to a hospital.

Before the day was over, the transportation system in New York that had seemed the safest and most immune from the snow and ice had proved to be no better than the omnibuses, the street railways, and the steam-powered railroads. By the end of the day on Monday, fifteen thousand commuters would be stranded at various points along the elevated tracks, high above the city streets, scared, angry, frustrated, and cold.

ON WEDNESDAY THE WEATHER turned again. This time for the better. A few more inches of snow fell to the north, but Philadelphia, New York, and Boston all saw temperatures climb back to forty degrees. Tracks began to thaw, roads began to clear, and when a hundred Italian shovelers finally dug out the Boston *Express* at Fifty-ninth Street, trains began to move again.

THE FIRST TRAIN THROUGH, read the headline in *The Times* on Thursday, March 15.

As for the nightmarish prediction of a widespread famine, it never happened, though there were some disastrous, long-term effects from the storm. Horses and cows froze to death. Thousands of pounds of butter and thousands of gallons of milk had to be destroyed after going too long with no refrigeration, valuable losses for farmers, who would need months to recover. Ten thousand coal and iron miners in Pennsylvania were laid off when the railroads lost so much revenue.

There was one bright moment to emerge from the storm. At the New York Infant Asylum north of the city in Westchester County, four hundred children between the ages of two weeks and six years old, along with two hundred unwed pregnant women, normally went through about eight cans of milk a day, supplied by a nearby dairy. With local roads closed, the blizzard cut them off from the dairy, and without their milk for a week or more they could have been at risk. But a few days before the storm hit, instead of the typical order of twelve dozen cans of Borden's canned condensed milk, the asylum was left with twelve gross, or 1,728 cans. The cans were usually for the older children, but now the infants had to drink them, too, and that concerned the physician in charge, Dr. Charles Gilmore Kerley. Cautiously, the staff diluted the condensed milk with barley water to see if the infants could tolerate it. Not only did they like it, but the babies who had been struggling to gain weight suddenly started to fill out. Because of a simple paperwork error, and one forced experiment, canned evaporated milk for infants, with Dr. Kerley's urging for the next fifty years, went from being shunned to being embraced.

The three-day storm cost businesses in New York about three million dollars in sales, though one store that had no problem moving product was E. Ridley and Sons, where John Meisinger's foolhardy Friday purchase of three thousand wooden shovels paid off handsomely when every one of them disappeared in a few hours on Monday. The "blizzard sale," as he called it, netted him $1,800 in less than twenty-four hours. Those Italian laborers also capitalized. The day after the snow stopped falling, they stopped shoveling and went on strike to demand a raise to two dollars a day. The rich railroad magnates wasted no time agreeing. And, finally, there were the deaths. Four hundred was the number estimated by officials in the days after the storm, but it was clearly much more than that. Almost a thousand bodies arrived at cemeteries around New York in the weeks after the blizzard, and the final tally did not include the deaths in other cities and towns up and down the East Coast.

The blizzard of 1888 was the trigger that cities needed to finally acknowledge that the horse-pulled carriages, the steam-powered elevated trains, the cable-pulled trolleys, and even the electrified street railways all suffered from the same flaw that could no longer be ignored. They were at the mercy of the skies. Rain, snow, ice, and scorching heat had shown they were capable of crippling a city or, at the least, making its streets miserable. And too many people needed the trains to get them where they had to go. From 1887 to 1888, the elevated rails saw an increase of thirteen million passengers. And down on the streets, where

William Whitney was showing a greater interest in controlling the street railways, that same period saw five million more people take a trip. Ridership was exploding, and there was no room above ground to put more cars. "Who will be the Moses to lead us through this wilderness of uncertainty?" asked *The New York World*.

6

NEW YORK CITY'S MOSES

TWO YEARS. THAT WAS HOW LONG Abram Hewitt ran the city. The streets of New York were filled with the stench of manure and uncovered, overflowing trash bins, and they were overcrowded with streetcars and street railways. Prostitutes had their own avenues, and saloons defied every attempt to shut them down at night in accordance with the laws. Change would not come overnight, but those streets would never be the same after Hewitt was through with them.

It was his fortuitous timing that his brief tenure was sandwiched around the three days of the blizzard of 1888. But it was his savvy politics, brilliant scheming, engineering know-how, and dogged persistence that helped ensure that those two years would go down as two of the most important in the city's history and would become a time when Gotham started to clean up its act and when the first seed for the New York City subway was finally, and firmly, planted. "The Father of Rapid Transit," they would call him. He also fathered six children. And when any of them asked for a toy, he had a ready response. "I won't buy them, but I'll give you materials to make them." Oh, he wanted his children to succeed in life, just not by taking. By building.

· · ·

ABRAM STEVENS HEWITT WAS BORN in a log house forty miles
north of New York City on July 31, 1822, in the village of Haverstraw. His
family was poor. His father, John, was a skilled mechanic whose cabinet-
making business had gone bankrupt, and his mother, Ann, a pretty, sweet-
faced daughter of a farmer. What he lacked in resources at home, where he
ate mostly porridge and almost no meat, Hewitt made up for in his studies.

After beating out twenty thousand other boys to earn a scholarship
to Columbia College, young Hewitt moved to New York. He supported
himself by teaching and excelled in his math and science studies, so
much so that when he graduated in 1842 he was at the top of his class.
After graduating, he tutored grammar school children, sometimes earning as much as $150 in a term from a single pupil. It was this work that
introduced him to a young man named Edward Cooper. The two had
actually been Columbia classmates, but when Cooper got sick and fell
two years behind Hewitt in his studies, he needed assistance, and Cooper's
father, Peter, agreed to pay Hewitt to tutor his son. Edward Cooper and
Abram Hewitt would be linked for life from that day forward and would
launch a formidable business partnership. There was only one point of sadness to Hewitt's time at Columbia. So immersed was he in his books day
and night that his vision began to fail him, and by the time he graduated
he was, in his own words, "nearly blind."

From his poor upbringing to his studies at Columbia to his fading vision to a near-death experience at sea while returning from an adventure
in Europe, Hewitt emerged into adulthood as a wizened twenty-two-
year-old young man. "It taught me for the first time that I could stand in
the face of death without fear and without flinching," he said. "It taught
me another thing—that my life, which had been miraculously rescued,
belonged not to me, and from that hour I gave it to the work which from
that time has been in my thoughts—the welfare of my fellow citizens."

Hewitt flirted with becoming a lawyer, but when his eyesight continued to fail him, he and Edward Cooper decided to go into business together. Not only would their relationship net Hewitt his wife, since he

married Cooper's sister in 1855, but their partnership turned into an American industrial force. They got their start when Peter Cooper, one of the richest men in New York, a distinction he owed to his success in business manufacturing and some savvy real estate investments, with no hesitation gave to his son and his son's friend the iron manufacturing branch of his business. Cooper, Hewitt & Co. was born. The two friends started slowly, making rails for the railroads, but it was also the age of telegraphs, and strong, sturdy, unbreakable wires were becoming the most desired commodity. That's where Hewitt turned next.

A CABLE DISPATCH ON January 23, 1862, changed Hewitt's life. In fact, he might have decided against ever entering a career in politics later in his life were it not for the message it contained. He was at the home of Peter Cooper on a Sunday evening in the early days of the Civil War. Dispatches at the time typically arrived by messenger and were printed on slips of paper, but this one addressed to Cooper, Hewitt & Co. was unusually long.

"I am told that you can do things which other men declare to be impossible," the telegraph said. "General Grant is at Cairo [Illinois], ready to start on his movement to capture Fort Henry and Fort Donelson. He has the necessary troops and equipment, including thirty mortars, but the mortar-beds are lacking. The Chief of Ordnance informs me that nine months will be required to build the mortar beds, which must be very heavy in order to carry 13-inch mortars now used for the first time. I appeal to you to have these mortar-beds built within thirty days . . . Telegraph what you can do. A. Lincoln."

President Lincoln had never met Hewitt. But Lincoln knew of Hewitt's reputation as an honest, hardworking manufacturer of iron, and Hewitt felt obliged to help his president in time of war, even if his own Democratic politics did not always align with Lincoln's Republican values. A mortar bed was the foundation on which mortars were mounted and elevated into firing position, and they were critical at ensuring accurate firing. If General Ulysses S. Grant could successfully take Forts Henry and Donelson, it would be a crippling blow to the railroad bridges and shipping abilities of the Confederate army, which Hewitt, who had followed the war closely, knew.

Grant was building momentum, and Lincoln did not want it stalled for months by military manufacturing delays, which is why he reached out to Cooper, Hewitt & Co. After reading the dispatch, Hewitt rushed from Cooper's house to the nearest Western Union office and had a cable sent back to the White House. If he could find a bomb carriage quickly that he could use, he would let the president know within a day if the task was possible. The War Department located a bomb carriage in Newport and, at the president's order, had it sent to Hewitt. It arrived by boat in New York Harbor on Tuesday morning, just two days after Hewitt first heard from the president, and Hewitt took one look and believed the request was doable. He cabled Lincoln, and not even two weeks later, after a furious, round-the-clock production schedule, on February 8 the first four mortar beds were put on a train and sent westward. The remaining twenty-six were sent out within the week, and on each box, Hewitt painted in big black letters, U.S. GRANT, CAIRO. NOT TO BE SWITCHED UNDER PENALTY OF DEATH.

Grant, who had successfully taken Fort Henry on February 6, 1862, received Hewitt's mortar beds a week later, and on February 17 he was able to capture Fort Donelson. "If that is so," an excited Hewitt wrote to a friend when he received the news, "the backbone of the rebellion is broken."

In three weeks Hewitt had fulfilled the president's wishes, a remarkable feat considering that every plate, bar, spring, and loose part had to be made from scratch. Hewitt was a modest man, but even he wanted to make sure his efforts were appreciated and that he was appropriately compensated. It had cost Cooper, Hewitt & Co. $21,000 to finish the work, and they did it with no advance payment from the government. "No effort has been spared," Hewitt wrote in a cable to Washington. "And as usual when people are in earnest, the work has been accomplished. This brings to a close the most remarkable mechanical achievement, so far as time is concerned, that we have ever witnessed . . . To serve the country in its time of trial is the dearest wish of our hearts and we hope that the

Department will avail itself of our services at any and all times when we can be useful."

True to his nature, Hewitt dramatically undercharged the government for his work. But when days and days passed and he had still not received any payment, he boarded a train for Washington on March 12 to meet personally with Lincoln's trusted war secretary, Edwin M. Stanton. Stanton explained to Hewitt that the unpaid bill was tied up in government bureaucracy, but he promised to get a note to the president, and the next thing Abram Hewitt knew he was being walked into the White House and shaking hands with Abraham Lincoln. He had seen him once before, when Lincoln delivered a speech in New York, but he was still overcome. It was quite the meeting, the six-foot-four Lincoln peering down in astonishment at the slight Hewitt, who barely stood five foot eight.

"Are you Mr. Hewitt?" Lincoln is said to have asked.

"I am," answered his guest with his usual straight face.

Lincoln could not contain his laughter. The towering president had assumed such a heroic task had been achieved by a man of equal stature, not someone so short. "Well then," Lincoln said, smiling, "I expected to see a man at least eight feet tall." Hewitt did not mind, but after listening to the president he presented his problem. He had not been paid for the work he had done. Lincoln, who had no idea, was stunned. He quickly called Stanton into his office for an explanation.

"Do you suppose that if I should write on that bill, 'Pay this bill now,' the Treasury would make settlement," Lincoln said to Stanton.

When Stanton shrugged his shoulders and explained how only the president could cut through the red tape holding up the payment on Hewitt's submitted bill, the president sat down, took out a pen, and wrote "O.K. A. Lincoln" on the piece of paper, assuring that it would be paid promptly and in full. He then ordered Stanton to walk personally with Hewitt to the Treasury Department and see that the bill was paid. On March 24, 1862, Hewitt received a draft of $21,000, and he saw the impact one could have as a chief executive. Lincoln may not have been Hewitt's mentor. And to that point, politics had not even entered Hewitt's mind. But Lincoln was a model for him to follow if he so chose, and twelve years later he took his first step.

IN 1874, HEWITT CHANGED HIS residence from New Jersey, where he lived most of the year in the town of Ringwood, to New York City, where he also owned a house and where he believed he could make the greatest difference. A short man with a brisk walk, sharp wit, and quick temper, he began to explore a run for political office, and he quickly learned of a humorous public misunderstanding that would serve him well. His first name was often misspelled in the newspapers as Abraham, and it led the significantly growing Jewish population in New York to believe Hewitt was one of them. How much of a role that played in his first race is difficult to know, but in the fall of 1874 Democrat Abram S. Hewitt was elected to Congress, narrowly beating Irishman James O'Brien by less than a thousand votes to win the Tenth District, which covered mostly the Lower East Side and Gramercy Park.

Though the House of Representatives was controlled by Democrats for the first time since 1861, the president at the time was a Republican, the same man Hewitt had helped secure victories for in key battles during the Civil War, Ulysses Grant. Hewitt set aside his emotions and went to work to help Democrats oust Grant and retake the White House in 1876. It was the beginning of a twelve-year stretch in Congress that shaped Hewitt's politics, beliefs, and values. And when New York Democrats organized to create a single, unifying voice and stand up for change in New York City, Hewitt was a natural choice; another was the city's corporation counsel, William C. Whitney. The election paved the way for both men to reach their own pinnacles.

ON NOVEMBER 2, 1886, Abram Hewitt was elected to what many at the time believed was the second most powerful executive position in the country, mayor of New York City. On the night of his victory, he was as humble as always. "I will make no promises or confessions," he said. "I know that it is the fashion for men elected to high office to make them, but I prefer to act as my conscience dictates. Let me be judged by my acts."

With one and a half million people, New York City was still far bigger than the second and third largest American metropolises, Chicago and Philadelphia, neither of which had yet to reach a million residents, though Chicago would close the gap soon. Washington may have been the capital city, but it was only the fourteenth largest in the country, even behind Pittsburgh, New Orleans, and Buffalo. New York City was the cultural and financial and entrepreneurial capital, and its mayor occupied an increasingly powerful position. Hewitt easily defeated a loudmouth, corrupt, Philadelphia-born economist named Henry George, who represented the United Labor Party, and a young, aspiring, reformist Republican assembly member named Theodore Roosevelt. Roosevelt had initially promised Hewitt he would work for him during the race, but then changed his mind and mounted his own aggressive campaign. When he lost by more than thirty thousand votes, Roosevelt said, "This is the end of my political career," and he set sail for London to marry his second wife. Roosevelt was twenty-eight years old.

The newspapers were supportive of Hewitt, whom they saw as an anticorruption, big-idea leader. "It is expected that it will mark the beginning of better government, of more honest methods, in our municipal affairs," *The World* newspaper wrote on January 2, 1887, the day Hewitt was inaugurated. Hewitt, despite health issues, including sciatic rheumatism, headaches, and insomnia, jumped into city affairs with vigor, sleeping four or five hours a night and running on an endless supply of nervous energy.

As mayor, the clean-living Hewitt, a man who hated to drink and viewed the saloon as the root of many of society's woes, but who also could be prone to bursts of anger, learned right away the limitations of his office. New York City was still merely a state entity, and therefore often at the mercy of what state legislators wanted to do, even when it was not in the best interests of the city or its residents. Undaunted, he latched on to two causes right away that stirred up deep passions inside of him.

They defined his brief tenure as mayor. And they changed the way New Yorkers lived.

IT WAS A STRANGE AND unsettling time for the city. The economy was strong and innovation was thriving, but if you lived in Manhattan the troubles were impossible to overlook. Corruption remained rampant, poverty was abysmal, and morality was laughable. Despite so much upheaval, the city's culture scene was bubbling, with stage performances of *La Tosca* playing at the Broadway Theater and Shakespeare's *A Midsummer Night's Dream* at Daly's Theatre. The Lyceum Theater, New York's first playhouse to be lighted by electricity, was crowded nightly, and so were the Bijou, the Casino, the Empire, and the Abbey, all thriving in what was known as Longacre Square (soon to be Times Square). A decade earlier, it had been a largely desolate and dark stretch of the city, but now it glowed nightly and could not have been more crowded with theatergoers and diners. The hottest ticket in town cost fifty cents and provided entrance into Madison Square Garden to see P. T. Barnum's dazzling circus extravaganza.

Sex was everywhere when Abram Hewitt took office, and he did not like it. On one of his first days in office, rather than ask the top police officials for a state of his city, he walked the streets himself and could not believe what he saw. Brothels on every block, right in plain view, making very little effort to conceal what was happening behind their doors. What was happening was commercial sex for the city's hardworking male laborers, who would pay one to two dollars for a fifteen-minute roll. The madams who ran the sex shops took half of the income from their mostly young teenage girls in exchange for weekly room and board. The expectation was that the girls would do their business quickly and efficiently, allowing no time for pillow talk. Some of the busier houses would sometimes see lines form outside, and in a good week a hundred transactions would take place at a single operation. If, however, a man wanted a woman, and not a girl, all he had to do was make his way over to Ladies' Mile, which stretched from Thirty-fourth Street down to Fourteenth Street on Sixth Avenue and was lined with prostitutes from dusk till dawn. And if it was a black woman he wanted, well that was one block away, Seventh Avenue, nicknamed African Broadway.

"Can they be closed up?" Hewitt asked the police superintendent William Murray one day.

"Certainly," Murray replied. "It is only necessary to give the order to have them closed up." Hewitt was puzzled. He asked Murray why they have never been shut down if they were so blatantly flouting the law.

"Well," Murray answered, "you had better ask some of your political friends about that." Murray told Hewitt that the most regular clients at the places the mayor wanted to close were not only the mayor's friends but also his biggest donors. But the police boss, a gruff veteran of the force for more than twenty years, underestimated the morals and the values of the new mayor.

"It does not make any difference to me who they are," Hewitt said. "The places have got to be closed up."

The two men parted, and by March police were shutting down the worst offenders and ordering the rest to straighten up or suffer the same fate. Harry Hill's popular saloon, a notorious host of criminals, changed into a dairy restaurant. At 27 Bowery, a dirty, popular spot called Plymouth where prostitutes could always find clients, a shooting gallery filled the space. De Lacy's, one of New York's most popular and shady pool halls, didn't even put up a fight and just closed its doors.

HEWITT NEXT TURNED HIS EYES to his other annoyance, the filthy, smelly, overcrowded streets. On January 25, 1888, Hewitt received a short letter from Boston. An inventor there by the name of Joseph V. Meigs had been trying to convince Boston to adopt the steam-powered elevated monorail he had invented, but so far he'd been unable to get it built. It was unproven, but Meigs told Hewitt that his invention was safe, powerful, and able to move a great number of passengers. It is "an absolute solution of the problem of rapid transit," Meigs wrote.

Hewitt was not convinced. And four days later, on January 29, 1888, he laid out his own vision for New York's transportation crisis in his annual message to the Board of Aldermen. "The time has come," Hewitt said, "when the growth of the city is seriously retarded by the want of proper means of access to and from the upper and lower portions of the city." With 94 miles of elevated railways; 265 miles of tracks on the streets, where cars were pulled by horses; and another 137 miles of old omnibus routes still clogging up the city, New York claimed by far the world's largest network of urban transit. It was time, Hewitt said, to modernize.

He proceeded to lay out a plan that reflected his thinking as a businessman with an engineer's mind and a politician with a citizen's heart. It was visionary and yet practical, so simple that the only thing more striking than the plan was that nobody had proposed it sooner. It was equal parts transportation and economics, because Hewitt, after studying for years all of the failed efforts to build a cohesive transit system, knew that nothing ambitious would ever be built unless it was clear to everyone—citizens, politicians, railway companies—how it would be paid for and how nobody would be left in financial ruin. Most important, he told the aldermen, it would reaffirm New York's "imperial destiny as the greatest city in the world."

His plan was rooted in the belief that New York had to find a way to take greater advantage of its vast land north of Eightieth Street, into Harlem and Washington Heights and especially north of the Harlem River. Unless that area was developed more, with rapid transit providing a way for the people to get from there to downtown, the lower portions of the city were doomed to unbearable overcrowding, and New York was sure to lose people to New Jersey, Long Island, or anywhere else they could easily move. The first half of his message he dedicated to improving and rebuilding New York Harbor and the docks and then paving and smoothing the streets. He described the lower part of the city, south of Canal Street, as being in "deplorable condition" and in need of being "entirely repaved." It was from there that he turned to "rapid transit," and said that he would waste no time explaining how "inadequate" the facilities were.

His first point was speed. Rapid transit, he said, must live up to its name, and that meant forty to fifty miles per hour, something that makes the horse-pulled carriages and even the elevated trains look as if they were crawling. Next, he said, no longer can the rails be linked from one pillar to the next with no guardrails to protect derailments. The speed of what he desired would not allow it. The only way rapid transit will work is if the rails are "laid below the surface of the streets" or if they rest on an embankment above so that it's no less sturdy than the underground surface. Any routes, he said, must be designed to take people where they want to go and "not on a route that takes them away from the centres of business." In what was surely a dig at the men who were convinced that elevated tracks would solve the city's woes for decades, not merely a few years, he wrote that any plan must factor in future population and ridership growth. And whatever it costs, it must be built in such a way as to not raise fares from the existing five cents. That was the populist mayor speaking.

To solve the economic conundrum, Hewitt proposed an imaginative solution. The city would pay for construction of the system, but it would be built by a private enterprise, hired through a bidding process by the city. The winning company would then lease the tracks from the city to control and operate the trains and pay for any necessary equipment. Additionally, the company would pay the city interest on the bonds that were used to pay for the work, plus 1 percent every year from the revenues generated by the system. It was brilliant. Everybody would win. The city would not go bankrupt building the system. A private company wins an expensive contract to construct and operate it. And when thirty-five years expired, the debts would be gone, the bills would be paid off, and the city would take ownership of the system with the hope that it becomes and remains a source of revenue.

In writing his annual message, Hewitt seemed to suggest that he suspected any objection to his plan would not be over the financing details but over making a subway the cornerstone of his proposal.

"Objections will be made by those who have not fully studied the subject to the fact that considerable portions of the routes indicated are in subways," Hewitt wrote. "Those objections are based upon the character of the underground tunnels in operation in London, which are not properly lighted and ventilated." He went on to say how much has been learned from London's smoke-filled Underground, but that "as long as the tunnels are operated by steam engines they will be more expensive to ventilate." And so the future of the subway, he wrote, was something other than steam engines. "The electric motor is being daily improved and what is known as the 'fireless engine,' propelled by super-heated water or by compressed air, is in successful operation in Europe and in several places in this country."

It was as bold a proposal as any that a New York City mayor had ever presented, and it came only a few months after the equally radical idea Henry Whitney had proposed for Boston to tunnel a subway under the Common. The New York Chamber of Commerce expressed its approval of Hewitt's proposal, and so did the powerful Real Estate Board.

THE MAYOR'S BIG SCHEME, read the headline in *The Times* on February 1, 1888. "Mayor Hewitt has fulfilled the promise he made recently of submitting to the public a comprehensive system of rapid transit," the story said. And while *The World* sneered suspiciously that the plan was not original, *The Times* disagreed in its editorial, writing enthusiastically about it and singling out the unique financing proposal. "The entire plan is worthy of the most careful consideration," the editorial read. "The time has come when the city should no longer be a prey to scheming jobbers in consequence of its needs in the matter of rapid transit . . . The mayor seems to have no motive but the public good and the advancement of the city's interests and all that he needs to distinguish his administration by the initiation of a grand system of rapid transit and general improvement is the full support of public sentiment."

It was a rousing endorsement, and six weeks later, on Friday, March 9, just as the blizzard of 1888 was at New York's door, Hewitt sent a bill to Albany. He called for a Rapid Transit Board that would include the public works commissioner, the city comptroller, and, of course, the mayor. Public hearings would let New Yorkers voice their opinions on everything from what should power the trains to what the new fare should be and even let them contribute to the route and construction method. Hewitt was sure his bill pushing for municipal ownership of a subway would sail through.

Instead, he severely underestimated how many people he had angered in his short time in office. By sweeping out popular but corrupt officials; by taking on the Irish and the Italians, too, in their requests to fly their flags over City Hall; and by closing down saloons and brothels, Hewitt had alienated many of the people who made his election possible. New York was a far better place. But Hewitt would pay for his deeds. The Board of Aldermen loathed him and wanted nothing more than to see him fail as mayor and be ousted at the first chance they got. They never even let his plan out of committee so that it could be voted on by the full board, never mind be subjected to public hearings. And a few months later they got their wish. Hewitt was soundly defeated in his bid for reelection by the New York County sheriff, Hugh J. Grant, who, at thirty years old, was the youngest mayor New York ever had. At nearly seventy years old, after one eventful, tumultuous, and historic term in office, Hewitt was done with politics. But he was not done with his subway.

7

WILLIAM WHITNEY'S MISSED OPPORTUNITY

WHENEVER WILLIAM WHITNEY TOOK ONE of his horses out for a ride in Central Park, the young Irish rector of St. George's Episcopal Church in Stuyvesant Square frequently joined him. A native of Dublin, the Reverend Doctor W. S. Rainsford was ten years younger than Whitney and was as tall and straight as a reed. He was also one of the most politically well-connected religious men in the city, thanks to his tight bond with the financier J. Pierpont Morgan. Perhaps it was because Whitney trusted Rainsford, or because Rainsford helped him find a governess for his daughter, or simply because Whitney valued how frankly the preacher spoke his opinion, but whatever the reason, on one of their many rides together in the park Whitney confessed his ambition to his friend. And it was not, as many suspected, to occupy the White House.

"Mr. Whitney," Rainsford said, "I suppose you will be our next president."

"Oh no," Whitney answered. "I am done with politics. I must make some money. It is time I did. Mrs. Whitney has money. I have none."

Of course that was an exaggeration. Whitney did have money, from his law practice, his political work, and his stock holdings from his late father's steamship company, but what he meant was that he did not have the enormous riches of his wife's family. That was what he desired, and to achieve it he had a plan.

"I am going into the New York street railroads," Whitney told Rainsford.

"Well," Rainsford replied to Whitney's pledge, "they are in such a tangle you will need a lot of legal work."

"Tangle" did not begin to describe the state of New York's streets in the 1880s. *The New York Herald* had described New York's street railways this way: "The driver quarrels with the passengers and the passengers quarrel with the driver. There are quarrels about getting out and quarrels about getting in. There are quarrels about change and quarrels about the ticket swindle. The driver swears at the passengers and the passengers harangue the driver through the straphole." It was a daily scene that left women disgusted and embarrassed and that alarmed children to the point of tears.

Crossing Manhattan, from the Hudson to the East River, required switching from one car to another to another and another. There were four different lines and each time riders switched they had to pay a new fare, to go one block or twenty. Free transfers were not an option. More than thirty different street railway companies ruled the streets, each independently owned, and they reported their business to nobody. Most coaches had no ventilation, no source of heat other than a thin bed of hay, and faint light at best, so not only was the smell horrendous but passengers were cold and virtually blind inside. It was a system in drastic need of consolidation and control. And nobody knew better than Whitney the inner workings of New York City politics, thanks to his time as corporation counsel. That knowledge, along with his supreme self-confidence and his growing number of powerful and wealthy friends, was enough to inspire him to believe that he could be the one to transform New York's streets.

Whitney had been drawn into the business back in 1884. Driven by greed and a good-hearted desire to improve the quality of life in his city, Whitney was poised to take on the man who was making life miserable for New Yorkers and who was about to make it a whole lot worse. Whitney had been watching for years as Jacob Sharp became the king of New York City's street railways through the strength of his Broadway & Seventh Avenue Railroad, and, like other wealthy New York businessmen, Whitney was determined not to let Sharp control any more of the city's streets without a fight. There was too much money at stake for one man to have so much power. Old Jake Sharp's vehicles were filthy, and passengers often had rats as company. And by choosing the routes where his vehicles operated, Sharp could maximize his revenues. New York had more people living per acre south of the Harlem River than London or Paris, most of them in slums, a fact that no doubt contributed to a death rate in the city that was higher than any in the country and among the worst in the world. Sharp already ran horsecars between Fifty-ninth Street and Union Square, but he wanted more, and in particular he wanted to run his line all the way down Broadway to the Battery. If Sharp won control over all of Broadway from Central Park to the wharf, he would essentially be able to hold the island of Manhattan hostage for whatever he wanted and earn a fortune in the process. With the city's elevated lines already at their capacity and horses clogging the streets worse than ever, New York City stood at a critical moment.

JUST AS LONDONERS GREW TIRED of their dark, dank, smoke-filled Underground, New Yorkers quickly grew weary of their Els. The city's four elevated lines had no more room. They were at full capacity on almost every trip and running as close together as possible without posing a danger. The pillars were not strong enough to support longer trains and heavier locomotives, and when the idea was floated to build additional elevated lines to relieve the pressure, New Yorkers said no more. The giant structures on which the tracks rested cast long shadows over the streets all day long, turning sunny days into what *The Times* called "a perpetual city of night." The steam-powered elevated trains were so packed, sluggish, and loud that the only task harder than conducting business during the day over the rumbling was sleeping through it at night. Property values plummeted, as did the morale of New Yorkers.

As if the vibrating, the noise, and the long shadows did not provide enough misery, as one unfortunate British tourist discovered, steam-powered elevated trains could be dangerous and dirty, too. Walter Gore Marshall was in Greenwich Village crossing the intersection at Sixth Avenue and Twelfth Street one day in 1880 when he decided to pause and look up at the El passing overhead. He regretted it the moment he did. "It was lucky I had not my mouth open at the time," Marshall recalled, "for as I gazed with my face upturned, I was saluted with a large pat of oil from one of the axle-boxes of a car, which besprinkled my countenance and neck-tie." Splattered from head to toe, he rushed into a nearby barbershop to clean himself off. "Oil drippings from passing trains are a source of constant annoyance to foot passengers crossing the roadway beneath, a nuisance that could be easily remedied by a proper sort of hard grease," Marshall said.

The elevated trains were not as bad as residents insisted, but there was no denying that steam power, for all of its reliability, was just not suited to coexist with city living. And while Chicago and Brooklyn were quick to follow Manhattan and build their own Els, Saint Louis, Philadelphia, and Boston all saw the flaws and decided that steam trains passing overhead and dropping oil, cinders, and soot on pedestrians below was perhaps not the future, after all.

Decisions had to be made about what should power the city's transportation system in the future and how it should be expanded to cover more territory so that residents could spread out more. Horses were trusted and reliable, but they were slow, they smelled, and they were at the mercy of the weather. The steam-powered elevated trains were speedier and above the crowded streets, but the shadows they cast on and the dangers they posed for pedestrians below were slowing down momentum for their expansion. Cables were quiet and smooth and seemed promising, but installing them was wildly expensive, and they worked best on long straight roads, which worked well for portions of New York but not the entire island, and also posed a severe limitation in how far east and west on Manhattan they could go.

Was the city willing to experiment with electric traction on its streets, which was still in its infancy but showing promise? Or was New York ready to follow London's lead and build the world's second subway, and America's first? Tunneling was now being done much faster than it was when London dug its subway in the early 1860s. In 1869, a new shield had bored 1,350 feet, or a quarter of a mile, beneath the Thames River in just five months, unheard-of speed. Fifteen years later, in 1884, London's Parliament authorized the use of a shield with additional improvements for digging a pair of railroad tunnels starting near London Bridge. The combination of tunneling with electric traction could be the greatest achievement yet. Clean, quiet, and underground.

A myriad of issues faced New York, and William Whitney was eager to take them all on, even if doing so meant splitting his life between Washington and New York.

Secretary of the navy was never a passion or a career ambition for Whitney. President Cleveland, who had not yet married his twenty-year-old girlfriend Frances Folsom, was a social oaf in Washington, and he relied on the Whitneys for companionship. The two men played in a poker group regularly, and Flora held so many lavish parties, always inviting the president, that Whitney had to tell his wife to be careful about earning Cleveland a reputation as a rich, party-going elitist. Cleveland treasured how Whitney watched out for him. "Mr. Whitney had more calm, forceful efficiency than any man I ever knew," Cleveland later said of his friend. "In work that interested him he actually seemed to court difficulties and to find pleasure and exhilaration in overcoming them."

It was an accurate description, and it explained why Whitney could not resist the pull of New York even as he was restoring the navy to its glory.

IN THOMAS FORTUNE RYAN, an aggressive Irish-American, Virginia-born stockbroker, Whitney found a mate to go to battle with and to take on Jake Sharp. The two men became fast friends and mutually set out to rip from Sharp's hands his most prized possession: Broadway, the spine of Manhattan.

Whitney and Ryan helped form what they called the New York Cable Railway Company. And only a few months later, in early 1885, they joined forces with a trio of Philadelphia transit men, William Elkins, Peter A. B. Widener, and William Kemble, who were behind a cable road that was recently launched on Market Street in Philadelphia, where they dominated the city's street railways. It was a formidable team these men created, and they would form one of the most famous alliances of wealth and power in American history. They would in a few short years acquire aging horsecar lines that covered Columbus Avenue, Lexington Avenue, Fulton Street, Thirty-fourth Street, and Twenty-ninth Street. With one deal after another, sometimes buying, sometimes leasing, other times overpowering, they soon controlled virtually every horsecar line in Manhattan. They were not profitable lines, but the businessmen had other schemes in mind for making a fortune. They believed the money wasn't in the subway itself but in the utilities required to operate it, namely gas and electricity. What Ryan and Whitney lacked in transit experience they made up for with their powerful connections, legal expertise, and deep knowledge of the ways of New York politics. And while the Philadelphians were outsiders to New York, they brought with them experience in street railways and in promoting cable streetcars. Together they were five men with vast amounts of money, influence, experience, and connections, and they shared the mutual goal of bringing to New York a streamlined street-transit network. If there was a weak link to their group, it was Whitney. His partners worried whether he could remain committed to taking down Sharp and taking over New York's street railways while rebuilding the navy from Washington. Whitney assured them he was on board, even as he became more entrenched by the day in the political and social scenes of Washington.

ON MAY 28, 1886, a letter arrived at Whitney's home at 1731 I Street in Washington's Northwest District that proved how important a man he had become.

"My marriage with Miss Folsom will take place at the White House on Wednesday (June second) at seven o'clock in the evening," President Cleveland wrote to his close confidant. "I hardly think that I can creditably demean myself unless you and Mrs. Whitney are present to encourage and sustain me in the new and untried situation. May I expect to see you both on the occasion?" Cleveland had been courting Frances "Frank" Folsom for years. She was the daughter of Oscar Folsom, his former law partner from his time in Buffalo. Oscar Folsom had been killed in a carriage accident and left Cleveland in charge of his estate, asking him to help his wife raise their then-twelve-year-old daughter, Frances. By the time Cleveland was elected president, she was an attractive brunette in her early twenties and he was rotund with thinning hair and approaching fifty. Still, their relationship evolved from paternal to romantic, and they traded letters for years until the spring of 1886, when he proposed in the mail and she accepted.

On June 2, beginning at 6:30 in the evening, William and Flora Whitney joined the other cabinet couples as they were ushered into the Blue Room at the White House for a small intimate ceremony. Flowers, ferns, and palms, all from the White House greenhouse, decorated the floor, and John Philip Sousa, the marching music king, led the Marine Band in the Wedding March. The engaged couple, with no ushers or bridesmaids leading them, descended the stairs together, with the bride leaning on Cleveland's left arm, and they stopped beneath a chandelier covered in flowers in the Blue Room. He wore a stately tuxedo, but all eyes were on his young bride, who wore an elegant white satin dress with a long silk veil, fifteen-foot trail, and low neckline and adorned with real orange blossoms. A brief ceremony led by the Presbyterian minister Reverend Byron Sunderland was understated, and it ended with him placing his hand over the clasped hands of the couple.

"Grover, do you take this woman whom you hold by the hand to be your lawful wedded wife, to live together after God's ordinance in the holy estate of wedlock?" the minister said.

"I do," the president answered, and he then fussed into his waistcoat pocket for the wedding ring and slipped it onto her finger.

The minister repeated the question for the bride, and she, too, answered in a clear voice with no hesitation. "I do."

"Whom God hath joined together let no man put asunder," Sunderland said in conclusion, and the only wedding that has ever been held in the White House was complete.

WHILE FLORA WHITNEY WAS PREGNANT with their fifth child in the fall of 1886, her husband was deeply immersed in the matters of the navy and plotting his takeover of the New York street railroads. What he was attempting was not illegal, but it was certainly unwise politically since it gave the appearance that Whitney was more interested in earning a fortune for himself in private enterprise than he was in repairing the navy's image. Most of his visits to New York passed without any notice, as he was able to sneak in on the train incognito, hop straight into a carriage, hold meetings at his Fifty-seventh Street mansion, and return to Washington just as quietly. But when *The New York Tribune* and *The Times* got wind of his repeated visits to New York, they began a crusade to publicly embarrass him.

"The Secretary of the Navy has spent much more time in this city recently than the general public is aware of," *The Tribune* wrote, "but he has not been occupied with naval business." It reported that he was solely in town to pursue his plan to seize control of Sharp's Broadway railroad. "Mr. Whitney was in town a week ago yesterday, although few New Yorkers discovered it. He did not proclaim his presence on the house-tops." Instead, he huddled in his home with Ryan and the rest of the Philadelphians, focused entirely on Jake Sharp.

They knew that they could never build a complete transit system in New York if they controlled only the streets running across the island and not the boulevards that ran down the middle as well. "The system could not be perfected with crosstown lines alone," Widener argued at a public meeting in 1886, "and no trunk line could be used with so much advantage to the system as that of the Broadway and 7th Avenue roads."

Broadway, in particular, was to New York what Market Street was to Philadelphia. And all five of the men knew that whoever controlled the busiest thoroughfare in any city controlled the city itself. In the mid-1880s, in New York, that was Jacob Sharp.

If Whitney and the others knew one thing, it was how to start a fire. And when Sharp, who by now was pushing seventy years old and dying of diabetes, pushed back against their efforts to buy him out, and even brazenly raised his asking price, they had their opening. New Yorkers became enraged at his refusal to consider a sale or to improve their way of life by allowing changes to the transportation system. Whitney's group took advantage of the public ire and persuaded one of Sharp's stockholders to file a lawsuit against him and demand access to review the company's books. That suit became irrelevant when it caught the attention of the New York State Senate, which opened its own investigation into Sharp. And in a matter of a few weeks, Sharp was under fierce attack. His bribes to city officials were exposed, and the aldermen, branded as forty thieves, were publicly excoriated; some of them even fled for Montreal rather than face the possibility of a corruption trial and jail time. As for Sharp, when he too confronted the possibility of incarceration at Sing Sing, he finally caved. He sold to his powerful rivals all ten thousand shares in his Broadway & Seventh Avenue Railroad, valued at almost three million dollars, and, finally, Whitney had his prize. Broadway!

FOR ALL OF THEIR GRANDEUR, raw power, and beauty, horses were becoming a real nuisance as the chief mode of transportation in American cities. The biggest problem was that horses are useful for only three years of hard work, and the city's streets were less forgiving on their legs than the soft dirt and grass of farmland. And then there was disease. In 1870, a mild panic erupted when a street railway driver named Michael O'Keefe died of a sickness called glanders. It is a bacterial disease seen in animals and is extremely rare in humans, but those who die from it are almost always found to have obtained it from a horse. The symptoms are obvious, and included rashes, lung infection, diarrhea, and enlargement of the spleen. O'Keefe's death caused so much worry that he was buried immediately without an autopsy. Two years later, in October 1872, an influenza outbreak among horses in Canada quickly spread south into North America and caused much more widespread panic. Michigan, Ohio, Illinois, all across New England, and as far south as Louisiana and Florida and eventually Cuba all reported similar cases in which horses suddenly were too weak to stand in their stalls, much less pull heavy loads of several hundred pounds. In New York, more than thirty horses died every day during the outbreak. Those that did survive could be heard coughing violently for months. The Great Epizootic Outbreak, as it was called, struck thousands of horses and ground much of the country to a standstill. Streetcars disappeared from city streets or were just abandoned. Coal couldn't be delivered to locomotives to provide their power. Firefighters could not respond to blazes. Soldiers in the army were forced to pull their own wagons when their horses broke down. It got so bad that in December of 1872 the Mexican government had to supply healthy horses to the United States.

The horse had served America well for half a century, but its time had come. The piles of manure they left behind—and a big horse could produce as much as fifty pounds of it a day—were no longer tolerated. City residents were tired of the smell. And while there was a time when a stable owner could make a hefty profit by selling horse manure to farmers, who used it for fertilizer, those days were gone, too. Bird excrement, or guano, along with man-made fertilizers, became more readily available, and the value of horse manure plunged. In 1860, the Second Avenue Street Railway in New York City could collect as much as $4.60 per horse for its manure annually. By 1885, that figure had dropped to $1.10, and some stable owners were losing money on manure because it cost them so much to cart away.

AS MOST NEW YORKERS SLEPT early on the morning of May 27, 1887, shouts cried out from inside a long building on the city's west side, startling the night watchman standing guard out front. He recognized the voices of his own men, but he had no idea what was causing their panic. It was the start of an unimaginable tragedy that would essentially be over in six minutes, and it came only a few months after New Yorkers had celebrated one of the most thrilling days in their city's history, the dedication by President Cleveland of the Statue of Liberty on October 28, 1886.

Even after the dramatic efforts of men like Alfred Beach and Abraham Brower at improving transportation on the streets of New York, the truth was that by the spring of 1887, fifty years after the first horse-pulled carriages started rolling through the city, very little had changed. Horses still ruled the day.

Nowhere was that more evident than in the three-story structure that filled the entire block of Tenth Avenue between Fifty-third and Fifty-fourth streets. From the outside, it looked as solid as any block-long building in New York, brown brick stacked upon brown brick from the street to the roof. And it was only fourteen years old, built in 1873. Inside, however, wood beams were attached to the walls and scattered throughout the interior. And hundreds of individual stalls were filled with all the comforts necessary to keep the 1,230 horses that belonged to the Belt Line Street Railway Company happy. Each horse was a valuable piece of property, valued at $130, for a collective total of $154,000. That's why there were four thousand bales of hay, five thousand bales of straw, and twelve thousand bushels of grain inside the stable. It was one giant inferno just waiting to be lit, and when smoke started pouring out of a first-floor paint locker, it was like taking a match to a cotton ball. In seconds, flames were licking across the floor and up the walls and across the ceiling.

The night depot master at the stable pulled the fire alarm, while other workers rushed up to the stables on the second and third floors and tried to shoo the horses downstairs into the streets. But when the flames spread, fueled by a brisk wind off the river, and it became obvious there would be no stopping them, the men fled and left their frightened animals behind, along with more than one hundred and fifty streetcars. Two of the stable workers couldn't make it to the stairs in time and jumped out of the second story. By the time firefighters arrived, the scene was too hot and the flames too high for them to get near the building. The sounds from inside, of horses neighing and crying and bucking against their stalls, was agonizing for those on the streets. Meanwhile, the fire was growing out of control.

The firemen could not prevent the flames from leaping across Fifty-fourth Street and setting fire to the new six-story silk factory at the corner. From there, the fire kept on spreading, rustling awake the residents inside a row of tenement houses and flats east of the silk factory and forcing them to flee for their lives out onto the sidewalk. Because the fire quickly blocked their front door, many of them raced out the back, where firemen tore down fences to help them escape. Adolph Kruger's liquor saloon, at the northwest corner of Tenth Avenue and Fifty-fourth Street, was next to go, and soon two entire blocks along Tenth Avenue were ablaze. When the fire threatened a shanty and some tiny wooden sheds filled by poor families along with their cows and horses on the north side of Fifty-third Street, firemen rushed over to get them out, too.

When the sun finally came up, Tenth Avenue looked like a Civil War battlefield, with dead horses strewn over three acres, charred streetcars, and arching streams from the fire hoses spraying into the ashes. The stench of burned animal flesh still wafted over the neighborhood when officials from the Belt Line Street Railway Company arrived to tally their losses. The catastrophe was staggering. Just 45 of their 1,230 horses made it out to safety. Of their 156 cars, 145 were destroyed, along with 3 track sweepers and 4 snow plows. The valuable straw, hay, and grain were all gone, not to mention five safes that contained more than six thousand dollars. The total loss just from the stable was calculated at $504,450, and when the neighborhood's losses were added to that, the overall figure was well beyond a million dollars. The only brief moment of joy on the day after the fire came when the stable's five pet cats crawled out of the rubble.

It rained the day after the fire, helping to douse any remaining cinders in the ashes of the stable. Also that day, the members of the executive committee of the Belt Line railroad met. Their purpose was not to bemoan what had happened but to look toward the future. They had quickly begun to buy more horses to keep their business operating, but, as *The*

Times reported two days after the tragedy, the Belt Line officials recognized that horses were no longer a worthy investment. "There is growing public sentiment that big stables in a crowded city are dangerous nuisances," *The Times* wrote. "Three kinds of propelling power will be tested by the Belt Line company if possible. They are the cable, the electric station, and independent electric motor systems. The promoters of all of these methods have been in contact with the company since the fire."

IT WAS PRECISELY THIS SORT of problem that Whitney and his Philadelphia cohorts hoped to solve. While Whitney was in Washington, Ryan and the others incorporated a new operation they called the Metropolitan Traction Company. It served as an umbrella over the group's assets, of which they soon had an abundance. Spending millions of dollars in only a few short months, the company bought out the Houston Street, West Street & Pavonia Ferry Railroad Company, the Chambers & Grand Street Ferry Railroad Company, the South Ferry Railroad Company, and others, all of which became one called the Metropolitan Street Railway Company. The Metropolitan Traction Company was not in the business of building or operating roads itself, but rather it served as a "holding company," the first one in the United States, and it would become a model for the future of big business and financial empires.

Finally, with all the roads and real estate that they had amassed came the responsibility to do what Jake Sharp had not done for years: make getting around New York easier. One of the first changes they made was to reroute the lines, so that passengers could stay on a single car longer to get to their destination faster. But for those passengers who did have to switch from one line to another, the group implemented a second change to the system. They began to allow passengers to transfer from one car to another, one route to another, for free, something Sharp had long resisted because of how much he believed it would have cost him. The new owners believed otherwise. They saw free transfers as a moneymaker. Under the new system, a single fare of five cents was all it cost to ride New York's transit system anywhere, for any distance. It reduced the cost for riders, essentially charging them one fare for two rides, while at the same time encouraging more people to ride. And it worked. In less than a year the Metropolitan issued more than a million transfers, a huge portion of which it learned were from passengers who otherwise would never have boarded a car at all. The free transfer would be one of Whitney's greatest gifts to his city.

But there was an even more pressing decision that needed to be made by the new leaders of New York's street railways: what would replace the horse as the source of power for New York's street railways as they entered the twentieth century?

IT HAD BEEN ALMOST six years since September 4, 1882, the day Thomas Edison, sporting a new Prince Albert coat, stood inside the Drexel, Morgan building at 23 Wall Street in downtown New York, flipped a switch, and watched as a direct current of electricity fed into his system and eight hundred lamps in the Drexel building and over at the *New York Times* offices flickered on. J. P. Morgan's Madison Avenue mansion was the first private home in the city to convert to incandescent lighting, though the first attempt saw an explosion that scorched Morgan's carpets and walls. Within a year, more than five hundred of the city's wealthiest homes were glowing brighter than they ever had.

Almost overnight, Manhattan came alive. Daytime businesses like printing and machine shops, piano factories, and lawyers' offices switched over and found the lightbulb to be so much more pleasant to work under than the gas lamp. But it was the change in nightlife that most excited New Yorkers. The formerly dark, nighttime storefronts of department stores lit up, and window browsing became a popular after-dinner activity. Theaters and restaurants were brighter, and so was the Statue of Liberty, the torch in her hand suddenly shining more brightly for ship captains to see her easily. More than fifteen hundred street lamps were alive in the city by 1886, and the number was growing by the week.

By 1888, a sea of wires that stretched from pole to pole, rooftop to rooftop, filled the air over New York's streets. The idea of burying lines in the ground had not yet been embraced, and so when New Yorkers gazed upward, their view was blocked by a dizzying collection of ugly black lines. In addition to Edison's, there were wires from Bell Telephone, the Gold and Stock Ticker Company, the fire and police departments, private alarm companies, Western Union, and more. There was little incentive to share a power line, and so a single fifty-foot pole might carry a dozen or more wires. To no one's surprise, the weight was often too much for the poles to hold, and they might snap and bring down dangerous live wires to the street. An attempt to legislate the crisis failed when the biggest companies simply ignored an order to put their lines underground and received no punishment.

FROM THE CITIES TO THE heartland, innovation was thriving in America. Out on the farms, a new combine harvester called the Sunshine was making farmers more productive, allowing them to move greater amounts of wheat, oat, barley, rice, and corn and increase their profits. In the big cities, electricity was generating an exciting nightlife scene, and Edison was already working on his next idea, combining sound with motion pictures in a device he called the kinetoscope. An electric-trolley experiment in Cleveland had worked successfully, and now other cities, most aggressively Richmond and now Boston, were implementing the idea. In Washington, the finishing touches were being put on the world's tallest stone structure, the 555-foot obelisk known as the Washington Monument. In New York, the waters surrounding the island had seen two exciting symbols of progress open in the past five years, the Brooklyn Bridge and the Statue of Liberty.

As fast as New York was growing, Chicago was growing faster. It was expanding its boundaries and growing its population through the annexation of more than a hundred square miles of suburban neighborhoods. The 1890 census would find that Manhattan was not as dominant as it once was and that Chicago, with 1.1 million people, was gaining on New York's 1.5 million. It was more than a number. If Chicago overtook New York in population, there was no telling the impact it would have on the cultural, political, and economic worlds of Gotham. Would banks see New York as weakening and the heartland as the new strength of America and shift their headquarters there? "New York would undoubtedly lose a great deal in prestige the world over—and in actual dollars and cents too—should Chicago or any other city on the continent count a larger population," *The Real Estate Record* wrote. When Congress soon awarded Chicago, and not New York, the right to host what would be the grandest World's Fair in celebration of the four hundredth anniversary of Christopher Columbus's famous voyage, it was a shove for New York to grow or be passed by.

"The elevated roads may be able to cram more people into their cars but they have long since passed the limit at which they can comfortably provide for their passengers during the busy hours of travel," *The New York Times* wrote in a blistering editorial in the spring of 1888. "Moreover they do not afford rapid transit at all. What electricity may do on the surface is yet to be proved, but rapid transit cannot be furnished on the surface, and as for cables they will only obstruct and delay the solution of the question. There is urgent need of underground rapid transit roads."

There was just one problem with electricity and the electric streetcar, and a few minutes after one o'clock in the afternoon on October 12, 1889, New Yorkers witnessed it firsthand in a horrifying way. A sturdy, thirty-year-old lineman for the Western Union Telegraph Company climbed up a pole at the southwest corner of Centre and Chambers streets right in front of Fire Engine Company number 7. His task was to cut out the dead wires of the company.

Like most of the tall poles in the city, the top was a confusing maze of live and dead wires. There were lines for the police and fire, telephone wires, and multiple Western Union telegraph wires. The worker had one foot resting on one of the half dozen crossbars atop the pole when he reached out for a wire he intended to cut and suddenly his body began to shiver and tremble. With pedestrians watching from below, and screams bringing people to their windows, a flash of bright sparks and blue flame shot out from beneath his hand. His body slumped and fell forward onto a network of wires that caught him and suspended him in a ghastly image forty feet over the street, with flames and blood shooting out of his mouth and nostrils. It took his fellow workmen more than an hour to carefully climb up, cut him loose, and lower him without receiving a deadly shock themselves. But once his lifeless body was removed, it was as if New York City itself had received a jolt.

There was genuine anger about the public death, and there would be an investigation and weeks of public hearings that followed. Mayor Hugh Grant, who only a few months earlier had personally taken an ax to a pole in a symbolic gesture of his desire to put wires underground, now had a horrific exhibit to bolster his case. If horses were the past and electricity was the future of street transportation, those wires would have to be underground.

OR SO IT SEEMED. The contingent of men controlling New York's streets had other ideas. Kemble, Ryan, and Widener had a vested interest in cable car systems because they had installed one in Philadelphia. They could not go one way in Philadelphia and another in New York City without raising questions. In the late winter of 1889, the men exchanged letters in which they debated the merits of cable versus other modes of transit power, including electric. Finally, on March 4, 1889, Widener penned a strongly worded letter to his partner William Whitney that took note of what Henry Whitney was building in Boston and urged the younger Whitney brother to look the other way.

"The work your Brother is doing in Boston whilst good would sink into insignificance when compared with it as I am satisfied it would solve the question of local transportation in New York," Widener wrote. "I say without fear of successful contradiction that if you place such a cable road on Broadway as we would build, it would be the greatest work of your life and one which you could always point to with pride."

Though Henry and William had remained close into their forties, exchanging letters and visiting frequently with their widowed mother in Brookline, they were also fiercely independent. They were enjoying their increasing clout in their respective cities. And Widener's letter reflected how they went about their business independently of each other, while at the same time paying attention out of the corner of one eye. Boston was small enough that one powerful businessman could have enormous influence over the streets; as the owner of the world's largest streetcar operation there, Henry Whitney was that man.

New York was much bigger, and it was harder there for one man to wield as much influence, but if William Whitney and his group could successfully transform the streets and make life more pleasant for the one and a half million residents, he would be close to the equivalent of his brother in a much larger metropolis. But to do that, the younger brother would have to suddenly change his stripes. Throughout their lives, William had been the smart, safe, and conservative brother, preferring to stay in the background while leaving his mark, while Henry had been the risk taker, unafraid to fail. Proposing to dig a subway tunnel beneath the cherished Boston Common was daring. So was switching his streetcar operation from horses to electricity before the electric streetcar had truly shown itself to be a worthy alternative.

Widener's 1889 letter to Whitney was striking for its stubbornness, in that it ignored the impact electricity was already having on street railways and focused instead on a technology that had severe limitations and was costly to install. There were some nine hundred miles of electrified tracks in the United States, three times as many miles as cable. For the Metropolitan Traction Company, and for the citizens of New York, Whitney's handling of the letter would be another critical moment.

The Philadelphians had enlisted Whitney because of his influence and connections in New York. They knew that his opinion mattered more than theirs when it came to the company's New York operations. If Whitney wanted to ignore Widener and follow in the footsteps of his older brother, he surely would have met resistance from his partners as they were dead set against using electricity. He also would have been ignoring the venerable *Street Railway Journal,* which had analyzed the question and weighed in emphatically, saying "the cable system was far superior to any form of the electric, and would never be superseded."

Widener's letter must have struck Whitney. He did not follow his brother's course and instead set his company on a path to pursue cable as a major source of streetcar power in New York. The Metropolitan Traction Company began to move forward with the slow, arduous, and expensive task of replacing the horses on New York's streets with a system powered by cables. It was, they believed, the most sensible solution, a compromise between the ugliness of steam and the uncertainty of electricity. At Broadway and Fourteenth Street, cable-pulled cars were soon whipping through a sharp, double turn so dangerous that passengers took to calling it "Dead Man's Curve." Of all the important moves that William Whitney would make in his life, his choice to pursue a fading technology like cable rather than to follow his brother's lead and embrace the electric streetcar would be his greatest miscalculation.

It was only a few months after that decision when another big city, not a smaller one like Boston, showed just how foolish and shortsighted Whitney was being.

ON NOVEMBER 4, 1890, a bright, sunlit morning in downtown London, thousands of people gathered at King William Street near the Monument and looked out for Albert Edward VII, the Prince of Wales, as well as the Duke of Westminster, the Duke of Clarence, and other lords, chancellors, and British dignitaries who were expected to arrive by carriage. It was a tense time in the city. For almost two years, a serial killer was believed to have slaughtered at least eleven women, mostly around London's Whitechapel district, and he was assigned the name Jack the Ripper after an anonymous letter later believed to be a hoax surfaced. Farmers who slaughtered cattle, along with butchers, physicians, and especially surgeons were all eyed suspiciously by investigators because of the way the women were mutilated, but in the end, after more than a hundred suspects were questioned, nobody was ever arrested.

At least for one morning, the gloom of the Ripper murders lifted off the city and smiles emerged. Together, along with the South African–born engineer James Henry Greathead, the royals in attendance stepped into an oversized hydraulic lift that could hold fifty people and enjoyed a smooth descent sixty feet below the street and into London's Underground. Once on the station platform, their eyes almost had to squint from the glare of the bright lights off the white glazed tiles. Red DANGER signs also shone brightly at tunnel entrances, near where a brightly colored train car decorated in flowers sat quietly.

When the chairman of the Underground handed the Prince of Wales a specially made gold key, the prince turned a switch and an electric current started up the train awaiting them. There was no rumbling. No burst of black smoke in the air. No whistle screaming. When the royal passengers took their seats in one of the three carriages, the train pulled slowly away from the platform, quickly zooming up to fifteen miles per hour without a hitch. Their entire journey lasted eight minutes. London's newest subway line was just a three-mile stretch, from the Monument to the south bank of the Thames River in Stockwell. But instead of being powered by steam or by cable as was first intended, its cars moved by electricity. A steel channel was run alongside the rails and iron "scoops" fixed on the bottom of the locomotives picked up the current. This was the world's first electrically powered subway.

At a luncheon after the journey, the Prince of Wales spoke about the significance of the electrified Underground and how its clean air was immensely more enjoyable. "It must be a matter of deep thought to all of us, the ever-increasing growth of this city, and the consequent increasing difficulties of the means of travel," the prince said. "This, the first electric railway in England, will, I hope, do much to relieve the congestion of traffic which exists in the city. Businessmen who have great distances to come will by this means find an easy way of leaving the city and of enjoying the fresh air of the country."

"Hear, hear!" the crowd shouted back.

Over time, as the City and South London Railway took on more passengers and expanded, there would be gripes about the cramped small carriages that had no windows, the annoying ringing sound that could be heard as the train whisked through the tunnels, and even the slower-than-expected speed at which the trains moved. But there was no denying that the electrified trains were more pleasant than the steam-powered ones on London's other lines. And among all the speakers who took to the podium at the luncheon on the day the electric subway was unveiled, it was a bearded, seventy-three-year-old British civil engineer who specialized in the construction of railways who posed the question on the minds of everyone, not just in London but around the world.

"Can this electric railway," Sir John Fowler asked, "be looked upon as a guide for the future?"

Back across the pond, another civil engineer half the age of Fowler, who had studied in London as a young man and closely followed the success of the Underground, was asking the same question.

8

THE ENGINEER AND THE
PIANO MAKER

THERE WERE FOUR GANGS, EACH WITH ABOUT half a dozen men, and on a sunny and warm weekday in early June of 1891 they swarmed over the streets in lower Manhattan like small armies on the move. They were mostly recent Italian immigrants, with names like Giuseppe, Luigi, and Alfonzo, but there were Irish and blacks, too. It was hard labor that paid $1.50 a day, and there was no shortage of men lining up for it. They wore hats with oversized brims and baggy overalls, and most of them had suspenders, too. They all had the hands of laborers, weathered, scratched, scarred, and perpetually stained with dirt or grease. Each group had the same peculiar load of machinery, and when one of the gangs arrived at the corner of Front and Whitehall streets, they immediately attracted a growing crowd.

One man cast an especially long shadow in the summer sun as he watched their progress, day after day, night after night. Always serious, he kept his beard scraggly and full around his chin and his thinning hair combed over on top to hide a balding head. He often wore a hat that covered his thinning hair and was pulled low over his deep-set eyes. At more than six feet, four inches tall, he was Lincolnesque in stature and because of the attention that his presence commanded. When he would arrive at one of the construction sites, the pace of the work quickened, and any laughter stopped. Occasionally he would pull a pencil from his jacket pocket and jot down a note. Later in his life, *The New York Times* described him as "city-born, city-bred, and city-minded," and as he watched these workers with intense interest it was an apt description. To William Barclay Parsons Jr., the work he was witnessing would determine not only how he would spend the next decade of his life. It would set in motion his personal legacy and that of one of the great engineering companies in the world.

On this June day, from the back of the flatbed carriage that came with them, the laborers took out a pump that was mounted on a petroleum barrel; carried out dozens of pieces of wrought iron pipe, some of them an inch in diameter, others two inches; and then wheeled out a small pile driver. Once they seemed to have everything positioned properly, they went to work. First, they lifted up a block from the pavement as close to the street corner as possible. A few feet away, a worker took one of the sections of two-inch pipe and tapped it into the soil until it was securely standing up, at which point the pile driver was positioned over the pipe. Next, a pulley from the pile driver was raised over the pipe, a rope was connected to the pipe, and, when the signal was given, WHAM! A one-hundred-and-fifty-pound hammer drove down on top of the pipe and slammed it into the earth. When it disappeared, a worker reached down into the ground, unscrewed a cap from the top of the pipe, and took hold of another section and screwed it into the pipe in the ground, thereby doubling its length and leaving a new piece for the pile driver to hit. WHAM! It was hammered again, and the process was repeated, each time a new piece of pipe adding another four or five feet to the growing pipe in the ground. It was a mystery how far down it would go before it struck something solid, and that was the whole purpose of the exercise.

A reporter for *The Times* was among the crowd watching when a man approached him. In a thick country drawl the inquisitor asked the reporter about the work that was going on, as he assumed the newspaperman would have the answers. "About how far'll they have to go daown to git to water?" the man asked. The reporter explained it wasn't water they were digging for. It was bedrock, or Manhattan schist, as it was known.

They wanted to know how deep the soil went at precisely this corner of the island.

As it turned out, the soil didn't go deep at all. After about five good whacks from the pile driver, the pipe could go no farther. It was some twenty feet into the ground. And it was then that the second stage of work began, which would provide the second set of results of what they came to learn. A narrower, one-inch pipe was hammered into the two-inch pipe, and it brought back to the surface dozens of soil samples that were collected in pails. Each pail was designated to hold a sample from a particular depth in the ground. That way, a complete register could be kept of every five-foot section of soil-covered bedrock. Most of the pails were filled with nothing but water and sand. But when the narrow pipe was pushed deeper into the ground, the samples coming back got thicker, first with vegetable matter and then with dark clay. That change was revealing, because it told Parsons which parts of the city could handle a trench and which parts might require tunneling.

These small groups of men scattered across the streets along Broadway from the southern tip at South Ferry up to Fifty-ninth Street. Their job had never been done before, but it was quite simple. They were going to collect accurate measurements of the actual shape of the rock on which New Yorkers were living. Until this day, only estimates had been made as to the depth of the soil, and they would be proved wildly inaccurate.

Canal Street, in particular, was expected to pose a huge problem. For years it was assumed that a subterranean creek flowed beneath it, creating an underground muck that would make it too weak to support any sort of tunnel. Instead, workers did not discover any creek there and determined that the ground south of Eighth Street was mostly gravel and stones the size of chestnuts, ideal for supporting a tunnel. Workers believed, in fact, that the tunnel might be built faster beneath Canal Street than in any other part of the city, perhaps as brisk as fifteen to twenty feet per day. As the workers discovered with the holes they punctured in the island, it was shaped like an upside-down mountain range, with peaks and valleys of all shapes and sizes from one neighborhood to the next.

At various points along Whitehall Street, rock was struck with a pipe at twenty feet, sixteen feet, twenty-eight feet, and as deep as thirty-four feet at Beaver Street. But the workers over at Exchange Place had to put a lot more pipe into the ground before they struck bedrock. The bedrock was sixty-one feet down at Wall Street; sixty-three at Rector; seventy at Pine; seventy-three at Cortland; eighty-three feet at Fulton. It was 112 feet at Park Place and a foot deeper at Murray Street. The deepest spot measured was Duane Street, where the pipe was hammered 163 feet into the ground before it struck bedrock. In contrast, when a pipe was hammered into the ground at Thirty-third Street, it went just four feet down.

FOR AN ISLAND THAT STRETCHED only seven miles long, Manhattan presented an unusual array of engineering nightmares. The softer rock had a grainy texture, almost like sugar, and was known as dolomitic marble. It was mostly at the island's northern end. The more solid, challenging rock, Manhattan schist, was dangerous to bore into because it could fracture more easily and collapse on workers. It was at the southern portion. The island's widest point stretches only about two miles, from river to river, near 125th Street, but just north of that it narrows quickly like a soda bottle. And though it appears flat to pedestrians, most of the city's terrain is actually quite rolling and rocky, especially between Twenty-third Street and the northern tip of Central Park. North of 110th Street the island has a steep rise in elevation that tops out at 268 feet above sea level, Manhattan's peak, in Inwood near Fort Washington Avenue and 185th Street. In this northern portion, there were two hurdles for major digging. The bedrock of Manhattan has two major cracks, or fault lines, one at 125th Street and the other further north near what is now Fort Tryon Park, that have existed for millions of years. Although gravel, sand, and silt deposits have mostly filled them in, the faults weaken the structure of the bedrock hundreds of feet beneath the sea.

WILLIAM BARCLAY PARSONS JR. came from a life of privilege. He was born on April 15, 1859, in New York City. His father, William Barclay

Parsons, was a businessman who owned a firm that imported chemicals, and his mother, Eliza Glass Livingston, raised their four boys at their home on Bleecker Street. It was his father who passed down to William Jr. two traits that would serve him well in life: patience and persistence. "When I squeeze lemons, what I'm after is lemon juice," Parsons said one day late in his life, after his greatest achievements were behind him, among them designing the Panama Canal and the Cape Cod Canal. "My method is to get all the juice out of each lemon before I tackle the next one."

His parents came from prominent families in England and Scotland. When William was just eleven, his parents sent him to a private school in Torquay, Devonshire, where he studied with tutors and explored Europe at any chance he got. His time overseas shaped his values, and he came to appreciate and admire the aristocracy for the way he believed it demanded civil discourse and implored accepting responsibility for one's actions. So much was he taken with his British roots that when he came home and moved back in with his family at their Fifth Avenue brownstone, he asked to be called by his middle name, Barclay, which sounded much more English than plain old William or, good heavens, Bill.

Tall and mature-looking for his sixteen years, he enrolled in 1875 at Columbia College, where, despite a few instances of rebelling, including one when talking during chapel services almost got him expelled, he sparkled. Though he was born in New York, Parsons behaved less like a New Yorker and more like a conservative Brit, dressing in somber clothes and adopting a more serious demeanor than his classmates. Still, they took to him and dubbed him Reverend Parsons.

He was hardly a shut-in, debating with the Philolexia Society; participating on the tug-of-war team; filling the role of sports editor for the school paper, *The Spectator;* being chosen as class president; and rowing for his college on the Harlem River. Long after his graduation, members of the crew team would brag about one particular race, when an accident at the start left them hopelessly behind and Parsons, to their amazement, somehow stroked them to improbable victory. By the time he graduated in 1879 with honors, he was tall, big-boned, muscular, athletic, and handsomely confident. Not quite sure what to do with his bachelor of arts, Parsons decided to take an engineering course at Columbia's School of Mines. It changed his life. He was absorbed by the subject, and when he graduated in 1882 with a degree in civil engineering, it was with the highest scores on record at the school.

Entering America's workforce as a bright young engineer, his timing could not have been better. Construction of the Brooklyn Bridge was nearly finished, and it was not only going to have a dramatic impact on the way of life in New York but also going to make civil engineering one of the hottest fields for graduating students. Columbia School of Mines graduates were attractive commodities, and Parsons, the most sought after of them all, took a job working for the Erie Railroad. He had only been in his new job for a short while when his supervisor received a letter from his worker's proud but worrisome father.

"He has never given me, an anxious, watchful parent, one single cause of complaint," William Barclay Parsons wrote. "I know he is good through and through, capable, highly educated professionally and otherwise, full of ability, energy, industry and integrity." A short time later, a reply came, informing the elder Parsons he had no reason to fret. "The young gentleman is all that can be desired," the supervisor wrote back, "and will by his industry and faithfulness force himself to advancement."

To show off his work, the son invited the elder Parsons to the Erie job site and took him on a train trip along the Rochester stretch of tracks, where Parsons Jr. was overseeing their reconstruction. During the beginning of their journey, he explained what he was doing and how bad the tracks were that he was in charge of fixing. But only a few minutes into their trip, his father was puzzled, as the tracks they were traveling on seemed perfectly smooth.

"Oh, but this is the part I have rebuilt," the son explained. "We'll come to the end of it in a minute and then you'll notice the difference."

Seconds later, as the driving wheel of the locomotive attempted to brake, the train hurtled off the tracks. It bounced down a fourteen-foot embankment, landing upside down at the bottom. The two Parsons men, as calm and controlled as ever, were stunned but somehow unhurt, and they found themselves sitting next to each other on the ceiling of the wrecked car.

"There, what did I tell you," Parsons the engineer said to his father.

"Yes, son," his earnest father said back, "it is rougher."

When Parsons was promoted to road master with the Erie Railroad, one of the first letters of congratulations he received was from a New York congressman who had his own interests in railroads and engineering, Abram Hewitt. Hewitt would keep his eye on the young Parsons from that day forward.

PARSONS CAME TO NEW YORK in 1886, and he opened an engineering consulting office. He was by now a taken man, having married Anna DeWitt Reed, like him a descendant of a colonial family. Anna Parsons accompanied her husband on some of his most important trips around the world, volunteered for the American Red Cross, opened an orphanage, and became the person that he turned to most often for early reads on his writings. She would also bear him two children.

Parsons was just twenty-seven when he moved to New York. He needed a partner, and so he and his younger brother, Harry de Berkeley Parsons, a budding mechanical engineer himself who would later design the reptile house at the Bronx Zoo, opened a firm together in lower Manhattan at 22 William Street. They were close, yachting together most weekends, but they were different. Harry was more shy, three years younger and narrow in his thinking. William had grand ambitions. And it was William who quickly got written up in *Engineering News* for experience that "will place him in the front rank of the profession in this city." Their small engineering firm quickly established itself as a force.

In their early days, William and Harry took on railroad projects, new water systems, and even hydroelectric plants, going wherever the work took them, from Ohio to Colorado to Maine to Pennsylvania to Illinois to Texas to California to Maryland. Railroads, in particular, became their specialty, and in 1887 Parsons was named general manager and chief engineer of the Denver Railroad, Land & Coal Co. But even as he traveled the country, Parsons did not lose touch with his home. Reports about New York City's need for some sort of rapid transit system were intensifying, and Parsons wanted to be there. "During these years I was engaged in various private practice in railroad and other engineering work in different parts of the country," Parsons wrote later, "but never absent for any length of time from New York, or accepting any assignment that would permanently take me away from New York, in order to keep in touch with the rapid transit problem, which I believed would eventually come to pass."

The two most promising New York underground railways, the Arcade Railroad and, after that, the New York District Railway, would both fail. But for Parsons it was for the best. He was still a young man with little experience managing others and only a few years spent working on railroads. But the opportunity gave him a chance to begin exploring the terrain of New York City, not only on the surface but underneath the streets. He studied the maps that were available to him, and, after trekking through the streets himself, he began to create his own topographical maps. In time, Parsons mapped out the entire island. The bedrock in midtown, as he learned, lay much closer to the streets than in most other parts, making midtown far more suitable for the construction of taller buildings, but also more challenging to place a subway tunnel under. He came to understand that in order to design a subway for New York, he would have to resolve not only the best route but also the best tunneling method and the mode of power for train operation.

There was something else Parsons learned during his climb in engineering circles. In order to achieve anything monumental, he would need friends in high places who believed as strongly in a subway for New York as he did. He already had the attention of Abram Hewitt. In January of 1888, Parsons had even written a letter to Hewitt, asking the mayor to keep him in mind for any future subway commissions. "I've had considerable experience in this subject and have given it close study," Parsons wrote. "I would be much indebted if you should submit my name for consideration." But it was another unlikely bond that he forged with a likable, hardworking, German-born manufacturer of the world's finest pianos that gained him his most valuable friend.

WILLIAM STEINWEG WAS BORN on March 5, 1835, the fourth of six children in a tiny German village called Seesen. Their father, Heinrich, was a piano maker and anticipated bringing all of his children into the business with him. But then his third son, Charles, at risk of going to war at a time when revolutions were breaking out across Europe, fled for New York, joined the piano-making business there, and then wrote home to his family that they should come, too, because the piano factories in the city were thriving. In 1850, they did come, sailing into the harbor just as the summer began. It was not long after they arrived that their family name, Steinweg, was anglicized into Steinway.

The children all got jobs in piano manufacturing, but their father preferred to keep the work in the family, and in 1853 he opened a family piano-making business. In a short time, Steinway & Sons was winning prizes and being recognized for its beautiful pianos, and soon it was big enough to open a large factory that stretched the entire block of what was then Fourth Avenue (now Park Avenue) between Fifty-second and Fifty-third streets. A musician at heart who played the piano and was an outstanding tenor, William Steinway, who spoke English more clearly than anyone in his family, also possessed a certain charm and devotion to his craft that made him easily likable. He was a natural choice to take charge of the company's finances and sizable real estate dealings. Steinway & Sons blossomed into a giant in its field, and Steinway, in his dealings with lawyers, shipping magnates, local businessmen, bankers, newspaper ad salesmen, and politicians became an American business force.

With his thick, dark beard; bushy head of hair; and upright posture honed from years of sitting straight on a piano bench, William Steinway cut an impressive figure. Almost single-handedly he helped the piano become a symbol of middle-class success, an instrument that reflected being cultured but not pompous. At the 1867 World Exposition in Paris,

American and European pianos commanded great attention, and Steinway & Sons and a Boston company called Chickering & Sons received the highest honors for their work. But as the company grew into a worldwide machine, with William as president, sending pianos across Europe and into homes and palaces, it was not the musical side of Steinway & Sons that drew the attention of New York's mayor, Hugh Grant, to Steinway in the early 1890s.

Over the years, Steinway, who had cultivated good relationships with his workers, developed swaths of woodland and open meadows in a part of eastern Queens called Astoria for an enormous factory. He boosted property values wherever his company went and even bought his own horse-railway line to make it easier to access a previously remote part of Queens. Inside his piano-making complex overlooking Bowery Bay, he could store mountains of lumber and giant stacks of iron and steel, and he could receive barge deliveries right up to the building. It was an ingenious development plan, and it did not go unnoticed by Grant. A man like Steinway, who was able to juggle so many tasks, disarm anyone he came in conflict with, and convince politicians to give him what he wanted was a man who the mayor recognized could be invaluable for a sensitive job like getting a subway approved.

After New York's governor, David B. Hill, signed into law the Rapid Transit Act of 1891, signaling that the city was finally serious about solving its congestion woes, *The Times* gushed with its headline: NOW FOR RAPID TRANSIT. Grant named Steinway to run the transit commission. Among the other commissioners, Grant also picked a rising figure in New York City, August Belmont Jr., whose banker father had died a few months earlier and left him with an enormous sum of money and influence. The commission quickly named two engineers to study the various options and design one or more plans to be considered. At seventy-two years old, William Ezra Worthen, a sanitary and hydraulic engineer, was one of the most experienced engineers in the country, and he was named the commission's chief engineer. At the recommendation of Abram Hewitt and with Steinway's backing, thirty-two-year-old William Parsons was named as the commission's deputy chief engineer.

On the day Governor Hill signed the Rapid Transit Act into law, Steinway said to a group of reporters that the decision facing New Yorkers was not as obvious as some believed: "The question is practically narrowed down by the conditions under which we are to have rapid transit to the choice of two systems," he said. "It is to be either a viaduct or underground."

But there was another decision that needed to be resolved even before that, and it was the problem Abram Hewitt foresaw back in 1888. The Rapid Transit Act left the burden of paying for a subway to private industry, in an attempt to remove any chance that history might repeat itself and allow a corrupt politician to block construction and pocket millions of dollars in kickbacks, just as Boss Tweed had done. The commission would tackle the responsibilities of deciding what routes a new elevated line or a subway should follow and what private company should be in charge of building and operating it. But that's it. It was as if the city was shirking any responsibility in solving its biggest crisis and was instead banking on a Carnegie, a Vanderbilt, a Whitney, a Belmont, or anyone else with tens of millions of dollars at their disposal and a strong interest in rapid transit, showing up unannounced at the doorstep of City Hall with a bag of cash and a shovel.

IN NEW YORK CITY in 1891, two downtown buildings that stood only a few feet apart near Exchange Place suddenly became the most important places to be. One was a restaurant. One was a boardroom. It was not unusual for deals that were struck over steak at the former to be approved over paper and ink at the latter.

Delmonico's, with its third-floor, private dining room, a luxury few restaurants could afford, and a basement wine cellar stocked with more than ten thousand bottles, had a long history in the city. Giovanni Del-Monico opened a small shop in 1827, where he personally bottled casks of wine. When he and his brothers opened a café and pastry shop, they dropped the hyphen from their name, and soon they were taking over various locations around lower Manhattan, including one that became a favorite haunt of Thomas Edison, who liked to visit with his wife while coming to the city for a weekend getaway. When a group of nearly two hundred wealthy financiers feted their candidate for president, James G. Blaine, with a dinner at Delmonico's in 1884, *The World* newspaper called it "the Royal Feast of Belshazzar." In 1891, the newest Delmonico's restaurant was opened at 2 South William Street. Eight stories tall, and the first to feature electric lights, it still had touches of the Old World, like its lavishly decorated dark wood inside and two Pompeii pillars framing the front door on the outside. Its private dining room became the newest destination for anyone who was out to cut a deal, legal or otherwise, and wanted a discreet location to do it.

Almost diagonally across the street was 22 William Street. It was the engineering office of the Parsons brothers whose company became the host for the public hearings and board meetings of the Steinway commission.

THE FRUSTRATION OF THE STEINWAY commission boiled over late in the afternoon of October 2, 1891. Steinway invited dozens of reporters to come in, and the commissioners proceeded to dump nearly a hundred typewritten pages onto the table. Then they told the reporters to see what they could make of them. Among the papers were maps, drawings, and reports of the commission's experts and engineers, and the commissioners were bluntly honest about their own review of the documents. They were divided and unable to make a decision almost a year after they got started. The commissioners thought that by showing the public just how difficult their decision was, they would garner some sympathy for how long it was taking them and gain some useful insights into how passengers felt.

Two plans were on the table. The Worthen plan, as it was called, had four tracks, two for local trains and two for express trains. And they were all on one level, essentially a four-track road, with a concrete base and supported by wrought iron girders and posts. The ceiling was a plate-iron cover that was coated with a coal tar that would seal it off from water and help preserve the iron. Worthen, however, did not address what to do with the myriad of water, gas, and electrical lines that were already buried in the streets and would have to be disturbed during the tunneling.

Parsons's plan called for digging deeper into the ground, with two double-deck tunnels, for local and express trains. One side of the street was for trains headed north, or uptown, and the other for those headed south, downtown. By stacking the tracks instead of placing them side by side, Parsons required two deeper tunnels, but he also created space in between the tunnels, where he proposed burying the pipes and conduits for the utilities.

There was no question that Worthen's plan was the simpler of the two, which is why three of the four consulting engineers the Steinway commission hired to review the plans and make recommendations preferred it to Parsons's plan. But the lone holdout was not just anyone. It was Octave Chanute, the outspoken French-born president of the American Society of Civil Engineers. Chanute's preference for the Parsons plan, with his own modifications, created a headache for the Steinway commissioners. Now, instead of having two plans to choose from, they had three.

MORE RAPID-TRANSIT TALK, the *Times'* headline said the next day. The story singled out Chanute for holding up the process. "It is undoubtedly this report which has caused hesitation and delay in coming to a definite conclusion on the general question of construction. With only the other reports before them they could probably have reached a decision on this; but Mr. Chanute's report has given them so much to think about that they have declared that no decision will be given out for several days."

THREE WEEKS LATER, THE Steinway commission announced its decision. Two separate routes would branch off one main line. The main line would start at South Ferry and head up the west side beneath Broadway to the Bronx. The second line would commence off the main line at Union Square and go up the east side under Madison Avenue and also cross the Harlem River into the Bronx. The tunnel would be built with a shield designed especially for the project, but the depth of the tunnels would be decided by the contractor. The trains would most likely be powered by electricity, though the commissioners remained skeptical about that. On the express lines, it was estimated the trains could reach forty miles per hour, a speed that seemed supersonic for a city that had been riding on plodding horses or congested Els for half a century.

ON JANUARY 1, 1892, a fifteen-year-old Irish girl with rosy cheeks and fair skin named Annie Moore was the first of 148 passengers to be escorted off the steamship *Nevada*. She and the others were placed onto a small transfer boat that was colorfully decorated in bunting, and when it docked a few minutes later Annie was hustled into a new building for arriving immigrants in New York harbor. Foghorns and whistles clanged to signal her arrival, and, after a brief stumble, she walked up to a registry desk, where she was registered as the first arriving immigrant at Ellis Island. She was handed a ten-dollar gold coin, the most amount of money she said that she had ever held, and then she explained to the throng of witnesses, workers, and reporters that she was here in America with her two younger brothers to join their parents on Monroe Street in New York City.

If there was a moment that signaled how desperately New York needed a subway, the arrival of Annie Moore was it. In 1877, sixty-three thousand immigrants arrived in New York City, passing through what was then the arriving station for immigrants, Castle Garden. When the Bureau of Immigration was put in charge of registering immigrants in 1890, it was clear that Castle Island could no longer handle the arriving flood of immigrants. A new station was needed to screen for fleeing criminals or merely the sick and the homeless, and the immigration bureau quickly settled on the empty landfill Ellis Island, which opened for business New Year's Day in 1892. In its first year, Ellis Island registered 445,987 immigrants, more Germans and Irish than any other group and more than seven times the total that had arrived fifteen years earlier. It was all the evidence needed to prove that New York City had to do more than merely expand its livable space to accommodate its surging population. It had to create a better way for all those new people flooding into the metropolis to get around.

IT TOOK MORE THAN A YEAR for the Steinway commission to write up a detailed contract outlining how the subway would be built, who would operate it, and how the fare money would be disbursed. Only then could the date be set to auction off a 999-year contract to build and operate a New York City subway: December 29, 1892.

A financial meltdown overseas in London back in 1890 triggered by the collapse of the city's oldest merchant bank, Baring Brothers & Co., had begun to cause financiers around the world to hold on to their cash a little tighter. This would have far-reaching implications. And when the king of New York's elevated trains, Jay Gould, died suddenly on December 2, 1892, it threw the city's transit future into greater turmoil. A few days later, when Steinway was cornered by a reporter at a transit commission meeting, he acknowledged that times had changed in the two years since the subway talks began in earnest. There was even a new yet familiar president of the United States. Once again, with the backing of his old friend William Whitney, Grover Cleveland had taken the White House in the 1892 election, winning revenge against the incumbent president, Benjamin Harrison, who ousted him from office back in 1888. The Democrats were again in power, though this time, unlike Cleveland's first term, the country was on much shakier financial ground, and a collapse seemed all but imminent. Despite so much upheaval, Steinway insisted he was not worried about the subway contract.

"I haven't the slightest doubt that capitalists would have eagerly sought the opportunity now presented to them in the rapid transit scheme for New York had it not been for the unfortunate failure of the Baring Brothers of London," Steinway said to a *Times* reporter in mid-December. "That financial disaster made capital everywhere very sensitive and overcareful in undertakings involving large sums of money. But evidence is not wanting that the financial market is recovering and that the undertaking we have on hand will be carried through successfully. I am confident that we shall get a bid for the franchise on the 29th of this month and that work will be inaugurated early next year."

If no bids were received, Steinway said the commission would simply wait a few months and offer it again. And if still no bids were made, the city would then be wise to consider the idea put forth by Abram Hewitt: build the subway and lease it out to the highest bidder. It would take a few years to bring the city a return on its investment, he said, but passengers would flock to the subway, and revenues would eventually soar. "When this is accomplished," he told *The Times*, "merchants and their clerks, who now stand and sit about downtown restaurants for their lunches, will jump aboard these cars and get home in five, ten and fifteen minutes for luncheon with their families. They could do this for ten cents and inside an hour, which will be far more economical to themselves and add to the dividends of the road."

They were confident words. But what he said publicly did not match how he felt privately. Steinway was nervous. On Christmas Eve, he stayed home with his wife, who had been suffering migraines, and his daughter Maud. He tipped his younger, hardest-working servants one hundred dollars apiece and his older servants and private coachman twenty-five dollars each and let them go for the evening to be with their families. And at eleven o'clock, the piano king and president of the Steinway commission climbed into bed, closed his eyes, and drifted off, dreaming that burglars were sneaking into his house. In fact, a nightmare far worse was imminent.

THE SOARING ROTUNDA INSIDE THE New York City Hall building is a stunning piece of architecture. A wide marble staircase twists on opposing sides up to the second floor, and light pours in from first- and second-floor arched windows and bounces off the gleaming white marble floor. When Abraham Lincoln visited New York in 1861 as president-elect, he spoke from the rotunda, and when he was assassinated four years later, his coffin was placed on the landing eight stairs up, where he lay in state. Ulysses S. Grant lay in state in the rotunda as well, as did the first Union officer killed during the Civil War, Elmer Ephraim Ellsworth, who had been a friend of Lincoln's and whose death sparked a Union rallying cry, "Remember Ellsworth!" In the late nineteenth century, whenever there was a major celebration or announcement or a day of mourning with state and national implications, only the White House carried greater importance than the rotunda of New York City Hall. On December 29, 1892, the awarding of a contract to build what would be the first subway in America was such an occasion deserving of the rotunda.

The entire first floor of City Hall was packed, as was the staircase leading up to it, as some of the most important men in New York came to witness the proceedings. The crowd was so big that Steinway's plans to make the announcement on the first floor had to be scrapped, and he was forced up to the landing between the first and second floors. William C. Whitney was there representing the Metropolitan Traction Company. Melville C. Smith was there on behalf of the Arcade Railway. Mayor Hugh Grant was there, as was his newly elected successor, Thomas Francis Gilroy.

At noon, Steinway asked for quiet. He explained that the law required that the terms of the sale and specifics of the construction be read first, and for the next hour Parsons shared in the task of reading the entire forty-three-page pamphlet. It was explained that any successful bidder would have to pay expenses of the commission that totaled $111,594, plus the $25,000 fees for the commissioners. A last requirement was that any serious bidder must be prepared at that moment to hand over 10 percent of their bid, in cash, as a show of good faith. The details finished, Eugene Bushe, the commission's secretary, shouted out into the vast rotunda for any bidders to step forward. Silence filled the room. He called out again, and again there was no response. Then, on a third call, a voice shot back from the crowd.

A tall, skinny, clean-shaven man stepped forward, moving with a nervous energy. He announced his name as William Amory, a resident of West Ninety-fourth Street, and he said he was prepared to make his bid. In a room full of powerful and important men who controlled the majority of New York's transit operations, a puzzled state fell over the room.

He said that he bid five hundred dollars for the franchise, plus half of 1 percent of the gross receipts per year. By his estimation, the city would collect fifty thousand dollars a year for a total over the life of the lease of

$50 million. His bid was stunningly low, but it was the only bid. The commissioners, joined by Gilroy, quickly huddled, and when they broke they said that Amory's bid failed to meet the requirements.

"In what respect is it defective?" Amory shouted back.

"The commissioners will consider that matter," Bushe said, "and give you an answer afterward."

Amory quickly said that he was withdrawing that bid and submitting another. He said that he now bid $1,000 outright for the franchise. The commissioners were silent briefly, as they hoped desperately that Bushe could pry out one more bid from the crowd. But when no one else came forward, Amory was told to follow the commissioners into the mayor's private office. The entire event was barely an hour old. Once inside, Amory handed over one hundred dollars, which was the required 10 percent of his bid. The commissioners asked who his financial backers were, since they were convinced he was not rich enough himself to take on the subway project, but Amory refused to answer. He was handed a receipt for his money and guided out into the hall so the commissioners could meet in private. In his mind, he was now the rightful owner of the New York City subway project. He had bid and paid his 10 percent, and the commissioners, by taking his money, had accepted his offer. But a half hour later, Amory was called back to the mayor's office. He was handed his one hundred dollars along with a piece of paper.

> Resolved: That the bids made this day by W. Nowland Amory, as follows, namely: One bid of $500 and one half of 1 percent upon the gross receipts of the proposed railroad and the other bid of $1,000 cash are not deemed by this commission to be advantageous to the public and the City of New York or its interests and the bids are hereby rejected pursuant to the right reserved by the terms of the sale, and that the sum of $100 deposited by him be returned to him.

For the next few days Amory was the fascination of every New Yorker. Two days after the auction, *The Times* ran a lengthy profile of him. The newspaper described him as a man "of fine personal appearance," thirty-five years old, from a financial and military family of Massachusetts. He was born in Arkansas, where his father had been stationed as an infantry officer, and he attended the prestigious St. Paul's private school in Concord, New Hampshire. When he settled in New York, he worked as the secretary for the New York District Railway, successfully convincing hundreds of property owners along Broadway and Madison Avenue to permit the railroad's construction. Even though the railroad never happened, he had proved he was a formidable businessman with strong powers of persuasion. But he was unable to persuade the members of the Steinway commission that he could find a way to pay for the construction of their subway, and as 1893 got under way Amory was soon nothing more than a footnote in the seemingly never-ending New York City subway debate.

STEINWAY WAS MORTIFIED AT THE outcome of the commission's two-year effort. A few hours after the auction ended, he met with reporters back at 22 William Street. The disappointment in his words was obvious, as he knew that the commission was no closer to getting a subway built than any of the men before him:

> Much has been made about the objections to underground transit. All this, however, is answered in the fact no well-planned and equipped tunnel, properly ventilated and lighted and free from the gases of combustion, has yet been in operation; but we all know that the achievements of modern science make these conditions now obtainable.
>
> It is unfortunate that New York is not to lead in this matter, for Broadway is probably the only existing artery of the world where such a line of transit could certainly be made successful from a financial point of view.

And with that he said the commission had no choice but to forget about building a subway and pursue an extension of its elevated system, anything to help the city develop its land to the north and encourage

people to move out of the overcrowded downtown and midtown neighborhoods. "Something must be done quickly to relieve the pressure," Steinway said, "and to give renewed impetus to the city's growth in a northerly
direction." It was his first acknowledgment of failure, and Steinway, whose
body at the age of fifty-eight was starting to break down, since his knees
caused so much pain that he needed a cane to walk, began to suffer not
just physically but also emotionally. In his diary, he jotted down a reflec-
tion on January 14, 1893. "To my dismay I see I stand alone in my stand
to guard the City from being further disfigured in streets," he wrote. "I
feel dreadful."

Two months later, on March 4, 1893, the day before Steinway's birth-
day, his wife, Ellie, died of a heart attack. Only a month earlier, Steinway
had sent a condolence telegram to his friend, William Whitney, who was
mourning the sudden loss of his wife, Flora, at the age of fifty. Flora was
buried in a marble grave next to their daughter Olive, and on the front
page of *The World* it was reported that the elegant Whitney mansion "has
become a house of mourning, and the man who could have any office in
the gift of President-elect Cleveland and would accept none is prostrated
by the bier of a dead wife." Now another member of New York's establish-
ment, William Steinway, was in mourning, too. In his diary from that
day forward, he would note repeatedly how Ellie's death destroyed him.

ANOTHER FINANCIAL MELTDOWN SAVED STEINWAY. The ripple
effects from the collapse of the mighty Baring Brothers bank in London
three years earlier were still lingering. One by one, the pieces of string
that held together America's economy unraveled. First the Philadelphia
and Reading Railroad, then the mammoth rope manufacturer National
Cordage Company, and finally the banks toppled. The country's credit
system folded, stock prices plummeted, and fortunes disappeared. More
than 140 national banks went under, and by year's end sixteen thousand
businesses were gone, too, making the panic of 1893 worse than those in
1873, 1857, and 1837. Police went house to house and found some seventy

thousand people unemployed. At least twenty thousand homeless people camped at police stations and shelters.

New Yorkers did not realize it at the time, but the panic of 1893 saved them from living without a subway for years to come. It became clearer than ever that any citywide massive-transportation project would have to be paid for by the government, not private businessmen whose fortunes could vanish in a flash. Six years after Abram Hewitt first proposed his financing plan, it was back on the table.

HEWITT SO DESPISED ANYONE he believed was standing in the way of progress that he made no attempt to hide his contempt, even when that person might one day become president of the United States. William Whitney was such a man. Hewitt and Whitney in the early years of the 1890s were at their zeniths of power. Despite their differences, they were both being talked about as Democratic presidential candidates. And their opinions on the matter of transportation in the city were as influential as any. Hewitt had established himself as the leading advocate for a subway and was putting all of his efforts into promoting his plan for city ownership rather than leaving it in private hands. Whitney controlled those private hands, as the owner of the Metropolitan Traction Company, the mammoth street-transit company. Had the two men managed to think alike and work together, there is little doubt a subway would have been built much sooner. Instead, their opposing views, stubbornness, and independent interests kept them from ever joining forces in the interests of New Yorkers. The tension that existed between Hewitt and Whitney came to life when the two men were vacationing in London. Whitney was coming down the steps of the Bristol Hotel just as Hewitt was walking up, and they were stunned to see each other on the other side of the pond.

"Hello, Hewitt," Whitney said. "Are you going back to the states soon?"

Hewitt shot back, "No."

"Well, you ought to go back and take the nomination for the presidency. You deserve it," Whitney said politely. Though Whitney, a former navy secretary, was actually being mentioned more favorably than Hewitt, an ousted mayor, for the nomination, he had clearly indicated that he had no interest in running for office. But Hewitt did not receive the words kindly from a man he respected so little.

"You ought to go back and stand trial for the Metropolitan Street Railway operations," Hewitt snapped at Whitney. "You deserve to get a jail term."

Whitney laughed at first, only to stop when he realized the former mayor was not joking. The two men, as powerful as any in New York City, would never become close. For Hewitt, the living conditions in New York were the responsibility of those who could bring about real change, from politicians to wealthy financiers, and in his eyes Whitney had never done his part. Because they traveled in the same social circles, their paths crossed often. But to Hewitt, Whitney stood for all the evils of big business, a millionaire who built his fortune through inheritance, consolidation, and, he believed, even corruption, although there was little evidence of the latter. As the man who controlled New York's street railway operations, Whitney could have pushed for more radical change, more innovation, than he did, but to Hewitt it seemed all Whitney wanted was to make incremental changes, like free transfers, that helped his transit company's bottom line but nothing else. Hewitt would have probably enjoyed a better relationship with Whitney's brother, Henry, in Boston, a man who proposed tunneling under the sacred Boston Common despite fierce opposition and who pursued Frank Sprague's electric streetcars before any other major city had such foresight. William Whitney's conservative and questionable decision to choose cable over electricity was exactly the sort of backward thinking that galled the forward-thinking Hewitt.

Whitney's cable streetcars, along with Gould's elevated lines, were dominating New York's streets. The Metropolitan Traction Company was becoming a monster, swallowing up smaller companies that controlled Houston Street, Sixth Avenue, Ninth Avenue, Twenty-third Street, Lexington Avenue, Broadway, and others, planning cable extensions for all of them. Whitney's biographer would later call it his "Empire on Wheels."

The "nerve center" was a nine-story building, called appropriately the Cable Building, at 621 Broadway, which dwarfed its neighborhood at the corner of Houston Street. The headquarter offices were on the eighth floor, but it was in the basement where the power plant was a sight to see. Enormous cables wrapped around giant belts went around and around for miles in an endless loop. It was impossible to imagine a cable snapping, as they were made of six steel strands with nineteen twisted wires, and each one weighed about forty tons. But inevitably they did break, and the fixes, costly and time consuming, would bring the huge steam engine that powered them to a halt.

NOWHERE IN NEW YORK were the conditions more desperate for relief in the mid-1890s than Manhattan's Lower East Side, where a mass of buildings that were typically seven stories high crammed more people inside of them than seemed possible. While New York City as a whole had seventy-six people per acre of land, the Lower East Side had almost ten times that amount, anywhere between three hundred and seven hundred per acre. It was one of the most crowded places on the planet. The living conditions were dark, wet, cold, rancid, and vermin-infested, and diseases like diphtheria and tuberculosis were common, thanks to poor sanitation and the lack of private toilets and adequate ventilation. Staying clean in a neighborhood filled with horse stables, brothels, slaughterhouses, and saloons was impossible. And yet there was nowhere else for the immigrants to go. Moreover, because they were at least living among others who spoke their language, understood their traditions, and practiced their religion, they were reluctant to assimilate and seek out change.

New York, like Boston, Chicago, and other big American cities filling up with immigrants, was not so much a melting pot yet as a countertop with separate piles of different immigrant groups. Changing that would take one issue that would benefit both the rich and the poor, that could improve the way of life across an entire city, and that the men in power could unite behind. As the last decade of the nineteenth century reached its midway point, that issue was rapid transit.

London had three times as many residents as New York, but New York had more miles of mass transit. And while the average London resident took just seventy-four rides per year, about one every five days, New Yorkers were going gangbusters on their systems, taking almost three hundred trips a year, making it a part of their everyday existence. The only problem was that thousands of immigrants were streaming in through Ellis Island every month and the cable streetcars and elevated trains could not keep up. It was almost as if for every steamship of immigrants that arrived, a ferryboat full of New Yorkers left the city, tired of the overcrowding. The system needed to get faster. It needed to go farther. And it needed to run beneath the streets. And it needed to be built now.

ON MAY 22, 1894, Steinway got his shot at redemption. The state legislature of New York passed a second Rapid Transit Act, which had one major difference from the act of 1891. As the embarrassing public auction had shown, rich, private capitalists had no appetite for taking on the burden of a subway. This time, the city would own the subway and lease it to a contractor, just as Abram Hewitt had first proposed six years earlier. Hewitt also got the man he wanted named as the new commission's chief engineer, William Parsons. And as yet another sign of how serious this new commitment was, the new Board of Rapid Transit Railroad Commissioners held their first meeting on June 8, 1894, only two weeks after the act passed. They wasted no time debating elevated lines versus a subway.

Parsons was dispatched to visit Europe, where the cities were more advanced than Chicago or Boston in their rapid transit plans, even though Boston residents were about to vote in a few weeks on their own subway. Parsons, who set sail in July, had already been to Berlin, where he saw urban train systems that ran at street level with mixed results. Now he was to visit other cities. In London, of course, the Underground was a model for the rest of the world. In tiny Liverpool, an electric elevated train more advanced than Chicago's was running. Paris was also on the brink of approving a subway. And Glasgow was digging a subway tunnel that was intended to be cable operated, but for which electricity was also being considered. Parsons's orders were to go and study them all and to return with a report that settled once and for all whether the tools and technology were there to bring to New York a subway with electric-powered trains. Parsons was skeptical.

His appointment as chief engineer had not been unanimously embraced. Despite his experience from the earlier Steinway commission, he was still only thirty-five years old, and there were far more seasoned engineers in the city. Many New Yorkers said his hiring "was a mistake," as the writer Arthur Goodrich wrote in a profile of Parsons for the magazine *World's Work*. "But the commission wanted a young man—no one but a young man could possibly complete the inevitably immense plan they were beginning." And, as Goodrich wrote, no one knew the underbelly of New York quite like Parsons.

Shortly after his appointment, there came an incident when he was put on a witness stand to testify about the work that would be required to dig a subway tunnel. Courtroom observers could not believe the level of detail he was able to spout off, about what sewer pipes were at what corner and at what depth beneath the street. It was as if he had a snapshot of the guts of New York in his brain. After hours of questioning from lawyers who were opposed to a subway, they gave up, acknowledging that they would not be able to fluster him. "The devil take him," one of those lawyers was overheard saying. "He's making fools of all of us."

When he was asked whether he had "the maturity to see this plan through," Parsons didn't hesitate in answering.

"Success doesn't depend on age, nor does it depend on will or enthusiasm," he said. "It depends on the rigorous analytical methods of a trained and educated mind." It was what he believed, and it explained why he often liked to quote the famous Greek mathematician Archimedes, who, it is said, once proclaimed: "Give me a lever long enough and a fulcrum on which to place it and I'll move the world." It could have been a motto for Parsons.

Parsons also engendered goodwill among those who worked for him. When the Civil Service Commission changed its rules to require that a special exam be taken for every pay raise of $150 in salary, Parsons angrily convinced the commissioners to withdraw the action. He was modest by nature, because, as one man said, "he doesn't know any better." It was a trait that made his workers want to please him more. Later in his life, Parsons would take a moment to reflect on his appointment as chief engineer for the subway, and he realized how it was a job that required a man with patience. "I am glad I was not older," he said. "I doubt if I could now undertake or would undertake such a work under similar conditions. But I had the enthusiasm of youth and inexperience. Had I fully realized all that was ahead of me, I do not think I could have attempted the work. As it was I was treated like a visionary. Some of my friends spoke pityingly of my wasting time on what they considered a dream."

PARSONS SAILED BACK FROM EUROPE in September 1894 and went to work on a report for his commissioners. In the meantime, New Yorkers had ballots to cast. Only four months earlier, they had read how the citizens in Boston narrowly approved construction of a subway. Now New Yorkers had their turn. On November 6, the election of a new mayor was relegated to an afterthought. In addition to voting in a Republican dry-goods salesman named William L. Strong as their new leader, New Yorkers overwhelmingly said, *Yes to public ownership!* Of the 184,035 ballots cast, 42,916 voted against city construction and ownership, while 132,647 voted in favor (399 ballots were deemed defective).

The 1894 Rapid Transit Commission had achieved in four months what the 1891 Steinway commission could not in more than two years. New York City was on its way.

9

THE RISE AND FALL OF HENRY WHITNEY

AFTER HENRY WHITNEY RETURNED HOME from his trip to Richmond, where he witnessed Sprague's successful experiment, he immediately placed his order. He asked the Sprague Electric Railway & Motor Company to supply thirty cars for Boston and to electrify the line that ran along Boylston Street from Park Square to West Chester Park (a street that today is Massachusetts Avenue), and then along Beacon Street, out toward his home in Coolidge Corner in Brookline and to the Allston railroad station in neighboring Brighton. It was an ambitious order in total, giving Sprague control of thirteen miles of track, and it would cover a large portion of the West End Street Railway's traffic. Whitney envisioned the day when the electric trolley would quietly whoosh relaxed passengers into and out of the city, encouraging growth farther out into the suburbs while reducing congestion downtown. It would not happen easily.

"We went to work vigorously on the contract," Sprague said. "But Mr. Whitney ran into a snag with the city fathers."

That snag almost doomed the business relationship between Sprague and Whitney before it had even begun. One of the biggest questions that arose during the race to electrify streetcars in the early 1880s was whether the current of electricity was best strung through overhead wires connected by poles or underground conduits, and when Whitney told city leaders of his plans to use overhead wires, he was told that option would not be allowed. Sprague preferred the overhead wires, no doubt because one of his other inventions was the electric trolley pole. His twelve-mile system in Richmond relied on a long network of trolley poles strung together. Whitney and Sprague decided that to get their way, they must once again run an experiment and convince the decision makers.

On a fall morning in 1888, Sprague arranged a demonstration and invited the Boston city councilors to ride aboard his electric streetcar. Determined to prove once and for all his design was the future, Sprague pushed the car to its limits, even though he knew he risked jumping the tracks. Fifteen miles per hour, then twenty, and finally twenty-five miles per hour, faster than anything Bostonians had ridden before. Almost five times as fast as the typical horse-pulled car. The little electric car cornered the rails with a slight lean and remained in constant contact with its overhead wire, but it never felt in danger of tipping, and when he finally pulled it to a stop, the dazzled city officials were won over.

"They gave Mr. Whitney permission to erect overhead wires throughout the city," Sprague said.

IN BUILDING HIS STREETCAR EMPIRE, Henry Whitney needed more than the electric motors provided by Sprague. He needed his own engineer to oversee the conversion of his entire system from one powered by horses to one powered by electricity. It was a massive undertaking, but Whitney didn't have to look far.

As a young boy growing up in Medford, Massachusetts, a few miles north of Boston, Frederick Stark Pearson, the son of an engineer who died when he was just fourteen, wasted little time proving to his teachers that he had a special ability to decipher complex ideas that grown men struggled with. His teachers learned to no longer be surprised after one day Pearson was seen engrossed with a book on metallurgy. While studying at nearby Tufts University, Pearson worked at the Medford Hillside train station, taking tickets, counting money, managing the telegraph,

Henry Melville Whitney, owner of the world's largest streetcar company, proposed tunneling under Boston Common. (*Courtesy of Lee Sylvester*)

William Collins Whitney, New York transit king and Secretary of the Navy under President Cleveland. (*Courtesy of Lee Sylvester*)

Late in his life, Henry Whitney loved spending time with his children. (*Courtesy of Lee Sylvester*)

Alfred Ely Beach

New York mayor Abram S. Hewitt was in charge when the Blizzard of 1888 struck. (*Library of Congress*)

Marc Isambard Brunel, the engineer behind London's Underground. (*National Portrait Gallery, London*)

William "Boss" Tweed used corruption to kill Beach's tunnel. (*National Archives*)

Samuel Meredith Strong, the boy caught in the Blizzard of 1888. (*U.S. National Library of Medicine*)

Engineer Frank J. Sprague, whose electric motor was a critical development. (*Courtesy of John Sprague*)

William Barclay Parsons, the engineer behind New York's subway. (*Parsons Brinckerhoff*)

New York subway contractor John B. McDonald.

Tufts engineer Frederick Stark Pearson was used by Henry and William Whitney. (*Cyclopaedia of American Biography [artist unknown]*)

William Steinway ushered the piano into living rooms and the subway into New York City. (*Courtesy of the Henry Z. Steinway archives*)

New York subway financier August Belmont. (*Library of Congress*)

Frank Sprague in the New York alley where he tested his electric motor. (*Courtesy of John Sprague*)

The hill in Richmond, Virginia, that Sprague overcame with his electric motor. (*Courtesy of John Sprague*)

…he unbearable congestion on Tremont Street in Boston. (*State Transportation Library of …Massachusetts*)

Dangerous overhead wires and the Blizzard of 1888 triggered subway construction. (*New-York Historical Society*)

Wall Street during the Blizzard of 1888. (*New-York Historical Society*)

The cut-and-cover tunnel under way in Boston in 1896. (*State Transportation Library of Massachusetts*)

The steel work begins along Tremont Street. (*State Transportation Library of Massachusetts*)

Workers digging the tunnel under Boylston Street take a rest. (*State Transportation Library of Massachusetts*)

More than 900 graves were discovered during Boston's construction. (*State Transportation Library of Massachusetts*)

It was up to horses to carry out the tons of dirt from the trench. (*Historic New England*)

On March 4, 1897, a gas line explosion in Boston killed pedestrians, passengers, and horses. (*Print Department, Boston Public Library*)

A dead horse was ignored as workers rushed to the injured after the explosion. (*Print Department, Boston Public Library*)

The Hotel Pelham suffered the most damage in the explosion. (*State Transportation Library of Massachusetts*)

Trolleys veered around the construction in Boston, but it was still a major disruption to businesses. (*Print Department, Boston Public Library*)

The trial run of Boston's subway in August 1897. (*Print Department, Boston Public Library*)

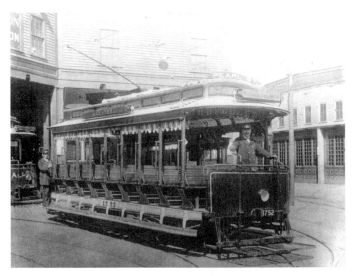

Motorman James Reed steers out America's first subway car. (*State Transportation Library of Massachusetts*)

The first subway trains emerge from beneath Boston on September 1, 1897. (*State Transportation Library of Massachusetts*)

William Parsons strikes the first pickax on March 26, 1900, to launch New York's subway construction. (*Parsons Brinckerhoff*)

Early tunnel digging in lower Manhattan in 1900. (*New York Transit Museum*)

Subway construction on New York's Park Row in November 1902. (*New York Transit Museum*)

The tunnel had to be dug deep beneath New York's streets in the city's northern half. (*New York Transit Museum*)

A rock slide in 1902 beneath Park Avenue at 38th Street nearly collapsed the tunnel and forced buildings to be supported. (*New York Transit Museum*)

Tunneling shields like this helped bore through the Manhattan schist. (*New York Transit Museum*)

New York celebrated its subway groundbreaking with great cheer on March 24, 1900, unlike Boston's almost invisible ceremony. (*New York Transit Museum*)

When New York's subway was ready to open, John McDonald was right in front and William Parsons was behind him. (*New-York Historical Society*)

and manually operating the signal system. When he grew tired of racing
back and forth from campus to the station half a dozen times a day just to
drop the signal arm after each train pulled out, Pearson invented an ingenious solution. He rigged a tripping device from the chemical laboratory
to the tracks that could raise and lower the red signal arm by electricity.
He taught at Tufts after graduating and then started two businesses, the
Somerville Electric Light Company and the Woburn Electric Light Company, supplying entire communities with electricity and light. On the banks
of the Mystic River, Pearson had quite the little power plant going. And
when Whitney went searching for an engineer, he took a ride to Somerville; after two interviews, he offered Pearson $2,500 a year to be the chief
engineer of the West End Street Railway Company.

The twenty-seven-year-old Pearson quickly put his mathematical mind
to work. He determined that to power an entire streetcar system by direct
current electricity would require a central power station like nothing else
that existed. West End's power was coming from a small plant in Allston,
as well as the Cambridge Electric Light Company, but combined they still
were not providing anywhere near the power that Pearson needed. Pearson set out to build the biggest power station in the world. He built it on
Albany Street at the intersection with Harrison Avenue. The chimney, at
250 feet high, was the tallest structure in Boston, thirty feet higher than
the Bunker Hill monument. And when his experienced mechanical engineer challenged the twenty-seven-year-old Pearson for pushing the work
too quickly, Pearson had a ready answer.

"It's got to be done," he said. "Whitney has promised it."

Pearson was soon besieged with job offers from around the country.
And while he did accept a few consulting positions, he remained loyal to
Whitney for having hired him at such a young age for an enormous task.
Whitney would not forget.

A FEW MINUTES AFTER MIDNIGHT on January 1, 1889, while bells
were ringing out the cold and ringing in the new year, two new electric
streetcars quietly pulled out of the Allston railroad depot. There was no

crowd to witness the start of the historic journey, the first ride of the West End electric streetcars, and there were no passengers on board other than Henry Whitney himself. They merely drove off into the night, with Frank Sprague manning the controls of one car and one of his electricians driving the other. They had a precise route to follow that Whitney and Sprague had mapped out, from Allston to Park Square downtown, passing through Coolidge Corner in Brookline.

The ride was going smoothly, with both the overhead wires and underground conduits working to perfection, until they reached the corner of Boylston and Church streets, where a bad patch of track caused both cars to fall off the rails. But they were quickly returned to the tracks, and by 12:30 A.M. they had reached Copley Square, where a crowd was still lingering from the new year's celebration. Whitney, so pleased at how the trip went, told Sprague he wanted to load up both cars with as many passengers as they could fit and drive them up Beacon Street and back, to let them be the first to experience what the future for their city held. The next day's *Globe,* under the headline PRESIDENT WHITNEY'S TRIUMPH, said, "Both cars were quickly filled and were soon speeding over the rails."

THE ELECTRIC STREETCAR WAS QUICKLY embraced by most, but not all, Bostonians. Soon after the first cars started running, a wealthy woman wrapped in pricey furs walked into the offices of *The Transcript* newspaper in Brookline to complain how it was a shame that she could not drive out to her country home without being bothered by the sight of the ugly electric cars. Others referred to them simply as "great electric monsters," and when an overhead cable crashed down and killed two horses one day, it only heightened the fears of those who longed for the days of being pulled safely and slowly down the street by a handsome four-legged animal.

No business highlighted the shortfalls of the horse more than the department store, which saw its rise in cities coincide with the transition of transit systems from horse-pulled to electric-powered. Market Street in

Philadelphia, Canal Street in New Orleans, State Street in Chicago—all saw departments stores act as magnets for women who would come in during the morning, browse, buy, or sometimes just window shop; enjoy lunch in the enormous new stores; shop some more; and eventually return home in the late afternoon. It was a new paradise, a place where, as one shopper was moved to write, she could find everything "without having been obliged to leave the store."

W. H. Macy's, the onetime upscale dry-goods store that had blossomed into an enormous and diverse department store, had its own stable on West Nineteenth Street in New York and employed dozens of helpers, drivers, and wagon boys to handle the fastest-growing part of its business—deliveries. As the 1880s wound down, Macy's was delivering more than a million packages a year, and after years of insisting it would only offer delivery to Manhattan, Brooklyn, and Jersey City, it quickly saw the potential of expanding its circle. On purchases of five dollars or more, Macy's began to provide free delivery within one hundred miles of its New York store, and soon there were busy routes out to Long Island and western and central New Jersey. The volume alone should have made the longer routes profitable. But instead Macy's lost money. The extra miles put an enormous strain on the horses, which forced the company to buy more animals and erased any windfall that long-distance delivery might have provided.

Boston's version of New York's Macy's was Jordan Marsh and Company. Started in 1851 by Eben Jordan, it became as famous for its blueberry muffins and afternoon concerts as for its luxurious shopping experience. Like Macy's, Jordan Marsh struggled with its reliance on horses to move its goods through Boston's crowded downtown from its flagship store.

IN 1889, THE WEST End Street Railway Company abruptly announced that it was withdrawing its plan to build a subway and instead wanted to pursue building an elevated rail line. It might have been a shocking change of direction for another company, but for one owned by Henry Whitney it was hardly a surprise. In the two years since he had proposed tunneling beneath Boston Common, much had happened. He had consolidated all competing railway lines into a single operation. He had created the world's largest streetcar company. He had begun weaning the city off its reliance on horses and introduced electric streetcars as the future of transportation.

Back when Whitney first set his sights on transforming Boston's street railways, horse-drawn streetcars generally went no farther than four miles from Boston's downtown. With more and more of his system being powered by electricity, six miles became the new reach. His company's ridership increased by 25 percent in its first four years, but it was not doing the one thing the people of Boston were demanding: reducing congestion. If anything, things were getting worse.

When he made his annual report to West End's stockholders in 1890, Whitney explained what a roller-coaster ride it had been. "Experience has shown," he said, "that wherever electric lines have been installed, travel has enormously increased; and indeed travel over the line increases so rapidly that it is well-nigh impossible for the company to keep pace with the demands upon it."

That demand was overwhelming, he explained, increasing by an average of thirty thousand per day over the previous year. "The number of passengers transported by the street railways in 1880 was about 160,000 per day; it is now nearly 360,000 people per day," he said.

What prompted Whitney to abandon the project that he had proposed and that would have transformed the city and made him a hero to its citizens? He never said. But as the final decade of the nineteenth century began, deciding precisely where to dig a subway tunnel was an argument that was dividing the city. The roads that were most in need of relief, mainly Boylston Street, Park Street, Tremont Street, and Washington Street, all happened to run directly alongside or around Boston Common, or were very close to it, and they formed the busiest intersections in the city. If building a subway meant tearing up even the fringes of Boston Common, never mind going right through the heart of it, well that was one decision some Bostonians just could not imagine making.

. . .

THE REVEREND WILLIAM BLAXTON was living alone on top of a small hill on a grassy plot in Boston in the year 1634. Thirty-nine years old, and with no family, he had chosen his spot because it was on the southwest slope of Beacon Hill and seemed to receive just the right amount of shade and sun. There were only a handful of trees on the field at most, and his only companions were the sheep and cows that grazed there, but its gentle slopes kept the land from flooding in the rain or becoming too hot during the summer and made the spot perfect for planting an orchard. For these reasons, Blaxton built his small cottage where he did. An ordained Anglican priest, he had arrived in America in 1623, and when his fellow travelers returned to England he decided to remain, making him the first European settler in the city of about three thousand people. He spent much of his time reading from the two hundred or so books in various languages that he had brought with him from England. His story is an unremarkable one in Boston's rich history, except that when he left for Rhode Island and vacated his land in 1634, he sold back forty-five acres to the city in return for thirty pounds and kept six acres for himself in case he decided to one day return.

Blaxton never did come back. And more than 250 years later, the land where he settled was at the heart of the city's subway debate. The Common, by its very name, was a symbol for the everyman in Boston, where the rich and poor could sit side by side on a bench or cross paths as if they were from the same bloodline. But as Boston developed, and as its downtown became a thriving commercial hub, this enormous park of untouchable land, with its increasing number of winding paths and rows of towering trees, became as much a blessing as a curse for the city. Every tree had its history, every hill had a legend, and every man and woman could share a story about romping through the Common as a child like it was their personal playground. There were those who held little regard for the park and had no problem sacrificing it for the greater good, especially if it meant a faster travel through downtown or to their outlying neighborhood. Then there were the protectionists, who believed that Boston would not be Boston without Boston Common and that everything must be done to protect it from development. "A stake may as well be driven here that no such desecration of 'the people's birthright,' the Common, will be permitted under any circumstances," wrote *The Boston Evening Transcript* on April 5, 1892.

HENRY WHITNEY WAS NOT OBLIVIOUS to the passions the Common stirred, but he argued that nothing should be sacred ground when it came to trying to solve the transit crisis, which affected people of all classes. He had a plan. He had the money. He had the political connections. And he owned a company that had more than a million dollars in cash and assets, a huge sum. He was the world's largest street railway operator. And on top of it all, business for the West End Street Railway Company was booming. The number of round trips that passengers were taking and the ticket revenue the company was collecting were both on a steady climb.

If there was one curiosity to Whitney's rise to prominence, it was the lack of any hard skepticism he received from the city's hundreds of reporters. If he had a speech to make, it was often printed verbatim in many of the papers, more like a paid advertisement than a news article, and often accompanied by a story that simply reported his appearance and quoted from his talk. In 1890, Boston had nine daily and four semiweekly newspapers. Yet day after day Whitney was portrayed only in the most favorable light. It was as if the papers were afraid of him or indebted to him. Or both. Not everyone, however, stood in awe.

As Whitney stood on the cusp of being a hero to his city in early 1888, a small group of young lawyers, journalists, college professors, clergymen, students, and distinguished writers, mostly in their twenties and thirties, formed the Young Men's Democratic Club of Massachusetts. They met in taverns across Boston. And in a short time they would begin to muster the strength to confront Whitney, to accuse him of scandalous and unethical behavior, and would ultimately aim to topple him.

• • •

ON THE EVENING OF January 6, 1891, a steady stream of carriages rolled down Commonwealth Avenue, one of the most famous boulevards in the world. Two hundred and fifty feet wide and more than a mile long, it was lined on both sides by the most beautiful homes in all of Boston, with tall windows, gothic columns, and enormous, glittering chandeliers visible from the sidewalk. The avenue was split down the middle by a tree-lined park dotted with benches, statues, and a straight-line walking path. Under the light of gas lamps along the mall, the carriages formed a line as they stopped in front of the six-story brick Algonquin Club around six o'clock to unload their passengers for a long night of revelry. Inside the Algonquin Club, bright lights danced off all the gold, silver, and glass while the smell of freshly cooked venison, clams, and duck wafted through the spacious rooms with twenty-five-foot ceilings. Every table had a colorful arrangement of flowers. The Boston Cadet Band was warming up, and the call of an auctioneer, shouting "going, going, gone," could be heard in the background and out on the sidewalk.

The club was founded as a social clubhouse for the city's elite, a private place to relax with a drink and a cigar and maybe strike a late-night deal. The winding central staircase, towering fireplace hearths, alabaster columns, vaulted ceilings, museum-worthy paintings, glittering chandeliers, wainscoting, stained glass windows, and leather reading chairs created a luxurious warmth for those who could afford it all. It was also known in town as the place where Henry Whitney offered bottomless glasses of liquor, endless helpings of free food, and fare-free carriage rides to bribe legislators to get what he wanted.

Every important businessman in Boston was at the club—real estate brokers, bankers, merchants, and city and state officials. Being held this evening was the annual formal banquet of the Real Estate Exchange, but the reason for the added excitement was that it was also a chance to celebrate the election of Boston's newest mayor, Nathan Matthews Jr., who was expected to make an appearance and even say a few words.

After Whitney led an informal reception that ended at eight o'clock, he invited the crowd up to the third-floor dining room, where dozens of tables covered in white cloth and fine china were set for the formal dinner. Once Matthews arrived, late and to loud applause, the head table became quite the collection of power and politics. To Whitney's right sat Willis G. Jackson, president of the Chicago Real Estate Exchange, and Thomas N. Hart, the former mayor of Boston, and to Whitney's left sat Matthews and Aaron W. Spencer, former president of the Boston Stock Exchange. Directly across the table sat Col. Francis Peabody Jr. of the banking house Kidder, Peabody & Company and Governor William Russell.

Polite clapping greeted Whitney when he stood to make his opening remarks. Ridership for the West End Street Railway Company was soaring. In 1890, 114 million passengers rode the company's cars, an increase of 10 million from the previous year and almost double the number that rode streetcars in Boston in 1880. Those passengers brought the company $5.7 million in revenue, and as the company reduced its reliance on horses and electrified more miles of tracks, it became a more efficient operation. Not only was Whitney's business thriving, but his wife, Margaret, was newly pregnant with their fifth child. It was no wonder he was in a good mood as he stood to talk.

"I am in my capacity as president of a transportation company brought every day in contact with vast numbers of people," he said. "I see day by day and month by month the throngs in our streets, which testify to the prosperity of our city."

Barely twenty-four hours after Matthews had been sworn in, Whitney begged Boston's new mayor to give real estate developers, like those filling the very room in which he spoke, what they needed to continue the prosperous times. "Give us on the main avenues wide streets; give us room for the development of transportation interests. And I am saying nothing at all on behalf of the West End Railway Company, but I am saying what is absolutely essential for the future prosperity of the city."

The real estate leaders stood and roared for Whitney. But what Whitney was only just beginning to realize was that Matthews had his own ideas for how a city should grow and prosper. And they did not align with Whitney's.

To Matthews, it was completely acceptable for a big business like the West End Street Railway Company to earn enormous sums of money, as long as it was honest and respectful in the way it treated its customers and its partners. But it was not, in the mind of Boston's new mayor, the job of the West End Street Railway Company to dictate the course of the city, to decide which neighborhoods got trolley stops or wider streets and which ones did not, or to determine how far into the suburbs the transit lines went. Most important of all, Matthews believed that it was irresponsible of the West End company to be so indecisive as to hold the city hostage over the question of building an elevated rail or a subway, when at least one of those, or possibly both, was so badly needed.

Just one day earlier, in his inaugural address, Matthews had said, "The City of Boston is no longer a New England town on a large scale; it is a great commercial and industrial city, the metropolis of New England, with a population greater than that of the whole state of New Hampshire." As their mayor, he pledged that it was time to take back the streets from the corporations that ruled them and return control to the people.

Matthews dedicated the greatest portion of his words to the subject of rapid transit, and he expressed his frustration with Whitney's company. "Many schemes have been suggested during the past few years, none of which, it is safe to say, are entirely satisfactory," he said. "On the other hand, the demand for rapid transit is a genuine one, and should be met at an early date. I believe that the city government itself should grapple with this problem and endeavor to settle it to the satisfaction of the people, rather than leave the matter entirely to the interested action of private corporations." He recommended the appointment of three people to a rapid transit commission, "to consider the whole subject of rapid transit, including elevated roads, tunnels, routes, systems, companies, and in particular, the best means of protecting the financial interests of the city as a corporation."

Matthews was well informed. A traffic count on Tremont Street had recently showed that 332 streetcars passed by a single point in one hour.

That was the equivalent of a car passing by every eleven seconds, unacceptable to the new mayor. From the moment he set foot in office, Matthews set out to make sure that the city of Boston, not the West End Street Railway Company, was working to solve the transportation crisis.

WITH HIS ROUND SPECTACLES, prematurely gray hair, youthful face, deep brown eyes, and bushy, well-groomed, silver and black mustache, Matthews swept into office behind a change in momentum that saw Democrats seize control of Massachusetts after a long reign of Republican leadership. By the time he chose to leave City Hall after winning four one-year terms, Matthews would carry with him a legacy as the "father of the subway."

Born in Boston's West End neighborhood in 1854, he attended the prominent private school, Epes Sargent Dixwell, before going off to Harvard College, traveling in Europe and returning home to attend Harvard Law School. He embarked on a life of law and serving the citizens of Boston. As much as he loved the law, Matthews embraced politics even more. Massachusetts was a Republican state in the early 1880s, but a shift was under way as the ranks of Irish Yankee Democrats gained strength. Matthews joined the wave of supporters who got behind Democrat Grover Cleveland in 1884, and he befriended important men, like the first Irish mayor in Boston, Hugh O'Brien. When a group of his friends set off to form the Young Men's Democratic Club in 1888, Matthews signed up, and they tapped Matthews to lead them. *The New York Times* described him as a "brilliant orator, and a fearless champion of clean politics and decent methods in administration." Matthews ran for mayor in 1890 and trounced the Republican Moody Merrill.

He was joined in victory by the newest Democrat on the Boston Common Council, nicknamed Honey Fitz because of his warm disposition; those who knew him called him Johnny Fitz. But John Francis Fitzgerald, born in Boston in 1863 to Irish immigrants, did not become one of Boston's greatest politicians because he was a pushover. He earned his respect from an early age. His favorite neighborhood growing up was by the water, the North End, a place where wagons and pushcarts filled the streets and he could watch how people worked from sunup to sundown and still earned barely enough to have a place to sleep at night. His first job as a newsboy at fourteen saw him rising at 3:00 A.M. to get his papers, shout out the headlines, and sell as many as he could before the workday started. As a boy he played baseball, and he was the fastest runner among all his friends, luring them to race and never losing. He was sixteen when he got a brief tour of a manor house on Beacon Street that happened to belong to a Harvard professor and future U.S. senator named Henry Cabot Lodge.

The teenage boy could not have known that as a young Irish man growing up in Boston, his interest in politics came at the absolute perfect time and that his heritage would help him rise to prominence alongside the owner of that Beacon Street mansion. He got into the prestigious Boston Latin School and eventually into Harvard Medical School, and soon enough he was serving on the Boston Common Council. Honey Fitz would go on to be a mayor, a senator, a congressman, and, late in his life, well into his eighties, he would teach his grandson, the future president John Fitzgerald Kennedy, the tricks of running an aggressive political campaign.

THERE WAS NOT MUCH to like in Boston during the days when horses ruled the streets. The city smelled. The rides were bumpy. All the clopping of hooves made such a racket it was impossible to carry on a conversation on the sidewalk. And crossing the street could be an exercise in futility at rush hour, as there was so little space between the back of one streetcar and the front of the next one. On the other hand, the horses moved at such a slow pace that at least it was easy to anticipate their movements, and any sure-footed pedestrian could cross a street fairly easily in front of them with little worry of being struck. If a horse got too close, a quick swipe of a cane, a swing of a shopping bag, or a wave of an umbrella usually was enough to shoo the animal into slowing down or veering to the side. The horse became more efficient when streetcars were put on rails instead of cobblestone streets, making it easier for horses to do their work, but it was the introduction of the electric streetcar that spelled the beginning of the end for horse-pulled cars. For the passengers, the rides were quieter and smoother and the smell was gone. For pedestrians, the adjustment was more challenging. No longer could they simply hop in front of a horse trotting along at five miles per hour. And no cane or umbrella or shopping bag was going to slow down an electric streetcar.

The electric streetcar in the early 1890s was not, as it turned out, the only new sight taking over Boston's streets. A two-wheeled invention called a safety bicycle became popular very fast, especially among children. Quiet side streets on warm nights were crowded with people of all ages learning to ride these bikes. The more adventurous ones made their way over to Columbus Avenue, where they learned to ride amid throngs at Colonel Pope's bicycle rink. There were many models of bicycles, but the more expensive Columbia, which sold for about $100, and the cheaper Lovell Diamond, for about $85, were the most popular. One young boy born in 1887 in Boston vividly recalled a typical evening in the city as the bicycle was growing in popularity. "From dusk to about 10 p.m.," wrote the historian Samuel Eliot Morison, who turned five years old in 1892, "the street was filled with young people learning to ride the bicycle, and resounded with tinklings, crashes, squeals and giggles."

THREE YEARS AFTER WHITNEY had won permission to create the world's largest streetcar operation it was obvious the experiment had failed. In the one-third square mile of downtown Boston, there were 16 miles of track, 55 miles of various wires, 714 tall posts, 195 street crossings, 257 switches, and 149 junctions of intersecting tracks. Boston was once again grinding to a standstill and patience with the West End Street Railway Company was waning.

In 1871, 34 million passengers rode the street railways within a ten-mile radius of downtown Boston. A decade later, the ridership had doubled to 68 million, and another decade after that, in 1891, it had doubled again, to 136 million passengers. There were too many people and not enough seats for them, and in June 1891, a city desperate for relief finally acted. Matthews, after ordering that a commission be formed to study the problem and present a solution, had set aside $20,000 for its work. It was called the Commission to Promote Rapid Transit for the City of Boston and Its Suburbs. On June 10, the members were named; on June 18, they were confirmed by the city council; and on June 20, they met at the mayor's office for the first time.

Among the commission members were Henry Lee Higginson, a Civil War hero and philanthropist who, a decade earlier, had founded the Boston Symphony, and John Quincy Adams, a Harvard-educated lawyer and the great-grandson of President John Adams and the grandson of President John Quincy Adams. After four years of dickering and debating with no progress, one new, swift-acting mayor, in a span of just seventeen days, had put the pieces in place for Boston to finally solve its transportation crisis. The commission's first order of business was to hear from the public.

AT ITS FIRST HEARING ON June 25, 1891, a dozen or so citizens, including Henry Whitney and several prominent businessmen and railroad leaders, came to City Hall at the corner of School Street and Tremont Street. At eleven o'clock, Mayor Matthews called the meeting to order, and he noted how much time the commission had. Its deadline, he said, was April 1892, at which point it was expected to submit a detailed report.

As the hearing commenced, Whitney volunteered to go first, but he had only a few words to say. He said that his West End Street Railway Company had submitted a number of proposals for the city and the commission to study, and he asked only that the plans be kept private unless his company agreed to release them. The most serious of those proposals, he explained, was being prepared by the company's chief consulting engineer, who outlined an attractive plan that included a subway and an elevated structure, both for electric trains.

After Whitney spoke, one man after another stood up to speak. A former Boston mayor from the late 1870s, Frederick Prince, now a seventy-four-year-old man with a bushy gray mustache that turned down at the tips, showed up to ask if the hearings were open to everybody, or only those with ideas to suggest. "We intend to hear everybody," Matthews replied. A retired physician, Ira Moore, who represented a trust that held millions of dollars of downtown property, stood up to say only that he was firmly in the camp against any and all elevated roads, while a Brookline gentleman, W. W. Toussaint, said he had plans for a tunnel beneath the sidewalks. Even the American Express company sent a representative, who proposed tracks straight across the Common. After the meeting ended, the only decision reached was a logistical one. If so many citizens were going to be coming forward with their own plans, the commission agreed a stenographer needed to be on hand to record the ideas on a typewriter so they could be reviewed in detail by the commission.

Ten months later, and after fifty more public hearings had been held and two commission members had traveled across Europe to study how other cities were handling their overcrowded streets, the commission's work was done. On the morning of April 5, 1892, a 296-page report was submitted for approval to the general court.

"The length of this report is greater than we had expected," it said on page 103. Perhaps that explained why a few months later Matthews confessed that he had yet to find a single person who had read the full report. No document would be so detailed, so meticulously researched, so full of questions. It's no wonder it divided the city into factions. Who would build and operate and pay for the next project, private businesses like the West End Street Railway Company or the government? How could the steam railroads be improved to handle the growth in the suburbs and the growing wave of people riding the trains into the city? And, finally, would Boston get a subway, elevated tracks, or both?

The report of the commission did not signal the end but the beginning of the debate over subways versus elevated tracks. And nowhere in the report was that more clear than in a brief section titled "Tunnels." During the summer of 1891, Congressman John Fitzgerald, who was appointed to the commission by Mayor Matthews, and *Herald* editor

Osborne Howes Jr., a state appointee, traveled together to London, Paris, and Berlin, cities that had built or were building rapid transit systems.

When Fitzgerald visited London, the city had a mix of steam and electric trains running underground, and he went anticipating that the electric underground would prove to be the future for Boston. He left disappointed. "As a piece of engineering I presume it is perfection," he wrote in his report to the transit commission. "But as a mode of conveying human beings from one part of a great city to another I should much prefer some other method, and some other feeling when travelling than the buried-alive feeling which one experiences in this tunnel." Most surprising to Fitzgerald was that the underground steam system actually impressed him more than the underground electric trains. "I traveled over this [steam] road several times, and found it did not contain so much smoke as I expected, because not only do they burn smokeless coal, but their engines also consume their own smoke," Fitzgerald wrote. "In addition to this, they have open spaces wherever it is possible," which made the journey more enjoyable because of the frequent bursts of light that shined down into the trains. But the electric cars, he said, moved at fifteen miles per hour, not as fast as he expected, and were too loud for his liking. "The noise is like the roaring of the ocean after a storm, and many persons whom I interviewed told me they always experienced a headache for some time after leaving these cars," Fitzgerald reported. "I must confess I experienced a similar sensation myself."

But even Honey Fitz's skepticism could not dissuade the commission. In its conclusion, the members indirectly pointed at the lack of progress made by the West End Street Railway Company. "The well-worn list of public works which have proved inordinately costly, interminably slow in building, and outrageously inadequate in every way when finished, is brought out and rehearsed once more," the report said. It also pointed out that public ownership would always mean fending off constant demands and requests for costly extensions and cheaper fares, both of which would be impossible to grant. But despite all of that, the commission recommended that the government should build a new system and then try to lease it to a private company, like the West End Street Railway, for operation. That allowed city and state officials, and not private businessmen, to decide how much a ride should cost, where transit stops should be, what streets should be widened, and what suburban neighborhoods should get their own streetcar lines.

The commission summarized the other recommendations in just a few short paragraphs. There should be two main railroad stations in the city, one called North Union for passengers coming from the north, at the corner of Causeway and Leverett streets, and a second called South Union, on Kneeland Street, for passengers coming up from the south. The streets, especially in the center of Boston, should be widened and extended in certain places and policed more aggressively to make surface travel more convenient for all vehicles and pedestrians. Two elevated railroads should be constructed, one from South Boston to Charlestown and another from Roxbury to Cambridge.

And finally, in a nod to what Whitney had first proposed five years earlier, the commission said that the street railway system should be reorganized by removing a large number of tracks from the narrow downtown streets and replacing them with a tunnel about one mile long beneath Boston Common and Tremont Street, "which shall take the greater part of the through cars to the southern and western portions of the city."

If they were all adopted, the recommendations would transform Boston, which is probably why the report ended on a somewhat pessimistic note. "If anything is to be undertaken," it said, "let it be ample and thorough and complete in its kind. Short of that, it were wiser to stand still where we are."

That was a position nobody in Boston wanted to consider.

MIDWAY THROUGH THE SUMMER of 1893, the patience of Boston's mayor expired. He quietly sent off a letter on August 5 to his city engineer, William Jackson:

> Dear Sir,
>   You asked me the other day to jot down my ideas as to the matters which require the most pressing attention on the mat-

ter of rapid transit. I would suggest investigating with a view to ascertaining the following facts: First, as to Sub-Ways, sketch out a four-track subway under Tremont Street from some point at the North or West end, where it would come out upon the surface, to Boylston Street. Thence two tracks diverging down Boylston Street and adjacent to Park Square, the other two tracks going up Tremont Street and coming out near Shawmut Avenue. Also a subway for the two tracks under the proposed elevated railroad. This would give six tracks, with stopping places at the cross streets, and would enable the city to get rid of all the surface cars between the Common and Atlantic Avenue.

After laying out more specifics, Matthews wrote that this, of course, was all "a very crude idea." But it was an idea he saw great promise in. "If it could be worked out and we could get a four-track elevated railroad system through the heart of the city, partly at the same level and partly on two levels, and all the present surface cars were put underground, we should have a system which should be worth a good deal of money to the people of Boston," he wrote in closing.

If Boston's biggest streetcar owner wasn't going to solve the congestion problem, Boston's mayor was.

ON THE MORNING OF September 7, 1893, the headline in *The Globe* reverberated across the city: WHITNEY OUT. RESIGNS AS PRESIDENT OF THE WEST END.

Henry Melville Whitney was fifty-three years old. He was the definition of an American capitalist, a man who grabbed opportunity when he saw it without fear of whether it would shower him with riches or wipe out his very last penny. When an entrepreneur had come to him with samples of bottled orange juice, he didn't laugh. He brought them home for his children to taste and imagined the fortunes that could be made. It was not to be. "They were uniformly horrible," his daughter Josie recalled.

In his official capacities, Whitney was serving as president of the West End Street Railway Company and of the Metropolitan Steamship Company, and, most recently, he had taken on the leadership role at the Dominion Coal Company in Nova Scotia. He was also the father of five who enjoyed spending more and more time riding horses with his children at their summer estate in Cohasset. He had built a half-mile track nearby, and soon, when Josephine was a few years older, he would spend hours there, standing with a stopwatch and timing his colts on their laps. He gave Josephine a strawberry-colored pony she named Merry Legs, and he rode alongside her through nearby wooded trails. Their favorite spot was a peak called Turkey Hill, where they could gaze out over the towns of Nantasket and Hingham and relax in the breeze.

By late 1893, six years had passed since he had first proposed building a subway tunnel under Boston Common. His biggest achievements had been to consolidate all of the competing streetcar companies into one giant monopoly, to electrify the tracks, and to expand routes farther into the suburbs. He had built the West End Street Railway Company into a hugely profitable operation, taking a business that functioned mainly in a two-square-mile area and expanding it to run almost ten miles out of downtown. The company finished 1892 with $6.3 million in gross earnings and $1.8 million in profit. Almost two-thirds of its tracks were being powered by electricity. After starting with 8,000 horses in 1887, the company had whittled that total in half, down to 3,754 in five years, providing a huge cost savings as it operated more than 260 miles of track. These were enormous accomplishments. But they could not overshadow how Whitney had never addressed the most critical issue of all, downtown congestion, a point he hinted at in his September 6 letter of resignation to the West End board.

"The time has come when I feel that I have not the strength to manage so many important interests in justice either to those interests or to myself," he wrote. "It seems to me that it is on the whole a propitious time to give up the presidency of the railway company . . . I admit that I give up the care of the office with a strong feeling of regret, because the relations between myself and community, as well as with the officers and employees of the road, have been pleasant and a source of gratification to me under the many trying circumstances which have occurred during my administration; and while I am aware that we have been criticized more or less, yet on the whole I feel that the public have appreciated the work in which we have together been engaged."

That may have been true at first, as Whitney insisted on a flat five-cent fare for all rides and pledged to lessen the reliance on horses and speed up the streetcars. But by the time of his resignation, there was little sadness to see him go. In a letter that Matthews wrote to Whitney just a few months earlier, the mayor referred to the "pleasant, personal relations" the two men shared, but then questioned why Whitney never came forward with a realistic, detailed proposal for the legislature to consider. No response to his letter came. And a few months later, it was clear why. Henry Whitney was ready to move on. So were most Bostonians.

THE MOST IMPORTANT TASKS of the transit commission were to assess how long it would take to build a subway and how much it would cost. Very quickly it was realized an initial estimate of $2 million was wishful thinking and that a more realistic number was $5 million because of how many buildings and how much land the city would have to acquire. City bonds would pay for the work, and the city would lease the tracks to a transit company to operate it and earn back the cost. It all seemed quite logical, and, as the weeks passed, one question after another was put to rest. Yes, travel would be faster, perhaps shortening some trips by one-third the time. Yes, Tremont Street would be blessedly free of tracks. Yes, the damage to Boston Common would be minimal, and the only new visible structures would be the stations on the surface for people to walk down into the subway. Yes, as doctors from Harvard Medical School and Massachusetts General Hospital explained, proper drainage of water and ventilation of stale air would make the subway perfectly sanitary and safe. For the supporters of the subway, it was difficult to imagine why anyone could oppose the plan if they took one look around downtown, and yet, sure enough, any time a hearing was held, there was at least one outraged voice and oftentimes many.

. . .

THOSE VOICES WERE HEARD at a hearing on Monday morning, March 26, 1894. Beginning at ten o'clock, one by one, people stood up before the commissioners, some of them reading statements from a piece of paper, others just spouting venom. Samuel J. Byrne, who ran a small dry-goods store on Tremont Street, claimed to represent two dozen other merchants, from theater owners to bankers to lawyers and accountants. He said they all feared that the construction would destroy their businesses by making it impossible for shoppers to access their storefronts. In the end, Byrne would prove to be the most successful organizer of opposition, sending three hundred signatures to the legislature and promising that he had twelve thousand in total. "Construction would seriously interfere with travel and traffic," the petition read, "proving ruinous to hundreds of merchants and in the end failing to relieve the congestion or promote rapid transit." Henry A. G. Pomeroy had a much briefer argument than Byrne. He told the commissioners he was convinced the temperature underground would be much colder than above ground and could not possibly be safe. John Stone, a seventy-one-year-old former mayor of Charlestown who owned a grocery store, said he had no desire to dump his money into a hole and he'd just as soon have "pirates and misers" take it instead. And still others trotted out the same arguments that had been heard a few years earlier during the public hearings that led to the 1892 report. One man said he was terrified for his mother going "down in that tunnel with her grey hairs, not knowing where she is going." Half a century after Marc Brunel's Thames Tunnel opened, fear of the underground still lingered.

Arguments were also heard from a group calling itself the Merchant's Anti-Subway League. Led by a jeweler named John W. Wilson, the group bombarded the newspapers with letters to the editor, and the papers responded in kind with headlines like SUBWAY SCARE: MERCHANTS FEAR INJURY TO THEIR TRADE. Wilson and his brother, Ed, had started out in business together early, selling newspapers in the city's West End neighborhood as young boys. They were known on their corner for being the most aggressive newsboys around, and it worked, as they saved enough to open Wilson Brothers jewelers on Tremont Street. They may have been good businessmen, but in the subway fight, they were disorganized. Wilson showed up at one hearing just to complain that the voice of the merchants was being ignored, only to be calmly told that every hearing had been advertised well in advance.

One surprising voice against the subway was Michael Meehan, a resident of Jamaica Plain and one of the hardest-working contractors in the city. When some merchants asked Meehan to give his expert opinion on the project, to be attached to the petition they were submitting to the legislature, Meehan happily obliged. He looked at the subway proposal and saw a complicated network of water, sewer, and gas lines that would all have to be rerouted to make room for the tunnel. The subway, he believed, would provide only minimal relief, and it would hardly be enough to justify the exorbitant cost of building it. "I think that it is a very expensive method of solving that problem, and I think we are not going to get proper results for the expenditure," Meehan wrote in his statement. It was a curious position for a local contractor to take. If a subway bill eventually was passed, and the city sought bids to build the multimillion-dollar project, would Meehan throw his hat in after voicing such a negative opinion of it? And if he did, would the city officials care that he had criticized them for moving forward with it?

IT SEEMED AS IF THE arguing was done and as if lawmakers were ready to pass a bill, proposed by Matthews, that called for building a subway and for purchasing the necessary land to begin planning an elevated route outside downtown for a private company to control. It was a savvy compromise by Matthews that seemed sure to pass since both elevated and subway supporters could claim victory. But it was not to be. An old challenger resurfaced at the last possible moment, determined to stir up trouble.

Joe Meigs, or Captain Joe to those who knew him well, had managed to build a short, experimental, steam-powered monorail between Boston and Cambridge a few years earlier and had even written to Abram Hewitt in New York about considering a monorail for his city. Meigs had been given permission twice to build a longer elevated rail and failed to raise the money or start construction, so it was hard to imagine legislators trusting him a third time, especially since the panic of 1893 had bankrupted so many potential investors. But Meigs had a new strategy. He sensed there was growing interest in an elevated line outside downtown, to connect with a possible subway tunnel, and so he smartly lobbied suburbanites for his downtown monorail, knowing they carried a growing influence with legislators. He requested yet another charter, this one to build an elevated line clear across Boston, from Charlestown out to Roxbury, covering a total of thirty-six miles of streets. It was an outlandish plan that would have ripped downtown Boston in half and shut down the business district for months or maybe years during construction. And yet, to the astonishment of nearly everyone in town, Meigs got his wish.

On April 30, 1894, the legislature chose to ignore Matthews's reasoned bill and instead to look more closely into the proposal from Meigs. The outrage was immediate. Accusations flew that he had bribed his way back onto the scene and that nowhere in his charter was there an explanation of how it would be paid for and who would reimburse the businesses that would undoubtedly be damaged during the construction. For three months, the city was in a confused uproar, and nobody was angrier than its mayor. Finally, some level of sanity was restored on June 28. Lawmakers hastily added a measure to the bill giving voters the final say and restoring the important pieces of Matthews's proposal, namely a subway in the business district and a clause banning any elevated tracks downtown.

But instead of the final bill being seen as a compromise, it was now viewed as a weak attempt to merely placate all sides. Nobody was pleased. The elevated supporters loathed seeing the subway plan in the bill. And the subway backers could not believe Meigs had wormed his way back in to get an elevated charter approved. Even the Citizens Association, which all along had favored the subway proposal, backed off its support because of what Meigs had achieved. On July 2, well after midnight, both the House and the Senate passed the new bill and sent it to Governor Frederic Thomas Greenhalge. He signed it immediately, and Mayor Matthews set July 24 as the date for the citizens to vote on their future.

ON JULY 23, 1894, the New York Giants visited Boston to play a game of baseball. It had been a big year of change for the game, and for the Boston Beaneaters. Two months earlier, an enormous fire in Roxbury destroyed South End Grounds, the Beaneaters' home field, along with more than two hundred other buildings. It left two thousand people homeless and leveled almost twelve acres of the city. The team was forced to move their home games to the Congress Street Grounds, and that's where the Beaneaters hosted the Giants the day before Bostonians voted on their subway. No doubt tired of all the transit talk, 3,333 people came out on the warm summer day for the game. The polls opened the next day at six o'clock. They would stay open for ten hours, closing at four in the afternoon.

It had taken Boston seven years to get to this day—seven years from Henry Whitney's 1887 speech first suggesting the city tunnel under its congested downtown to build an electric-powered subway. Whitney had since moved on. Three mayors had been in charge. Blizzards and fires had leveled portions of the city. Tracks had been electrified and extended the city's limits six miles out of downtown. A bizarre elevated monorail had briefly made an appearance. And finally a compromise had been reached. But would it pass?

The same debate had been raging in New York, launched by Mayor Hewitt after the blizzard of 1888. Almost seven years later, New York was also nearing a vote. The Rapid Transit Commission had finally approved a recommendation from its chief engineer, William Parsons, to build a subway and set a tentative date, November 1894, for the public to vote on it.

Incredibly, half a century after the Thames Tunnel opened and a quarter century after Alfred Beach's secretly built one-block subway opened, years that were filled with rancor and debate over how to build a safe and comfortable subway that American cities could rely on, Bostonians and New Yorkers were now going to vote on that issue just four months apart.

IT WAS WET AND WARM on July 24 in Boston. A steady rain fell from morning to night, and the temperature hovered in the seventies. Maybe that's why not even thirty thousand people turned out to vote. Or maybe they were tired of all the talking. Or perhaps they just assumed there was no possible way, with the addition of the elevated line to be built by Meigs, that the final bill would be passed. They were wrong. The final vote, counted by hand, was reported differently in nearly every newspaper in town, perhaps because the clerk who had been in charge of the "No" column miscounted the tally at first by more than one thousand votes. But in the end, the result was the same. The referendum was passed. *The Globe* reported the final result as 15,458 in favor, and 14,209 opposed, meaning that, by a slim margin of 1,249 votes, the citizens of Boston said they were ready for a subway. It was hardly overwhelming support.

Sam Little, who had replaced Whitney as president of the West End Street Railway Company, said on the evening after the results had been announced that he was surprised at the total number of people who voted and at the closeness of the vote. "I really thought a large number of people demanded an elevated road, from all the talk to that effect in the newspapers and one way and another, but the result doesn't seem to indicate it."

That was one way to look at the results. But another was that fears about the subway, despite assurances from respected doctors from Massachusetts General Hospital that the subway's air would be just as clean as the air above it, still had not been put to rest in the minds of many. "I don't believe in a tunnel or a subway," a local undertaker said after voting no. "I expect to be a long time underground after I am dead, but while I live I want to travel on earth, not under it."

Over in room 12 at Young's Hotel, the celebration was loud, and Joe Meigs could not stand still. His attorney told the throng of reporters that his client was not available to speak but that he was elated that his proposal for an elevated railway had been approved after so many years.

"The people have spoken," George V. Towle said. "The citizens of Boston have pronounced in favor of our system and there is nothing more to be said." As seven o'clock in the evening passed, the chamber room at City Hall was so packed that there was no room to move. Aldermen, department chiefs, city and state politicians, and citizens fascinated with the project all gathered to mingle and discuss the results. Surrounded by well-wishers, Nathan Matthews answered questions from reporters.

For Boston's mayor, the vote was the victory he had pledged to achieve in his first inauguration speech in 1891. It had taken more than three years and created sharp divisions in the city, but the mayor was convinced that there was no other option. "The election shows that however the citizens may differ upon the merits of elevated railroads, subway routes, etcetera, a majority of them voting at a special election are in favor of a system of subways to be constructed and leased on public account," Matthews said. "The verdict should be accepted as final and as a reasonably satisfactory conclusion to the rapid transit agitation."

"What is to be done next?" a reporter shouted at him.

"I should assume that the main plans can be prepared," the mayor answered, "and the work of construction begun and possibly well advanced before the close of the year."

Part Three

TRAGEDIES, TRIUMPHS

BIDDING TO BUILD HISTORY

THEY GATHERED AT 11:30 IN THE MORNING on March 20, 1895, a group of about twenty men in the small downtown office of the Boston Transit Commission. Eight months had passed since the rainy day in July when voters approved the combined subway and elevated plan. Now it was a sunny Wednesday with spring just around the corner. When the door to the room opened, all eyes turned to the large tin box being carried into the room by B. Leighton Beal, a former newspaper editor who had recently left the business to become the transit commission's secretary. With one swoop, Beal hoisted the box up and turned it over, and in dramatic fashion twelve large envelopes flew out onto the table at the front of the room. Beal neatly stacked up the envelopes right next to another stack, this one of twelve smaller envelopes. The smaller ones each contained a $5,000 certified check, for a total of $60,000. The larger ones contained the figures that would decide in whose hands the citizens of Boston would place the building of the first section of their subway.

Sitting at the front table were the commission's five members, led by George G. Crocker, a likable gray-haired, clean-shaven lawyer and former president of the Massachusetts State Senate. Of all the commissioners, Charles H. Dalton had the most important role. A former parks commissioner, his presence was supposed to reassure those who feared that the subway would destroy trees all over the Common. There were 150 trees in the park standing over portions of the subway route, and 57 of those were too tall to be uprooted and transplanted, while many others were young and just taking hold. It was always assumed that many trees would have to be sacrificed for the subway, but Dalton's hope was to restore the Common to its full beauty.

The other men in the room with the commissioners were strangers to one another, but they were all too familiar with this process. They had come to find out if their bid, which required a $5,000 check just to be eligible, might win them the contract to build the first section of the Boston subway. These were not the twenty- and thirty-year-old tough Boston Irish laborers who would soon be putting in nine or ten hours a day and taking home $1.70 per shift for their sweat. These were businessmen, the contractors who would hire the laborers, and they were some of the most respected contractors from the East Coast.

All of them were well aware of the stakes as the meeting got under way. This was no $10,000 sewer job. The subway was projected to cost $5 million, a figure that included $3.5 million for constructing approximately 10,000 feet, or 1.8 miles, of tracks, plus $1.5 million to purchase the land needed for the stations. The most expensive purchase by far was the old Haymarket Square railroad station, which was no longer being used by the Boston & Maine Railroad and which cost the city $750,000. If the subway opened on time and close to budget and proved to be successful and safe, the lead contractor was sure to be in demand for years. But if it failed, or worse, if there was a construction disaster, it might be impossible for a contractor to ever recover, especially if there were multiple and preventable work-related deaths on the job.

ON THE DAY OF the hearing, Boston was still rejoicing from another momentous moment only nine days earlier. On March 11, the Boston Public Library, which since 1848 had been housed near the Common on Boylston Street, unveiled an Italian Renaissance–style building in Copley Square designed by the famous New York firm of McKim, Mead and

White. With thirteen arched windows facing the square, it felt more Roman than Bostonian. The public was dazzled and proud to host the first publicly supported lending library in the United States and to reinforce Boston's reputation as the country's scholarly and literary capital. With enormous bronze doors; two lion statues out front by Augustus Saint-Gaudens; sculptures by Daniel Chester French; murals by Sargent, Whistler, and Edwin A. Abbey; and a cavernous reading room with vaulted ceilings, the books felt almost like an afterthought.

Meanwhile, despite the urgings of former mayor Nathan Matthews, who insisted that Boston must begin acting like a major city rather than a large New England town, the city retained a small-town feel. Its entire downtown district could be walked across in twenty minutes, since it was about the same size as the Mount Auburn Cemetery across the river near the line of Watertown and Cambridge. Because it was surrounded on three sides by water, Boston's downtown was like a balloon blowing up while trapped inside a box. Each new surge of immigrants arriving to live or work downtown swelled up the balloon to its bursting point, and that bursting point seemed to be here.

In 1790, Boston was the third largest city in the United States behind New York and Philadelphia, with 18,320 residents. Fifty years later, it was still the third largest, but with 136,881 residents. And fifty years after that, in 1890, while its ranking had dropped to sixth, its population had more than tripled to 448,477. In describing life in Boston, *American Architect and Building News* said in the early 1890s that people were "elbowing each other off the sidewalk into the gutter" and the city's sidewalks were "jammed to suffocation with pedestrians." Since the sidewalks were suffocating, the subway was supposed to provide the burst of fresh air to keep everyone breathing.

A week after the library opened, the city was poised to start its next historic chapter by moving forward with building the first subway system in America.

There would be eleven sections to the subway, each one built by a different contractor with their own contract. It would stretch just 1.8 miles in total. And it would open in two stages. The first phase resembled an L shape, running from the entrance of the Public Garden, near Boylston and Arlington streets, up to the corner of Boylston and Tremont streets and then turning left to the corner of Park Street across from the Park Street Church. The second phase would run from Park Street along Tremont through Scollay, Adams, and Haymarket squares and ending at North Station.

For the contractors bidding, it was an enormous opportunity. Not since John Roebling designed the Brooklyn Bridge two decades earlier had there been such a prestigious, high-profile, and complicated public works project as the one Boston was about to embark on. Their job was to dig the city a safe and secure subway tunnel, not to design it.

In fact, the wording for the job was quite specific: "An inclined open entrance to subway in the public garden, between Church Street and Charles Street, subway under Charles Street and Boylston Street mall of Boston Common to a point about 160 feet from Tremont Street and under Tremont at mall of Boston Common from a point about 110 feet north of Mason Street to a point near the southerly line of West Street." Among the expectations listed for the project were that 6,870 cubic yards of dirt would have to be dug up just for the inclined entrance to the subway, 1,150 additional cubic yards outside of the subway trench would have to be excavated, and 1,020 tons of iron and steel would have to be set and secured in the earth, along with hundreds of tons of brick and stone masonry, concrete, and spruce lumber.

It was a big job, but it was nothing like what London had achieved with its Underground. The London subway was a true tunnel that required boring through the earth without tearing up the surface. Boston's was not even as challenging as Alfred Beach's one-block pneumatic experiment in New York, which had been dug deep beneath New York's streets in secret. Boston had neither the ambition to dig so deep as London, nor the desire to be secretive like Beach. Its plans were quite simple.

The Boston subway would be built just beneath the surface of the streets, so that passengers would merely have to step down a few dozen stairs to reach the tracks. Workers would use what engineers called the cut-and-cover method, which described the work perfectly. Cut a trench in the ground. Install the necessary tracks and lighting to run the trolleys from station to station. And make sure the tunnel is sealed off from water and protected from collapse. Cover the trench. It sounded simple enough, and it would soon be a method that cities around the world adopted, but in an era before there were steam shovels to do the digging, the subway trench would be backbreaking work for men wielding picks and shovels, who would fill up wagons with dirt that horses dragged away.

The contractors who showed up at the Boston Transit Commission meeting to see their bids unsealed knew all of this. They came from Brooklyn; Manhattan; Westchester County; New York; Franklin, Massachusetts; the Boston neighborhood of Jamaica Plain; Providence; and downtown Boston. Just before noon, the chairman, George Crocker, welcomed everybody and began to unseal the envelopes one by one.

J. W. Hoffman and Co. from Philadelphia bid $181,206. John McNamee from Brooklyn bid $138,484.10. Washburn and Washburn from Westchester County, New York, bid $189,787.50. McCarthy Bros. and Co. from Franklin, Massachusetts, bid $191,910. Wearing Booth and Company from Boston bid $182,135.90. Crawford and Company from Brooklyn bid $173,423.25. R. A. Malone from Boston bid a competitive $146,604.50. F. C. O'Reilly and Company from New York bid $183,057.90. H. P. Nawn from Boston bid $212,602. Everson and Liddle from Providence bid $230,765. Woodbury and Leighton from Boston bid the highest, at $231,625.50, almost a full $100,000 higher than the lowest bid. And Jones and Meehan bid $139,602, right behind McNamee's lowest bid. Jones and Meehan was a local contracting firm, and its bid was noteworthy because Michael Meehan had spoken out against the subway during the debate. Now here he was bidding for the right to build it.

THE NEXT DAY, WHILE THE other contractors anxiously awaited word, J. Edwin Jones and Michael Meehan decided they were too close to sit by without putting up a fight. Their bid was only $1,118 more than the lowest one submitted by John McNamee of Brooklyn. Losing by such a paltry dollar amount, especially to a New York contractor for a historic job that would completely reshape their hometown, was too much for the Jamaica Plain businessmen to bear. They requested an immediate hearing with the transit commissioners, before a decision had been reached on the bids.

Jones and Meehan made for a good team despite their many differences. Meehan, who was self-taught and had minimal schooling, was a battle-tested mechanic. Jones was an educated, experienced engineer. What they shared was an intimate knowledge of the streets and topography of Boston and its surrounding suburbs, and they were both savvy to the ways of how local politics worked.

Meehan was born in Ireland in 1840 and moved to Boston when he was fifteen. As a young man he served in the Union navy during the Civil War for three years, surviving an attack on the frigate *Minnesota* and swimming to shore. Back home, he briefly worked as a reporter for *The Globe* before becoming active in politics, being named as secretary of the state Democratic committee. In the mid-1880s, he and Jones first worked together. Jones was the superintendent of streets for Boston, a job that paid $4,000 and came with the use of a horse and vehicle, and Meehan was his deputy. Jones studied engineering at Harvard and worked as a civil engineer at the U.S. Navy Yard in Portsmouth, New Hampshire, before leaving to run a Maine railroad line for two years and the enormous Croton aqueduct sewer system in New York. He arrived in Boston to work as the assistant to the city surveyor and worked his way up to run the streets department. When his city work was completed, he joined with Meehan to open a civil engineering office.

In a small office on Rockview Street in Jamaica Plain, the two men soon built a formidable contracting business that would land some of the biggest sewer and bridge jobs in Boston and Cambridge. Meehan's brother, Patrick, a banker and one of the richest men in Jamaica Plain, helped them get their business off the ground. Once they did, they gained experience and confidence. Both of these qualities were on display when they sought out the transit commissioners the day after the bids were unsealed and argued that as residents and taxpayers of Boston, they should be given preference over a contractor from outside the state.

There was no legitimate reason to award them the bid. They were not the lowest bidders. And their chief competitor had built the foundations for elevated trains in Brooklyn and would go on to help build the Inter-borough subway in the same city. He was well deserving of the Boston job. But he was not local. And the commissioners were warm to the idea of having local men build the Boston subway. They took a second look at the bids and decided that Meehan's bid more accurately reflected how much dirt would be dug up for the tunnel. Three days after they opened the bids, the commissioners curiously adjusted Meehan's bid to be $782.10 below McNamee's. Just like that, the job belonged to Jones and Meehan.

And less than a week later, on the morning of March 27, 1895, the two contractors from Jamaica Plain took their first walk along the subway route and over the Common. They took particular note of all the trees and burial grounds they would have to contend with.

THE TEMPERATURE ON MARCH 28, 1895, never got above 35 de-grees. The skies were dark, the ground a soft and sticky mud, and light flurries were starting to fall. A Harvard student was rescued from the freezing water of the Charles River after his rowboat capsized. *Hamlet* continued its run at the Tremont Theater across the street from the Com-mon while, down by the harbor, a number of boats remained washed up after the previous day's snow squalls. Warm coats were on sale down on Washington Street for as little as three dollars. It would have passed as an entirely uneventful day if not for the brief and quiet proceedings that oc-curred in the morning on Boston Common.

A dozen men gathered by a collection of wheelbarrows, all of them bundled up tightly in long dark coats and wearing winter hats. Governor Greenhalge, a bald, mustachioed Englishman who first came to the States as a boy, walked down from the statehouse a few minutes before nine o'clock and watched as a stake was driven into the ground to signal where the first shovel of dirt should come from. The governor's opinion on the subway had been a thing of mystery from the day he took office in January 1894. Dur-ing his inaugural address, he barely mentioned rapid transit other than to say it was an important issue facing the city and the state, and he left his citizens to wonder exactly where he stood. Soon the governor was joined by all the members of the Boston Transit Commission; the winning contractors, Jones and Meehan; and two Boston city councilors. A few citizens stopped outside the fence and gazed in, drawn by the sight of their portly governor but unsure what they were witnessing. Within minutes the watchers numbered close to a hundred. The plan had been to put the ceremonial shovels in the ground at nine o'clock, but when the bell tower of the Park Street Church began to ring on the hour, it occurred to George Crocker that the Boston mayor, Edwin Curtis, was absent. Crocker sent an aide to rush to the nearest telephone and call the mayor's office.

"The mayor is too busy to attend the proceedings," the aide was told. "If necessary, he will send his private secretary, Mr. Courtenay Guild, to represent the city."

When the word got back to the group, they were shocked. Curtis had succeeded Nathan Matthews when Matthews decided not to run for re-election the prior year after serving four terms. As strongly as Matthews supported the subway, Curtis opposed it, believing it was only a short-term fix. But city funds were helping to pay the projected $5 million bill. Curtis was a stubborn man and did exactly as he said he would. On the day work was to begin on a subway for Boston, a historic moment in the nation, to be sure, the mayor went off to visit some South Boston businesses and sent his private secretary to be the city's representative for him. It was a move that did not sit well with his citizens, who, when given the chance later that year, voted him out of office and replaced him with Josiah Quincy.

At nine minutes after the hour, Governor Greenhalge handed a shiny new spade to Chairman Crocker. "Mr. Crocker of the transit commission of Boston," the governor said, "I hereby tender you this spade, with which will begin the work on the subway that has been designed for the city of Boston, and I trust that great relief and comfort will come to the municipality when the plans laid out by you and your associates shall have been fully carried out."

As Crocker took the spade from the governor, he said, "I now proceed to take out the first shovelful of dirt in the inauguration of the great undertaking that has been entrusted to me and the other gentlemen of this commission." He reared back and plunged the shovel into the soft dirt with great might, only to see it sink a few inches into the ground. Crocker lifted out a measly sum of dirt and dropped it into the wheelbarrow next to him. The entire ceremony lasted less than five minutes, and there was no great applause to acknowledge the moment. It was brief and understated, and as soon as it was over the men inside the Common scattered, and so did the passersby who'd been watching from a distance. Only the contractors remained.

BY NOON, A DIFFERENT AND more sizable crowd had gathered at the Park Square gate entrance to the Common: five hundred workmen hoping to be picked for the job. They did not care that it would demand they work days, nights, and weekends and right through the winter with no breaks. As a group they were asked to recite an oath that said they were all naturalized citizens, and they gave their names for a list that was being compiled for Jones and Meehan. They were told to return the next day. The first group would be hired, handed shovels and picks, and told where to start digging.

II

MEEHANVILLE

THEY CALLED IT MEEHANVILLE. THE COMMON QUICKLY filled up with wagons, lumber, and tipcarts loaded with dirt. Piles of picks and shovels were all over, and every morning before the sun came up there were dozens of men, sometimes a hundred, jostling for position to get noticed.

The most important person who stood guard at the front door was not Michael Meehan but his son Robert Emmet Meehan, easily spotted by his bowler hat and the piece of paper always in his hand. The contractor's office was fitted with a rolltop desk and comfortable chairs, and nobody was allowed in without the password. Meehanville was the makeshift village set up on the Common for the duration of the project. Three shanties were erected and given fresh coats of paint, as places for the laborers to eat their lunches, take a breath, mend their calloused hands and sore feet, or sometimes just wait for their next assignment. No smoking was allowed during working hours, so at noon the shanties also became a place where pipe smoke filled the air.

From the day the first shovel went into the ground, Robert Meehan was entrusted by his father to take down the names and addresses of the able-bodied workers who would congregate around Meehanville every morning. He was also the timekeeper on the job and the general utility man who answered all questions. Each morning, he would take down the information of the men who'd gathered and explain that if and when their services were required, they would receive a letter in the mail and be expected to arrive promptly at seven in the morning on their assigned day. At first, only twenty-five men were needed, but that was expected to grow to fifty, a hundred, and possibly more than a thousand per day, working day and night shifts, as more equipment was brought in, the trench got deeper and longer, and the process of sealing it up with concrete and steel beams began.

As soon as the project started, neither Meehan nor Jones, whose faces had appeared in the papers enough times to make them familiar to the average citizen, could walk anywhere without being cornered and pressured for work. They were celebrities, and every day letters begging for work were thrust into their hands. Meehan spoke pleasantly to each man and referred them to his son, except in those instances when they were not up to his standard.

"Do you want to pick and shovel?" he asked one of the men who approached him.

"No, I want something easier," the man replied.

"Well," Meehan huffed, "there are no snaps around here." And he laughed.

Another man tried a different approach, appealing to Meehan's softer side with a plea.

"If I don't get work today, I'll get 'Hail Columbia' when I get home tonight," he said, a reference to a popular patriotic American anthem. "My wife told me not to come home tonight without a job, and she means business, too." It worked. "Well, I'll save you the time," said Meehan, a family man himself with a wife, two sons, and four daughters at home. "Take a shovel and go to work."

Most times, his instincts were right and his men showed up on schedule and put in their honest day's work. Only occasionally did a workman disappoint: in one instance, an Irishman on the job for several weeks stopped showing up, was spotted frequently imbibing at a nearby tavern, and then was arrested for stealing tools from the construction site.

But those incidents were rare, as Meehan and Jones tried their best to hire men they had worked with before and trusted. In fact, there were two well-known ways to get hired for sure, as Meehan had made no secret of them. The first was to be citizens of the country. The second was to come from the same neighborhood as Meehan, Jamaica Plain.

Meehan made no secret of his affection for the Irish and his disdain for the Italians who showed up at the site every morning. One morning Meehan spotted a group of Italian men sitting by themselves and talking only in Italian, and he knew right away they would not make his list. "The Italians, you see, they are not wanted," he said. "They hold aloof from the others. I told them that none but voters would be employed. And why not? I'm going to employ my friends. I never lost anything by standing by the men who supported me." That was not entirely true. He lost money. The Italians would have worked for lower wages, but Meehan didn't care. "If I hired Italians at $1.20 a day, as other contractors are doing, and worked them ten hours, I could make a good deal more of money on this job," he said. "But I'm not doing business that way."

Of the first twenty men Meehan picked to work, nine were laborers who had worked for him before from Jamaica Plain. The rest came from other parts of Boston. Meehan kept true to his word about the Italians. As long as they kept speaking Italian and isolating themselves from the others, they would have to wait for their opportunity to work in Meehanville, at least until the demand for more bodies was greater.

THE POTENTIAL OBSTACLES THAT CAME with building a subway ranged from the benign to the disastrous. There were big questions like what to do with all the tombs along the subway route and how to properly ventilate the tunnel so passengers could breathe fresh air. And there were smaller issues, like how many trees in the Common might need to be replanted and where to put all the dirt that would be dug up to make way for the tunnel. The chief engineer for the transit commission, Howard Adams Carson, left none of them to chance.

He was born in central Massachusetts in the town of Westfield in 1842, left high school to serve as an engineer during the Civil War, and graduated from Massachusetts Institute of Technology in 1869. Most of his experience had been with water and sewers when the Boston Transit Commission hired him as chief engineer to oversee the building of the subway. But Carson had other appealing qualities. He had traveled through Europe to study various sewer systems, which was appealing because a similar trip would likely have to be made to study European cities that were building or making changes to their own rapid transit systems. Carson had also shown tact in dealing with private contractors and public citizens in his work, and that was critical given the raucous debate over the subway. His tact also became a big reason why, late in his life, both Philadelphia and New York would seek out his opinion on tunneling their own subways. Carson was described as having "scrupulous honesty and impartiality, moderation and modesty in all things, and faithfulness to the point of extreme self-sacrifice."

And he wasted no time after the transit commission appointed him to head overseas. He visited London, Budapest, Glasgow, Paris, Berlin, and Cologne, all cities that happened to be building subways or elevated structures. He even spent time meeting with the British engineer James Greathead, whose improved metal circular shield was the key to digging London's latest subway branch. Carson came home on the largest and fastest passenger ship afloat in the 1890s, the British ocean liner *Campania,* which crossed the Atlantic in six days. So anticipated was his return that before he could even step off the ship, the longtime *Globe* political reporter Michael E. Hennessey snuck on board and intercepted him to find out what he had learned.

"What's the news in Boston?" Carson asked Hennessey with a smile. Their pleasantries were brief, and Carson shared with candor his lessons from abroad.

"Over on the other side they are discussing the transit question with the same degree of earnestness as we are in Boston and New York and other American cities," Carson told the reporter. He said most of the tunnels were poorly lighted and not very welcoming and that the plans Boston had drawn up compared more than favorably to anything he saw in Europe. But he did take away some useful bits.

In Berlin, he enjoyed how passengers dropped their money into a slot and got a ticket in return, eliminating the need for ticket sellers at every station and reducing the system's operating costs. In Liverpool, the ventilating system was the best he had seen. And he was also struck by how easily London's elevators whisked people up and down into the stations from the surface. But the more he thought about that for Boston, the less inclined he was to push for it. The London tracks were so far down beneath the streets that reaching them by stairs would have been an exhausting, time-consuming exercise. Boston's tracks could be reached in probably no more than twenty or thirty stairs, a far more doable task. But Carson did begin to think about some sort of lift or moving staircase that might help the elderly or injured into and out of the subway. With those same passengers in mind, Carson considered how other cities were handling slippery stairs during inclement weather. Some covered their iron steps with rubber, but that wore down quickly and was costly. Others had wood stairs, but those would not last long. When he saw one city using little ribs of steel on its steps, he said he knew that was the best option and made sure to jot down some notes in his pad. It was that sort of attention to detail that made Carson the perfect man to oversee the Boston subway. But even Carson's estimable presence could not quiet the subway's loudest protesters back home, who remained determined to squelch the project even after it was under way.

TWO DAYS AFTER THE GROUNDBREAKING for Boston's subway, in Charlestown a *Globe* reporter knocked on the front door of the blustery state representative Jeremiah J. McCarthy. A stout man with a pointy nose, McCarthy had just offered a resolution to the legislature that asked for the subway acts to be reconsidered and submitted for a revote and for any work being done to stop at once. He was convinced that the subway would cost much more than the citizens had been promised and that it would leave the city bankrupt and unable to perform any future maintenance or to extend rapid transit out to the suburbs.

"I regard the subway as a big humbug," McCarthy said. "It will rob the citizens of Boston of $20 million before it is completed, and rapid transit will not be secured." He much preferred an elevated rail instead. "The subway, if ever needed, will not be popular with the people, as they will not use it when opportunity is afforded to travel overhead," he said. "Subways are damp and unhealthy, and mostly constructed for crossing a river when no other way is offered." The next day's *Globe* gleefully blared McCarthy's best quote across the front page: IT'S A HUMBUG.

But his resolution went nowhere, and when it died on the afternoon of April 29, a young courier raced straight from the statehouse across the street to the Common, hat in hand, hair rumpled and breathing heavily, to deliver the news to Meehan himself. Though great progress had been made in just one month, McCarthy's blabbering had made the transit commissioners nervous and halted them from placing all the necessary equipment orders that Meehan needed. He had expected most days to have more than a hundred men working, but instead it was usually closer to fifty, and so the news of McCarthy's defeat brought great relief.

"McCarthy was buried out of sight," the young boy said, as he explained that the repeal bill was defeated.

"Good," Meehan said to the small crowd that had gathered around him. "Now the subway will be pushed along, and don't you forget it. I'm mighty glad that the house has the sense to refuse to pass the bill repealing the subway. In the first place we would be the laughingstock of the country, and in the second we have not pushed the work as rapidly as we wished, owing to this agitation."

McCarthy may have lost, but he and others who favored elevated travel over the subway did win one concession in the planning of the subway. Because it was agreed that one day the subway might need to connect seamlessly with a future elevated line, an assumption that would prove correct, every height, width, and curve that was included in the design of

Boston's subway was measured so that one day, a car identical in size to the ones being used by the Manhattan Elevated Railway could easily fit into the tunnel.

THE WORKERS WORE BAGGY PANTS, suspenders, long-sleeve shirts with the sleeves rolled up their forearms, and hats to protect their hair and eyes from flying dirt and rocks. They started at the corner of Boylston and Tremont and made their way down toward Charles Street. The carts with their big wooden wheels were slowly pulled out of the hole by horses and replaced by an empty cart, which was quickly filled and pulled away just the same. It was tedious, but in the course of a nine- or ten-hour day, with more than three dozen men applying their muscle nonstop except for a thirty-minute lunch break, fast progress was made.

The commission agreed that the subway should be built as close as possible to the surface of the streets. And the tunnel would also mirror the grade of the street, so that if the street took a slight upward tilt, so did the tunnel. The London Underground tunnels were typically between one hundred and two hundred feet down, which was why the invention of the Greathead shield had been such a critical breakthrough. The Boston tunnels would be no more than fifty feet down, and there were three reasons for this. A shallower trench could be dug faster and would produce less dirt to cart away. The likelihood of damaging neighboring buildings was greatly reduced if the tunnel was closer to the surface. And a shallower subway meant fewer stairs for passengers to have to walk up and down to get into and out of the stations.

In the first month, a routine was quickly established for how the trench would be dug. For the first ten feet in depth, workers simply shoveled the dirt into carts that were hauled out at one end of the trench. But as they got deeper, more effort and equipment was needed. The trench was dug in sections, ten feet long by twelve feet wide and six feet deep. Wooden braces were fixed against the dirt walls to prevent a cave-in and were placed across the top of the trench to provide the foundation for where bricks would be laid. Also, a derrick was brought alongside the trench. At this point, the dirt would be shoveled into skips, which were hoisted to the surface by the derricks and then dumped into small, steam-driven trains. The derricks were also used later to handle all the stones, timber, and beams for the retaining walls. As the trench got deeper, the steel support beams were laid along the sides of the walls and along the top, perpendicular to the tracks. The tunnel was then being constructed in two places. Underground, workers in the trench poured concrete, laid the floor on top of it, and then put down a bed of crushed stone. Wooden ties were sunk into the stone while steel rails were hammered into them with heavy iron spikes. Back on the surface, laborers placed bricks on top of the steel beams and sealed them in place with mortar. Once the roof was sealed with more concrete, a final layer of soil was dumped on top of it so that the road and sidewalk could be restored to its original condition.

There were occasionally exciting moments during the monotonous days of digging, when a shovelful of dirt brought up a piece of history. The two sons of Michael Meehan, Edward and Robert, were always on the lookout for souvenirs while standing along the Tremont Street ditch. One day early into the construction, Edward spotted a workman turn over his shovel and toss aside a black piece of metal. The young Meehan jumped into the trench to grab it and, after examining it for a few minutes, came to the conclusion that it was a piece of metal from a Revolutionary War cannon. Not long after that, his brother Robert was near Charles Street when he found a French coin dated 1636.

The deeper the workers went, the greater the risk for them. They were digging around water pipes, gas pipes, and sewer lines, and a leak from any of them could prove disastrous. When Thomas Roy and Michael Grogan emerged from the trench near the entrance to the Common on Charles Street one morning shortly after ten o'clock, they both had a dizzy look about them as they explained to their boss why they could no longer work.

"What's the matter?" Meehan asked them.

"The gas has knocked me out," Roy answered him. "My eyes are so blurred that I cannot see anything with them." His partner added, "Mine feel as if I had been peeling onions all the morning." Both men left for the hospital to be checked out, never to return to the job.

In the weeks and months before the contract for the subway was awarded, land surveyors had walked the route to bore holes in the ground at sixty-seven different spots to determine just how hard or soft the ground was and how deep it went before it struck something solid. The shallowest holes went twenty-five feet down, the deepest fifty feet. The topography and soil were nothing like what Parsons encountered in New York four years later. Engineers mapped out precisely where, underneath the narrow streets of the route, the gas pipes, water pipes, sewer pipes, and electric conduits were resting. This work proved especially tricky because many of the maps engineers had to rely on were imprecise, using scales of fifty feet to the inch or even one hundred feet to the inch, which made their markings more like guesswork.

Even though the tunnel was expected to go deeper into the ground than the foundations of the buildings nearest to the planned route, it was critical to know where those foundations were, so that nothing was done during the digging that might weaken a building's structure or, in a nightmarish scenario, cause it to topple over. Workers went into the basements of buildings with levels to check the flatness of the floors so that they could be rechecked if there was a fear that the digging might be causing a building to lean. Measurements were taken of every building along the route, and every manhole, sidewalk, street lamp, electric post, and streetcar track was plotted onto a map. To satisfy the demands and fears of the Boston Common protectionists, every tree in the park was also marked on a map, and a topographical survey was made to show what areas might be regraded with dirt from the subway trench.

Perhaps the biggest challenge was creating a detailed outline that showed all the streetcar lines that would be affected by the subway. Twenty-three different maps were drawn showing the various streetcar routes and where they ran through the subway route. There were seventy-six streetcar lines total, seventy-one of them controlled by the West End Street Railway Company and five others by the Lynn & Boston Railroad. With so many lines, stations were mapped out that were very close together. Stations were plotted for Tremont Street, at Boylston; Tremont, at Park Street; Scollay Square, just south of the Park Street station; Adams Square; and finally Causeway Street, or what would later be known as Haymarket Square.

The question of designing the actual tunnel came next. Walls had to be built and, even more important, the roof over the tunnel needed to be strong enough to carry the weight of moving cars and people. The tunnel needed to be airtight, aside from the openings to accommodate staircases in and out, and, even if it was never tested this way, it had to be capable of floating by itself in the ocean without letting a single drop of water inside. Three plans were studied for the tunnel, all of them similar but with critical variations.

One called for masonry sidewalls and a masonry arched roof. A second plan also had masonry walls, but the roof was composed of masonry arches resting on steel beams that were laid crosswise over the subway tracks. The third plan had the same roof as the second plan, but its sidewalls were masonry, strengthened by steel beams.

The first plan was ruled out because the masonry arches were thought to be vulnerable to cracking if they were used alone for the roof so close to the surface of the streets with nothing else to support them. They would be better for a deeper subway, but not Boston's. The concern about the second and third plans had to do with the steel beams. On one hand, the steel would be at full strength the second it was laid in the ground, unlike concrete, which would take months to harden. But would the iron and steel weaken over time from oxidation? Engineers investigated the question, and, after learning that the Romans had used iron beams to strengthen the stone masonry of the Colosseum and that many of those beams were still there, virtually unchanged, they put their fears to rest. Lead, cement, and concrete could help protect the beams from weakening, and the price of steel was also at a level that made the third option the cheapest of all. After the transit commissioners took the three options and asked a number of leading engineers in the country to render an opinion, they unanimously supported the third design. And so it was agreed that the first section of the subway, to run from the corner of Tremont and Park streets to the corner of Tremont and Boylston streets, would be built with masonry walls strengthened by steel beams and topped by a roof of masonry and steel beams lying crosswise over the subway.

Thanks to Frank Sprague, ventilating the Boston subway was not expected to present the same challenges that London faced in 1863 when steam locomotives first operated underground. But to reassure Bostonians that every precaution was being taken, the transit commissioners sought the opinion of a regular citizen. S. Homer Woodbridge, a heating and ventilating engineer and professor at the Massachusetts Institute of Technology, was asked to submit his opinion. He estimated that if steam locomotives were used in the subway, then at least thirty times more fresh air would have to be ventilated into the tunnels than if electric trolleys were used. The commissioners were satisfied that their focus should be on removing any stale air rather than blowing in good air, and they decided they would stand large electric fans inside the stations that would draw air from deep inside the tunnels and expel it through specially created vent shafts.

IN MID-APRIL, THE DAY ARRIVED that everybody who had followed the subway debate knew was coming. The living and the dead came face-to-face. Dr. Samuel Green, a former mayor of Boston and one of the city's kindest and most distinguished physicians, arrived at Park Street and Tremont Street early in the morning of April 19, 1895. The workers stood by, holding their shovels and picks, as the sixty-five-year-old physician, a rotund man with a thinning head of dark hair and a long, scraggly white beard, made his way onto the construction site. Green bent down to pick up some tiny fragments from the ground that looked like small rocks or twigs. Had they been found anywhere else in Boston, they would probably have been tossed aside. But Green knew precisely where he was standing and what he was holding. The workers had dug up pieces from a human skeleton. There would be no more digging on this day.

Green knew the discovery of human remains in the place where Boston was digging its subway tunnel would stoke the fears people had about going underground to ride a train. During the long debate in Boston about whether to build a subway, one skeptic, after visiting London, said the subway gave him a "buried alive" feeling. Yet another asked officials if they had any desire to go underground before it was their time. He certainly did not.

Green had tried to reassure the public that such fears were misplaced in his first report to the transit commission. "I would say that there would be no danger whatever to the workmen," he wrote. "The earth is a good disinfectant and a burial of more than half a century would wipe out and destroy any germs of disease that might still linger after death."

But Green's report had been forgotten by the time the bone fragments were discovered four months later. On the morning Green arrived, the Boston newspapers had heard about the workers' discovery, stirring up the decade-long debate about the safety of a subway and whether building it was worth all the trouble. Almost fifty years had passed since Marc Brunel successfully dug his tunnel beneath the Thames River in London, and yet much of the public around the world remained skeptical about how safe underground travel could be. "The dead are not allowed to rest quietly in their graves," *The Daily Advertiser* in Boston wrote. "The subway must be passed through the Boston Common, even if sacrilegious hands are to be laid on the dust of Boston's historic dead."

Green didn't know what else he could do to reassure people. But he also knew this was only the beginning, not the end. There were more skeletons to be found. He ordered boxes for the workers to collect the bone fragments, and he made sure that great pains were taken to try and put the bones of one person into one box to avoid mixing up collections. When the fragments of two tombs were identified, they were quickly taken by members of those families so they could be reinterred elsewhere. That was rare, unfortunately. Most of the coffins had decayed so much that they were filled with bones, rocks, and dirt, and it was near impossible to separate the human remains from the earth, never mind identify who the remains belonged to. Day after day, workers carted away new piles of remains. By the summertime, more than nine hundred fragments had been removed and reburied. Opponents to the subway became angrier as the public learned the names of the dead whose remains were disturbed, taken from the inscriptions on the tombs: Lydia Kimball, died October 29, 1821; Solomon Hawes, died January 30, 1834; Zeal Skidmore, died February 7, 1827; Gideon Williams, died January 23, 1830. No longer were the fragments anonymous bones.

Other than its taverns, the most revered places in Boston are its old burial grounds. They tell the city's history, and the survivors of the deceased treat their granite tombstones like family heirlooms. Along the proposed route of the subway that Boston was building were tombstones bearing the names Hancock, Revere, Cushing, Winthrop, Bowdoin, Faneuil, Adams, Paine, and Otis. There were signers of the Declaration of Independence, governors, war heroes, victims of the Boston Massacre and the battle of Bunker Hill, and the parents of great Americans like Benjamin Franklin. But there were also ordinary citizens, mothers and fathers, grandchildren and grandparents. Their tombstones were the book jackets of Boston, weathered, beaten, cracked, and chipped but still able to tell a good tale.

A week into Green's work in late April 1895, workers lifting a huge flagstone were surprised to find a tomb beneath it bearing a solid silver plate that bore an inscription:

William Keith Spence Lowell.
Aged 9 years 4 mos.
Died Feb 12, 1823.

Green had remembered being contacted recently by a Commonwealth Avenue woman, Frances P. Sprague. Her maiden name, she explained, was Lowell and she knew that the Lowell family tomb was buried in the vicinity of the subway excavation. When Green contacted her after the discovery, she confirmed that the five bodies in the tomb were indeed her family's remains, and she arranged for an undertaker to hold the remains until she decided where she would reinter them. Green was relieved to have made the connection.

The Lowell family was no ordinary clan. The great-grandfather of Frances P. Sprague was a judge appointed by President George Washington, and Sprague's brother, John Lowell, was appointed to the judicial bench by President Lincoln. Sprague's other brother, Augustus Lowell, was a prominent businessman and philanthropist whose children achieved great prominence of their own. A daughter, Amy Lowell, became a celebrated poet; their eldest son, Percival Lowell, founded the Lowell Observatory in Flagstaff, Arizona; and another son, Abbott Lawrence Lowell, became president of Harvard College for more than two decades.

For Green, it was a rare and gratifying episode during the project of identifying remains and trying to put them into the hands of surviving relatives. Throughout the excavation process, a line of buried tombs from one corner of the Common to the other was discovered, and Green was usually left frustrated. Some had been completely destroyed; others were in good condition. Inside the tombs, the coffins were mostly rotted to nothing and the bones were scattered and decomposed. And in many cases, the brick arches that had once covered the tombs collapsed on top of them and created a mess of stones, dirt, granite slabs, and bone fragments that was impossible to sift through.

THE CHARLES STREET SIDES of Boston Common and the Public Garden were often damp and putrid year-round. They were the lowest parts of the parks, and they were dumping grounds for city workers looking for a place to put snow and ice and mud and street refuse in the winter. Additionally, the Public Garden had been built upon a salt marsh of fibrous peat, which, when uncovered, gave off an eye-watering rotten-egg smell. The result of all this was a moist stew that reeked and that was a mess to walk over, steering people to other parts of the park. The only solution was to raise the grade with additional soil and then to make sure it was no longer used as an unofficial city dump. But the enormous amount of dirt needed was always too costly, and the problem was continually avoided. It was estimated that 9,000 cubic yards were needed for the Public Garden, and 62,000 cubic yards for the Common. With a single cubic yard weighing about 3,000 pounds, that was roughly 14,000 tons of dirt for the garden and a whopping 93,000 tons for the Common.

But suddenly, there it was.

In the summer of 1895, thousands of loads of dirt had been dug up and the wagons carting it all away were struggling to keep up with the fast-moving workers. In anticipating this possibility, the transit commission had said, "So rare an opportunity for making this important improvement at a trifling cost should not be lost." And so it was done. A plan was drawn up that called for plowing up portions of the parks, putting down the new dirt to create an undulating surface, planting new grass seed, and inviting lawn bowling, lacrosse, and other games onto the grounds. In fact, any game was welcome, except for baseball. In the end, the new surface in the two parks was in some places a full six feet higher than the old, and 3,500 square feet of new paths were created.

On the last day in April, more skeletons were unearthed while three different derricks helped workers push deeper into the ground and get past the layer of dirt to where the soil was stiff blue clay. The clay was a critical discovery because it ensured a stronger foundation for the subway.

NO VISITOR HAD AS MUCH history with the subway as the man who first proposed it eight years earlier. When Henry Whitney, who still kept a home in Brookline, stopped by the Common briefly on April 30, it did not go unnoticed. The West End Street Railway Company of 1895 looked nothing like the one he founded back in 1887. Instead of eight thousand horses housed in sixty different stables across the city, the company owned fewer than a thousand horses, and that number was continuing to dwindle fast. And a transit operation that started out owning zero electric motors now had 1,842 of them. Virtually every mile of track had been electrified by 1895, including most recently the ones that ran into Brookline near Whitney's house.

What had not changed was West End's growth and prosperity. It was earning a thousand dollars more per day from passenger rides than the previous year, a success story that no doubt would have made Whitney proud. During his visit to the subway site, the fifty-six-year-old Whitney made little fuss and did not wish to talk to reporters, especially since it was difficult for him to hear through all the racket. But he left impressed, and he said only that he was pleased that something he had suggested so long ago was finally happening. A subway, Whitney said before leaving, was the only practicable and possible solution for Boston's rapid transit woes. Savvy Bostonians must have been left shaking their heads, wondering why the man who had been in charge of the West End Street Railway Company for so many years and who brought them electric streetcars never made a serious effort to fix the broader problem himself.

BY EARLY MAY, 130 ELM trees that were in the subway's path had been replanted, with forty of them going along the sidewalk of the Public Garden by Arlington Street. On May 21, 1895, the site was a bustle of activity. An enormous pile driver was slamming its hammer into the ground with a great loud thud to loosen the dirt for the workers, who quickly shoveled it into the wagons and waited for the next drop. A stout iron chain kept back onlookers fascinated by the powerful, 2,300-pound pile driver, and every time it slammed down with a whack, whack, whack! a collective "ohhhh" shot up from the crowd.

Nearby, a large wagon was pulling slowly onto the site behind four horses. The wagon was loaded up with giant granite blocks, and as it came to a stop, laborers prepared to wrap a chain around one of the stones so it could be hoisted out.

David Keefe, a young worker from Charlestown, was shoveling out dirt that had been loosened by the pile driver when he momentarily lost his whereabouts and leaned too far forward without looking up. Before he could react, the wicked blow from the swinging hammer grazed his forehead and arm and knocked him to the ground unconscious. His co-workers instantly assumed he was dead, that nobody could survive a blow from a hammer that size dropping eighteen feet. Miraculously, the hammer had only stunned Keefe. Had his head been another two inches forward, he would surely have been crushed. He regained consciousness quickly and was taken to the hospital to have his gash dressed and broken arm mended. It was the first serious accident on the construction site. It would not be the last.

There were certain buildings in Boston near the construction site that were given special care to make sure no damage came to them, either because of their proximity to the tunnel or their historic place in the city. There was no more important church in Boston than the Park Street Church, and the subway was going to raise its visibility even higher because it stood directly across the street from the first station scheduled to open, and exiting pedestrians' first sight as they climbed the stairs would be the church's majestic white steeple.

On the evening of Sunday, November 24, the Reverend Isaac J. Lansing, an odd-looking pastor with a small chin, bushy mustache, and big ears, who earlier in the year had caused a great uproar when he called President Cleveland a drunkard, was about to begin his sermon, titled "The Sin of Sodom, Ancient and Modern." Suddenly there was a loud crash from his private office. Reverend Lansing rushed upstairs to find a powerful jet of water had crashed through his glass window and was flooding the luxurious room, soaking the silk upholstered chairs, his desk, carpet, and bookcase. A worker outside had accidentally struck a main waterline with his pickax, and there was immediately a fear that the church's foundation was being weakened by the water. The water was shut off, but the damage would not stop the evening's proceedings. Determined to go on with his sermon, Lansing told his members that working on the Sabbath was an outrage. Of the subway, he said, it is "an infernal hole, in more ways than one." He said the boss of that hole was not Michael Meehan. Lansing paused for effect, and then shouted, "It is the devil!"

The devil was apparently an efficient leader, because as the end of 1895 approached, the finishing touches were being put on the section of the subway from Park Street all the way down Tremont to Boylston Street. The tracks were laid. The walls were almost sealed. All that was left was to fill in the top of the subway with concrete, bricks, and the steel beams. And if the devil himself wanted to help in any way, Meehan surely would have hired him for $1.70 per day. Especially if he came from Jamaica Plain.

AS CHRISTMAS APPROACHED, A NOTICEABLE change occurred on the construction site under Jones and Meehan. The Italians joined the Irish. Meehan had initially dismissed them as isolated, but when he decided to reduce the pay he gave his laborers, from seventeen to fifteen cents an hour, his more experienced workers refused the pay cut and left the job. The Italians, he discovered, were more than happy to take his new rate. Meehan's face lit up as he looked around his job site at his newly invigorated work crew.

On March 28, 1896, a large party gathered at the Hotel Thorndike, which had opened on Boylston Street across from the Public Garden in 1887. Governor Roger Wolcott was there, along with all five members of the Boston Transit Commission, the legislative committee on metropolitan affairs, and more than a dozen senators and representatives. At ten o'clock sharp, Crocker, the commission's chairman, wearing a light-colored spring suit and a tall, festive hat, stood up. He explained to his audience the significance of the day, and he told them that because of Representative McCarthy's early efforts to stop the subway, very little work other than digging was done in the first two months. But since then, great progress had been made. "The Boston Transit Commission has nothing but praise to bestow upon the contractors and engineers for the ability, zeal and indefatigable efforts to secure the prompt completion of the work which they undertook," Crocker said.

When Crocker singled out Boston for having "no counterpart in the world," it was a reference to two specific milestones. The first, of course, was that Boston's subway system would be powered by electricity, the trains thanks to Frank Sprague and Fred Pearson and the lighting in the stations thanks to Thomas Edison. The second was more technical but no less critical to the subway's success. Boston's subway would be the only one to avoid any track crossings at the same grade by trains moving in opposite directions. By designing the subway tracks in a way that junction points at certain spots kept the trains from ever having to cross, the risk of collisions was negligible, delays would be reduced, and the capacity of the tracks was increased.

Crocker asked everyone to follow him. "I now invite your inspection of the subway," he said with great confidence. He took the governor's arm, and they marched across Boylston Street, attracting a growing crowd with each step. It was a significant moment for both men. Crocker's job was to convince the opponents that this really was the best thing for Boston and to reassure the supporters that they had made the right decision. For Wolcott, who became governor when Thomas Greenhalge died of illness midterm, this was his first official visit to the subway. As the group walked down the incline at the corner of Boylston and Charles streets, the morning light from above faded, and when they reached the bottom everybody stopped moving, suddenly nervous about taking an awkward step in a dark, unfamiliar place. There was no odor or sense of dampness, and the only visible water was drizzling down the inclined path from the sidewalk.

With no warning, one of Crocker's attendants pushed a button and flooded the entire space with light, more than one hundred feet down the tunnel. In one startling moment, the entire group was bathed in bright white light, and some men even had to squint for a brief second. The electric current worked! Meehan had tested it before this day, but he knew that was no guarantee it would respond when he needed it most. And it had. Of all the fears from citizens that had been expressed during Boston's long debate about a subway, one of the most often repeated ones was that walking down into a tunnel would feel like walking to your death. Dark. Damp. Scary. Those were just some of the words heard throughout the public hearings, and yet here was a subway tunnel that was bright, clean, dry, and odorless with shiny white walls and a sparkling white roof.

The dryness of the tunnel was particularly striking to the visitors. Engineers were well aware that the deeper they dug, the more likely they were to encounter springs of water in the ground directly beneath where the tracks would lie, and they had to keep that water from seeping into the tunnel. Drains were being installed in the stations at the lowest points, where water might pool, and there were pumps powered by electric motors, Frank Sprague's electric motors, to push the water out. "This subway is like a ship," one engineer said of the tunnel. "You build a ship and she floats in water. So this subway can be built, immersed in water and yet on the inside be perfectly dry." As an extra precaution, waterproof coating was being applied throughout the tunnel, and special measures were taken to keep water from percolating through the walls. It was all quite elaborate, and it was clear to Crocker that he had the group's attention. They were eager to see more.

When they had first stepped into the tunnel, Crocker asked that only three of the incandescent lights be turned on at first. It was plenty bright enough to cause the governor to glance down at the report of the Boston Transit Commission he'd been given and say, "Ample for one to read by, without the aid of glasses." But that's when Crocker really wanted to impress. At his signal, three more incandescent bulbs lit up, and then three more after that. Nine bulbs in total were now lighting the tunnel, and it went from feeling like a comfortably lit restaurant to the Tremont Theater when the curtain comes down on a show and every single light in the house comes on, as if nighttime became daytime in a heartbeat.

"Now," Crocker told his guests, "we will ascend by this ladder through ventilating chambers and see another portion of the subway." Most of the men were wearing business attire and shoes that were not ideal for climbing a ladder, but they all managed their way back up to the street without incident. Next, they were heading for the corner of Boylston and Tremont streets, where the work of Jones and Meehan along Tremont would intersect with the work of a fellow contractor, Edward W. Everson, from Providence, who was handling the Boylston Street stretch. Like Meehan, who had Meehanville, Everson had his own village of shanties, dubbed the Everson Stockade.

When they reached the corner of Tremont and Boylston, the pace of the work taking place was impossible to dismiss lightly. Giant derricks were hoisting huge granite stones into the air or placing them into the ground, a stream of horse-pulled wagons was carrying away piles of dirt or dumping load after load of gravel, and there were at least one hundred men hard at work, not one of them standing still. Crocker then led his troops on foot along the Tremont Street mall to the northern section of Meehan's work, where the first station, at Park Street, would be. Instead of an incline, here the men had to use a ladder inside a wide ventilating shaft to climb down to the grade level of the subway.

On their way down, Crocker told them it was "the finest example of concrete work to be found anywhere on the American continent," and no one questioned him. One detail that was shown to the visitors was a feature being built into the sidewalls throughout all the tunnels. Notches, about the size of a human being, were being carved out of the walls at close intervals, for workers down in the subway to leap into in the event an oncoming train catches them by surprise and they need a quick escape. As for any doubts about the strength of the subway walls to hold up beneath the weight of overhead traffic, those were put to rest with a simple explanation. First, there was a back wall of concrete one foot thick, plastered and waterproofed. On top of that were two inches of ribbed tiling, a layer of clay terra cotta, four inches of brick, half an inch of cement mortar, half an inch of asphalt waterproofing, and finally three more solid feet of top-grade concrete. The walls were more solid than a rock.

EVEN AS MORE CITIES AROUND the world moved closer to having their traffic underground, a new competitor was emerging that would simply replace one vehicle on the streets with another. Any hope that cities may have had of their streets becoming quiet and safe and pedestrian-friendly in the absence of all that streetcar traffic would be short-lived.

A young man from Michigan was putting the finishing touches on an idea for a horseless carriage powered by gasoline. He called his five-hundred-pound invention the quadricycle, because it was no more than a bicycle with four wheels and a place to sit and steer. With its two-cylinder engine powered by ethanol, it motored along all by itself, and Henry Ford was so eager to show it off that in the summer of 1896 he traveled to New

York to attend a convention of the Association of Edison Illuminating Companies. When the thirty-three-year-old Ford met the world-famous Edison and described his gas-powered car, Edison was instantly intrigued and fired questions at the young inventor. Hearing the answers, Edison supposedly banged his fist on the table. "Young man, that's the thing. You have it! The self-contained unit carrying its own fuel with it! Keep at it!" Ford would keep at it.

AS THE NEW YEAR ARRIVED, anticipation in Boston began to build about the opening of the subway. An important step was achieved on the first day of 1897, resolving one of the biggest problems Boston and New York had struggled with during their debates about how to pay for a subway. Henry Whitney back in his day had demanded that the West End company design, build, and own the system, retaining total control over every piece of the subway. He did not want the city's interference, and he wanted to be able to determine where the tracks went and how frequently they were traveled. But the Boston Transit Commission had grown wise to the flaws of that plan, and Boston's citizens had made it clear they were tired of the West End monopoly.

With Whitney out of the picture and the subway nearly complete, a deal was struck between the West End Street Railway Company and the Boston Transit Commission, and it was approved by the Boston Board of Railroad Commissioners on January 1. The West End company would lease exclusive control of the subway tracks from the city for twenty years and pay the city a fee of 4⅞ percent of what it would cost to operate the system. Fares for passengers had to remain at five cents, and free transfers would continue. And if, for whatever reason, the West End company could no longer operate the subway, the city would retake control of it. The contract put the system in the hands of the city, not a private company, which meant the city would decide where, when, and how it could be expanded. The West End Street Railway Company would prosper as long as it provided clean, safe, and swift travel in the new subway.

In February 1897, a gigantic new piece of equipment designed by an assistant city engineer arrived on the scene and caused great excitement among the laborers. It was an unusual shield, and it weighed twenty tons and had a span of almost thirty feet. Shaped like a crescent moon and not a complete circle like the Greathead shield, it had a much simpler purpose: It was a roof shield.

One of the trickier parts of the subway work proved to be digging a sufficiently smooth surface at the very top of the sidewalls of the tunnel in order to properly seal it off. The workers spent weeks swinging their shovels and picks, trying to knock loose the hard dirt above them. With the new shield, workers could move through the tunnel dislodging the hardest dirt at a much faster pace than a group of diggers ever could. The machine was hailed in the newspapers as a "labor and time saving machine," and it was hoped that the new shield might cut weeks off the final preparations of the tunnel. It had cost $10,000 to make but paid for itself in the amount of time and labor it saved. By the time the shield arrived, very little cutting in the cut-and-cover method was being done, and most of the work involved covering. Citizens could no longer peer down and see an enormous dirt trench at most spots along the route. The trench had been covered by hundreds of beams, and workers were preparing to put down the masonry arches and concrete and begin the process of sealing off the roof.

During the construction, the city managed to keep its busiest streets open to traffic and to close them only after 11:30 at night, allowing just enough room for fire trucks to get by. The path of the first leg of the subway ran almost directly above the sidewalk down Tremont Street, but building the tunnel required a much wider construction site than the mere width of the sidewalk. The cutting and covering of the tunnel extended far into Tremont Street, directly into the path of the street railway tracks. But rather than eliminate street railway service for more than two years, which would have caused enormous hardship to citizens and businesses along the route, the engineers took the extraordinary step of designing a detour of the tracks, which was constantly shifted to accommodate the tunnel work. The temporary tracks coming down Tremont Street from Scollay Square veered toward the Common directly in front of the Park

Street Church and made a wide turn in the shape of the letter C before veering back into Tremont Street. That took the streetcars around the construction work, no more than fifteen feet from the laborers, before they continued on their way down Tremont.

BY MARCH OF 1897 ALMOST two years had passed since the work on the subway began. It had not been an accident-free project, but there had been no massive catastrophes. At one point early on in the work, Meehan had said, "I had hoped to go through with this job without injuring a man. In all the work I have ever done I have not had a man under me hurt." That may have been true. But it was safe to assume that Meehan had never taken on a job with so much potential for disaster. Forty-foot steel beams swinging from a boom. Enormous scoops of dirt and concrete hanging from above. Gas leaks. Flooded trenches. Deep holes that could claim a life with a simple slip. There were so many ways to get hurt.

One worker was killed when a sheet of concrete paving foundation fell on his head. Another died when he was crushed by a piece of falling masonry. Digging a two-mile stretch of subway was proving to be less dangerous and not nearly as challenging as the decade-long building of the Brooklyn Bridge, which required thousands of miles of cable and claimed the lives of almost thirty people along the way. But the subway construction site provided unique perils.

Two friends and laborers, Patrick Gaffney and Michael Powers, were badly injured one morning when they carried lighted lanterns into a sewer tunnel where gas was leaking from a pipe. The loud explosion threw both men to the ground with badly burned faces and caused a small cave-in. Three men were nearly crushed to death when an engineer raised the dirt-filled scoop on his derrick too high, causing the scoop to break free from its boom and fall into a trench. In the crash, Edward O'Donnell had his foot crushed, Michael Eagen injured his back, and John McCue bruised his foot. And on the same day, only a few hours later, another scoop broke free from its eighty-foot boom and rained a load of concrete down on John Micher, a laborer working in the trench. After Micher was dug out, scared but unscathed, Meehan was fed up. He fired the engineer who lost the concrete-filled scoop. "I'll have more careful men if I change engineers every hour," the boss said.

But no matter how careful his men were, nothing could have prevented two gruesome accidents that occurred four days apart in the fall of 1896. During the night of September 16, Charles McMullen, a fresh laborer who had only started work that evening and who was unfamiliar with the terrain of the project, stepped backward and fell into a deep shaft in front of the Park Street Church. He dropped forty-two feet to his death. A similar tragedy nearly ended the life of William Doherty days later. Climbing out of the same shaft on Tremont Street, Doherty's feet slipped off the ladder, and he plunged back down almost thirty feet, where he struck a bucket. He was badly hurt and lost an eye, rendering him incapable of hard labor.

By early 1897, the pace of the subway construction was almost frantic. The site was an around-the-clock operation. The early days of a few dozen workers were long gone. It was more typical now for there to be a few hundred laborers working in shifts from noon to midnight and back again. The tunnel was complete, and the focus had shifted to making sure the thousands of sewer, water, and gas pipes underground were rerouted, connected, and sealed; that the roof and floor of the tunnel were secure enough to begin piecing the streets back together again; and that any excess dirt was either carted away or packed back into the ground. A date was scheduled for the opening, September 1, and at the rate the work was progressing, only an unexpected disaster could prevent America's first subway from opening on time.

~

12

BOOM!

EARLY IN THE MORNING OF March 4, 1897, James Groake took hold of a lantern with a candle burning brightly inside and went underground. It was 3:00 A.M. Because of the temporary bridge that had been constructed over the tunnel trench near the corner of Boylston and Tremont streets, he had to lift up some of the planking in order to go down below. He was looking for a place to dump two carts filled with dirt. When he found a good-sized cavity, he instructed the men with him to shovel the soil through the hole in the planking that he had made. It took them almost three hours to empty the carts. As they were finishing, the dark sky was just beginning to show the first signs of light and the early risers of the day were strolling down the sidewalks.

Groake's men had dumped dirt into the hole. The Italians arrived to distribute it around and to pack it in tightly against the pipes. They had iron rammers with short handles, each weighing about ten pounds, and they would pound the dirt into the ground, flattening it as much as possible. It was not delicate work, but it did require concentration because of one factor. There was a six-inch pipe filled with gas and held aloft by steel supports right in the cavity where they were working. It was dark, and the spot where they were standing and swinging their rammers was tight. They had to be careful to avoid striking each other, let alone nicking the gas pipe. If the pipe was fractured or, worse, if it was cracked so slightly as to be unnoticed, gas could slowly leak up and pool just below the surface of the street.

When Groake left the tunnel, there was nothing to alarm him, and there was certainly no smell of gas, which he would have been sure to notice. It was seven o'clock in the morning when the Italians finished their pounding and emerged back on the street. Groake watched as the planks he had lifted up four hours earlier were hammered back into the ground and the bridge was returned to the exact condition he had found it in. He headed home, confident that the traffic of the day would drive safely over the spot where his men had been working overnight and that pipes sitting in a maze only a few feet beneath the surface were as airtight as they'd been when his shift started. "So far as I know," Groake would say later, "no pipes or supports were touched while our men were at work there that morning."

As the day began and the sidewalks and streets grew crowded, the corner of Tremont and Boylston once again became the intersection around which the city functioned. The biggest attraction besides the subway project was an enormous painting inside the Masonic lodge. Measuring thirty-one feet by twenty-four feet, *Le mort de Babylone,* or *The Fall of Babylon,* by the French artist Georges Antoine Rochegrosse, had been on exhibit since December, and it was attracting hundreds, sometimes thousands, of people every day. Art students came to study and talk about it or just to attend the daily lectures about the history behind the painting. The story went that Rochegrosse took ten years to complete the work. The painting depicted in rich colors the conquering Cyrus amid a royal feast. Nude women lying on their backs and drunken men dotted the foreground. Rich draperies, gold and silver vases, and flowers and crumbs from the feast filled out the canvas. The angel of death was visible in the center toward the top of a monumental staircase, awaiting the band of invaders at the gates. Perhaps it was the grim tone of the painting that drew the crowds, but it turned a busy corner into the most congested spot in Boston.

. . .

JUST AFTER EIGHT O'CLOCK IN the morning, Wolf Koplan, a fifteen-year-old boy wearing a black cap and lugging a satchel over his shoulder, turned the corner from Washington Street onto Boylston Street in downtown Boston and headed up one block to the corner of Tremont Street. A powerful smell of gas greeted him as he strolled, but that had become a daily occurance.

All morning, the number of people who smelled the gas had grown by the minute. Thomas B. Hosmer, a dentist whose office was on Boylston Street, tried to use his gas, but he could not get enough of it to reach the required temperature of 180 degrees. Another dentist, Leonard Howe, whose office was in the Hotel Pelham, could not summon enough gas to use his Bunsen burner and was forced to give up when the flame would go down after two or three minutes. Somebody found the smell so strong that they telephoned the gas company to report it. From December 22, 1896, when the first gas leak was reported on Boylston Street, to this day, March 4, more than two thousand leaks, or about twenty per day, were reported.

Although the smell of gas should have been an ominous sign, it could not quell the feeling of optimism and excitement in the air, in both Boston and the country. In just a few hours, five hundred miles to the south, in Washington, D.C., William C. McKinley was going to be inaugurated as the country's twenty-fifth president, renewing hope among Americans that the depression hanging over the country since the panic of 1893 was in its final days. And in six months, Boston was planning to open its subway.

Wolf Koplan's home was about fifty miles northwest of Boston in the town of Fitchburg. But lately he had been living with family in Boston so that he could work and go to school in the city. The streets of big cities in the late nineteenth century were crowded with young boys earning good wages typically doing one of two jobs, selling papers as newsboys or shining shoes as bootblacks. The leather badge on Koplan's black cap contained the word LICENSED along with his license number in polished letters. The badge also had the letter B on it, which identified him as a bootblack to the adults passing by and the truant officers patrolling the city. The license was free, but the badge cost a dollar and a quarter. And no bootblack received a license unless they attended school at least two hours every day. Most went to school in the morning so they could work in the afternoon, but some, like Koplan, chose the afternoon for school because the morning hours were most profitable.

At the corner of Tremont and Boylston, where he set up his stand, pavers were starting to smooth out the street after two years of disruption. Just beneath the street was about five feet of empty space on top of the roof of the subway barrel. That cavity carried a network of pipes belonging to the Boston Electric Light Company, the Edison Electric Company, or the Boston Gas Light Company.

As streetcars filled the downtown district on this late winter morning, a conveyor system moving large steel buckets ran above them with a clickety-clack sound. The buckets moved in two directions along thick cables, some taking the last piles of dirt away from the subway project, others delivering cement to be used for the tunnel's sidewalls and foundation. The conveyor system was tedious, but using dump wagons would have meant bringing more vehicles onto city streets that were already beyond capacity.

When Koplan got to his corner in front of the Masonic lodge, he stopped and emptied his pouch on the sidewalk. He took out a hand towel, a soft bristle brush, and two jars of shoeshine, and he prepared for his first customer to come by for a shine. He hoped that on Inauguration Day the men of Boston would want to look especially dapper, because he knew the easiest way to accomplish that was with a quick polish.

THE SMELL HAD BEEN GETTING worse for months. The leaking gas was presumed responsible for killing a cat in the basement of Walter Pratt's health food store on Tremont. But when Pratt called the gas company to complain, they sent a man out to replace a pipe in his basement, who told him not to be surprised if the smell returned. "The subway people [are] to blame," the workman told Pratt. It had become a common refrain for Bostonians. Business was slow—blame the subway project. The streets were too loud—blame the subway project. Traffic was a nightmare—blame the subway project. The city smelled of gas—blame the subway project.

The country was in economic turmoil, and Boston's retail district, already struggling, was being hurt even more by the subway's construction. Washington and Tremont streets, parallel thoroughfares, were cluttered with stores specializing in wool, dry goods, fresh produce, leather, and meat. Most of the shoppers who came downtown walked in from two neighborhoods. To the north lay Beacon Hill, where gas lamps lined the streets, brownstones housed the wealthiest families, and for a penny a hungry young boy could stick his arm into a giant goldfish bowl at Greer's Variety Store and pull out an enormous green pickle. In the other direction, the West End and North End were home to Boston's working class immigrants, gritty communities filled with saloons, flea markets, and fishmongers.

WHEN THE POLICE OFFICER Michael Whalen first detected the smell of gas, he didn't panic. He knew the odor had snaked its way through the neighborhood for months. He knew about the dead cat. He knew apartment dwellers were forced from their homes because the smell got so bad. But each time a gas leak was reported, within a few hours the smell faded and all was forgotten, until the next time and the calls started anew. On this morning, though, the odor didn't go away. It kept getting stronger. When a young black worker on the subway project left his job site and walked over to Whalen, he asked the obvious question.

"Do you smell that?"

"Yes, it's pretty strong," Whalen answered. "Can you tell where it's coming from?"

They both looked around puzzled. Whalen tried to follow the smell, but when he walked across the street, it was less strong, and then as soon as he walked back to the Hotel Pelham, there it was again. He remembered there had been a gas leak six weeks earlier at this same location that had caused the gas supply to be cut off for two days, and he was determined this time to find the source.

At seven minutes after eleven o'clock in the morning, the phone rang at the Boston Gas Light Company, and Nellie Harmon answered.

"Are you the Boston Gas Light Company?" a man's panicked voice said.

"Yes sir," Harmon said.

"Will you please send some men to the corner of Tremont and Boylston streets right away?"

"What is the trouble?" He told her there was a bad leak and to send someone fast. Harmon reached for her complaint ticket and wrote down, "Corner of Tremont and Boylston. Leak bad."

"Who are you?" she asked the caller. But all he said was, "Mason temple" and "Thank you."

As each minute of the gas leak passed, it had spread so far that it made its way into the basement of the Masonic temple a block away on Washington Street. Because that was where the call to Harmon came from, she sent her workers there, assuming the cause of the smell was a building leak. Except it was not. So while the temple was being evacuated shortly before noon, gas continued to pool a block away, in the actual site of the leak, just below the surface of the street at the corner of Tremont and Boylston, feet away from Wolf Koplan's shoeshine stand and directly over the workers putting the finishing touches on the first subway in America.

A few minutes before noon, three crowded streetcars rounded the corner at Boylston and Tremont. Each car had a different destination as signified by its sign. One, which said BACK BAY, the neighborhood nearest to the intersection, was on its way directly across Tremont Street. The second said RESERVOIR, a station farther out in the wealthy town of Brookline. It was turning right from Tremont onto Boylston. The last of the three cars, trolley 461, with the words MT. AUBURN on its front was the one that caught the attention of Whalen. As it screeched around the corner, the officer looked down at its wheels and saw them grinding on the sand scattered over the rails, causing sparks to fly off the side. Up on board, the passengers nearly gagged from the smell of gas, and some turned their heads in search of a breath of fresh air. Then, with no warning at all, the ground shook, and the sound of a cannon boomed.

THE EXPLOSION WAS SO POWERFUL that the clock in the tower of the Young Men's Christian Union building recorded the precise moment, stopping at 11:47. The two streetcars that were rounding the corner at the precise moment of the boom soared into the air in a burst of flames, splintering into pieces and drowning out the shrieks of the horses and the screams of the passengers. As Wolf Koplan gave one last wipe of his rag across the shoe tops of his customer, he stood up and was slammed against the side of the Masonic building and knocked out cold. He cut his right thumb badly. It took a few minutes for some pedestrians to help revive him and get him to his feet, and only then did he realize he had more than a pounding headache. He could hardly hear out of his right ear, a loss that would stick with him for the remainder of his life.

The hole in the surface of the street looked like a gaping wound. A tangled mess of badly damaged gas main lines, electric wires, pipes, and the rails and wooden planks from the street railway tracks were left dangling just over the roof of the exposed underground tunnel.

An umbrella-shaped black cloud rose up from the street, followed by an even bigger puff of white steam that seemed to push the black cloud high into the air. The two gray horses that had been attached to the Back Bay car pulled free from their vehicle and dashed across Boston Common, somehow not trampling over the workers and people in the park. The Mount Auburn car, after soaring into the air, twisted and in an instant came crashing down on its side, directly on top of its horses, a crash so loud that none of the screams from inside it could be heard. The second it hit the ground, the streetcar burst into flames, sending a bright orange plume at least fifty feet into the air. The explosion caused the Hotel Pelham's windows to break and rain down shards of glass on the sidewalk.

"The people didn't have a chance for their lives," said one passenger who survived the blast, James Hardeman. "For as soon as the car rolled over on its side a sheet of flame shot up."

No building suffered more damage than the Hotel Pelham. Every window on its ground floor was smashed; skylights in the roof were cracked or broken. A barber on the hotel's second floor was in the midst of giving a trim when he was thrown clear across the room.

Paul Klein, the longtime owner of a popular first-floor drugstore at the corner of Tremont and Boylston, was sitting at his desk sifting through bills when the explosion occurred. His two giant plate-glass windows came crashing in on the store, taking down bottles, jars, vases, and other supplies. Klein himself was lucky. He suffered only a few deep cuts in his head from flying glass. One man standing just outside the front door of the drug store had his hat blown clear inside and was killed almost instantly in the blast.

With the entire street corner a ball of fire, witnesses screamed for help for the victims trapped with bloody faces and broken limbs inside the cars and beneath the rubble. It was only seconds before the clanging of approaching fire trucks started to drown out the groans and cries. John Carroll, a carpenter who had walked past only minutes earlier, rushed back to the scene and saw four men dead on the ground. He picked up one of the lifeless bodies, carried it away, and returned to the scene, where he comforted two elderly women. Mary Stone, a music teacher, suffered a bad injury to her scalp along with a fractured left thigh, right kneecap, and right ankle. The one person who cheated death more than any was surely Paul Hackett, the conductor of the Mount Auburn car, who sustained two broken legs, but nothing more.

Reverend W. A. Start, the Tufts University bursar, was walking up Tremont Street and might have been the closest pedestrian to the corner when the explosion occurred. The back of his scalp was badly sliced, his left leg was mangled all the way from the ankle to the hip, and his forearm was fractured. He died right there on the sidewalk. Two wealthy sisters, Amelia M. Bates and Georgianna H. Bates, had left their home on nearby Arlington Street for a drive around town on the pleasant morning. Their carriage was almost directly on top of the hole that burst. Amelia Bates was thrown to the front of her carriage and could not be saved because of all the fire around her. Her sister escaped harm, but their driver fell off into the flames and died instantly. William Vinal, the private secretary of a prominent banker in town, was on his way to collect his boss's daughters when his carriage was hurled into the air and both he and his driver were killed. He might have been saved by a doctor who tried to get to him with some brandy for his wounds as he lay on the sidewalk, but the crowd was so dense and the scene so frantic that the doctor could not get through, and Vinal took his last breath with a crowd of helpless people standing over him.

Within minutes at least 150 police and fire officers, along with hospital workers, were on the scene. Their first challenge was keeping back the crowd of more than a thousand witnesses, including many who wanted to rush to the aid of their neighbors and shopkeepers. The ground all around the scene was littered with shopping bags and purses, left by women who had been injured or merely dropped them and ran off. The police, frustrated by their crowd-control efforts, finally warned the onlookers that another explosion was imminent. It was a lie. But the crowd scurried back and allowed the rescue workers to work more freely amid the debris, the carcasses of the dead horses, and the torrents of water being poured on the fire.

As the rescue workers began finding bodies, there was relief there had not been more fatalities; in all, ten would be killed. But by early afternoon, once the fire was doused and the rubble was being carted away, the attention of everyone turned to the cause of the explosion. There was no question that leaking gas played a part, but what ignited it? A discarded match? A broken trolley wire? Or the most plausible theory, a spark from the wheel of a car passing over the pool of leaking gas underground?

Both Mayor Quincy and Nathan Matthews, the ex-mayor, visited the site to comfort the injured and the workers. But they had broader concerns, too. They needed to learn whether the subway tunnel had been damaged. "It certainly seems that this accident could not have occurred unless there had been negligence either on the part of the contractors or of the Boston gaslight company," Mayor Quincy said in the afternoon. "And that responsibility must be divided between them."

And it would be. Wolf Koplan would be the first of many to file a lawsuit, and when the legal wrangling was said and done, the city of Boston, the West End Street Railway Company, and Boston Gas all paid out settlements to families of the victims and victims themselves. It took a jury all of seven hours in Koplan's case to blame the gas company for his injuries and award him $3,000 in damages.

In the hours after the blast, Howard Carson, the chief engineer of the subway, was immediately concerned not with who or what caused the explosion but with how badly it damaged his tunnel. Workers from Boston Gas Light Company and the Edison Electric Company wasted no time in setting to work to repair the damage. Within hours, two eight-inch pipes and one six-inch pipe were being closely inspected, and it was obvious to everyone that while the bigger pipes were new, the smaller one was older and had a fracture in it that seemed certain to have played a part in the accident.

CARSON WASTED NO TIME touring the tunnel, and at an emergency meeting of the Boston Transit Commission held just a few hours after the accident, he assured the commissioners that it appeared secure. Because the explosion occurred between the roof of the subway tunnel and the surface of the street, he explained, the inside of the tunnel was not damaged.

"It appears to be in perfect condition, and not injured in any way by the explosion of gas this morning," Carson said. "Whether the exterior may in any way be injured I cannot say until it is more nearly uncovered, but I do not expect to find any injury unless possibly to the tiling on the exterior." And even if the tiling was damaged, he added, it would not weaken the strength or stability of the subway tunnel. "The explosion occurred entirely above and outside of the subway and none of the employees in the subway were hurt."

He hoped his words would have a calming effect in the wake of the tragedy. Carson was no fool. He knew how apprehensive the citizens of Boston had been about a subway, and he assumed the coverage of the explosion would only reignite their strongest fears that it could never be entirely safe, not when they would be traveling along the same ground where gas lines were buried. All he could do was push his contractors to keep working and hope that in six months, when the subway was expected to open, the accident would be long forgotten.

On March 5, 1897, all the city's newspapers were filled with long front-page stories of the explosion and detailed eyewitness accounts. The coverage of the emergency meeting of the Boston Transit Commission, where Carson sought to reassure the public, was relegated to seven small paragraphs in *The Globe* under the headline SUBWAY IS NOT INJURED. Reading the day's coverage, it was as if the country's biggest news of the day never even happened. "It isn't often that home news outshadows the inauguration of a new president on March 4," *The Globe* wrote the following day, "but it did so most gloomily on March 4, 1897."

ON JULY 3, 1897, Sam Little invited a dozen reporters and a few high-ranking members of his West End Street Railway Company to join him for a test ride. At precisely two o'clock, a single car dipped beneath the road on Boylston Street in front of the Public Garden and zoomed into a brightly lit tunnel. From the moment the electric engine hissed to life, the passengers seemed in awe. The train went straight under Boylston to the sharp turn at Tremont and, without stopping, continued on to the Park Street station, where it slowed, completed a loop turn, and went right back to where it started without a single stop. It could not have gone smoother. The polished tracks glistened. The white walls were so bright they almost required squinting in the lights. The bed of crushed stones covered every inch of ground between the spiked-in rails and wooden ties. And almost entirely out of sight, embedded in the ceiling of the tunnel, a black electric cable followed the path of the tracks below. "Pure air, true light, perfect ventilation, express speed, absolute safety," *The Globe* reported the next day.

But even more important was its headline: RAPID TRANSIT INSURED: SUBWAY SAVES NINE MINUTES IN RUNNING TIME FROM PUBLIC GARDEN TO PARK STREET. The subway was scheduled to open in less than two months. The blue and gold sign boards were up to tell passengers where to catch certain cars bound for the right destination. The ticket offices and turnstiles were almost finished, and two railings were being installed on the stairways to try and separate the entering and exiting crowds. If there were any doubters left, nothing would change their minds.

ON AUGUST 25 THE JOYOUS mood of the city was nearly crushed by a five-ton derrick. Another tragedy, one week before the opening of the subway, would not only cast a pall over the day, it would erase all of the good feelings that emerged out of Sam Little's public relations coup in July.

Thomas Ryan, a twenty-four-year-old engineer, was working along with laborers Maurice Connors and Bernard Rodder in a fifty-foot hole on a later section of the subway being built in Scollay Square, a few blocks from the Park Street Church. The arm of the giant derrick was swinging over a fence on the construction site and getting ready to reach into the hole to lower a five-thousand-pound granite block into it. The derrick suddenly lurched and tilted, and even though the engine cut off it began to lean forward and slide into the hole, right on top of Ryan, who was trapped in a corner, and Rodder, who was scrambling to climb out on a rope. As the ground caved in around the hole and the derrick toppled over, Rodder and Ryan managed to dive out of the way and fall on top of each other, just feet away from the wreck of a giant machine. Ryan twisted his left leg and his chest took a hard blow, while Rodder cut his head and right arm. But a tragedy had been averted, both men had cheated death, and it seemed now as if the city was poised for its historic day.

A few minutes after ten o'clock on the night of August 30, a well-dressed crowd of about two thousand people spilled out of the cozy Tremont Theater and onto Tremont Street. In less than eight hours, America's first subway was scheduled to roll underground. The audience filing out had just seen a dramatic opening-night performance of *The Sunshine of Paradise Alley*, a play featuring a young girl who comforts troubled souls and sets them on a stronger path. It was playing in Boston just as the country was emerging from the worst of times following the panic of 1893, a point that was not lost on critics of the day. In previewing the performance, *The Globe* said, "It will teach those who live in luxurious homes that amidst squalid surroundings and under ragged clothes there beats many a warm heart and exists many a sunny nature; that in such poverty-stricken districts many deserving people may be found."

As the theatergoers streamed out of the theater across from Boston Common, a strange sight greeted them. The sidewalks were crowded with audiences emerging from several theaters on the block or the nearby restaurants, such as the fine French bistro Locke-Ober; the more casual German spot, Jacob Wirth Company, known for its bratwurst, pea soup, and dark rye bread; or the Parker House, famous for its warm rolls, Boston cream pie, and codfish. But as crowded as it was downtown, the streets were almost entirely empty of traffic. On a night when Tremont Street should have been bustling, most of the streetcars that normally choked it were otherwise occupied. The managers of the West End Street Railway Company were running their final preparations for the next day, and in the process they were giving Bostonians a sneak peek of their future. Clear streets at last.

The Boston Daily Globe could hardly contain its excitement. Two weeks earlier, *The New York Times* had tweaked Boston with an article that expressed disappointment and surprise at losing the race underground, proclaiming it "remarkable" that "so conservative an American town should happen to be the pioneer in adopting this." Now, on the day of its subway opening, Boston's largest paper volleyed back with a dig of its own.

On the morning of September 1, 1897, Bostonians awoke to a headline in *The Globe*, NOW FOR THE SUBWAY. It was only a short piece, five paragraphs in total. But in closing, the editorial pointed out that Boston's project had been followed for years from around the world and that today was an accomplishment worth cheering. "Boston's experiment in subway construction has been watched with a great deal of interest elsewhere. Its success will mean setting the pace for greater Gotham, not to mention many smaller cities in our land."

Had he seen *The Globe* article, William Barclay Parsons would surely have cringed at the thought of little old Boston setting the pace for New York City to follow.

13

"FIRST CAR OFF THE EARTH!"

SHE MUST HAVE BEEN QUITE THE SIGHT. It was not yet five o'clock in the morning when the young woman, still fastening the strings of her bonnet, realized she had better start running. She heard a rooster crow from a remote backyard and hoped that she still had time. Down the empty sidewalk in the Boston neighborhood of Allston she ran as fast as her long dress would allow, under a dark sky streaked with pink. Only when she came gasping around a corner onto Cambridge Street and she saw a group of railway men standing and chatting on the sidewalk did she know that she had made it. She stopped for a moment to catch her breath and to finish straightening her bonnet, and then she approached the group with a smile. When one of the men saw her, he congratulated her on showing such pluck at an early hour and invited her into the car shed. That's where the open-air trolley number 1752 with a SUBWAY TO PARK ST. sign on top was waiting.

It was one of the newer models in the West End's system, built just two years earlier by the Massachusetts Car Company in the town of Ashburnham, and so it was not yet showing too many signs of wear. With its freshly polished brass fixtures and nine shiny rows of wood benches it looked almost new for its special trip. The worker helped the young woman take a seat in the front-row bench, right alongside the spaces that were being reserved for the half dozen newspaper reporters. Within minutes she was joined on the car by thirty other early-rising passengers, each one more giddy than the next. Together, they sat and they waited.

It had been a remarkable two years for the City on a Hill, as John Winthrop, the first governor of the Massachusetts Bay Colony, had unwittingly nicknamed Boston in a fiery sermon he delivered in 1630. The opening of the Boston Public Library was followed a year later by a publishing story for the ages. A little-known graduate of the Boston Cooking School named Fanny Merritt Farmer released a cookbook of nearly two thousand recipes that gave home chefs precise measurements to help them make their own angel cakes, baked beans, chowders, and puddings. The home kitchen was never the same. For a city that was already a medical mecca with Boston Floating Hospital, New England Baptist Hospital, the Tufts School of Medicine, Massachusetts General Hospital, and the Boston Lying-In Hospital, the opening of another prominent institution, New England Deaconess Hospital, solidified the city's place in the world of healing. The subway capped a string of achievements that secured Boston's spot as a birthplace of innovation.

And yet there were no speeches planned for the morning of September 1, 1897. There was no official program. There was no formal invitation extended to President McKinley or Governor Wolcott or the former mayor Nathan Matthews, the "father of the subway," or even the man who first proposed the idea of tunneling a subway a decade earlier, fifty-eight-year-old Henry M. Whitney. The current mayor, Josiah Quincy, apparently thought so little of the event that he spent his morning at the Plaza Hotel welcoming two hundred members of the Catholic Young Men's National Union to Boston.

The final hours before America's first subway rolled under the streets of Boston were spent on the details, polishing the brass fixtures in the stations, checking the oak railroad ties one last time, applying a final coat of white paint to the picket fences between the underground tracks, and making sure the words "No Smoking" appeared on enough of the white posts. After a decade of debate, Bostonians needed no reminder that this was to be their day. And the men who built the subway decided that the achievement should speak for itself. They did not need dignitaries to affirm what they had accomplished after two and a half years of digging. Their puritanical values told them that no pomp was necessary. And so as "birds were bubbling with the exuberance of morning and the sun was kindling mock fires in east facing windows," as *The Globe* described the dawn, it was almost shaping up to be an ordinary Wednesday for Boston, aside from the early risers who were starting to gather on the streets downtown.

If there was a practical reason why the subway's opening did not generate much excitement outside Boston, besides the city's own unwillingness to celebrate, it might have been that the actual first leg of the subway was so short. Of the eleven total sections being built, only sections 1, 2, and 3 were ready to be unveiled on September 1. The rest of the subway, connecting past Park Street out to Haymarket Square in one direction and from Boylston Street away from the Common out to Pleasant Street in the other, was not far behind. Even those legs would only extend the entire distance of the subway to 1.8 miles. But those three sections traversed beneath the two streets that defined Boston as much as Fifth Avenue and Broadway epitomized New York.

Standing at the corner of Boylston Street and Tremont Street, where the deadly gas line explosion occurred six months earlier, looking in both directions, up Tremont and down Boylston, provided a glimpse into Boston's history and to its future. The two streets rimming Boston Common and the Public Garden bustled with activity. Tremont Theater was there, and down a nearby alley off Boylston so was Locke-Ober, two establishments that provided many an evening's entertainment of acting and dinner. "Ladies' Street," a row of retail stores, began at the corner of Tremont and Winter streets and was crowded most days with the city's most fashionable shoppers. There was one of the city's most revered buildings, Tremont House, with its distinguished reading room and heavy dark granite walls, a place where Andrew Jackson, the Prince of Wales, Charles Dickens, and Henry Clay had all come to read, to write, or just to think. "It has more galleries, colonnades, piazzas, and passages than I can remember or the reader would believe," Dickens once wrote of it. A little farther down was City Hall, at the corner of Tremont and School streets, a handsome building with a white granite front, tall arching windows, and towering bronze statues of Benjamin Franklin and Josiah Quincy out front. Just a few feet away was the hotel Dickens once called the finest in America, Parker House, and around the corner was one of the country's oldest bookshops, the Old Corner Bookstore. Boylston was lined with taller buildings than Tremont, many of them occupied by the Boston Conservatory of Music and half a dozen piano manufacturers, who gave the stretch the nickname Piano Row. It was a place William Steinway had visited frequently, to see the showrooms where his pianos were being sold.

WHENEVER ONE OF THE WORLD'S engineering marvels of the second half of the nineteenth century had been completed, they were accompanied by orchestrated celebrations. On January 9, 1863, the night London opened its Underground, a banquet at the Farringdon Street station was held to toast the feat. Seven years later, in New York City, when Alfred Beach unveiled his one-block pneumatic subway tunnel, he did not let the moment pass quietly. Ever the showman, he invited dignitaries down and crowed to the world that he had solved the urban transportation nightmare. On May 10, 1869, when the last hammer swung to finish the transcontinental railroad, thousands gathered in the flatlands of Promontory, Utah, and stood in a circle or sat on the idling trains to watch as a gold spike was hammered into the ground. Within minutes, President Ulysses S. Grant received a telegram telling him the railroad was complete. In May 1883, when the Brooklyn Bridge opened, President Chester A. Arthur attended the festivities, as did hundreds of thousands of citizens on land and in the boats in the harbor. Children skipped school, workers skipped work, vendors made small fortunes hawking their wares, and there was an hour of speeches followed by a parade. And two years later, President Arthur came out again for the dedication of the Washington Monument, the tallest building in the world, and he led a procession to the Capitol Building, where he greeted passing U.S. troops. For each occasion, no detail was overlooked, and there were often buttons, pamphlets, balloons, and bands to mark the occasion.

But on this historic morning for Boston and the country, there would be no boastful proclamations, no processions, and no celebratory spikes of the last subway rail. The only question to be decided was, Who was going to drive the first subway car in America?

EACH CAR WOULD HAVE a motorman and a conductor, one to drive, the other to collect the tickets from the passengers. Strapping James Reed, or Jimmy as he was known, short and muscular with a thick mustache and weathered and bronzed face from nearly thirty years of railway driving, and Gilman "Gil" Trufant, one of the oldest and gentlest conductors in Boston, were two of the most experienced transit men in the city, and so it was decided that their Pearl Street–Allston car should be the first through the tunnel.

Reed grew up in a small brownstone on Tyler Street and attended public schools downtown until his family moved to the grittier Charlestown neighborhood. He enlisted in the army for the Civil War, but when he was told he wasn't old enough to shoulder a gun, he was made a drummer. He came home frustrated after his enlistment ended, feeling as if he had not done his part, but he quickly grew bored and reenlisted, this time as a private, and his second stint earned him his stripes since he took part in some of the war's fiercest battles. When the war ended, he came home to Boston and took up in the railway business. He drove his first railway car in 1868 for the Middlesex Railroad Company, from Boston up to Malden, and later joined the Metropolitan and the South Boston companies, before Whitney's West End merger swallowed them up. When the day arrived for Boston to unveil its subway, he was a natural choice to man the first trip. He knew his job so well that he would entertain his passengers with a joke or by telling them exactly how many railroad ties there are in a mile.

. . .

WHEN JIMMY REED WALKED INTO the Allston shed, looking nattier than usual in a new, trim-fitting uniform, a single-breasted dark blue coat with seven gold buttons, and a cap with a straight visor and two bands of gold, he greeted his passengers and confessed with no hesitation that he was tired after a night of restless sleep. Dreams of his trolley rushing to reach the subway tunnel first and on time kept him awake, he said.

One of the last passengers to arrive was the chief inspector for the West End Street Railway Company, Fred Stearns, who took up a spot on the car's footboard so that he could warn boarding passengers to keep their hands and heads inside to avoid bumping any posts or trees. After one final inspection to make sure the car was ready, the doors to the garage opened and the passengers let out a hearty cheer as the electric motor sent the Allston trolley on its way. The nine rows of benches were not filled yet, but they would be soon enough. Outside, a small group of onlookers waved their handkerchiefs and shouted out words of encouragement at the popular motorman. "Get there, Jim, old man, and don't let any of 'em get ahead of you," one cry went out.

Reed smiled. But he turned serious as his car rounded a bend, and he braked to a stop to allow another dozen passengers on board. "All aboard for the subway and Park Street," he shouted with confidence. A voice shouted back at him, "That's right, Jim, you did that without a stutter!"

"Dling, dling, dling," the bell rang out, and the car pulled away again. The journey from Allston through Cambridge to Boston took about twenty minutes most mornings, but the unusual number of passengers at this hour delayed it a few extra seconds at each stop. By the time the car reached Pearl Street in Cambridge, just across the Charles River from Boston, an older gentleman wanting to get on board found there were no seats left, and he was told he'd have to wait for the next car. Not a chance, he shouted back.

He announced that his name was C. W. Davis, that he came all the way down from Dickerson Street in Somerville to enjoy this privilege, and that he deserved to make history with the rest of them. He said that back in 1856 he had ridden on the first horse-pulled car of the Metropolitan Railway line and that he wanted to achieve another first today. "The running schedule called for a car every half hour in those days," he told his audience. "And that was thought to be fast running. People have learned to live and move faster in these days." The passengers on board could not refuse the charming Mr. Davis, and they scurried to clear a space for him as he climbed up and hung on to an upright pole. When a photographer hollered at Reed to let the historic trolley sit for a minute at Pearl Street so he could photograph it, the motorman refused, too nervous about falling behind schedule.

As the car got closer to Boston, the crowds along the street grew in numbers, with men, women, and children waiting and waving their hands high. Flower bouquets that Reed and Trufant had been handed were visible up front, but they were being crushed more with each stop. The car by now was brimming over its edges, with passengers standing on the footboard and dangling off the side and limbs visible out of the windows despite the pleas of Stearns to keep all parts inside. As Reed steered his car down Boylston Street, both sides of the street were lined with a sea of people and the roar became louder. Up ahead, he could barely make out the entrance to the tunnel, a black hole surrounded by a sea of people dressed in black.

At the final stop before the tunnel entrance on Boylston between Arlington Street and Charles Street, when it seemed there was not a single inch of room left inside, two more people reached up from the sidewalk and grabbed hold of an arm that was being held on to by another arm, and they were pulled on board and swallowed up by the excitable mass.

"The spaces between the seats were filled with standees," *The Boston Evening Record* wrote of the car, "the platforms were packed like sardine boxes. Each running board was two deep with humanity, while both fenders were loaded down until there was not enough room for a fly to cling!" A car with seats for forty-five passengers and standing room for a few dozen more had 140 passengers. With Reed at the controls, the Public Garden on his left, and the clock on the Arlington Street church pointing at six o'clock, car number 1752 crept to the summit of the subway tunnel's downward slope.

. . .

IF THERE WAS A TIME to stop and acknowledge the moment, this was it. Perhaps a speech from Mayor Quincy was in order, or from the ex-mayor Matthews, or Henry Whitney, or Governor Wolcott, or the chief engineer, Carson—anybody who had a hand in bringing America's first subway, an electric subway, to this day. Not only was it completed on time, in two and a half years, it came in at $4.2 million, under the $5 million projected cost. Along with the ten killed in the gas explosion, four others died in the building of the subway, and it was constructed without as much disruption to the streets as had been anticipated.

Municipal governments (as New Yorkers would surely agree) at the time were notorious for being small-minded, underachieving bureaucracies too easily intimidated by business interests and susceptible to corruption. Boston had defied all of those labels and even managed to preserve the one piece of land its people cherished the most, Boston Common. The uncovering of 910 bodies in the path of the subway route was an unfortunate finding, but Dr. Green's delicate handling of it had mitigated the public's worries. The subway was a success by every measure before it even opened. And as small flags waved amid the deafening cheers, the crowd almost seemed to be clamoring for someone to stop and recognize the achievement.

It had been ten years since two men, Henry Whitney in Boston and Abram Hewitt in New York, first made serious overtures about tunneling beneath their cities. A decade later, one of those cities stood at the brink of history while the other had yet to put a shovel into the ground. For Boston, that was satisfaction enough. By now Reed's car was so crowded it seemed in danger of tipping over, and it was difficult to imagine the electric motor having enough power to move it. Trufant pulled on his strap signaling that he was ready, Reed clanged his gong and switched on the electric current, and Allston car number 1752 eased forward, crested the hill, dipped down the incline, and disappeared beneath Boylston Street. The passengers in the front seats stood up on their tiptoes and leaned forward, peering ahead to see what sights awaited them. And from the rear, a shout rang out. "Down in front!"

. . .

A "HORROR OF TUNNELS," is how one Chicago resident once described the idea of a subway. One Bostonian used more vivid terms, saying subways gave him a "buried-alive feeling." Even John "Honey Fitz" Fitzgerald, a member of the 1892 Massachusetts Rapid Transit Commission, came back from his trip overseas and described the noise of the London Underground like "the roaring of the ocean after a storm." But then along came Frank Sprague and Thomas Edison, and suddenly it was possible not only to use quiet, clean, and safe electric trolleys underground but also to light up those tunnels with bright-white electric lightbulbs. At the start of the nineteenth century, barges were still stacking up at the entrances of canal tunnels as their nervous crews argued over who would steer into the darkness first. By the middle of the century, the Thames Tunnel was complete and the London Underground was operating. Now, near the dawn of the twentieth century, public opinion in America had officially swayed. And when Jimmy Reed guided his trolley underground, any lingering fears were quashed for good.

"Oh, dear, isn't it delightful!"

"I thought it would be quite dark and gloomy looking."

"Oh, come, and let us ride around again."

"My, how white it is."

There were no screams of fear or groans of disgust or complaints of rank odors. Nobody was more impressed than old C. W. Davis, who found no comparison between the trip he took above ground in 1856 and this one forty years later. "What a difference there was in the ride this morning," he said the moment his journey from Somerville to Cambridge to Boston had ended. "Why you could not scare up as many people on a dozen trips as we had on that car when it reached the subway. And the cars! Think of a car that would hold comfortably about twenty persons, drawn by one horse, and not a fast one at that. None of the comforts of open cars then. The door was at the rear end and the driver was conductor as well."

The reviews were glowing. Only the draft blowing through the car elicited complaints. It was bright enough to read, with the white bulbs bouncing off the white enameled brick walls and combining with the sunlight that peeked down through the staircases and in through the overhead vents to make it feel like noon on a sunny day. It was dry enough to sit on the ground, thanks to automated electric pumps tied to the city sewers that took care of the water that leaked into the stations from the inclines at Arlington and Park streets. And the air was clean enough to take in one long deep breath and not notice any difference from above ground. It smelled no different than a crowded church or theater. That was aided by ventilating chambers and large, inconspicuous fans installed along the route.

The first car in moved slower than it might normally because of its overcrowding, and Reed took the curve smoothly beneath the corner of Boylston and Tremont streets. But it must have been a bizarre moment when, in a place that once housed thousands of coffins and where hundreds of human skeletons were found only a few years earlier, a passenger on board the first subway car, too joyous to contain himself, broke out in old Irish song. "O, Mister Captain, stop the ship! I want to get out and walk." Another voice hollered back in tune, "What's the matter with riding?" to which the first singer replied, "There are 19 elbows planted against my spine, there are two boys on my shoulders, and 14 feet on my pet corns. Do you blame me?" Laughter broke out on the car as it pulled into the Boylston Street station.

Reed was thankful to see only a few people waiting for him, and they agreed to wait for the next car. He pulled away, with cheers filling the tunnel, and at 6:06 A.M., car number 1752 arrived at the Park Street station, its first voyage complete. More than three hundred were standing and waiting, hats waving in the air. "Bravo, bravo," the cries rang out. "Bravissimo," a group of dark-skinned Italians hooted. But when another man hollered out, "Three cheers for the subway!" in an attempt to start a hip-hip-hooray chant, he found himself shouting all by himself, the crowd too distracted to join him.

Half of the passengers disembarked and quickly filed through the turnstile that led them up to the street again. But the other passengers were too excited to get off, and they remained on board as the car took on more passengers, turned around in the loop, and headed back for Arlington Street. Those who boarded at Park Street were the ones who had purchased the day's first tickets, with numbers like 000002 and 000240, which they no doubt kept as souvenirs.

Inevitably, there were some who simply found the bustle too much to take. "Damn me if I'll go through this again," one red-faced man blurted out after squeezing off his train and onto the Park Street platform. "I'll take my regular train the next time," gasped another. But they were outnumbered. When a young woman hopped off her train smiling, she could not hide her surprise at the whole experience. "I thought it would be cold, damp and dingy," she said. "But it is so bright and the air seems so pure."

Women like her were thought to be the hardest customers to please. They had complained that the subway cars should have settees on them for more comfortable seating after they'd had a long day of shopping. That complaint was all but forgotten on the first rides of the day as women carried on board their babies and their bundles, and their amazement at the tunnel seemed to make them dismiss their worries about their sore bottoms. They were even more enthusiastic than the men, holding their breath in anticipation and letting loose with an "Oh, dear" followed by "Oh, my."

They were especially admiring of the subway employees. "Such nice looking men," was a comment heard often in those first few hours, directed at the manly-looking West End workers in their crisp new blue and gold uniforms. Some women suspected they were a handpicked lot of the most handsome men employed by the West End company, to distract their focus away from the tunnel. As for the children, the subway took some getting used to. The crush of people, the strangeness of the underground, it was too much for the littlest ones at first, and in the early hours and days of the subway, they could be heard wailing whenever the car they were on started moving.

Car number 1752 was not alone in the tunnel for long. It was followed quickly by a second car, 1743, also from Allston; a third, 2534, from Cypress Street in Brookline; and soon a string of them, one after another, each one stuffed beyond capacity with passengers hanging off the sides and crammed into the rows of seats, cheering and waving like caged wild animals. Of the dignitaries in town, the earliest to ride through the subway was Sam Little, the president of the West End railway, who arrived at seven o'clock, an hour after the opening.

Within four hours, the typical trip from the entrance at the Public Garden by Arlington Street up to the Boylston Street station, around the corner, and to the end at the Park Street stop was taking between three and four minutes, depending on the volume of passengers or the timid nature of the motorman at the car's controls. That same trip on a typical weekday on the surface of Tremont and Boylston streets took at least ten minutes and sometimes longer, with cars sometimes sitting perfectly still for two or three minutes at a time while they waited for the one ahead of them to inch forward.

Even more impressive than the speed at which the subway cars moved was the rapid, machinelike manner in which passengers were able to board and exit the cars. Only seconds passed from the time that a car pulled into Park Street, unloaded its passengers, and took on a new group for the return trip to Arlington Street. It was a most unusual sight to see for anyone who had grown accustomed to the painstaking surface experience of loading and unloading. A hundred and twenty cars an hour pulled out of Park Street during the first day of operation, a shocking number.

Only one of them did not make it out unscathed. The tunnel was barely four hours old when it was the scene of the first subway accident in America. At 10:20 in the morning, car number 2022, bound for Jamaica Plain and marked with the sign HUNTINGTON AVE. CROSS-TOWN was emerging from the tunnel at the Public Garden when its roof nicked the crossbeam at the end of the covered portion. The motorman stopped the car immediately and joined his conductor in a quick climb on top of the car, where they assessed the damage, hopped back down, and had their trolley moving again in minutes.

THOUGH PUBLIC OFFICIALS DID NOT deem the day worthy of a special event, the city's biggest paper certainly did. Within a few hours of the first trip underground, paper boys were hawking *The Globe*'s special edition on the streets. FIRST CAR OFF THE EARTH! the headline blared. ALLSTON ELECTRIC GOES INTO THE SUBWAY ON SCHEDULE TIME.

"Out of the sunlight of the morning into the white light of the subway rolled the first regular passenger-carrying car at 6:01," the paper wrote. "The car was from Allston and it approached the immense yawn in the earth by way of Pearl St Cambridgeport and the Harvard bridge." In colorful language, the paper described how Reed's trolley car "hissed along like a brood of vipers."

Of all the new habits passengers had to get used to with their subway, there were two that caused great consternation from the very first trip through the stations. At the stairways, to control the flow of traffic out of the stations and back to the streets, eight-foot-tall wooden turnstiles were installed. Above each one, a sign read, LOITERING ON THIS STAIRWAY PROHIBITED, to prevent the platforms from becoming a place where people on the street came for shelter from rain or snow or the homeless came to loaf, panhandle, or sleep.

The turnstile was a new contraption for the times, and they were immediately deemed everything from an "irredeemable nuisance" to "clumsy, complicated things." People getting off their trains would stand and stare at the turnstile, unsure how to navigate it and wanting to see others go first or receive assistance from the handsome West End workers. Couples got scared at the thought of being separated even for an instant, and friends who insisted on going through together inevitably got jammed or bumped in the face or the rear by the swinging bar. Little old ladies cringed and closed their eyes as they passed through while men carrying baskets filled with groceries caught glares from those behind them as it took them an extra few seconds. The heavyset crowd especially loathed the turnstiles, as they found it embarrassing to squeeze through the turnstiles and draw attention to their girth. When one exceptionally overweight gentleman got stuck, he required a shove from behind by an alert, if sheepish, West End employee. But as annoying as the turnstiles were, they were effective. Sixty passengers could melt through the turnstile in sixty seconds if prodded. And they usually were.

The other source of immediate complaining was the ticketing system. Sam Little wanted the ticketing process for his West End company to be handled on the streets, in kiosks at the top of the stairs, rather than at the bottom inside the stations. But an old concern reared up again at that request—marring the appearance of Boston Common with ugly architecture. And so the battle was lost and the ticketing was handled underground. Passengers who came down the stairs had no choice but to stand in line and wait to be next up to the window to purchase a ticket for a nickel. Even though Park Street was equipped with four ticket offices, each with a roll of tickets to sell, the workers could not keep up with demand, as most people came in to purchase tickets for a ride, but plenty more simply wanted a ticket to keep as a souvenir and never used it. By 11:15 A.M., one office had sold 2,500 tickets, another 2,100, the third 1,500, and the last 1,250. As the day proved, a slow ticket agent was disastrous, since the time it took to count out the correct change and hand over a ticket caused lines to grow, passengers to fret, and the boarding system to grind to a standstill.

"Why can't the conductors take cash fares on the cars as before," one gentleman standing in line was heard saying on the morning of the first day.

A nearby West End worker heard the gripe and came over with his answer. He explained that the ticketing space was meant to keep people out of the subway who had no intention of riding and to allow the conductors to collect all the fares before the car leaves rather than try to hunt down passengers on board. Because the cars were moving much faster now, conductors would miss collecting fares from passengers before they exited. But those answers were not sufficient for one man, who suggested bluntly that if this were another certain city, the people would not stand for such foolishness.

"It's a shame to have such incompetents doing such work," the complainer muttered. "Of course they're new, but that's no reason patrons should be made to put up with such annoyance . . . You can just bet they would stand no such nuisance in New York. They have men there who know . . ." His voice stopped without warning as he looked out toward the tracks. "There's my car!" he hollered without finishing his thought, and off he dashed excitedly.

WHILE THE SUBWAY'S FIRST DAY progressed smoothly underground, the real measure of its success was on the streets. The transformation on the morning of September 1 was astounding. Tremont Street looked deserted, with greater distances separating the cars than had been seen in years, or at least since motormen went on a brief strike over Christmas the previous year. Standing at the corner of Boylston and Tremont streets, looking in both directions, it was sometimes two or three minutes before a single car would pass. Only one week earlier, fifty cars might have passed in the same period. Pedestrians didn't quite know what to make of this empty feeling, and some of them stood on the sidewalk, by force of habit, waiting for the crush of cars to come, only to realize how foolish they looked and to finally cross the empty street at a leisurely pace they hadn't tried for years. As they looked out at the streets, pedestrians began to wonder when the annoying tracks along Tremont and Boylston could be ripped out so the streets could become more friendly to cross. It would not be long.

On the concrete plaza at the corner of Park Street and Tremont, across from the Park Street Church, long lines formed outside the two stairway buildings leading down to the tracks. The buildings for the staircases, and there were eight of them now on Boston Common, were modeled after the subway buildings in Budapest, fortress-like with granite walls, white enameled brick, and glass and copper roofs. Including the staircase, each building cost $11,000. The crowd outside the stairways was overwhelmingly men, as they mingled in their bowler hats and dark suits. The women stood out because of the umbrellas they carried to shield them from the sunlight.

Because of how overcrowded the cars were on the first day, tracking how many people actually rode the subway on September 1 was impossible. But it was estimated that between 200,000 and 250,000 made the trip, and, in the words of *The Globe*, "Nearly everything went as smooth as the proverbial clockwork, and the opinion heard on all sides was that, as far as it goes, the subway is an unqualified success."

IT TOOK FOUR HOURS for the first delay to register a complaint. The transit commissioner, Horace G. Allen, a mutton-chopped man with wavy dark hair and wire-rimmed spectacles, wandered down into the Park Street station at 10:30 and announced how pleased he was at the morning, especially the lack of any injuries. "If a woman should fall," he said, "or somebody get thrown by a sudden start there would be a chorus of, 'Subway! I told you so!'" His smile disappeared, however, when he noticed passengers waiting on the platform and no car in sight. They had only been there for one minute, but for Allen that was too long. He wanted perfection, which is why he had even hired janitors, all of them black men attired in sharp white uniforms, to comb the stations and tracks with dustpans and brooms to keep things looking spotless for as long as possible. Allen asked for emergency rooms to be built into the first few stations, so that a sick or injured passenger could be tended to without hesitation in a room supplied with a cot, chair, table, and electric heater.

The longer that Allen saw passengers waiting, the more he fretted. He wanted their first trips to be memorable, so they would be sure and come back again and again. "Hmmm," he murmured out loud, "I wonder what's the trouble. There should be more cars along."

But before he could inquire, the rumbling of a car was heard and then a second and a third, and all three came into the station at the same time, discharged their loads, and carried off the next crowd. Relieved, Allen himself decided to join them. "I think Boston is going to like it and like it a great deal," he said smiling, as he stepped on board his subway car. "It will surprise them. Most people imagined that the subway was going to be a close hole in the ground. The sunlight and gas light, the white walls, general cleanliness and the facilities for handling any crowd will surprise and please them." And with that he vanished into the darkness of America's first subway tunnel.

14

THE BRAINS, THE BUILDER, AND THE BANKER

IT WAS TITLED "REPORT ON RAPID TRANSIT in Foreign Cities." And befitting its author, its sixty-six typed pages were crammed full of meticulous details, drawings, photographs, and charts. When William Parsons delivered it to his commissioners on November 20, 1894, two weeks after New Yorkers had voted in favor of a subway, it immediately became the research paper that would shape the course of New York's transit efforts for the next decade. From each city he'd visited, he drew lessons about the best methods for digging beneath a city's streets, for ventilating subway cars and tunnels of stale air, and for where to best place the doors on a subway car.

Of London, Parsons wrote about both the Metropolitan line, which was the first tunnel dug back in the early 1860s and was still using steam locomotives, and the City and South London Railway, which opened in 1890 and was dug using a different tunneling method and powered with electric trains. The steam locomotives used a high-quality coal that was free of foul-smelling sulfur and produced little smoke. And Metropolitan engineers were told to not push their engines too hard in the tunnels. But Parsons called the efforts a waste. "In spite of these precautions, however, the air in the tunnel is extremely offensive," he wrote. The City and South London line, on the other hand, impressed him greatly. "Inasmuch as the motors are electric, and the only fouling of the air is that due to the passengers, the amount [of air] required to be changed per minute is small," he wrote. "The air in the stations is quite fair, although susceptible of further improvement." However, there were other flaws. He described the cars as "small, badly ventilated and lighted, hard riding and noisy," defects he blamed on the construction. With a diameter of only ten feet, two inches, the tunnels were too narrow and small, forcing the use of small, four-car trains that could seat ninety-six passengers and move at an average speed of thirteen miles per hour. Building bigger tunnels lined with brick or concrete would make for a quieter, more comfortable ride, he said. He was especially excited about the reliability of the electric trains. He noted that the average repair cost per mile of one of London's electric trains was one and a half cents, whereas the Manhattan Elevated Railway was paying more than three cents per mile to repair its steam locomotives.

As advanced as London was, Glasgow proved to be more interesting and enlightening for Parsons. Glasgow already had one subway operating and two more under construction when he visited. The tunnel was plenty big, twenty-six feet in diameter, and it was dug through solid rock, shale, clay, sand, and mud. Because of how varied he knew the ground to be under New York's streets, the Glasgow tunnel was especially interesting to him. Some portions were tunneled while others were dug as a trench through the street, which is how he suspected New York's subway might be built. And one of the most important nuggets he took away from his trip was that it cost roughly eight times more to tunnel using a shield than it did to dig a trench in the street and cover it over. He praised Glasgow's engineers by noting that the only places where there appeared to be some settling of the street surface was where the subway was built, and no place else, meaning they had successfully secured the areas on the edges of the tunnel. But he seemed less pleased with their decision to light the trains using electricity yet to power them using cables. Parsons was coming to believe that cable streetcars were yesterday's technology.

In Paris, which was only just beginning to build its tunnel, he summarized conversations he had with their engineers and seemed energized by what they told him. Use masonry instead of iron, they explained.

Avoid using any special stones that might prove difficult to cut. Remove by train the enormous amounts of dirt and rocks that are dug up, instead of putting the materials on carriages to be pulled through the streets. That will only worsen congestion. And last, dig the tunnel as close as possible to the surface. Every inch you go down, they told him, the cost rises significantly.

Toward the end of his lengthy report, Parsons devoted space to two American examples that he said possessed "decidedly novel features." One was the elevated Intramural Railway that ran on electricity during the Chicago World's Fair. The other was the Baltimore Belt Railroad, which was built to allow passenger and freight trains to pass between New York and Washington through Baltimore without disruption. A tunnel beneath Baltimore's busiest thoroughfare, Howard Street, impressed Parsons, who wrote about the ease with which the trains passed through the hilly tunnel with engines built by the General Electric Company: "These motors are designed to attain a speed of fifty miles per hour, and do everything that a steam locomotive can do. These machines are far beyond anything before attempted in the electrical line, and will put it, as far as power is concerned, on the same footing with steam."

Where to place the doors on a subway car was a question that especially intrigued Parsons and also confused him. It was one of those details a less meticulous engineer might overlook, but for him it was essential to the passenger experience, and in every city he visited he saw that there was no consistent answer. In Berlin and in London, where side doors were in use on some lines, stops averaged between thirty and fifty-five seconds. On the elevated Liverpool line, side doors resulted in twenty-second stops, while the end doors on the City and South London line made for fourteen-second stops. He recommended end doors in his report, believing they allowed passengers to step on and off faster. "This is due largely to the confusion resulting from compartments, classes and many doors," he wrote. "Passengers run along platforms looking for good seats, while with the end door arrangement they enter the car at once and distribute afterwards."

His section on the doors was one of the few places were Parsons inserted a touch of humor into his report, even if it was unintentional. He explained how stops in New York were unusually fast, from a speedy four seconds to thirty depending on the time of day. Because they were so quick, he did not bother comparing them to the European cities, where it seemed passengers were less hurried to get on their way. He blamed (or credited?) the fast stops in New York on "the nervous and active temperament of the people." New Yorkers? A "nervous and active temperament"? Imagine that.

PARSONS WAITED UNTIL THE FINAL section of his report to tackle the one issue that was most responsible for the thirty years that passed between London's inaugural subway in 1863 and another city following its lead. "There is a wide-spread popular idea," he wrote, "that electricity has some mysterious properties which render vastly superior and more economical than steam as a motive power." He called that thinking "fallacious in the extreme." He went on to explain that while there was no debating that an electric subway would be cleaner than a steam-powered subway, it was important to look at the costs of the two. In great detail, he explained how coal was required for both, with one critical difference. The coal in a steam-powered train was needed on the train itself, where it was burned in its own boiler in the locomotive to help convert water into steam that powered the cylinder and piston rods that made the wheels turn. It was an entirely self-contained process. Not so with an electric train.

For an electric railroad, coal was still required, but it was used in a stationary boiler at a central location, where engines drove dynamos that created the electricity. Only when that electricity was conducted from the powerhouse miles away through the railway tracks and into the trains and the motors converted it back into power did the wheels of the electric train turn. Although both systems required coal, they could use a different type of coal, and that, Parsons explained, was a point that could not be ignored. "On [steam] locomotives it is necessary to carry the best quality of coal," he wrote, and it had to be lump size, not a powder, or else it would sift right through the grate bars of the boiler. "Coal of that quality commands an extra price. Under stationary boilers, however, the grate bars can be adapted to burn the cheap fine coal of an inferior quality."

That Parsons had gone so far as to study what grade of coal might make the difference for a New York subway showed just how deeply he cared about the project. In the end, on the subject of how the subway should be powered, he wrote plainly that "the balance of economy is in favor of electricity."

It was one of the most boring and, at the same time, most important sentences in his entire sixty-six-page report. But in reaching his conclusion, Parsons was not alone.

William Whitney had finally come around as well. With Chicago embracing electricity to power its trains in the early 1890s; London expanding its Underground; Glasgow, Budapest, and Paris all moving forward with subway tunnels; and even Whitney's brother, Henry, electrifying Boston's streetcars in the late 1880s, New York found itself in the strange position of falling behind other cities as the century came to a close. The Metropolitan Street Railway Company's horse-pulled carriages were old and slow, expansion of the city's elevated lines had been abandoned, and the flaws in the cable lines on Columbus and Lexington avenues were too many to count, from the snapped lines to the cost of maintenance to the congestion they continued to cause on the streets.

When city leaders ruled in 1893 that any future wires would have to be placed underground instead of overhead, Whitney grew desperate. He offered a $50,000 prize to anyone, presumably an engineer, who could show him a way to successfully place wires underground to power his trolleys. And when no one came forward, he wrote to his brother, Henry, in Boston. William hoped that Henry might have a recommendation for an engineer, and as it so happened he did. Henry wrote back to William that Fred Pearson, still only thirty-three years old, was as brilliant as any man and that William should grab him without hesitation. Will Whitney did hire the former Tufts University prodigy, first as a consultant and then as the chief engineer of the Metropolitan Street Railway Company. New York was a huge job that would earn Pearson a salary of $75,000, a long way from the $2,500 that Henry Whitney paid him back in 1888 to be chief engineer of the West End Street Railway Company.

Fifteen years had passed since their father died and the Whitney brothers went their separate ways. One of them used real estate to earn his fortune while the other married into money before finding success through politics and deal making. But eventually both men found themselves as the streetcar kings of Boston and New York, and their shared use of Fred Pearson was an unusual moment when their business interests and their brotherhood aligned. Over the course of the next decade, with Pearson's guidance, New York would gradually eliminate its cable and horse-pulled lines and see more than a hundred miles of streetcar tracks electrified, including some crosstown streets and nearly all of its long and straight north-south boulevards.

THE SUBWAY ROUTE THAT WAS mapped out by the 1894 transit commission mirrored the one passed by Steinway's 1891 commission, with one route up the east side from Union Square under Park Avenue to the Bronx and a second from South Ferry all the way up Broadway. But there was a wrinkle this time. The 1894 act insisted that the subway cost less than $50 million, and in an effort to save wherever possible the commissioners tweaked their plan in such a way that they hoped to trim $2 million without raising any opposition. They should have known better. That change proposed building cheaper elevated tracks instead of a subway tunnel on a one-mile, mostly vacant stretch between 92nd Street and 112th Street. Though virtually nobody lived in those twenty-two blocks on the Upper West Side, it was valuable land, with 320 individual plots worth between $20,000 and $50,000.

On March 12, 1895, fifty angry developers stampeded into a meeting of the Rapid Transit Commission. Leading the charge was a financier named Francis M. Jencks, who years earlier had joined with William Whitney and others in forming the New York Loan and Improvement Company to develop land on Manhattan's Upper West Side and Washington Heights neighborhoods. Jencks estimated that an elevated line up the west side would reduce the properties there in value by at least five thousand dollars, an enormous sum, and that instead of the land developing into hotels and restaurants and shops and beautiful homes, it would be used for nothing more than five-story flats and tenement housing.

"I feel that an elevated railroad would be ruinous to this property," he said. "The entire West Side from 72nd Street to the Columbia College property is one of the most important and beautiful residential neighborhoods in New York. The city expended millions of dollars in laying out Riverside Park and other places, and the only way for the city to justify this outlay is to preserve the character of the district." The president of the Chamber of Commerce, Alexander E. Orr, seemed interested in hearing Jencks, even if he was frustrated at the lateness of the argument.

"What character of construction other than a viaduct would you advise?" Orr asked.

"Either a tunnel or a depressed road," Jencks answered.

"You have spoken as a property owner," Orr countered. "As a citizen which would you prefer?"

"Why, an elevated road, which has more air, more light," Jencks said. "But as I understand, this viaduct is for but one mile and to save expense."

So strongly did Jencks feel that, a few minutes later, when Jencks was questioned by another commission member, Seth Low, he said that the property owners would be satisfied with no change at all to the transportation in their future neighborhood.

"How do you feel between no road and the road proposed?" Low asked Jencks.

"We would much prefer to see no road built," Jencks replied. His answer prompted loud applause from the other speculators in the room.

One week later, the Rapid Transit Commission emerged from another closed-door session prepared to issue a decision. Parsons was there. Steinway, hoping for redemption after his 1891 commission had failed, was there, too. And so were the angry developers. When the commissioner John Inman said, "I am prepared to act understandingly and to vote for an underground system," cheers erupted from the property owners. When other commissioners echoed Inman, the cheers grew louder. The developers had won. There would be no elevated tracks on the west side.

Even though the argument over those twenty blocks was resolved quickly, the timing of the dispute stalled the momentum of the subway project. By the time Mayor William L. Strong and the Board of Aldermen approved the transit commission's new plan, it was too late.

AS IT TURNED OUT, the property owners along the northern portion of the Manhattan route were not the only ones with strong opinions. Just as merchants in Boston along Tremont Street feared that construction of a subway would keep shoppers away during the digging, the same concern surfaced in downtown New York. The difference was that New York's property owners, unlike Boston's, had real powers to act. Each one had a vote, and the more valuable their property, the more weight their tally was given.

When they rejected the Rapid Transit Commission's new plan, the commissioners desperately turned to the New York Supreme Court to step in once and for all and clear the way for construction to begin. It was not to be. Though a three-man panel appointed by the court did approve the subway, it carried no authority. The final approval was needed by the appellate division of the Supreme Court. In a ruling issued on May 22, 1896, the presiding justice, Charles H. Van Brunt, scoffed at the plan, almost ridiculing it, especially the estimated cost of $30 million.

Van Brunt said that he failed to understand how the projected cost was not scrutinized more closely, and he took great pleasure in quoting from the Bible, a passage from Luke 14:28, to make his point. "More than 1,800 years ago," Van Brunt began, "it was said: 'For which of you, intending to build a tower, sitteth not down first and counteth the cost, whether he have sufficient to finish it.'" He was only warming up. "If there is a probability that financial difficulties will be met and the construction of this road will drag its weary length along for a time which no man can compute, and possibly its construction be absolutely abandoned because of the wreck of the city's finances, and the intervention of Constitutional prohibitions, it is manifest that great injury will result to the property of abutting owners for which they can never be compensated." He blamed the transit commission for having too much power and said that it could single-handedly destroy the financial credit of New York City. "The motion should be denied," he said. It was.

It was a crushing blow.

"IT MEANS THE END," the transit commission president, Alexander Orr, said bluntly. Eight years after Mayor Abram Hewitt first laid out his vision for how to pay for and build a subway, eighteen months after the citizens of New York had finally voted in favor of a subway, and one year after the transit commission approved a detailed route and plan, it was as if none of those events had ever happened. History was wiped clean, and New York was back at the starting line.

Nobody was more devastated at falling behind other cities in engineering breakthroughs than the engineer who had devoted the last ten years of his life to trying to build a subway for New York. When a reporter for *The New York Times* knocked on William Parsons's door at 51 East Fifty-third Street, he emerged grim and clearly in shock.

"You must excuse me," he said, "from making any comment about the decision of the court. The decision was a surprise—a complete surprise—and well, I do not wish to criticize the conclusion of the judges. I—none of us—know now where we are at. We may find out tomorrow. In the meantime I do not wish to say anything about the matter." But before he could turn and step back inside, the reporter asked him one question. "Will the work of the commission and the expense it involved all go for naught?"

It was the question Parsons had to be asking himself. "Yes, probably it will. But I cannot say positively. As I said, we are all at sea, and I would rather not say anything more on the subject tonight." With that, he disappeared, no doubt to wonder what his future held. Despite all the talk about progress, in 1896 New York's streets were still stuck in the past. The dreams of Alfred Beach, who had died on January 1 of that year, seemed so distant. There were thirty-eight miles of cable road, less than four miles of electric road, and the remaining terrain, hundreds of miles in and around New York, was still covered by horses and elevated trains. The subway remained elusive.

And when *The New York Times* ran a front-page story a few months later, announcing BOSTON'S SUBWAY FINISHED, it had to gall the competitive Parsons. It certainly seemed to gall *The Times*. The article carried a jealous tone, calling the project "exceedingly expensive" but difficult as well. It was the last line of the article that seemed particularly petty: "It is therefore not unlikely that within a couple of years Boston need not be ashamed of her transit facilities."

Parsons wondered if a subway for New York was not meant to be, and he began to explore new opportunities for himself. "We have the worst transit problem in the world," he said to a fellow engineer one day. "Are we to be the last to act?" It seemed that way.

IF ANYONE HAD MORE EMOTION invested in New York's subway than Parsons, it was the broad-shouldered piano manufacturer who came to America from Germany to start a new life half a century before. William Steinway was sixty-one. His health was declining and his battles with gout often left him bedridden. His longtime wife had recently died. And the transit commission that had been named in his honor in 1891 had failed in its attempt to get a subway passed. The 1894 commission was supposed to be his second chance, but now it, too, had failed. Steinway, in his final act, set out to make sure that the beauty of New York, something he cherished as dearly as the elegant curves on one of his grand pianos, was not ruined by the court's ruling and by the construction of more enormous concrete pillars and ugly elevated tracks.

TOGETHER STEINWAY AND PARSONS drafted a new plan for a subway, both men determined to finish what they had started. They mapped out a route that covered enough of the island to satisfy enough of its citizens, yet steered clear of spots where opposition to a subway was the most vocal or where construction would be most troublesome and thus expensive because of the makeup of the ground beneath the surface.

Wall Street was avoided. So was the Upper East Side and the stretch of Sixth Avenue between Tenth Street and Twenty-third Street. It was known as Ladies' Mile. Private carriages would line up three and four deep off the curb so that the most elegant ladies of the Gilded Age could shop. President Cleveland's wife used to come up from Washington to join Flora Whitney to look for new dresses at Arnold Constable on Broadway at Nineteenth Street or nearby at Lord & Taylor or B. Altman. And when Boston's grand dame, Isabella Stewart Gardner, needed new diamonds, she waltzed into Tiffany's on Union Square. Those were the exact customers that the merchants feared losing during the construction of a subway, and for that reason the route Steinway and Parsons mapped out avoided Ladies' Mile entirely.

The route was shaped like the letter Y. The stem covered the lower east side, and the two branches were above Central Park. Subway trains would start by New York City Hall and travel north to Grand Central Terminal at Forty-second Street on the east side. But there, trains would cross to the west side beneath Forty-second to Longacre Square at Seventh Avenue, what is now Times Square. The tracks would then curve north beneath Broadway and go all the way up to Ninety-sixth Street, at which point two branches would emerge. One would continue under Broadway up into Harlem, Washington Heights, and eventually what would become the Bronx. The second line would cross back to the east side at the northern tip of Central Park and run up Lenox Avenue and across the Harlem River and all the way out to Bronx Park. Under the plan, the east side north of Forty-second Street and the west side south of Longacre Square would continue to be served by the elevated trains of the Manhattan Railway Company.

It was a limited, imperfect subway route aimed at getting a shovel into the ground as soon as possible and sacrificed reaching all parts of the city. Express trains could run all the way from City Hall to 135th Street on the west side in twenty minutes or less, Parsons predicted.

This one seemed all but certain to pass. It even won the approval of an important figure from Boston. When Howard Carson, the chief engineer of the Boston Rapid Transit Commission, was invited to a hearing in New York to see what Parsons was proposing, he first walked a portion of the route between the post office downtown and Grand Central Terminal. He then described Parsons's plans as meticulous and perfectly accurate, though slightly more expensive than what the actual cost would probably be. Carson singled out the amounts Parsons estimated to pay for steel and for rock excavation as being too high, but they were not criticisms, merely suggestions. "They are very similar to our Boston plans," Carson said. "And I cannot condemn our own plans. I consider Mr. Parsons' plans and estimates as thoroughly practicable and within just limits." Before he left, Carson tried to assure New Yorkers of the greatest fear Bostonians had about a subway. "The air in the subway will be purer than the air you have in your churches, your theaters, your schoolrooms," he said. "Of course, if you want ideal conditions you would have to make use of some appliances as fans, but this will not be necessary."

HAD THERE BEEN A New York subway operating on August 5, 1896, that claim by Carson would have been tested. Temperatures soared to eighty-five during the day. The following afternoon, the Rapid Transit Commission was to vote on the route Steinway and Parsons drafted. Steinway's gout was not bothering him too much on this night, and he was able to walk with little pain, though he was anxious about the meeting. To help cool himself down, he drank a glass of pilsner at ten thirty before going off to bed.

The following day, shortly after three o'clock in the afternoon, the commission approved the plan, with Parsons again in attendance and Steinway voting in favor. This time, not only did Mayor Strong and the Board of Aldermen voice their approval, but so did the necessary group of citizens and merchants and, finally, the appellate division of the Supreme Court. The justices even praised the commission for accurately estimating the cost, a far cry from the first time around.

Not even three months after he cast his final vote, with his legacy secure as both a piano manufacturer and, finally, as a transit pioneer, William Steinway, a frail sixty-one-year-old, died at his home on November 30, 1896. He did not live to see the subway open, but he lived to make sure that it would.

WILLIAM WHITNEY, ANOTHER MAN who had brought about great change for New York, did little to quash speculation with his repeated assertions that politics did not interest him. *The World* newspaper polled thirty editors in the state of New York and reported that twenty-six backed Whitney. While visiting his mother and his brother, Henry, in Brookline, Massachusetts, Whitney granted an interview to *The Globe* and left his intentions clear.

"I am not and will not be a presidential candidate," he said. And yet it appeared unavoidable. On the same page in which its interview with Whitney appeared, a small article ran at the bottom with a dateline of Chicago, where the Democratic National Convention was to be held. WHITNEY FOR THE CANDIDATE WHETHER HE WANTS IT OR NOT, read the headline. At the convention a month later, delegates were spotted wearing WHITNEY FOR PRESIDENT buttons. Whitney ignored it all and watched as McKinley, a former Republican governor from Ohio, defeated Nebraskan Democrat William Jennings Bryan.

THE FOLLOWING SUMMER, WILLIAM'S SON, Harry Payne Whitney, traded vows with young Gertrude Vanderbilt, the twenty-one-year-old daughter of Cornelius Vanderbilt II, putting in motion a blending of two of the most important families of the late nineteenth century. Over the years, William Whitney and Cornelius Vanderbilt had been more than neighbors. They had vacationed together in Newport, Rhode Island, at the Vanderbilt mansion, the Breakers; in Bar Harbor, Maine; and upstate New York. They had shared a love of the opera, attending hundreds of performances together. And they had, on occasion, seen their business interests align. Now their families were merging. With the combined wealth of their families, Gertrude Vanderbilt Whitney, a sculptor and art collector, went on to become one of America's greatest patrons of the arts.

BY THE TIME OF HIS son's wedding, Whitney was no longer a single man. In September 1896 he married for the second time. His bride, Edith S. Randolph, was the widow of a British soldier. Their engagement had been brief and caught his family and friends by surprise, and it especially angered the Payne family, who had long questioned whether Whitney had been faithful to Flora before her death. But Whitney, who was now fifty-five, had been lonely, and that was only reinforced as he watched Harry walk down the aisle.

His children were happy for him, but his own joy would not last. Not even two years into the marriage, the Whitneys boarded a private railroad car and headed south to their estate in Aiken, South Carolina. On a February morning while riding with friends, they were chasing after a deer when the group began to spread out. Some of the riders came upon a low rustic bridge that required anyone on a horse to bend sideways to pass beneath it. Edith, who was riding a horse taller than what she was used to, thought that she had bent low enough under the bridge, but she had not. Her head slammed with a sickening thud against the overpass, and she was thrown to the ground unconscious and bleeding from the head.

Her daughter Adelaide, stepdaughter Dorothy, and William all rushed to her. When they were eventually able to take her back to a hospital in New York, doctors were less concerned with her six-inch scalp wound than they were with her limp arms. They feared she had fractured her cervical vertebra. Whitney himself was paralyzed with grief at the thought of losing a second wife so quickly after his first, and though Edith regained consciousness a few days later her prognosis was grim. In a touching display, when she was ready to go home, still in a cast and with her head supported by a metal frame, Whitney arranged for a special carriage with deep springs to soften her trip. As Edith's carriage moved slowly over the cobblestone streets of the city, her husband walked beside it, resting his hand on the window of the vehicle while she lay prone in a cot, and cleared the streets of any obstacles that might cause her pain. She lingered for more than a year before dying at home in the spring of 1899. Whitney never fully recovered, growing grayer and frailer at a faster rate than before from that day forward.

THERE WAS ONE LAST QUESTION New York needed to answer in order to start digging. Who was going to step forward to build the subway? Anyone interested in bidding had to invest at least $7 million of his own money, a sum that ruled out a huge number of potential contractors. They had to not only build the twenty-one miles of subway and elevated tracks but also agree to operate the system, another hurdle for many contractors.

The Times projected that if the new route carried two hundred thousand passengers a day, as some estimated, and each person paid the five-cent fare, that would bring in $10,000 in revenue daily. That was enough, The Times wrote, to one day yield a net of about eight percent for whoever won the job. "The contract," The Times summarized, "offers an attractive profit."

But profit was not the appeal of a subway, as one of New York's most famous lawyers, Wheeler H. Peckham, learned during a visit to Boston in October 1897. Boston's subway had only been open for a month, but Peckham found it to be perfect in every sense. "I rode wherever the cars went," he told New York's transit commissioners upon his return home. "I entered the car on a street corner, going down a short stairway. I found everything charming and delightful. The method of transit was as admirable as can be imagined. The cars were well-lighted, airy and comfortable. There was no feeling of being underground or oppressed by bad or close air." When Peckham was asked about the speed of the trains, he said it seemed like they went about eight miles per hour, but they were capable of going twice that fast. "Would you object to going forty miles an hour?" he was asked. "No; if I have forty miles to go, I want to go as quickly as possible." The commissioners all laughed at his reply, relieved to hear that at least one New Yorker had emerged from his subway adventure unscathed and unafraid.

Peckham had been so eager to ride on a subway that he had beaten New York's transit commissioners up to Boston. But three weeks after his visit, the commissioners journeyed north to see it for themselves. Even though Boston only had three stations open and a short distance of tracks, Carson, Boston's chief engineer, told the commissioners the subway had taken one hundred trolley cars per hour off Tremont Street. He added that the method of construction, digging a trench, covering it over so traffic could continue, and then finishing the tunnel, had been done with little disruption on the surface. New York's commissioners left Boston impressed and more determined than ever to find the right man to build their own subway.

EVEN THE STEADY RAIN and soggy snow falling on the night of December 31, 1897, could not dampen the mood of raucous New Yorkers flooding into the brightly lit City Hall Park. Their city was in the midst of a cultural building boom; there was good reason it was a period that came to be called the gay nineties. New York was already calling itself America's capital of entertainment, a place where dozens of kinetoscope parlors showed Edison's movies and vaudeville shows were a nightly happening. In various stages of construction were the New York Public Library, the Metropolitan Museum of Art, the Brooklyn Museum, and Columbia University. The recovery from the 1893 recession was complete, and an era of decadence was in full swing. Even the subway project had been approved, and the final details about the financing were all but worked out. This particular New Year's Eve was truly the dawn of a new New York. Bands played, choruses sang, bells chimed, and a hundred-gun salute shattered the night air while ferries and tugs parked in the harbor blew their whistles. The big moment came during the singing of "Auld Lang Syne" when a blue and white flag unfurled atop City Hall, and, just like that, Brooklyn and Manhattan were no longer two giant cities on opposite sides of the East River. A decade after the New York Chamber of Commerce had first urged Manhattan to swallow up Brooklyn, it was done. The threat of another American metropolis like Chicago surpassing New York in size was vanquished. The boroughs of Brooklyn, Queens, Staten Island, the Bronx, and Manhattan were now one giant New York City.

A FEW WEEKS LATER, on a January evening in 1898, the USS battleship *Maine* steamed into Havana's harbor with all of her guns fully loaded. She was not alone. German warships lay nearby, and on shore Spanish soldiers kept a nervous eye on her from the rocky hilltops. America and Spain had an increasingly tense relationship over Spain's efforts to quash the Cubans' push for independence. With each day the *Maine* sat off Cuba's coast, the situation intensified, until shortly before ten o'clock in the evening on February 15, moments after a marine bugler had played taps on board. With no warning, the *Maine* exploded into the sky. A fireball lit up the night as she sank quickly into the harbor. Of the Americans on board, 266 were killed and 89 survived.

America was at war, and though not everyone understood precisely what was being fought over, New Yorkers got behind President McKinley. A military march down Fifth Avenue, with loud bands and gunfire salutes, was watched by hundreds of thousands of flag-waving New Yorkers. The newspapers of New York assisted the war effort by relaying messages on behalf of the military. And Teddy Roosevelt used the war to launch himself onto the national stage. He had served as New York police commissioner and had been named by McKinley as assistant secretary of the navy, but when war broke out, he resigned from the navy and took his mishmash band of Rough Riders to Havana to assist the army in the fighting. When the war ended, Roosevelt was elected governor of New York, and, after campaigning with McKinley in the 1900 election as his vice presidential nominee, he found himself as president when McKinley was assassinated. It was a stunning rise in less than five years for the nation's twenty-sixth president.

Though the Spanish-American War was won in only a few months, it tested the strength of the fleet of warships America rebuilt under William Whitney. It also distracted the one man who had been waiting for more than a decade to build New York a subway, William Parsons. He volunteered to serve in the First United States Volunteer Engineers and climbed to the rank of captain. And after that, he traveled with his family to China. He'd been hired to survey the land and map out a route for a new railway. It was a rare opportunity, one of the first times American capitalists were willing to risk a fortune on a project that was entirely on foreign land. But those capitalists had the money to gamble with. One of them was J. P. Morgan. And the other was August Belmont.

Before leaving, Parsons penned a seven-page letter to the Rapid Transit Commission's counsel, Edward M. Shepard. He explained that if the commission disbanded, he wanted to make sure his detailed studies were not handed over to city leaders, whom he did not trust. "Those plans are a part of myself," Parsons wrote to Shepard, "and I should like to keep them." If, on the chance the commission was able to get the approvals needed to move forward, Parsons assured Shepard he would "come home if so ordered." But he insisted that Shepard not give that order "unless absolutely necessary."

In the summer of 1899, while he was finishing his work in China, Parsons received an urgent cable. New York City's infrastructure was under a massive upheaval, and there were contractors hungry to work and millionaires opening their deep pockets to back the projects that would bring them the most riches. There was only one job left to usher New York into the new century, and the cable Parsons received told him it was time to come home and build it.

AS THE CENTURY CAME to a close, William Whitney remained as determined as ever to leave behind a legacy. For a man who had lost his father to a premature heart attack and a child to a sudden illness and who had been widowed not once but twice, Whitney had proved time and again that he was resilient in life and able to compartmentalize his per-

sonal sorrow from his professional work. He controlled nearly every lighting, heating, and power line under the streets of Manhattan and Brooklyn,
under a company called New York Gas and Electric Light. In building his
Metropolitan Street Railway Company into an all-powerful monopoly,
Whitney had never shown much interest in a subway. If anything, he
viewed a subway as a threat to his "empire on wheels."

But Whitney was also too smart to ignore reality. With a subway so
close at hand, he knew that his company was one of the few that had
the money and connections to pull it off. He offered to build the subway
within three years in exchange for 5 percent of the annual gross receipts
and permanent ownership of the lines. The man who had introduced the
free transfer system proposed a more complicated system now. Five-cent
fares for all local rides, ten-cent fares for express lines and free transfers
from the express lines to his streetcars, and three-cent transfers from the
local trains. His offer also came with the promise of thirty-mile-per-hour
speeds on the express trains below Forty-second Street. Last, with a dash
of arrogance, he demanded that his company pay no taxes on the subway
until its costs had been recouped.

It was a detailed plan, and the numbers would actually prove over the
ensuing decades to have been a favorable deal for New York City. But New
Yorkers hated it. There was little desire to be at the mercy of the Metropolitan Street Railway Company for the foreseeable future, and the plan
was roundly rejected. There was much greater comfort in a plan where
the city paid for the entire construction cost and awarded the contract to
the lowest bidder, who would be obligated to pay for the equipment, operate the system, and lease it all from the city for fifty years.

Whitney was disappointed and said that he was insulted at having his
integrity questioned. In a statement released by his company on April 17,
1899, he said the Metropolitan was withdrawing its interest in the subway
for good. "Mr. Whitney and his friends resent the imputation that they
are trying to grab something," the statement said. "Inasmuch as they have
been inspired largely by public spirit in taking up this gigantic project,
they feel that the present drift of public sentiment places them in a false
position. Therefore they determined to drop the whole thing at once."

The man who had ruled the street railways of New York through the 1890s seemed ready to accept that if a subway was going to be built, it would be without his involvement.

THE FIRST SNOWFALL OF THE season was accompanied by a cold snap down to sixteen degrees that froze the ponds in Central Park with two inches of ice, thick enough to walk on but not for skating. The streets were blanketed in white as the city rose for the first day of 1900, covering the signs of revelry from the night before that included battered tin horns, mountains of peanut shells, and random pieces of clothing that were curiously shed through the night and strewn everywhere.

Two weeks later, a day that Parsons had been anticipating for more than ten years and that some New Yorkers had been looking forward to for as many as fifty years arrived. The city, after weeks and months of speculation, was going to learn who would build New York a subway. Parsons anticipated half a dozen contractors to bid for the job, but as the hour grew near he lowered his expectations. Bidders had to submit a check of $150,000, which undoubtedly would keep many away. "Money is not so cheap now that people are willing to sacrifice the interest on such an amount as that even for a day," he said.

On Monday around eleven o'clock, January 15, 1900, the large meeting room of the Rapid Transit Commission began to fill up. Citizens from all over the city came to watch the opening of the envelopes, and by noon all the players were in place and the room was overflowing. Mayor Robert Van Wyck took a seat, and so did Parsons.

At noon, the commissioners announced that they had received two bids, which must have been a relief considering the embarrassment the commission faced the first time when not a single reliable bidder emerged. The commissioners sounded confident they would find a contractor from the two formal bids. "These bids," Alexander Orr said, "show that we were right. They are satisfactory. It is splendid vindication for Mr. Parsons."

The first bid opened had a $150,000 check from National Park Bank, as required, and a promise to submit $1 million in cash and securities. It laid out the subway project in four separate sections, with individual costs for each one. The total bid from the contractor named Andrew Onderdonk was for $39,300,000, but it included one curiosity that gave pause to the commissioners. He offered to share a percentage of his yearly profits above $5 million with the city. He was bidding above the $35 million figure Parsons had projected with the promise of a return on the city's investment. It was risky, considering that nobody knew if the subway would make money or how long it would take to become profitable.

Onderdonk's qualifications were never questioned when his name was announced. He was already working with the state on a dredging project in New York Harbor. Fifty years old, and a trim man with a bushy dark mustache, his first big project was to build up the harbor in San Francisco Bay. But he also came with experience in railroads, retaining walls, and, most important, tunneling, having built a four-mile water-supply tunnel under Lake Michigan in Chicago.

When asked about Onderdonk's profit-sharing offer, Parsons said he had little doubt that $5 million in revenue would be achieved when the subway opened. He said that the eight tracks of elevated trains in New York produced $10 million in revenue a year and that it seemed reasonable to expect four tracks of subway to produce at least half that. "Mr. Onderdonk's offer will therefore have to be carefully considered," Parsons said.

Onderdonk's only competitor was a jovial character who came with even greater experience and whose bid of $35 million was $4 million less. Also like Onderdonk, John McDonald came with a complication. And it made the commissioners very nervous about hiring him.

JOHN BART MCDONALD WAS fifty-six years old and short in stature with a bald, flat head; broad shoulders; a puffed-out chest; a softly curved mustache; and warm hazel eyes that contradicted his otherwise gruff appearance. When he shook hands with his strong grip, he identified himself as a man who had spent a lifetime in hard labor, which he had. He was born in County Cork, Ireland, on November 7, 1844, a year before the Irish potato famine leveled the country in starvation and disease. Like many parents, Bartholomew and Mary McDonald fled from the famine with their children. John was three when they came to New York and settled in the Bronx. His father, an independent contractor, taught his boy from a young age the value of combining politics and hard work, making a fortune in labor while also serving as a city alderman. His son tried college but wasn't interested, and he dropped out to partner with his father in work. He quickly showed himself to be skilled as both a laborer and a manager.

One of his first assignments, which he landed through his father, was a low-level timekeeping job at the Croton Dam. His first railroad job was rebuilding Cornelius Vanderbilt's New York Central Railroad's Fourth Avenue tracks up around Ninety-sixth Street. It was a job that gained him notoriety and led him on a busy path around North America, from New Jersey to Canada to Western Massachusetts to Buffalo to Philadelphia to Wisconsin to Illinois to West Virginia. He settled for a while in Baltimore to work on a long and complicated tunnel for the Baltimore & Ohio Railroad, and by the time he returned to New York with his wife, son, and daughter, he was no longer a run-of-the-mill contractor. He was enormously wealthy and successful, regularly golfing and yachting with friends, a man who enjoyed big meals, smooth drinks, and good cigars. He was known as a good boss who didn't blow budgets or miss deadlines. He also enjoyed good company, which is no doubt how he rose in power among Democrats and in the powerful world of Tammany Hall politics. As a native Irishman, McDonald bonded easily with the Irish-American politicians of New York, like the Tammany Hall leader Richard Croker, who got Van Wyck elected mayor and who preferred a city where business was done with a wink and a handshake rather than a lengthy bidding process for every little job.

But that night, when he was found by reporters imbibing at the Hoffman House, one of New York's oldest hotels, McDonald was nothing short of arrogant in believing that he, not Onderdonk, was the man for the job. "I expect to get the contract," he said. "I have made arrangements for the necessary bonds and I can have the work started inside of thirty days from now if the commission promptly awards the contract." McDonald overlooked one detail in his assumption. His bid was certainly the lowest. And he was unquestionably qualified to build the subway. But while he was a wealthy man, he was not nearly rich enough to afford the $7 million the commission required of the winning contractor. Unless he could raise the money, he would never be allowed to put a shovel in the ground. And considering that Onderdonk was in no better financial position than McDonald, once again New York's subway was in peril.

Not surprisingly, given such an enormous issue, rumors started to fly the moment the bids were unveiled. There was talk that Onderdonk had approached McDonald in the days before submitting their bids and asked him to team up and submit one bid together and that McDonald replied that he preferred to go it alone. There was also gossip that after the subway was built it would be turned over to the powerful Metropolitan Street Railway Company, so that it could have total control over the streets and the subways and provide more seamless rides for passengers transferring between the two systems. But the day after the commission opened the bids, Orr, the commission's president, received a letter quashing that suggestion, from none other than the man behind the Metropolitan, William C. Whitney.

"My Dear Mr. Orr," Whitney wrote on January 16. "I cannot begin this day without offering to you and your associates my sincere congratulations upon the success of your long labor . . . The Metropolitan Company, I promise you, will do all in its power to aid the work." In the letter, Whitney also assured Orr that the Metropolitan company "has no connection with nor responsibility for either bid. The credit of undertaking this great work belongs to others, but we will aid them in all ways possible."

With that reassurance, the Rapid Transit Commission needed less than twenty-four hours to award the contract to McDonald. And Orr quickly put to rest another rumor, one that suggested if the Tammany-connected contractor did not win the job the subway would never get built. "Absurd!" Orr said. "Politics has had no consideration in this matter. The board in its wisdom decided that Mr. McDonald's bid was the better. That's all there is to it."

It was the better bid. But when he received word that he had won the subway job, McDonald was uncharacteristically silent. What only he knew at that moment was that the banks he had lined up to back his bid had, without any warning, dropped him. They had been told by the men from the Metropolitan Street Railway group, mainly Whitney and Ryan, that the subway was a dangerous investment unless the city awarded the contract in perpetuity rather than for a fifty-year term. The banks listened, and were convinced that a subway was a financial loser, and they backed away.

McDonald had made a bid for a $35 million job, and now suddenly he had no way of putting up any significant money toward it. Perhaps that's why, after receiving such joyous news, McDonald released no comment. He had ten days, under the commission's rules, to find $7 million to put down. While reporters scurried about town to find the burly Irishman, he enjoyed a quiet dinner and drinks at the Hotel Savoy before returning home to his apartment in the Dakota flats on the Upper West Side. He had no time to waste. He began lining up meetings with some of the wealthiest financiers in the city.

AUGUST BELMONT JR. WAS the spoiled son of one of the richest bankers in America. The young Belmont attended the Rectory School in Hamden, Connecticut; Phillips Exeter Academy; and Harvard College. When he was caught one time dousing people with water who were walking beneath his dormitory window and another time howling at the moon at five o'clock in the morning, he was merely scolded politely. But rather than punish him, his father essentially bribed him to behave better, buying him a sloop called the *Ariel* for about $1,000. Private tutors helped August Jr., but he bored easily and graduated Harvard only with the help of a last-minute cram session for his final exams. For his graduation and birthday, his father gave him two hundred shares of the Bank of the State of New York, a present worth $25,000. When August Belmont Sr. died on November 24, 1890, with an estate estimated as high as $50 million, there was no doubting who would take over his affairs. And his son's interests soon expanded beyond his father's.

A SECRETARY ARRANGED THE historic meeting. By the time John B. McDonald sat down with Belmont in January of 1900 to strike a deal, it was as if they were meant to do business together. Both men were short-tempered and cocky. And Belmont's princely life no doubt forged a bond between himself and McDonald. They both enjoyed drinking, sailing, fishing, golfing, and horses.

In a series of meetings the two men held, it became clear that McDonald needed more than a loan. He needed Belmont to put up the $150,000 certified check and to bankroll the entire project. The two men struck the historic agreement that would make New York's subway a reality, although Belmont, not a humble bone in his body, would not exactly view the agreement as an exercise in compromise. Like any shrewd businessman, Belmont told McDonald he was not going to simply hand over his money. He wanted power in return for his investment. The plan called for the city government to hand over to the contractor $37.5 million to pay for the construction costs and the land necessary for the station terminals. So Belmont agreed to organize a syndicate, which he later called the Rapid Transit Subway Construction Company, to raise the money and to pay for the subway construction, which McDonald would lead. And, because the Rapid Transit Commission also required the contractor to run the subway after it opened, Belmont set up what he called the Interborough Rapid Transit Company, or IRT. Last, McDonald agreed to spend his own money to build and purchase the subway cars, signals, and other miscellaneous equipment, which the city would buy back at the end of the lease. It was a straightforward agreement that made perfect sense. The builder would build. The banker would bankroll.

As to the question of what would power the subway trains, that debate was no longer in doubt. Steam was ruled out. Cable was too expensive and prone to break down. Electricity was the only sensible choice, and the reason was, once again, Frank Sprague. This time, New York, not Boston, would be the beneficiary of his genius.

Sprague was on the verge of perfecting a breakthrough even more significant than the one he had achieved in Richmond back in 1888. Sprague's latest technology was called multiple-unit control. The reason those trolleys had struggled so mightily to climb that hill in Richmond during that dramatic midnight run was because the front car was pulling the dead weight of the passenger cars behind it. But Sprague was never satisfied with that. It seemed so inefficient and sluggish. He spent the 1890s working on something he called multiple-unit control, where each car has its own electric traction system and can be controlled by a single motorman at the front of the train to work with other cars as a unit. So successful was the multiple-unit train that General Electric, which had tried to beat Sprague to the same idea and lost, would buy it from him.

On January 30, with all the major decisions in place, Belmont announced his involvement in the New York subway with a terse statement.

"Yes, I am Mr. McDonald's financial agent," he said in a brief appearance.

Three weeks later, on February 24, 1900, a few minutes after 10:30 in the morning, August Belmont walked into the offices of the New York City comptroller. He was soon joined by Mayor Van Wyck, McDonald, Parsons, and the members of the Rapid Transit Commission. Belmont handed over one million dollars in certified checks and the other required securities and bonds. It was precisely 10:49 in the morning when a gold pen was produced and the signing of the subway contracts began. One by one, papers were passed around a long table and signatures were affixed to contracts and receipts. The final man to sign was McDonald, who had been sitting quietly, beaming. When it was his turn, he stepped forward, accepted a round of applause, and turned to Belmont.

"Here is the gentleman who gives me the privilege of signing this contract," McDonald said. And then he sat down and signed. A debate that had been raging in New York City for half a century, since the day in 1849 when *Scientific American* published Alfred Beach's article proposing a subway beneath Broadway, was put to rest in a proceeding that lasted all of eleven minutes. Or so it seemed. Belmont, it turned out, still had one last problem to resolve.

TO FULFILL ALL THE OBLIGATIONS required by the Rapid Transit Commission, the owner of the subway also had to operate it for fifty years. Belmont was a banker. He did not own an actual transit company. McDonald was a builder. He had no interest in running a subway. "I am a contractor, not a railroad man," he told the commission. "And I guess I had better stick to my business."

The only way to start a transit company was to apply for a charter from the New York State legislature. It should have been an easy process for Belmont, considering that by this point there was near-unanimous support for the subway. But when Belmont began the paperwork to apply for a charter, he discovered that the men who owned the street railway companies, powerful and influential businessmen themselves who had forged deep relationships with the right politicians in Albany and the biggest banks in New York, were not exactly thrilled with the idea of a subway. To them it was competition. It would eat into their profits, and if it expanded into the suburbs, as was expected, it would probably destroy them in the end. When Belmont turned to the bonding companies and banks to support his financial commitment to the subway, institutions that had shown great willingness to work with him in the past, this time he could not find a single one to back him. The banks were either completely uninterested, or they demanded conditions he was unwilling to meet. At every turn, Belmont recalled later, "I found the door closed."

Belmont knew that he needed a friend who, like him, recognized that this charter was too important to be quashed by petty businessmen who were too small-minded to realize that a revolution was at hand for their city. He needed someone who could quickly and quietly push his charter through the legislature and did not need to be credited. He needed someone who took pleasure in helping others get what they wanted, as long as he believed it was for the public's good. But what he really needed was someone who knew how the street railways of New York operated, so that he could maneuver around them and get the charter to fulfill the subway contract. "I resolved to go straight to a man who was all powerful, or at least most influential with the powers that were, and I did," Belmont reflected years later. "I went to that man, told him just what I was trying to do, what the project meant for New York and how certain influences were trying to prevent me from carrying it out. He promised his help and gave it."

The man who delivered Belmont his charter, the man who cleared the final hurdle that allowed New York to finally get the financing for its subway, was William Collins Whitney.

Even though Whitney had briefly made his own play for the subway contract before it was awarded to McDonald, Belmont had a hunch. He reached out to Whitney for help. And he got it. It was a secret that Whitney took to his grave and was only revealed reluctantly by Belmont a decade later, when, under a courtroom oath, he was asked to tell the story about how he had finally received his charter.

ON THE FEBRUARY DAY in 1900 when Belmont signed the contract, he had one employee, John Bart McDonald. They made an odd couple, the bald, belly-bulging Irishman who had worked hard labor his whole life and the trim, snobbish, spoiled German Jew born into a life of privilege. They, along with William Barclay Parsons, the young engineer who had the entire route mapped out on his blueprints and knew the formation of the island of New York down to every last pebble, were now being hailed as saviors and protectors of a project that seemed doomed time and time again. And they had thirty days to hire a crew and start digging. They would not have to look far.

The news that New York was about to build a subway spread fast. Two dollars a day for eight hours of work was good money for a laborer. Engineers, axmen, levelers, steelworkers, inspectors, cement mixers, masonry men, accountants, stenographers, diggers, and even messengers were all suddenly needed. At the Municipal Lodging House on First Avenue at Twenty-third Street, skilled and unskilled laborers from around the country began to flock in day after day in search of a cot to sleep on and a penny to earn. There would be thousands of men within a few days.

A three-room apartment in New York, which rented for eight dollars a month, could be divided among three, four, or as many as six workers to reduce the cost. A dozen eggs was going for twenty-five cents, about the same for three tins of sardines, while a dozen pints of beer could be had for a dollar fifty. At the saloons, drafts were five cents, whisky shots ten cents. With those basics, a group of immigrant workers could be quite content, as long as they had paychecks to purchase them.

As for McDonald, arrogant as always, he vowed that digging twenty-one miles of tunnel through the schist of New York would be no more challenging than any other routine job he had handled.

"Constructing the tunnel will be simple," he boasted. "Just like cellar digging."

15

PLAYING WITH DYNAMITE

MOSES EPPS AND EDWIN ARLINGTON ROBINSON came from two different worlds at the dawn of a new century. Epps was a strong, twenty-five-year-old uneducated black man trying to support himself and to stay out of trouble in a time when racism was still very much a part of life in America. Robinson was a thirty-one-year-old white man with round glasses and a neatly trimmed mustache. He came from wealthy old English stock, studied at Harvard, and was on his way to becoming one of the country's most distinguished poets with a letter of praise from President Theodore Roosevelt and a shelf full of Pulitzer prizes. His poems, *The New York Times* glowed, "stood out like poppies in a dandelion field." In contrast, when given repeated chances to explore Epps's life, *The Times* had little to say, describing him over and over as simply a "colored man."

In the first year of the 1900s, Moses Epps and Edwin Robinson found themselves in the same city, on the same job, two struggling men looking for work who found it, of all places, in the bowels of New York City. One of them took work as a timekeeper, his only tools paper and pencil. The other worked as a powderman, handling the dynamite that was used to blow up the ground beneath the streets. The New York City subway project brought together men from all walks of life, like Epps and Robinson. It also brought together men from all parts of the world, from the rolling hills of Ireland to the small villages of Italy to the diamond fields of South Africa and the coal mines of Pennsylvania.

ON THE CRISP AND SUNNY morning of March 24, 1900, inside a tiny courtroom in Mount Vernon, New York, the county judge, Smith Lent, faced an unusually large crowd. More than two hundred people had packed themselves in, almost all of them young men. It should have been a Saturday of smiles and cheer, since they were all there for the same reason, to receive their naturalization papers to become citizens of the United States. But as the day's proceedings began, and each man came before Justice Lent, he grew more visibly annoyed. They were filthy, their hands and faces caked with dirt and their clothes like rags. They looked as if they hadn't bathed in days, and they reeked of body odor and pipe smoke. Smith found it disrespectful that they would come into his courtroom in such a filthy state. By the time a young Italian man from Yonkers stepped before Lent, he'd had enough.

"Haven't you any water or soap in Yonkers?" Lent asked him.

"Not much," the Italian answered.

Lent looked out to the room, incredulous. "You foreigners must wash your hands before you come before me," he shouted to the men, most of them Italians, Germans, Poles, and Scandinavians who spoke in their own slangs and jargons and understood little, if any, English. "Water costs nothing and soap is cheap. I would grant your application for citizenship with great pleasure if you were clean."

The men in the room nodded their heads and promised the judge they would keep clean from that day forward. It was a promise they should not have made. The reason they needed their immigration papers to be official was that they had come to America for one reason: to get hired to work on the rapid transit tunnel that New York was about to begin digging. In fact, at the same moment they were sitting in Lent's courtroom, a much larger crowd was beginning to gather at City Hall Park, where the final touches were being put on the subway's groundbreaking celebration, scheduled to begin in a few hours. If they were lucky enough to be among the thousands hired for the job, they would earn two dollars a day for ten hours of work, gouging a trench into the ground by swinging axes, picks, shovels, and hammers, hard labor that was sure to cover them head to toe in dirt and grime and sweat and blood. It was not exactly ideal work for men who had just promised a judge they would smell fresh and keep their hands clean.

IT WAS SUPPOSED TO BE a miserable day of rain. Instead, clouds gave way to a blue sky and bright sunshine. For an event that had been talked about for half a century, no detail was overlooked in planning the celebration to build a subway. For Boston's groundbreaking five years earlier, half a dozen officials just showed up and, with a small crowd looking on, stuck a shovel in the ground. So understated was it that the mayor didn't see a reason to attend. New York was not about to let its moment pass so quietly.

John Philip Sousa, the forty-four-year-old composer and conductor who had played for presidents, led his band in entertaining the crowd, drowning out the clanging church bells from the neighborhood. Pulitzer's *World* newspaper hired the Pain Fireworks Company of New Jersey to set off explosions of dynamite, and a twenty-one-gun cannon salute was planned. Out in the harbor, horns and whistles blew and fog bells rang. It was a cacophony of sound that was matched by the majestic appearance of City Hall. Half-moon American flags hung off the roof and outside windows.

The crowd began arriving as early as seven o'clock in the morning, with the throngs showing up two hours later and lining up behind the thousand police officers on hand to maintain order. But there almost weren't enough police as the pushing and shoving led to a crushing scene. One woman fainted and cut her head when she fell, and several small children had to be plucked from the crowd before they were trampled. The early birds watched excitedly as a few workers came out before noon and chipped a small hole into the ground with pickaxes, marking the spot where city officials would do the more official deed in a few minutes.

A few stones from the broken pavement flew into the crowd and were pocketed as souvenirs. As noon approached, dignitaries gathered on the balcony, while thousands of citizens crammed their necks from the windows in nearby buildings and from the sidewalks below, stretching in a solid wall from Broadway through the entire length of City Hall Park. Boston broke ground on its subway with no fanfare or celebration. But there was no chance of New Yorkers overlooking their own moment. It was estimated that 25,000 people turned out.

Nineteen hundred was a year when New York's biggest names were at, or near, their height of power, and right behind them stood a generation itching to seize their own day. Fiorello La Guardia, Jimmy Walker, and Franklin Delano Roosevelt were all teenagers growing up in the city. John Singer Sargent, Alfred E. Smith, William Randolph Hearst, and Teddy Roosevelt were the power brokers as the new century began, still in their thirties and forties. None was more powerful than J. P. Morgan, who was Wall Street's king after rebuilding the city's financial strength in the wake of the panic of 1893 by investing in steel and copper at outrageous profits. In his remarks on that March morning, New York's mayor spared no hyperbole about the significance of the moment.

"The completion of this undertaking," Van Wyck said shortly after one o'clock, "will be second only in importance to that of the Erie Canal, celebrated in this city seventy-five years ago." A few other perfunctory speeches followed, at which point the mayor was handed a spade. August Belmont, a man who spared no expense in life, was not about to let this moment pass without putting his personal stamp on it. He had asked Tiffany & Co. to make him a special silver spade for the occasion, with a wooden handle crafted out of one of the thirteen trees that Alexander Hamilton planted in Washington Heights in 1803 to recognize the original thirteen states. The coat of arms of New York was etched into the blade. It was more jewelry than tool. Taking a shovelful of dirt from the pile neatly prepared for the ceremony, Van Wyck deposited it into his hat, which he had removed from his head, a souvenir for his office.

"Bravo, old man," a voice shouted out, and a roar of cheers erupted from the crowd as fireworks boomed into the sky.

When John McDonald's turn came, he was surprisingly timid in the way he reached for some dirt and gently placed it to the side, acting more like a stiff politician than a burly contractor. Parsons, knowing that he'd be monitoring McDonald's work for the next few years, could not let the incident pass. "If your laborers shirk work like that, there will be trouble," Parsons joked.

TWO DAYS LATER, ON March 26, 1900, at the corner of Bleecker and Greene streets, the chief engineer himself took hold of an ordinary pickax. It was only a few blocks from where Parsons grew up. Chatting with those who had gathered, he said it was a poignant event for him to be able to strike the blow that broke ground on such a historic event, so close to his boyhood home. Just after eight o'clock in the morning, Parsons held the pickax low between two cobblestones in the street long enough for photographers to get their posed pictures. He then raised the tool high and slammed it into the earth with such force that it must have felt like letting ten years of frustration out with one single violent swing. The subway was officially under construction. Other cities had beaten New York. But their subways, with the exception of London's, were toy train sets compared with what New York was set to embark upon. The city's timing was perfect.

Trapped between its two rivers, New York trailed London in population but little else. With a century of enormous growth and the 1898 consolidation, it had blossomed from a village to a town and from a town to a city to a megalopolis. The Belmonts, Astors, Vanderbilts, Whitneys, Carnegies, and Morgans gathered for costumed galas at their Fifth Avenue mansions, sat in their private boxes to hear Italian arias at the Metropolitan Opera, and began to recognize that the Metropolitan Museum of Art was on its way toward becoming one of the world's great museums. It was already a home to classical antiquities, and its purchase of two pieces by Édouard Manet in 1889 had signaled that it was serious about building its collection of famous canvas paintings. Broadway was vibrant and repetitive, as the same plays often monopolized theaters for months or years. A single actor named Joseph Jefferson played Rip Van Winkle more than 2,500 times, and in *Monte Cristo* an older actor named James O'Neill, the father of Eugene O'Neill, starred almost as often. *Sherlock Holmes* was popular, and so were the plump ladies of vaudeville dressed in short frilly skirts in *Billy Watson's Beef Trust*. The most popular organized sports were not college football or professional baseball, which were growing but still in their early days, but more brutal activities suitable for small crowds, from dog fights to prize fights. Jazz was only taking shape in New Orleans and had not yet migrated north, but one area where New York shined was fine dining. Delmonico's, the Claremont, Shanley's, and the dining room of the Waldorf, for those who could afford the meals, served thick steaks and rich crepes drowned in brandy. At Sherry's on Forty-fourth Street and Fifth Avenue, the Carte du Jour offered Little Neck clams for twenty-five cents, filet of sole for forty cents, filet mignon for sixty-five cents, roast lamb for seventy, venison in a port-wine sauce for a dollar, and, the real splurge, chicken partridge for two dollars and fifty cents. For the working class, a meal for two at those prices was equal to a day's pay or more. For a Carnegie, it was pocket change.

IN A MATTER OF DAYS after Parsons's first swing, it looked like bombs had exploded all over the city. Downtown, uptown, midtown—swarms of men wearing baggy pants, heavy boots, brimmed hats, shirts with their long sleeves rolled up, and suspenders emerged with their sharp pickaxes and started swinging. In minutes the streets were reduced to rubble. As one group pushed forward inch by inch, another group behind them shoveled the loose rocks and dirt into wooden carriages attached to mules that carted it away. They made remarkable progress considering their primitive tools. In weeks, the streets were obliterated and the men were standing ten or twenty feet deep, often amid a maze of sewer, water, and gas lines that would need to be rerouted or lowered farther into the ground. So nervous were the crews about gas leaks that, instead of working around the pipes, they rerouted them above ground to get them out of harm's way.

In Columbus Circle, the imposing seventy-foot marble statue of Christopher Columbus, erected in 1892 to honor the four-hundredth anniversary of his landing in America, soon stood amid utter destruction, looking out over an intersection in chaos. The street railway tracks circling the monument were littered with debris and passed between piles of dirt or directly over newly dug trenches. Waiting passengers stood feet away from the work, and women with children stopped and stared at the progress. The deeper the workers went, the bigger the rocks that they loosened. And that's when the machinery was needed. The arm of a steam-powered crane would hang over the trench and drop a rope down, waiting for it to be tied to a boulder before hoisting it to the surface.

Throughout the city, diggers would discover coin chests and colonial weapons, and a crazy collection of underground brooks, springs, and even a small subterranean pond at Thirty-second and Madison. Giant mastodon bones surfaced near Dyckman Street, and the charred hull of a seventeenth-century Dutch merchant ship was found near the Battery. Fortunately, they would not, like the workers in Boston, stumble upon hundreds of bodies in cemeteries. Once a section of trench was long and deep enough, steel beams were laid in a grid across the top of it to begin the process of building the roof of the tunnel and of rebuilding the surface of the streets.

BECAUSE THE QUESTION OF how the trains should be powered had been decided, the next critical question Parsons faced was how deep to dig. His choice would affect the way New Yorkers lived and traveled from that day forward. Today, when New Yorkers merely bound down a dozen or two dozen well-lighted steps to most of their stations across New York City, rather than ride elevators much deeper into the dark underground, it's because Parsons had the foresight in 1900 to make his decision based not on how difficult it might be to build the subway but on how easy and pleasurable it must be to ride the subway day after day, year after year. As with everything he did, Parsons approached the question of how deep to dig practically, thinking like a passenger, and analytically, using the wealth of engineering knowledge he'd accumulated from more than a decade of drilling holes in the island.

There were two ways Parsons could instruct John McDonald to build the subway. He could tunnel through the earth, far beneath the streets, like London, causing little disruption to the streets during construction. Or he could scoop out a shallow trench right through the streets, like Boston had done.

Tunneling the subway meant boring deep through the earth by using giant shields, oversized drills essentially, which pushed forward inch by inch and carved out the path for the trains. But it also required blasting through rock. McDonald could not claim any firsthand experience in underground subway tunneling. Very few contractors around the world could. However, he did work on the Hoosac Tunnel in Western Massachusetts, a five-mile-long railroad tunnel carved through the seventeen-hundred-foot Hoosac Mountain. It was a disastrous job that dragged on for a quarter of a century, claimed nearly two hundred lives, and involved dozens of explosions, subterranean floods, and cave-ins. It came to be called the Bloody Pit. But it was not a complete wasted effort. On the Hoosac Tunnel, workers used dynamite for the first time to set off controlled explosions, a feat that would come in handy for McDonald. Of course, it was one thing to blow up dynamite inside a mountain in rural Western Massachusetts. McDonald would be digging his tunnel beneath four million people living, working, and riding in streetcars overhead in a city built of steel, iron, wood, and concrete.

PARSONS WAS NERVOUS ABOUT how a deep tunnel would be received by the public, and he worried about the long-term cost of maintaining dozens if not hundreds of elevators for the entire system. He imagined a station during evening rush hour, with hundreds of passengers waiting for a train to get home, having to stand on the street level for the next elevator car to rise up so that it could carry only a few dozen people down at a time. Passengers would have to wait twice, once for the elevator and again for the subway, an inconvenience Parsons could not ignore.

The inconvenience with the cut-and-cover method, he believed, was "confined solely to the period of construction." Life might be miserable for a few years, he knew, but if the trade-off was a more enjoyable subway experience for the next hundred years, then it made sense to sacrifice the short-term pain for the long-term gain. "When that is finished," he said of the cut-and-cover approach, "there will be the maximum of convenience." It would be close to the surface, approximately fifteen feet from street level, and therefore could be lighted not only by electricity in the stations but by natural sunlight peeking through down the staircases and grates.

"I am no prophet, but the great cities of the Old World show no signs of standing still," Parsons said in an interview with *The New York World*. "London, twice the size of New York, is still growing. We have no means of foretelling the ultimate fate of a modern city or assigning a limit to its growth. We only know that the great cities of ancient times—Babylon, Carthage, Athens, Rome—grew to the point of decay." He would not let that happen on his watch.

CONSTRUCTION WAS NOW IN the hands of McDonald and the subcontractors he hired and the thousands of laborers who had swarmed into the city from around the world. So desperate were men for work that hundreds of them gathered in front of City Hall on that first morning because they assumed that construction would begin there, but they would walk away disappointed when no contractors showed up.

James Pilkington didn't make that mistake. He was the first subcontractor on the job, and on March 26, 1900, he arrived at the intersection of Greene and Bleecker even before Parsons. He knew the sewer system of New York as well as any man, and that's why McDonald hired him. Pilkington was handsome and muscular, a former boxing and wrestling champion who was also an expert sculler. On the day construction began, he wasted no time in pleasing his bosses. His task was a routine and essential one—to lower nine hundred feet of sewer line from fourteen feet beneath the street surface to twenty-one feet below, putting it deep enough into the ground so that the tracks of the subway could pass above it. It was more complicated than it should have been only because all the old sewer and water pipes were laid in the ground in such a mess over the years that untangling them was like untying a double knot. Pilkington tried to take some measurements of the ground himself, but he was besieged from the instant he began.

Dozens of laborers, armed with their own picks and shovels, had gathered at the intersection and filled up an entire two-block area, an army of the unemployed. A mixture of Italians, Swedes, blacks, and Irish, they converged on Pilkington, many of them so skinny it looked like they hadn't eaten in weeks. They were desperate to catch his attention. Pilkington begged police to clear him a space, which they did, and he pointed at twelve men he recognized from previous jobs and told the rest to come back another day because he'd need about fifty in total for his contract. In minutes, the neighborhood had filled with the sounds of swinging pickaxes and the grunting of labor. The workers ripped up paving stones from the street, working inward from the curb. Others unloaded timber that would be used to brace the walls of the trench they'd be digging. Parsons and McDonald both stood by and watched, thrilled to finally see work begin, knowing that London, Boston, and Budapest all had subways operating and that in four months Paris would be opening its Metro.

Their smiles did not last. The agreed-upon fee for unskilled workers was two dollars a day. But skilled workers commanded more, $2.50 a day and $3.50 for overtime hours. One of the men Pilkington hired, Henry Russell, had been working the hoisting engine at the side of the trench, scooping up the dirt that was loosened by the Italians working in the ground and dropping it into the waiting wagons. After several weeks, Russell demanded that his pay be increased to at least $2.75 and up to $3.50, and his union, the Safety Association of Steam Engineers, ordered him to quit working until it was. On April 2 at ten o'clock, Pilkington showed up at Bleecker Street and saw Russell's engine idling and Russell smoking a cigar while standing nearby. He angrily confronted Russell about the delay.

"I'm on strike," Russell said to his boss. "And I want $3.50 a day."

Pilkington paused and figured this was a battle not worth fighting. "All right, go ahead with your work," he said. He would quickly regret giving in so easily. As soon as Russell moved toward his machine, the delegate for the union, a man named William Cheatham, shouted at Russell to stop.

"Don't you touch that engine until I tell you," Cheatham said, and then he turned to Pilkington. He told him there were fifteen other workers just like Russell who deserved the same pay. Pilkington had dug himself a hole, and now he had no choice but to agree to pay all of them the increased rate. Cheatham told Russell he could get back to work, and with the strike averted, Pilkington relaxed as he watched scoops of dirt once again fly out of the ground and into the carts.

THE CUT-AND-COVER WORK MOVED QUICKLY below Tenth Street for one reason: The ground in lower New York was a soft, granular soil, almost like sand. Those pipes that were pounded into the ground downtown went sixty, seventy, and more than a hundred feet deep in some places, making excavation a breeze. But the soft soil was also more challenging because of the danger of the hole collapsing.

Even as the guts of the city's streets were being torn up, the street railway tracks rerouted around the trenches, the sidewalks rendered almost impassable, and businesses along the route suffered exactly the sort of losses that they feared, the work progressed smoothly. New Yorkers proved to be a hardy bunch. At the northern end of Central Park, a mess of scaffolding and sewer pipes and steaming derricks turned the carriage road at 110th Street into something resembling a war zone. But there were also a dozen swinging steel buckets methodically dropping the dug-up dirt into carriages so that it could be carted away. Parsons and McDonald had decreed together that towering piles of dirt should not be left to linger across the city.

After a section of trench was finished, the next phase began, building the secure, leak-proof box to hold the actual subway. Solidifying the base was done with a four-inch sheet of poured concrete. The sides were also concrete, but they were additionally supported with steel I beams erected every five feet. The combination of the two—steel beams and concrete—was essential to supporting the weight of the street and traffic overhead. The final key step was waterproofing, which was achieved before the concrete was poured by applying a thick layer of felt and asphalt paper to the floor, walls, and roof.

If the entire subway could have been built using cut and cover, it would surely have been completed much faster. Parsons knew the truth. The island's topography required more rock tunneling than he anticipated, as north of Tenth Street it became apparent in many portions of the route that simple excavation was not going to work. It was too difficult to dig through rock and still keep the tracks on a flat level. The only way to keep the tracks from resembling the peaks and valleys of the Adirondacks was to tunnel. Tunneling meant dynamite. In the end, of the original twenty-one miles of subway tracks that were laid, only eleven of those miles were in tunnels built with the safe cut-and-cover method.

Just because the Manhattan schist was a rock did not mean it had any consistency to it. Soft enough in some places for a worker to easily chip away big chunks but so hard in other places that it was like pounding steel, the schist was McDonald's greatest challenge. If he worked too aggressively through it, he risked his crew being buried in a rock slide. If he worked too timidly, Parsons would be breathing down his neck, demanding that he pick up the pace. One thing McDonald knew. He couldn't just blast away like he had done at Hoosac Mountain. In New York, he had people walking on the streets and sidewalks directly overhead and electric streetcars riding over rails that could easily be bent or broken in a blast, which might send a car tumbling onto its side. This work required more care, and so it was no surprise when, late in 1901, McDonald began to worry. He discovered that he would need to use a huge amount of dynamite to bore through the earth beneath one of New York's most upscale, fashionable, and densely populated neighborhoods.

· · ·

MURRAY HILL ON MANHATTAN'S east side was named in honor of
the merchant Robert Murray, who in the late eighteenth century owned a
wedge-shaped farm on a tract that became the area between Thirty-third
Street and Thirty-eighth Street. Most of its development happened in the
late 1860s and early 1870s, boosted by a series of mansions built there by
men who made fortunes from the Civil War. The emergence of the
posh Ladies' Mile shopping stretch in Murray Hill forced faster growth,
and by the end of the 1800s Murray Hill was as built out as any neighborhood in the city.

It was home to Grand Central Terminal, and the Murray Hill Hotel,
which hosted President Cleveland and Mark Twain in its early years. It was
also a neighborhood that attracted the city's distinguished residents. Civil
War hero Rear Admiral David Farragut lived there. So did James Fargo,
president of American Express, and Marshall Clifford Lefferts, whose collection of rare antique books was among the finest in the world. And the
city's greatest architects rebuilt brownstones in Murray Hill with beautiful
touches, from wrought iron balconies to oval dormer windows to arched
main entrances. The arrival of Charles L. Tiffany, the son of the founder of
Tiffany & Co., into a Murray Hill mansion in the early 1900s was the cap-
stone to the neighborhood's fifty-year rise and marked it as the single most
desirable place to live in all of New York. As it turned out, however, Murray
Hill was like a glimmering diamond with an almost imperceptible flaw.

The area between Twenty-seventh Street and Forty-second Street and
between Third Avenue and Sixth Avenue, essentially the boundaries of
Murray Hill, sat on a portion of the schist that was particularly unstable.
It sat on a rock at such a steep angle that it was impossible to imagine a
dynamite blast not causing a rock slide underground. But there was no
way around it. All of the back and forth in laying out a subway route and
avoiding sections of the city where opposition was fiercest had forced Parsons to call for a tunnel right through the heart of Murray Hill.

There was little to do to make the blasting more tolerable. It was loud,
and the ground shook with terrifying vibrations each time there was a

detonation. The only attempt to ease the annoyance was to blast first thing in the morning, at the end of the overnight shift, so that the day-time crews could pile the rubble into carts and get it out of the trench. Digging the Murray Hill tunnel would be one of McDonald's greatest challenges, which he placed in the hands of a thirty-nine–year-old civil engineer and Spanish-American War leader.

IRA SHALER WAS THE only child of Alexander Shaler, a general for the Union army in the Civil War who received the Medal of Honor for his brave act of grabbing a flag and leading his men into the teeth of the Confederates at the second battle of Fredericksburg. Ira Shaler was never the war hero like his father, but he was called Major Shaler out of respect for the rank that he achieved while serving in Puerto Rico during the Spanish-American War. He was a star student at Cornell, and through the 1890s he became one of the most respected engineers in New York, which is how he caught the attention of McDonald.

Shaler was one of the dozens of subcontractors McDonald hired. They were the middle men, the bridges connecting the lowly laborers who earned twenty cents an hour shoveling, digging, hoisting, and blasting their way through the island and their buttoned-up bosses, from Mc-Donald to Parsons to Belmont to Mayor Van Wyck and his successor in 1902, the Brooklyn-born Seth Low. The subcontractors were the day-to-day leaders, following the orders of the lead contractor and the chief en-gineer to make sure the work stayed on course. They each got pieces of the job. There was the Canadian-born Duncan McBean, a silver-haired genius engineer whose $1.5 million bid won him the right to solve the problem of tunneling under the Harlem River. There were the McCabe brothers, assigned to dig the deepest tunnel in the schist, under Wash-ington Heights north of 157th Street. There was Holbrook, Cabot & Rol-lins, the construction company McDonald hired to tunnel beneath Fourth Avenue because of its experience five years earlier digging a section of the Boston subway tunnel. And there was Major Ira Shaler. His job was to not blow up Murray Hill.

. . .

"RUN FOR YOUR LIFE!"

A few minutes after noon on January 27, 1902, the clamor from the digging along Forty-first Street near Park Avenue was suddenly drowned out by the frantic shouts of Moses Epps. The country was in a sad place, still recovering from the shock of President McKinley's assassination in Buffalo four months earlier, which gave way to the rise of his vice president and New York's former governor, Rough Rider Teddy Roosevelt. But even as the chaos of the subway construction had been a welcome distraction for New Yorkers, the sight of a black worker wearing overalls and yelling with frantic wide eyes must have been terrifying. Epps came tearing out of a rickety wooden shack, trying to warn anyone within earshot to run fast and to run far. There were a dozen people who heard him, and flee they did. Most got only a few feet. Those who did not hear him, like the cashier at the cigar counter at the Murray Hill Hotel, a young waiter, and a wealthy Canadian businessman who was visiting New York with his wife and four children, simply went about their day oblivious to the sudden panic on the street.

"Run for your life," Epps screamed. "The powder shanty's on fire. I can't put it out!"

Dynamite was more than thirty years old by now. Contractors knew how it worked. But when there was as much dynamite needed in one city as there was for the New York subway, the odds of an accident increased dramatically.

On the morning of January 27, at least five hundred pounds of the explosive were crammed into one tiny wooden shanty, far more than the law permitted at one place. As if that was not enough risk, the shanty was being lit by two candles that were fixed to an inside wall to provide light and help warm the hands of the workers. A carriage agent who worked at the nearby Murray Hill Hotel and often peeked into the shanty said a subway worker once told him there was enough dynamite in there to "blow the whole hill to hell." Moses Epps was standing inside a ticking time bomb in the middle of New York City at noon on a busy workday, and when one of his two candles melted to its bottom, he tossed it to the floor and began to light a new one. All of a sudden, the one that he dropped ignited a piece of paper on the ground. He grabbed a bucket of water and threw it on the flame, but it was too late. A wooden shack with twelve boxes filled with seventy-five sticks of dynamite each was now on fire.

THE SOUND FROM THE EXPLOSION was louder than anything New Yorkers had ever heard. Some thought the city was under attack. "I thought the end of us had come," one witness said. The ground shook, windows shattered, buildings rocked, and a blinding glare was followed by a plume of white and blue smoke that shot hundreds of feet into the air. Epps was thrown to the ground unconscious, with deep gashes in his scalp and leg. The windows on a northbound Madison Avenue streetcar shattered without warning, covering its passengers in glass. The motorman, Henry Gaines, despite suffering a dislocated shoulder and other injuries, managed to safely bring his car to a halt.

In seconds, a dense cloud of dirty yellow dust turned a clear day into a foggy one and blanketed a ten-block stretch between Thirty-fifth and Forty-fifth streets with air so thick that it hurt to inhale. As the funnel of smoke rose up, hundreds of people rushed toward the shanty where the explosion occurred and came upon dozens of crying, screaming victims, lying or limping, with blood dripping down their faces from shards of falling glass or wood splinters from the shanty. The Manhattan Eye and Ear Hospital was evacuated in minutes, its rooms destroyed and unfit for patients.

The Murray Hill Hotel suffered the brunt of the blast. Not a single window on its Park Avenue front survived. But the hotel manager, a kindly fellow named Washington L. Jacques, did not hesitate in turning his building into a makeshift hospital. Victims were carried in and laid out, including his son, a bank cashier across the street who was badly hurt by flying glass while eating his lunch. A surgeon who happened to be nearby and was unhurt, Dr. Louis Livingston Seaman, followed the flow of victims into the hotel and began to triage the most severely injured. It was familiar work for him, since he had served as a battlefield doctor during the Spanish-American War.

Jacques feared that there were victims who did not survive the blast in his hotel, and he organized a search party to enter every single room. On the first floor, in the hotel cigar shop, they found Cyrus Adams, the popular seventy-year-old cashier known for his black velvet skullcap and nicknamed Old Adams, lying dead behind the register. On the parlor level, they found the mining businessman from British Columbia, Roderick Robertson, in his bed with his head crushed in, the furniture in his room shattered to bits. In the basement, Jacques stumbled upon a thirty-two-year-old black waiter from the hotel restaurant named James Carr. By the time a surgeon could reach him, he was gone.

The instant that the longtime chief of the New York City Fire Department, Edward F. Croker, heard the blast, he didn't wait for a call. He took off, dashing downtown when the first of four gongs clanged back at headquarters. "I knew that something big was on hand," Croker said. Within ten minutes, scores of ambulances from Presbyterian Hospital and Bellevue were at the scene, and so were fire vehicles, but the firemen had little work to do. The dynamite didn't spark an enormous blaze, only a few scattered flames in the basement of the Murray Hill Hotel and the shaft of the subway tunnel. The damage was the wreckage.

The financial cost was staggering, estimated at $300,000. The loss of life was devastating, but it was shocking that it was not worse. Six people died and 125 were hurt, most of them suffering cuts from flying glass and bruises from falling debris. Within days, Epps was arrested on murder charges, and so were his bosses, John McDonald and Major Ira Shaler. They were accused of manslaughter and violating city ordinances on the storage of explosives. For Epps, his troubles would be brief, once it was learned that he was more of a hero for warning people to run. McDonald, too, would escape without much penalty, claiming the amount of dynamite stored was exaggerated. But Shaler would not get off so easily.

While the case against Shaler moved forward and victims filed lawsuits against him, he went right back to work. Two months after the fatal blast, on the morning of March 21, 1902, a group of Shaler's workmen came running out of the Murray Hill tunnel screaming that it was about to collapse. Seconds later it did. They narrowly survived the avalanche of loose rocks and dirt, and as they stood on the street and looked down, they saw months of their work gone in a flash. The roof of the tunnel along Park Avenue between Thirty-seventh and Thirty-eighth streets had caved in, and, with it, the home of a lawyer who lived in a brownstone at 55 Park Avenue sagged forward so much that the front door could not be opened. Shaler stood with his workers, stunned at the sight of the cave-in and relieved no one had been killed. "This accident," he said while standing over the scene, "was one which could not be foreseen."

For the second time in two months, McDonald and Parsons rushed to a chaotic site on the subway route that was under the watch of Ira Shaler, who by now was being nicknamed the "Hoodoo Contractor" for his troubles on the job. The first time six bystanders died and several of the city's grandest hotels were nearly destroyed. This time, a beautiful block of Park Avenue was blighted. The Murray Hill tunnel was proving to be a disaster, just as the contractor and engineer feared when they studied the topography and learned how porous the ground was.

Parsons and McDonald stepped off a Madison Avenue electric streetcar at Thirty-eighth Street at four thirty in the afternoon of the collapse, and, after a brief glance down the damaged block, they trudged down into the tunnel to look over the wreckage. They estimated the damage to three homes at more than $250,000, but rather than question Shaler's competence, both men stood by him. Parsons agreed that the collapse could not have been predicted, and he said the tunnel would proceed on schedule. The damage, he said, was trifling. Parsons's leniency with Shaler after two disasters was puzzling given his demand for perfection, especially since Shaler was now facing a pile of legal bills and criminal charges that threatened to ruin him financially and emotionally. But Shaler was his friend, and Parsons, unlike McDonald, had expected the subway to pose engineering nightmares. Still, given the chance to turn over the work to someone else, Parsons declined. A few months later, his affection for his friend nearly got Parsons killed.

. . .

DESPITE ALL OF HIS TROUBLES in Murray Hill, by early June Shaler's work was almost done. His crew had finished building two separate tunnels extending from Thirty-fourth Street to Forty-first Street, and he invited Parsons and his assistant chief engineer for the Rapid Transit Commission, George Rice, to visit for an inspection. They arrived on June 17, a few minutes before eight o'clock, and all three men walked down into the ground. The easterly tunnel was the one damaged by the collapse, and Parsons was impressed by its rebuilding. The walls had been grouted, and the only step remaining was a concrete lining. It was a few weeks from completion.

The trio emerged from the first tunnel at Forty-first Street and walked over to the westerly one. This one caused more concern because the rock through which it was dug was less secure than the first. Shaler wanted advice on the best way to prop up the roof of the tunnel and avoid another collapse. As they neared the end of the tunnel, passing under Thirty-ninth Street, Parsons noticed a boulder overhead that looked precarious. His engineering mind told him that it was a soft rock, and, sure enough, when he stuck a long pole out to touch it, a piece dislodged and fell to the ground. That was a dangerous sign. If a simple poke could cause it to crumble, serious tunneling would no doubt bring it crashing down.

"That stone doesn't look right to me," Parsons said to Shaler. "I'm afraid we're going to have to turn back."

"With all due respect, General," Shaler answered, "the tunnel is perfectly safe." He even stepped out from beneath the wooden bracing in a show of bravado.

As the three men were discussing how to deal with the problem of propping up the roof, the exact boulder Parsons had poked suddenly broke apart, and a thousand pounds of rubble crushed Shaler to the ground, striking his head first, then his body, burying him alive. Parsons and Rice miraculously felt only a few pebbles land at their feet, and they rushed to dig Shaler out. They called for help, but when the laborers had heard the sound of falling rock, they ran up to safety and refused to come back in. Unable to move, but still conscious, Shaler looked up at McDonald and Parsons without any wincing or crying and said, "I think my back is broken."

By the time he'd been freed, hoisted out of the tunnel, and rushed to Presbyterian Hospital, his injuries included a broken spine, a severe scalp wound, and a badly injured leg. "It was simply Major Shaler's ill fortune that he happened to be in the wrong spot," Parsons said. "I might have been standing there." Shaler's wife, mother, and father rushed to be with him. Two weeks later, on June 29, his injuries were too much to overcome. Major Ira Shaler was not even forty years old. The next day's headline in *The Times* summarized the life of the engineer sadly: MURRAY HILL DYNAMITE EXPLOSION, ARMORY FIRE, AND A CAVE-IN RUINED HIM FINANCIALLY—THEN A BOULDER STRUCK HIM IN THE TUNNEL.

Shaler's death shook Parsons, and he briefly considered quitting, telling Belmont, "I've lost my best friend down there. I can't stomach this business anymore." Belmont convinced him to stay on, and in a rare moment of public emotion, Parsons called Shaler a man of integrity and charm. "His sense of justice towards his employees won the regard of all with whom he came in contact," Parsons said. "Therefore his sudden and sad death was felt as a personal loss by everyone connected with the work." True to his being, Parsons never let Shaler's demise slow down the subway's progress. He ordered the work in Murray Hill to continue without Shaler. And it was finished on time only a few weeks later.

THREE AND A HALF YEARS after Parsons slammed his ceremonial pickax into the ground at the corner of Bleecker and Greene, New York was looking like its old self again. McDonald and Parsons worked well together; even when they argued, it passed quickly. Their most public spat happened at a board meeting of the transit commission in September 1903, when McDonald griped that Parsons was holding up his work on lower Broadway by not issuing permits fast enough. "We have the tools and machinery but we are not allowed to work," McDonald complained to the commissioners. Parsons did not back down, and afterward he joked about the confrontation with a reporter who asked about the clash. "Clash?" Parsons answered. "I know of no clash, it is just a difference of opinion."

By the fall of 1903, there were still more than five thousand workers on the job, but nearly all of them were invisible to pedestrians. They were underground. The streets had been scooped up, the tunnels had been built, and the repaving was mostly complete. A stranger walking through the city for the first time would have no idea that only a dozen or so feet beneath them lay one of the most complex and impressive engineering feats man had achieved. Bright green strips of turf intersecting with gravel paths began to appear in the median of upper Broadway. New street lamps were installed. The scars of Major Ira Shaler faded away, and Murray Hill finally looked like Murray Hill again, as massive derricks and small toolsheds were taken apart and taken away. The pieces of white canvas in the windows were gone, and new glass filled the windows that had been damaged in the dynamite blast. For the first time in two years, a visitor to the Park Avenue Hotel would not look out a window at a neighborhood that appeared ravaged by a cyclone. Streets were smooth again, thanks to three separate repaving efforts and workers who got down on their hands and knees to smooth over the gaps between the cobblestones.

By the fall of 1903, if a curious sightseer managed to wander down into the tunnel at Columbus Circle, they would have seen a completely finished underground subway station, with walls painted bright white, lights turned on, and shiny reflectors gleaming to help guide the motormen through every inch of the finished tracks. The only thing missing were the trains.

There was, however, one visible sign on the surface of Manhattan that something was amiss. When the first subway contracts were signed back in 1900, William Whitney's Fifth Avenue neighbor, the sixty-five-year-old silver-haired Scottish-American industrialist Andrew Carnegie, was awarded the bid to supply the steel for the job, 72,945 tons. The $10 million bid was believed to be the largest single steel contract in history for one steelmaker to supply for one project. That one behemoth, the Carnegie Steel Company, was able to manufacture the entire subway's supply of steel was a sign of just how enormous the steel industry had become at the turn of the century, thanks to the fortunes of the Gilded Age robber barons. Though Carnegie had half a dozen steel-manufacturing rivals in the 1890s, none were serious competitors. During the decade, Carnegie's production exploded from 322,000 tons in 1890 to almost four million tons by 1900, a pace that was impossible to match. The subway project required enough steel to lay down tracks from New York to Cincinnati, about six hundred miles. The vast majority of it was to be used in the construction of the actual tunnels, where steel beams were placed to keep the streets from collapsing. But plenty was left over for the final critical part of the project: the tracks.

From the bottom of the island to the top, in one nearly continuous chain, four thousand tons of steel rails lay end to end wherever there was a tunnel underground. A passerby might walk down a street one day and see ten rails, return the next day and see six, see two the following day, and then see none. It was as if a monster from beneath the surface was gobbling them up one by one. The work could be heard but not seen, as the hundred-pound rails were slid into the tunnels on mule-pulled carts, hammered into the ground with spikes, and secured with closely placed hard pine cross-ties. Tracks in a tunnel were the best indication that the end was in sight.

THE REASON THE WORK HAD gone so quickly was the cut-and-cover method Parsons had chosen. New Yorkers became so accustomed to it that they began to sarcastically call the tunnels Parsons's Ditch. But up at 158th Street, from the first day construction began in the spring of 1901, it was apparent that no trench could be dug there. The ground was too hard, the schist too close to the surface. The tunnel needed to be dug through the schist so deep that Parsons planned for elevators big enough to carry dozens of passengers at once down to stations at 168th Street, 181st Street, and 191st Street, where the tracks would run 180 feet below the streets, to this day still the system's deepest station. Two miles of tunnel between Washington Heights and Hillside Avenue in the Bronx needed to be built, and the only way it could happen was by blasting through the earth with dynamite. This was where McDonald's experience might help. The only tunnel in the world that could compare to the Washington Heights work was the same long tunnel where dynamite was first used for controlled blasting, the Hoosac Tunnel.

Because working on the Washington Heights tunnel was different and more dangerous than creating a cut-and-cover trench, McDonald wanted more-experienced men on the job. It was more like mining. The moment the Miners' Union got word about the two-mile subway tunnel, its members came running from around the world, from Colorado, Pennsylvania, Ireland, Scotland, Canada, and Italy. They knew nothing about "subways" or "nickel fares" or "transfers," words that were meaningless to them. They were pugnacious and jolly, solid men who smoked pipes, told long yarns, and followed orders to the letter. They crossed continents and oceans for work with nothing but a bag on their back, and they put down a bed wherever it was cheapest and closest to their daily job. The drillers made the most, $3.75 a day, the ordinary miners the least, $2 a day. Their routine rarely changed. They climbed into the earth, grunted and sweated for eight or ten hours a day, and then emerged back into civilization coated in filth, blinking and squinting as they readjusted to the sunlight.

But for men who were used to working deep inside mountains, in isolated rural lands where the only company they could find were other miners, the chance to work in a big city surrounded by pubs and brothels and restaurants was irresistible. It's no wonder they came by the thousands and, almost overnight, transformed New York City into, of all things, a mecca for miners. Who needed sleep when a day of tunneling could be followed by a night of carousing or whoring or whatever else their few dollars a day could buy them?

As work began, they called their tunnel "the mine" to help them feel right at home. When they first flooded into New York, oblivious to where their piece of the job was, they crowded Bowery lodging houses on the Lower East Side. Once they realized their work was uptown, they found shelter in boardinghouses in a southern section of what is now Riverdale called Spuyten Duyvil.

Their presence at nighttime served to liven up the neighborhood, even if it was with more noise than their neighbors were accustomed to. But it was the racket of the tunneling that was the real bother. Because the work was happening so deep, compressed air was pumped into the ground. The monotonous "chug-chug-chug" of the machine was torture for the residents who, after weeks and months of it, were being driven out of their minds. Adding to the din was the dynamite blasting. Even though it was happening so far underground, each explosion caused a dull thud to ricochet toward the streets and a puff of smoke to follow it, evidence of yet another blast. What could not be heard on the streets was the sound of the men singing and laughing from below. It was, *The Times* wrote in the early days of the tunneling, as if "they are in love with life in the bowels of the earth."

THE MINE HAD TAKEN SHAPE nicely by the fall of 1903, and McDonald was so impressed that he visited the site and congratulated the men on winding up such a dangerous job with no accidents. The progress of the tunnel at the time was captured in a photograph that showed the enormity of the challenge. A dozen stern-faced men stand inside of a half-moon tunnel, its cavernous rounded ceiling lined with concrete. The floor is unfinished, a collection of boulders, smaller rocks, and towering piles of dirt on which the workers stand and climb. The men are grimy, all of them wearing hats, their hands by their side or tucked into their pockets or suspenders. A cart filled with debris sits, waiting to be pulled away. What little light there is comes from a row of bright bulbs fixed to the sidewall.

For two years, most of the rock that was blasted was solid mica schist. The explosions were clean, and there was little chance that they would cause the schist to become unstable. But when the miners encountered short stretches of soft rock, like they did at 155th Street or 193rd Street, they knew they had to be more careful and that they had to wedge timbers between gaps in the schist and the concrete lining.

Only a few hundred feet left of tunneling was needed to connect the tunnel the entire way through. The McCabe brothers, the subcontractors on the deep tunneling job, were eager to finish, knowing it was such a monumental feat. Rather than blast twice a day, they ordered three dynamite explosions daily. The remaining blasts were needed to widen the tunnel to its required twenty-five feet. It was about ten thirty at night on October 24 when the last blast of the day went off, 110 feet below the streets in the area near Fort George and 193rd Street. It was customary to wait a few minutes after a blast to let any loose debris fall, and so when the foreman on the job, Timothy Sullivan, went in after ten minutes to see if the walls were secure, he had little reason to be nervous. He looked around, saw no problems, and shouted back to his workers.

"Come on boys," he said, "let's get to work."

What Sullivan could not see were two veins running through an enormous boulder in the ceiling that weakened it to the point where the slightest quake, never mind a dynamite blast, could cause it to split.

A young German electrician named William Scheutte was the first in so he could string up the lights to brighten the way for the others. A pair of black miners, Michael Hargraves and Charles Crocker, followed, pushing in a tramcar to load up with rocks, and along with them came a line of Italians. The large group had barely set foot into the tunnel when they heard three separate blasts, followed by a loud, horrifying rumbling. The men at the back of the line who had not yet entered the cave turned around and sprinted back up toward the street. The others ahead of them never had a chance.

That three-hundred-ton rock, which measured almost five feet wide and forty-four feet long, came crashing down right on top of the workmen who had just arrived. Men were crushed, pinned, and buried. Small rivulets of blood began to drip down the side of the boulder. Six died instantly, and eight others were seriously hurt, including an Italian named Alfonzo Annetello, who had to have his crushed leg amputated in order to be freed. From the street, the cries of agony could be heard. Father Thomas Lynch, the sixty-year-old priest with a ruddy face and kindly blue eyes from nearby St. Elizabeth's Roman Catholic Church, rushed into the ghastly tunnel in his black robe, ignoring warnings shouted at him so that he could tend to the injured and dying. Kneeling in puddles of blood and water, with a red-shirted Italian by his side as an interpreter, Father Lynch gave the last rites to the most gravely injured, touching his crucifix to a dying man's lips. "Kyrie, eleison," or "Lord have mercy," Lynch said, and the others in the tunnel bowed their heads.

When other rescuers reached the tunnel, three men were found to be in such pain that doctors injected them quickly with morphine, but it mattered little as they died minutes later. And Alfonzo Annetello also died a few hours later. It took all night to get the bodies of the injured and the dead out, the last one emerging at ten in the morning. The ten who died were Italians, except for Scheutte and Sullivan.

The removal of Sullivan's body brought onlookers to their knees. His young son, Sammy, stood outside the tunnel all night long, waiting and watching. When a tramcar came to the surface carrying Sullivan's body, his face bloodied and disfigured, Sullivan's son walked beside the car, climbed into the patrol wagon with it, and left without shedding a tear, even when a police officer put his arm around the boy. "Sorry for you, little man," the officer said as they left.

Parsons was out of town when he got word by telegram the morning after the accident, and he ordered his deputy, George Rice, to rush to the scene. Hours after the bodies were removed, Rice compared the accident to the one that nearly struck Parsons down in Murray Hill. "Whether the falling in of the mass of rock was due to moisture or to fissures, or what, nobody will know," Rice said. "It is one of those things that happen every day in tunnel construction and the workmen all know what risks they are incurring. The accident by which Major Ira Shaler lost his life on June 17, 1902, was precisely the same as that which happened last night."

When Parsons arrived two days after the accident, he repeated in cold, almost robotic terms similar sentiments to what he had said at all the other accidents on his project. The proper precautions had been taken. The deaths were unavoidable, in this case caused by "a seam that could not have been detected."

Walking out of the tunnel, Parsons looked down at his hands, moist from a mixture of blood and water after he had rubbed them up against the fallen rocks underground. He refused to wipe them clean, however. And when a reporter tried to pry a reaction to the tragedy from him, Parsons could only muster a few soft words. "The rock was weaker than any of us knew."

THE ELECTRIC SUBWAY WAS GOING to speed up life in cities and expand their boundaries for miles beyond the crowded downtowns. That much was now clear. But as 1903 came to an end, another transportation marvel, this one targeted at making long-distance travel faster and easier, quietly made its debut trip a thousand miles away. On December 17, above a windy beach on the coast of North Carolina, Wilbur Wright piloted the first powered airplane for a record fifty-nine seconds, covering 852 feet. If the mission of the subway was for cities to feel a little bit smaller by quickening the way people could move from one neighborhood to the next, then Orville and Wilbur Wright had a similar goal. They were determined to make the whole world feel a little bit smaller. Their rickety 605-pound double-winged plane with a wingspan of forty feet and a twelve-horsepower engine was going to make the transcontinental railroad feel like a horse-drawn buggy and the steamship feel like a rowboat.

The following year was shaping up to herald the future of travel. And the New York City subway was not even the most exciting transportation innovation. As the Wright brothers perfected their airplane to make it fly farther and faster, a hundred thousand people crowded into Madison Square Garden in January 1904 to see how much the automobile had advanced since the turn of the century. They saw new rubber tires, powerful engines, and more comfortable seats, and they heard boasts about cars that could cover a mile in forty seconds, not quite as fast as steam locomotives but not far behind. Only the rich could afford to have a private automobile, and on the streets of New York they fought for space with the street railways. Inevitably, fatal accidents became more common.

But there was no turning back. The age of the automobile was coming, and the era of the subway was here.

. . .

ON NEW YEAR'S DAY of 1904, New York's newest mayor, George B. McClellan, joined Belmont, Parsons, McDonald, and others on a six-mile journey inside a handcar powered by the strong arms of nine cheerful Italians; they rode beneath their city to see how close the subway was to completion. Afterward, at a party at Sherry's, an unknown guest toasted McDonald: "We all want to thank you for giving us an opportunity to appreciate this great work," he said. Parsons, who was close by, scoffed. Perfectionist to the end, for him it wasn't done until it was done. "Pshaw!" he said. "There's no citizen so poor that he cannot appreciate it much more comfortably a few months from now—for five cents."

The subway's arrival and continued expansion was inevitably going to take passengers away from New York's other crowded transit systems, the elevated lines and the street railways. In one more sign of the times, the once-almighty Metropolitan Street Railway Company, which once controlled the streets of New York just as the West End Street Railway Company con-trolled the streets of Boston, dissolved with a debt of more than $20 million.

And what of its founder, a brigadier general's youngest son, who grew up from a lonely and shy boy reading books by a Massachusetts river to a man who helped elect a president, rebuilt the United States navy, raised one of the most prominent American families in history, and ran a powerful street railway company? Until his final day, William Whitney kept secret how he had helped August Belmont receive the critical charter that cleared the way for Belmont to build and operate the New York City subway.

On January 28, 1904, a Thursday evening, Whitney joined his secre-tary, Thomas J. Regan, for a performance of *Parsifal* at the Metropolitan Opera. Whitney did not feel well, and, after leaving his box early, he dis-appeared into a private room, threw his silk hat on the floor, and col-lapsed on the couch. He did not know it, but his appendix was inflamed. After six days of fading in an out of consciousness at his home, with his children by his side and his older brother, Henry, rushing down from Boston, William Whitney died on February 4, so peacefully that his doc-tors did not even notice his heart had stopped beating.

An appraisal of his estate confirmed the success he'd achieved, though it put him nowhere close to the fortune of his Fifth Avenue friends. Whitney's real estate and personal holdings were valued at nearly $23 million. William Hussey Page, a friend and Harvard lawyer who helped him argue his railway legal battles in New York in the 1890s, eulogized Whitney in the pages of *Harper's Weekly* a few weeks after his death. Four lines summed up the man perfectly:

> *Generous, magnanimous, and just*
> *Thoughtful for all, of station high or low,*
> *Lion in action, fearless, frank,*
> *In friendship true as steel and pure as gold*

Maybe it was because, by 1904, Boston, Budapest, Paris, Glasgow, and London were operating subways, millions of passengers were riding on them, and nobody was dropping dead from breathing the subterranean air. Maybe it was because, after half a century of watching subway plans come and go so many times that they had thrown up their hands in resignation, they assumed a subway would never be built in their lifetimes. Or maybe New Yorkers were just harder to scare. But for whatever reason, the same fears that Bostonians voiced for years throughout the 1890s—about traveling underground, comparing their subway to long underground coffins and insisting that the only people who should go beneath the streets are the dead—never materialized in Gotham with any real strength. The subway was more like a curiosity for New Yorkers.

As summer gave way to fall and the scheduled October opening approached, to put to rest any concerns once and for all, Dr. Thomas Darlington, New York's commissioner for public health, wrote an essay in the Sunday *World*. He had spent considerable time in the tunnels, measuring the quality of the air not only to assess its breathability but also to compare it to the air on the streets, as well as the air inside poorly ventilated places, like theaters, schools, cars, and berths of ships. He found nothing that concerned him, and in fact with 119 openings into the subway between City Hall and 157th Street, the air quality was almost identical above ground as below it. The subway air had plenty of oxygen, and it was not, as some suggested, poisoned by carbon dioxide. The subway was given a clean bill of health.

But New Yorkers had other concerns. Even before the subway opened, in the weeks leading up to the big day, passengers wanted answers to their mundane, even frivolous questions, to help them understand how this contraption worked and why they should feel assured that it would be operated safely. The questions were answered in the papers and by subway officials, who found themselves being cornered daily by eager, if slightly anxiety-filled, passengers.

If a fuse on the front engine burns out, will the entire train be stopped for a long time, blocking traffic in the tunnels? No, thanks to Frank Sprague, whose multiple-unit control system allows for the rear cars to have their own motors that can push the train forward. *How long will trains stop at stations?* Approximately fifteen seconds, depending on how many people get on and off. *How long will it take to get from Times Square to Grand Central if you're racing to catch a train there?* About forty-five seconds. *Can subway travel hurt the eyes?* Yes, looking at the long rows of white columns strains the eyes, so don't do it. *What do the green and red lights inside of the tunnels mean?* Green tells the motormen to go, the track ahead is clear, and red means stop. *Will every passenger get a seat?* No, but overhead straps in the cars are safe to hold during travel. *Could heavy rains flood a tunnel?* No, the walls are waterproofed, and the entrances are protected. *How fast will the express trains go?* Up to forty-five miles per hour. *Can you get a transfer from the subway to the streetcars or elevated lines?* No. *Can you stick your head out of a subway car like you can on a streetcar?* No, the lower windows are locked.

The questions were endless. Nobody was more curious than the city's children.

The day before the subway was to open, about fifty boys ventured to their new favorite place for hijinks. At the one place where the subway trains would be emerging from underground for a brief bolt through the outdoors, near 120th Street, the boys discovered a low barrier about four feet high right next to the tracks. At four thirty in the afternoon, the boys gathered to sit on the ledge and wait for a train taking a test run to pass by. Just as they heard one approaching, one of the boys, about twelve years old, lost his balance and fell right onto the tracks. The motorman fortunately was running at a slow speed and was able to apply his emergency brake, giving the boy just enough time to scramble to his feet and hustle back to his ledge, where he gleefully taunted the train as it passed.

OCTOBER 27, 1904

FOR OLDER NEW YORKERS, OCTOBER 27, 1904, had a familiar feel. Two decades earlier, on a cloudless, breezy May afternoon, the city had come out in droves to celebrate the opening of the Brooklyn Bridge, fourteen years in the making. Both engineering marvels had come at great sacrifice. Twenty-seven men died building the Brooklyn Bridge. Twice as many, fifty-four workers and civilians, perished during the four years of the subway's construction, from anonymous Italians whose bodies were never identified to former war heroes who oversaw construction to innocent onlookers and ordinary working citizens whose fate was decided simply by their proximity to an explosion. And, as with the Brooklyn Bridge, where the greatest fear of its builders were jumpers who saw the span as an adventurous challenge or an easy path to death, the subway men nervously waited for the first train to strike a person carelessly crossing the tracks. Both of those fears would be realized within days of their celebrated openings.

For the Brooklyn Bridge party, President Chester A. Arthur came. Governor Cleveland was there. Buildings were draped in red and white and blue bunting, and vendors peddled everything from bananas to buttons to flags to pictures to commemorative medals. Schools stayed open, and so did the stock exchange, but classrooms were almost all empty, and only a few brokers bothered to show up to the trading floor. When the speeches were finished and the ceremony was over, thousands flocked to rush across the 1,595-foot span above the East River. Brooklyn and Manhattan were still two cities at the time, but the bridge was a signal of what was to come a decade and a half later, when consolidation would link them officially as well as physically.

For the opening of the subway, an equally glorious, if slightly chillier day, the red, white, and blue flags and bunting returned, the boats in the harbor once again bellowed their horns, and the hucksters pounced anew. "Popcorn!" they hollered out in the crowd. "Git a programme, git a programme!" All the dignitaries turned out, too, except this time the most important one curiously skipped the festivities. President Roosevelt, the former police commissioner of the city and governor of the state, who owed his rise to the people of New York, sent his apology in a concise, formally worded telegram that must have disappointed the men behind the subway. "The president regrets his inability to accept the courteous invitation," read the note from Roosevelt's press secretary.

Aside from the president's absence, there was one other noticeable difference between the two historic days. The thousands who came out for the Brooklyn Bridge's unveiling flocked to the same place, the shores of Brooklyn and Manhattan, as if pulled there by a powerful magnet. The crowd that began to turn out early in the morning for the subway's opening fanned out across the city, lining up outside of stations from City Hall to Murray Hill to Union Square to Columbus Circle to Washington Heights. There was to be a noontime celebration, but it was for six hundred invited guests only.

The places to be, as New Yorkers smartly figured, were the stairways and kiosks of the subway. Trains were not going to accept passengers until seven o'clock at night, after a long day of speeches and a celebratory ride by public officials. But that didn't stop the crowds from gathering as the sun came up, and, in what was a preview of life in New York City in the twentieth century, there was pushing and shoving and kicking before the doors had even whooshed open. Expecting a crowd far beyond what the subway was capable of handling on a daily basis, Frank Hedley, the general manager of the subway, warned people to be patient. Never before, he reminded New Yorkers, had a single, giant railroad system been opened at once "on the tick of a clock," as he put it. "I don't want the public to pass judgment on the road for the first two days. It would not be exactly fair to us. After that, however, we are willing to submit ourselves to the most critical tests."

At one o'clock, Mayor McClellan led a procession into the alderman chamber of City Hall. The room could hold five hundred people, and there were at least that many inside. Ex-mayor Van Wyck joined him, as did the mostly unrecognizable members of the Rapid Transit Commission and the directors of the Interborough Rapid Transit Company. The wives of all the leading men were escorted in, along with judges; priests; business leaders; the president of Columbia University, Nicholas Murray Butler; and prominent engineers and railroad men, including Cornelius Vanderbilt. The crowd had mostly settled when the final three men entered, each receiving so much applause that the ovations blended together. Parsons, Belmont, and McDonald filed in together, weary after what had been a long night of drinking at Sherry's, where the tables were adorned with tall potted rosebushes, a miniature facsimile of the subway was laid on the floor, and Belmont was presented with a magnificent two-foot-tall silver cup. The initials A. B. were on one side of it, and on the other, an inscription: "Presented to August Belmont by the directors of the Interborough Rapid Transit Company in appreciation of his services as President in constructing the Rapid Transit Subway, October 27, 1904."

ONLY A FEW HOURS LATER, they settled into their seats to savor the moment more officially. The tall, bearded, brilliant engineer was the youngest, just forty-four; the short and stiff banker was fifty-one; and the bald, potbellied builder was the elder statesman at sixty.

Parsons had quieted any critics who had suggested he was too young to design the subway for the city. His mastery of the city's topography, his stern leadership, and his firm grasp of the latest technologies had all been proved, and he had brought the subway to this day on time and on budget. If there was a flaw in his leadership style, it was his almost cold-hearted response to the tragedies that occurred on his watch. But refusing to let emotions scare him into charting a new course was his way of remaining focused on the task, treating it like a business, not a family.

For Belmont, who had no intention of getting involved in the subway and was only drawn in when McDonald did not have the money, it was validation. "The subway would not have been built if I had not taken hold of the work," the arrogant Belmont reflected years later. "McDonald had a contract with the city, but he could not get the money to finance the work." It was true that Belmont put himself at risk with the deal, because if something had happened to McDonald, Belmont would have had to replace him. He said his lawyers warned him but that he was determined. "I told them I would take the risk and I did. If I had not, the subway would not have been built—at least not at that time."

McDonald could not make the same boast. If he had not been chosen to build the subway, surely someone else would have come along to do it. But tunneling through the schist of Manhattan had been a huge and dangerous challenge, nothing like what London had done by digging its subway through soft blue clay. Plus, London's Underground was only longer than New York's subway after multiple extensions over decades. New York's twenty-one-mile system, every inch constructed under McDonald, was the world's longest subway built in one shot. Boston's first subway along Tremont and Boylston streets, the first in America, was only one and a half miles long when it opened, though it now had more than five miles of tracks. To be sure, there had been collapses and explosions and careless mistakes under McDonald, like storing dynamite in a shed lit by candles, and more than fifty men had died under his stewardship. But after four years of construction, from that day in March of 1900 when the streets were torn up into rubble, the subway was a sight to behold, the air underground was a pleasure to breathe, and the trains ran fast and smooth. In the end, those were McDonald's gifts to the city.

As the three men walked into the overflowing room, Parsons blushed and Belmont glowed. McDonald smiled broadly, even though inside he was seething. He had not been on the original invite list for the day's events, and when he found out he flashed his Irish temper by raising a stink and calling a reporter to his office. "When the dirt is off your shovel," the man who built the subway groused, "Wall Street doesn't give a damn for you." His invitation arrived soon after.

MCCLELLAN OPENED THE PROCEEDING with a declaration: "Without rapid transit, Greater New York would be little more than a geographical expression." He went on to compare the subway to the Brooklyn Bridge and to discuss how the two projects brought the city into a new era that would help New Yorkers forget what part of the city they came from and instead unite them "in a common destiny." He then introduced his chief engineer.

For Parsons, this was a moment he'd almost given up on seeing. His trip to China was a distant memory. He had recorded nearly every single day of construction meticulously in his diary, aware of the significance of the achievement. But now, with a podium and an audience, and having a chance to finally exhale and talk about obstacles overcome; the lives lost, including his friend, Ira Shaler; and the revolution New York City was about to undergo, Parsons, wearing his customary long black coat, had no interest in the spotlight he richly deserved. "Mr. Mayor, Mr. Orr, and Mr. President," he began after the applause had died down, "I have the honor and the very great pleasure to state the Rapid Transit Railroad from the City Hall Station to the station at One Hundred and Forty Fifth Street on the west side line, is ready and complete for operation." As he stepped away, the applause lasted longer than his speech.

McDonald and Belmont had no problem embracing the cheers. McDonald came prepared with a speech that he unfolded and, after briefly fixing his eyeglasses, read in a voice so soft that he could hardly be heard beyond the first few rows. Perhaps forgetting his words from four years earlier, when he said building the subway would be like digging a cellar, he admitted being nervous about bidding for the work.

He graciously thanked Belmont and Parsons and, in his final words, the people of New York: "I scarcely believe that their patience and forbearance have been or will be equaled elsewhere, but I trust that the result will amply repay you all." Belmont spoke last and praised the city for embracing a public-private financial model that should be followed for projects from that day forward. After Mayor McClellan had stood and said, "I, as mayor, in the name of the people, declare the subway open," Belmont walked over to him and handed the mayor a mahogany case. There was one last act to complete before the subway belonged to the citizens of New York.

OUTSIDE CITY HALL, A SEA of more than five thousand people covered the steps, filled the plaza, and surrounded the kiosk of the City Hall station. It was almost 2:30 in the afternoon when a procession of men in tall silk top hats and long black frocks came bounding down the steps and marched briskly into a roped-off corridor lined on both sides by police, who fought to keep the pushing and shoving crowd back. As Frank Hedley, the subway's general manager, led the group toward the City Hall kiosk, they were greeted by cheers and applause that drowned out the tooting factory whistles, the horns of ferries and tugs from the nearby harbor, and the chiming of church bells. Hedley opened the station door, and the group, with McClellan still holding that mahogany case, descended the steps to the platform. A shiny silver subway train with eight cars attached sat there, and in seconds it was filled above its capacity with the officials and a few dozen thrill-seeking stragglers who'd managed to sneak in behind them before the station door was closed. In the front car, McClellan opened up the case to reveal a silver key, and Hedley took it and reached to slide it into a hole on the motor, only to be momentarily stymied.

"Doesn't fit very well," he said. But after tinkering for a few seconds, he succeeded, and with a sudden hissing noise the electric motor buzzed to life. Hedley leaned over to McClellan with some last-minute instructions. "Are we ready?" the mayor hollered. "All right," Hedley answered him while keeping his hand on the emergency brake. "Slow at first, remember!"

McClellan, young and clean-shaven with dark wavy hair, cut a dashing figure. A city alderman by the time he was twenty-seven, he was elected mayor over Seth Low in 1903 at the age of thirty-eight. His father had run against Abraham Lincoln for president and had been a famous Civil War general. Though McClellan had no formal role in the subway's approval or construction, he was savvy enough to realize that his citizens were clamoring for it, and on his first day in office he took a tour of the tunnels as a way to show his interest and appreciation for it. Unlike his most immediate predecessors, who were voted out of office in a year or two, McClellan proved popular enough to last five years, and during his term his fondness for huge public works projects grew as he oversaw the construction of the Queensboro and Manhattan bridges. For the subway, he merely benefited from arriving in office at the right time, and he made history when he pushed his hand forward and began the first subway ride in New York's history.

The car rounded a corner, and the lights of the Brooklyn Bridge station came into view. The car jerked to a stop without warning when the emergency brake was accidentally bumped, causing everyone on board to lurch forward. But the mayor got the hang of things and had the subway moving again in no time, picking up speed while Hedley blew the train's whistle to warn track workers they were coming. As they pulled into the Spring Street station, McClellan turned to Hedley. "Shall I slow her down here," he said, talking as if he'd been a motorman his whole life. "You're going slow enough," Hedley answered. "But aren't you tired of it? Don't you want the motorman to take hold?" Like a boy playing with his new toy, the mayor shot back with a quick reply. "No sir! I'm running this train."

Run it he did. Zooming up Fourteenth Street and along Fourth Avenue (which is now Park Avenue), McClellan pushed the train faster, his passengers behind him oblivious to how nervous he was making Hedley. They passed idling trains that had not yet been allowed to start and flew by track workers, ticket takers, and guards, who doffed their hats and cheered as the special train zoomed through. Into Grand Central Station they came, and then it was gone. A minute later, the passengers spotted a large electric sign four feet high and twelve feet long, with a single word glowing: TIMES. Here, McClellan shouted out, "Times Square Station," but instead of slowing, he pushed the subway harder, up to forty-three miles per hour, far faster than Hedley had anticipated going on what was supposed to be a leisurely pleasure trip. Up the west side they went, past Sixty-sixth Street, where Hedley turned to McClellan with a plea. "Slower, here, sloooow-er! Ea-sy for the curve."

They passed a worker, who neatly sidestepped the train when he saw it coming, and then glided toward the last express station at Ninety-sixth Street, where it slid over a switch in the ground onto the northbound local track. Nineteen minutes the trip lasted, about five minutes longer than the express ride from the Brooklyn Bridge to Ninety-sixth would normally take under the control of a professional motorman, but impressive nonetheless.

It was after Ninety-sixth when McClellan finally took his hand off the control and let the motorman on board, George L. Morrison, take over. McClellan, taking out a cigar that he quickly lit and puffed, shook his tired wrist. "Well, that was a little tiresome, don't you know," he said. "Why, you have to keep pressing that thing down all the time, for if you relax your hand the train will stop."

With Morrison at the controls, the train continued north, until, without warning, the passengers, who had been staring mostly at darkened tunnels, were suddenly looking out into the dusk. North of 122nd Street, the subway train emerged from the ground onto a viaduct that crossed Manhattan Valley. It was the only place where it ran in the open air, and New Yorkers who knew of this precise spot came out to cheer it on, shouting from the streets and rooftops. In response, Morrison blew the train's whistle before it disappeared back out of sight at 135th Street.

BY EVENING, THE CROWDS WERE on the verge of bursting through the doors of the kiosks to get inside the stations. A slogan that had been shouted out for years and written in big headlines at one point or another by nearly every newspaper in the city began to be chanted in all seriousness, as it was now possible. "Fifteen minutes to Harlem!" the cries rang out. Most of the men held nickels in their hands, while the women who lined up had five pennies, ready to hand over their coins in return for a green IRT ticket. In the next five hours, 111,881 passengers would pay to ride the subway, and it seemed like every last one of them was standing outside a station somewhere across the city.

The biggest crowds gathered at the express stations, from the Brooklyn Bridge stop to Grand Central to Times Square, where more than three hundred people filled the sidewalk and poured into the street. On the platforms underground, the ticket sellers braced themselves, worried about being unable to collect their fares and terrified of being crushed. Every New York police officer was on duty, sent out to protect the doors of the kiosks and stairways until permission to open them was received. It looked like a riot but felt like a carnival, since the pushing and shoving was of the friendly variety and anyone who had a hand free blew a whistle to keep up the party atmosphere.

A FEW MINUTES BEFORE seven o'clock in the evening of October 27, 1904, a familiar ringing sound echoed under the streets of New York. It was first heard in the uptown stations, and then quickly it began to be heard in the downtown stations. Alexander Graham Bell's telephone, thirty years after its invention, was now as much a part of everyday life in New York City as the subway was destined to become. Telephones had been placed inside the stations to allow for the different managers to call each other and for emergency calls to be placed in the event a train had to be stopped. The ringing at this hour lasted only a few seconds. For when the station managers of the Interborough Rapid Transit Company answered the calls at their different posts across the city, they were all greeted with the same three-word message: "Let 'em in."

EPILOGUE

IN OCTOBER 2012, THE UNTHINKABLE HAPPENED. And then four months later, it happened again.

First, New Yorkers got to feel what it must have been like in 1888, when that angry blizzard shut down the elevated trains and rendered horse-pulled carriages useless, grinding the city to a standstill. It was snow then, and 125 years later it was rain, from a hurricane named Sandy. With the streets of Gotham flooded, a system that had ballooned to 468 stations and covered more than eight hundred miles was essentially shut down. New Yorkers were paralyzed. And four months later, it happened in Boston, though it was a much more traditional blow that shut down America's first subway. A blizzard in February 2013 dumped foot upon foot upon foot of heavy snow, until the head of the Massachusetts Bay Transportation Authority said that it was too dangerous to keep the trains running and shut down the subway and the commuter rail.

Predictably, commuters in both cities griped about the shutdowns, confused about how they were supposed to get anywhere of any great distance if they could not ride their subway. And, just as predictably, when their systems churned back to life after the messes left behind by their respective storms could be cleared, those same commuters rejoiced as if they had just had air restored to their lungs.

· · ·

THE FIRST HOURS OF the New York City subway in 1904 were not unlike the first few hours of the Boston subway back in 1897. Carnival-like atmospheres saw passengers who could not wait to descend the stairs beneath their streets and clamber on board for a journey they had been debating for so long. Fear of the underground was gone, replaced by a palpable excitement at what the future held. In New York, between the public opening at 7:00 P.M. and midnight on October 27, 1904, more than 100,000 passengers took a ride on the subway, while in Boston, which had opened its subway at 6:00 A.M. rather than in the evening, more than 250,000 people took a trip on the first day. And then, in the blink of an eye, the subway was ingrained into the culture of the two cities. It didn't take days or weeks or months or years for the cities to adapt to their new world. It took hours, proof of how ready the citizens were for the change.

In Boston, on September 3, 1897, two days after America's first subway opened, a headline in *The Globe* read NOVELTY OVER. The story told of how the turnstiles in the stations were officially a nuisance, how the evening rush hour was handled without a hitch, and how the public's attention had already turned to the question of removing the railway tracks from their downtown streets to put the miserable past behind them as quickly as possible. So popular was the subway that when *The Boston Post* proclaimed in a story on September 12 that "hideous germs lurk in the underground air" and tried to frighten readers with the enlarged drawing of a hideous "subway microbe," with beady eyes and tentacles, the story was largely ignored and did little to dissuade passengers.

When a final judgment was able to be rendered months later, it was found that the subway was more than doubling the speed and capacity of the old surface lines. In the days before there was a subway, a survey of traffic on Tremont Street by the Boston Transit Commission had found that more than two hundred trolley cars per hour moved at a speed of two miles per hour, or about the speed of a crawling baby. Inside the subway tunnel, almost three hundred cars moved the same distance easily in an hour, and they traveled at eight miles per hour, or about the speed of a brisk jog. Subways may have been more expensive to build than elevated trains, but it was obvious from the first day that they were able to carry more passengers by far than any other mode of transit. They carried nearly five times as many as streetcars, eight times as many as motor buses, and fourteen times as many as private automobiles.

New Yorkers adapted just as quickly. Their subway had barely been open for an hour or two when a Philadelphia man named F. B. Shipley stood up from his seat as his train pulled away and offered it to a young woman. It was, he explained, the polite thing to do. Another passenger who took his inaugural train ride that first evening asked his conductor in a matter-of-fact manner, "Can I get a transfer?" as if it were a question he'd been asking his whole life. The men returning home from work that evening got off at their designated stations as if it had been their daily commuting routine. Even Mayor McClellan knew what to do, stepping briskly off his train with a lighted cigar in his mouth and bounding up the steps to head back to his office. And it took barely a minute of operation for the first theft on the subway to be reported, when a West Side resident named Henry Barrett told police that he took the first train at 7:02 P.M. and that one minute later his $500 horseshoe pin with fifteen diamonds on it was gone.

No neighborhood was more excited about the subway than Harlem. For years, the slogan "Fifteen minutes to Harlem" had been a rallying cry for what a subway could mean for helping develop uptown New York. And now that day was here, and it was true. When the first subway train carrying a full load of paying passengers burst out from the tunnel in Harlem and into the open air above Manhattan Street, a hotly contested baseball game in which a player had just smashed a home run came to a sudden stop. The olive-green subway train demanded the full attention of the spectators, and bats and balls dropped to the ground. Fans surged closer to the track to get a good look, and they waved their handkerchiefs and hats as the train shot past them.

FOR MOST OF THE POLITICIANS, businessmen, and engineers whose lives were defined by the subways in Boston and New York, the years that followed the openings were good. Some moved on to other challenges, furthering their legacy, while others slipped quietly into seclusion, satisfied with their accomplishments. Two of them feuded over their respective roles in history. Two others saw their lives end with shocking and tragic twists.

Sadly, the man who first proposed a giant subway system for New York and then used the blizzard of 1888 to convince his citizens that there was no other choice, was there to see the first shovel go into the ground, but he died a year before the subway opened. If not for Abram Hewitt's visionary thinking—to have the city pay for and own the subway system and hire a private business to build and run it—who knows when the New York City subway would have been built?

As for the bullish Irishman, John McDonald, he was briefly considered as a candidate for New York governor in 1904, at the height of his popularity, and he was said to have left behind a multimillion-dollar fortune from his work building the subway when he died peacefully in 1911. August Belmont also reaped millions from his decision to finance McDonald's work. But Belmont was already rich at the time, and the politics of New York took such a toll on him that he regretted ever getting involved in the subway. He much preferred the life of a sportsman, and it was at the stud farm in Lexington, Kentucky, that he inherited from his father, where Man o' War, Tracery, and Rock Sand, three of horse racing's star Thoroughbreds in the early twentieth century, were all bred. Belmont Park in Long Island, one of the greatest horse-racing tracks in the country, remains as much a monument to his life as does the New York subway. When Belmont died of blood poisoning at his Park Avenue apartment in 1924 at the age of seventy-one, the news rocketed around the worlds of racing, politics, and big business, and sympathy cablegrams and telegrams flooded the Belmont home for weeks.

A DECADE LATER, FRANK J. Sprague died. If one man deserves more credit than he's received for the birth of the subway, it's Sprague. The London Underground was a remarkable breakthrough for mankind, but its greatest flaw was the reason it was not replicated for thirty years. Steam trains in underground tunnels made no sense. Only once Sprague perfected the electric motor and the multiple-unit control system could cleaner and quieter subways be built around the world.

Sadly for Sprague, who died on October 25, 1934, the shadow of Thomas Edison proved difficult to escape, even after Sprague branched out on his own. The roots of the resentment Sprague felt toward Edison can be traced back to an article that appeared in *The New York Sun* in 1919. The writer, Edward Marshall, interviewed Edison about the electric streetcar. Marshall credited Edison with "the pioneer appliance of cheap, quick power street transportation in America. Naturally he is proud of it."

Sprague, who in the 1880s had led the fierce competition to electrify street railways, could not sit by quietly while Edison received what he believed was undue reward. Two weeks after *The Sun* article appeared, Sprague answered back with a long-winded response that ran in *The Sun* under the headline INVENTORS OF THE ELECTRIC RAILWAY: FRANK J. SPRAGUE PROTESTS AGAINST THE SHARE OF THE GLORY ASSIGNED IN AN INTERVIEW TO THOMAS A. EDISON. The dispute played out in the pages of *The Sun* over the next few months, two engineering greats demanding the other back off certain claims. Neither would. Sprague went so far as to take the fight to Congress, asking for a correction in the description of Edison's work that was used in awarding him the Congressional Medal of Honor. It was to no avail. Only long after Edison's death in 1932 and Sprague's death two years later did a third party attempt to resolve the matter. Sprague's widow, Harriet, his second wife, published a short biography, for which the title alone revealed where she stood: *Frank J. Sprague and the Edison Myth*.

As for another engineer who played a huge role in both cities, Fred Pearson, the Tufts prodigy, his life would be filled with one remarkable achievement after another before ending in a most shocking fashion. He died aboard the *Lusitania*, the British ocean liner torpedoed by the Germans in 1915. Pearson would owe much of his engineering legacy to the Whitney brothers.

. . .

OF ALL THE MEN who devoted years of their lives to one of the first two subways in America, it was the man who launched Sprague to his greatest fame and who first proposed the idea of tunneling under Boston Common who lived the most surprising years after leaving the subway behind. Henry Melville Whitney never could settle down, even with a wife and a rollicking houseful of children.

His Dominion Coal Company, the Canadian venture that lured him away from Boston, fizzled like so many others for him. He returned to Boston in the early 1900s, and he was there for his younger and more famous brother's death in 1904. But Henry Whitney could never quite convince the citizens of Boston to forget about the scandal that nearly doomed him and about his failure to push through his proposal for a subway tunnel. He ran for governor twice and lieutenant governor once, losing each time. But no matter, politics would never have suited Whitney. He could hardly hear a lick or sit still longer than a minute or two. He was happiest when he was out exploring the serious or the frivolous.

A rambling letter to his daughter Laura in 1914, written from his home in Cohasset after he turned seventy-five, provides some insight into Whitney's impatience and impetuousness. He wrote that he was feeling healthy and strong and full of new ideas. California, he said, was calling to him! The man who once brought his children foul-tasting orange juice was on to a new citrus taste. "Why not lemon juice?" he wrote. "The same as grape and lime juice, and varieties of other fruit juices, and I thought that there was some good reason why it had not been exploited before, that perhaps it would not keep its vitality." He said he had looked into the matter by speaking to chemistry professors and to the owners of S. S. Pierce, the big market in Brookline's Coolidge Corner, and that he had been assured that not only would lemon juice stay fresh, it would be a popular item on store shelves. "Nothing may come of all this," he wrote his daughter, "but it is surely something to think of and may possibly result in giving one something to do. I am certain that Whitney's Pure Lemon Juice would attract some notice in every store in Boston."

Nothing came of Whitney's Pure Lemon Juice, like so many of his crazy pursuits. But for Whitney, life was never about the reward. Or the money. It was about the chase. From steamships to streetcars, from oil to gas, from orange juice to lemon juice, he saw his fortunes rise and his fortunes fall. One of his last investments, into a Rhode Island coal mine, proved to be his biggest mistake. When he finally succumbed to pneumonia on January 25, 1923, at his home on St. Paul Street in Brookline at the age of eighty-three, nobody could have foreseen what they would discover. Whitney had recently divorced Margaret Green after nearly half a century of marriage, and she left him flat broke. The man who had popularized the notion of urban mass-rail transit in America, who electrified the street railways of Boston and created the world's largest street railway company, who came within a whisker of being elected Massachusetts governor, who owned a summer mansion on the beach and rode horses as a hobby, who dressed impeccably in pinstripe suits, and whose brother very nearly became president of the United States, died penniless and alone. Hundreds of millions of dollars had passed through Whitney's fingers during his lifetime. And all he left behind was $1,221.93, a $400 Dodge 1921 touring car, a $150 watch, a $75 fur coat, and $20 in books and miscellaneous belongings. It was an unfathomable end to the life of a man who had an enduring impact on everyday life in urban America.

ON A BITTER MORNING in February 1912, workers for the Degnon Contracting Company, along with a number of New York City officials, carried lighted candles and wormed their way into a ventilation shaft that took them beneath Broadway in lower Manhattan. They were there to scope out the challenges that lay ahead for them in building section 2 of the Broadway subway line. A few days earlier, *The Times* had written that workers should expect to come across "an interesting relic" during their project, in the vicinity of Warren and Murray streets. Sure enough, after climbing down the shaft, the group stumbled into precisely what *The Times* predicted they would: Alfred Beach's pneumatic subway tunnel, forty years after it had been sealed up for good. They could not believe what they saw.

It looked more like an archaeological find than the engineering marvel that it once was. The one-block tube remained in almost pristine condition, and while the rails in the ground had rusted away, the brickwork lining the walls remained dry and solid, a testament to how well it had been built. The fountain was there, rotted and dried up but intact, a bizarre reminder of Beach's vision for underground splendor. And a steam pipe was leaking hot air, but otherwise the air in the tube was comfortable. The car that had been blown through the tube by a giant fan, carrying two dozen excited passengers on each trip back and forth, was a wreck of rotted wood. Its wheels were nowhere to be found. But the shield Beach had designed to push safely through the earth was still there, or at least the rusted metal frame of it, leaning up against a far wall that it had once bored through inch by inch.

What should have been treated as a piece of history and at least photographed extensively to preserve its memory was instead regarded as little more than a nuisance in the way of progress. A few random artifacts were collected as souvenirs; pieces of the digging shield were offered to Beach's elderly son, Frederick, who had taken over as editor of *Scientific American*; and the laborers for Degnon Contracting got to work on the Broadway subway line. Quite quickly, most of Beach's tunnel was destroyed, and the portions that were preserved were blended in with the subway station at City Hall. In just a few weeks, workers had dismantled what had taken Beach twenty years to achieve, from the day he suggested a subway for New York in 1849, writing of "railway life down stairs, instead of railway life up stairs," to the day it opened in 1870. The man who had challenged, and beaten, the indomitable Boss Tweed surely deserved a more suitable honor.

NOT EVEN ONE YEAR AFTER the New York subway opened in 1904, William Barclay Parsons moved on to be the chief engineer of the Cape Cod Canal. He would not go it alone. Financing the project was none other than his partner on the subway, August Belmont. The canal, which connected Buzzards Bay and Cape Cod Bay through a two-hundred-foot-wide S-shaped path, fulfilled a dream of New Englanders that was three centuries old, and that had once interested George Washington in 1776 as a speedier way to move his Continental army from Boston to New York. Nothing came of Washington's dream, and it would be another 140 years before another great leader came along and built the canal. The hundredth anniversary of the Cape Cod Canal will be celebrated in 2014, and Parsons and Belmont are sure to be hailed.

Parsons's motivation to build the canal was not unlike what had drawn him to the subway. The work's difficulty, importance to businesses big and small, and ability to greatly improve the quality of life for thousands of people all appealed to Parsons. Circumnavigating the tip of Cape Cod, where the weather could be treacherous and the coastline was a jagged edge of the earth, had become a death trap for ships. One count tallied 2,131 shipwrecks along the coast of the Cape between 1845 and 1903, during which time 700 sailors died. Parsons believed a canal was more than just a way to shorten the trip for big boats by five or six hours, or seventy-five miles. It was essential for improving the flow of goods between Boston and New York and ensuring that the two cities remained the two dominant cities on the East Coast. His prediction that the canal would take three years to build proved only slightly optimistic, as the waters between the two bays blended together on July 4, 1914, when Parsons allowed his wife, Anna, and daughter, Sylvia, to lift a few ceremonial shovelfuls of dirt. With that act, they cleared the way for a rush of water to form one single winding route between the two bays. The Cape Cod Canal had taken five years to complete.

Between the subway and the canal, Parsons established himself as one of the greatest engineering minds in history, and it was a mind that every city in America soon wanted to borrow. Cambridge, Massachusetts; Cleveland; Washington, D.C.; San Francisco; Detroit; Philadelphia; Atlanta; Newark, New Jersey; and Westchester County, New York, all sought reports from Parsons on their transit possibilities. The small firm he started with his brother became a behemoth that thrives to this day.

Known as Parsons Brinckerhoff, it employs thousands worldwide and boasts a complement of projects that includes sports arenas, rail lines, canals, pipelines, and highway tunnels, including Boston's infamous Big Dig.

In a return to its roots, Parsons Brinckerhoff is responsible for the design of the Second Avenue subway now under construction in New York. This has been called the most complex, and one of the most expensive, public projects the city has ever undertaken. No longer reliant on picks, axes, and a crude tunneling shield to push forward, today's sandhogs, wearing neon-green vests and hard hats, are digging two twenty-two-foot-wide tunnels, eighty feet below the surface, using a wormlike machine that chews up the earth with its head of whirling steel discs. When they blast, it's a controlled blast that merely causes a bump or vibration on the surface. Windows are not shattered, and horses don't let out yelps of fear. But that's not to say the neighborhood hasn't complained or that the workers don't face risks. It is, after all, solid rock they are tunneling through.

On March 21, 2013, a present-day sandhog nearly met the same fate as Timothy Sullivan, one of the earliest sandhogs, the worker killed in the Washington Heights explosion in 1903. It was his son, Sammy, who watched as his body was carried out of the tunnel. More than a century later, Joseph Barone, a fifty-one-year-old sandhog from Lyndhurst, New Jersey, slipped while walking through a tunnel near Ninety-fifth Street and found himself pinned, waist deep, beneath plywood and amid freezing water and mud one hundred feet below the streets. One rescue worker described the predicament as "a hell hole." It took a pulley system, a backhoe, and a powerful griphoist machine, not to mention the muscles and determination of dozens of firefighters, to finally dig out Barone, who had hypothermia but suffered only minor injuries. "Everybody did what they had to do to get me out," Barone told his rescuers a month later. "Otherwise, I wouldn't be here—you'd be talking to a box." His words were a reminder of the dangers of tunnel digging, but the fact that he was alive to thank his rescuers was also a reminder of how far man had come since the earliest subway tunnels were built.

When it's completed, the Second Avenue subway will be a fitting

tribute to the founder of Parsons Brinckerhoff, who would have appreciated the challenge it presented. William Parsons, as much a writer as an
engineer throughout his life, was at work on a book about engineering
during the Renaissance when he died on May 9, 1932, after surgery following a pulmonary embolism at the age of seventy-three.

As the people of San Francisco, Washington, Miami, Atlanta, Chicago, Baltimore, Jersey City, Cleveland, and Philadelphia would discover
in the coming century, only the subway could successfully relieve their
overcrowding. Even Los Angeles, a city where people live as much in their
cars as their homes, is embracing the underground train, building a line
that will connect downtown with the Pacific Ocean in a project being
called the "Subway to the Sea." Subway ridership nationwide reached record levels in 2012, and New York and Boston were no exceptions. In
New York, 1.7 billion trips were taken on the subway, the highest total
in sixty-two years, while Boston recorded more than 400 million rides,
the first time that milestone has been broken.

WHEN ALFRED BEACH PROPOSED TUNNELING under Broadway
in 1849, the public reacted as if he had suggested that man should one day
fly to the moon. Preposterous! And he was laughed right back to his job
at *Scientific American*. Then, twenty years later, he blew a train down a
track inside of a glittering tunnel, and the public gasped in disbelief. All
Beach had done was to use the power of suggestion to push mankind to
imagine the possibilities of technology, to think big, not small, to always
ask, Why not? instead of merely, Why?

A century after Beach's dream died, an article appeared in the *Los
Angeles Times* under the headline L.A. TO N.Y. IN HALF AN HOUR? The
article in 1972 went on to describe the acclaimed RAND Corporation
physicist Robert M. Salter's dream of digging a tunnel along the routes of
U.S. highways that crossed the country. Tubes inside the tunnel would
carry trains that floated on electromagnetic fields—at top speeds of ten
thousand miles per hour. The cars would float on the fields just as a surf-
board rides on the ocean's waves. There would be no motors on the train

and no tracks. No friction at all. In the cases he studied, Salter, who died in 2011, suggested that in the ideal scenario, the trip from coast to coast could be achieved in twenty-one minutes. "Safe, convenient, low-cost, efficient, and non-polluting service is offered," Salter said in one of the many talks he delivered on his idea. "With short transit times, it is possible for a businessman in New York to travel to Los Angeles during his lunch hour and hold an afternoon/morning meeting and return at his regular quitting time."

Laughable? Of course. But Salter was no crackpot. He started out as an intern at General Motors and rose up to work for the military on anti-ballistic missile technology. He was, like Alfred Beach, a dreamer. And he was a student of history, who noted how tunneling under the English Channel was proposed during the era of Napoleon, only to be delayed for centuries, and how Henry Ford developed the automobile long before the government decided roads and highways were a worthy investment. Salter said that the obstacles to something as ambitious as a "vactrain," as it has come to be called for its use of vacuumlike technology, are not technological. They are political. And, in fact, engineers at the National Power Traction Laboratory in China are said to be working on a vactrain that could travel at unheard-of speeds of one thousand kilometers per hour. "The U.S. has the greatest industrial and technical basis in world history," Salter once said. "We proved that we could perform the prodigious feat of putting man on the moon. It would be useful to employ a small fraction of that capability to explore our future options in travel on this planet."

A cross-country supersonic subway with no motors and no tracks, powered only by electromagnetic charges? Why not, indeed.

ACKNOWLEDGMENTS

It was about halfway through the writing of this book when my family traveled to New York City for a summer weekend getaway. Most of my nights and weekends at that point were consumed by subway research, and, kids being kids, my two never came to understand why I couldn't just come outside and throw a ball around. "Do you have to work this weekend?" was a question that became painful for me to hear. Sometimes five-year-old Julia would tiptoe quietly into my office and squeeze my arm, or three-year-old Ben would come in with his favorite truck and fall asleep on the couch just so he could be with me. So this weekend away was special, and when we ventured down the steps in my old neighborhood, the Upper West Side, to the Seventy-ninth Street station, I could feel their excitement. As my wife and I sat and waited for the downtown number 1 train to pull in, Ben and Julia alternated between sitting with us and running up to the yellow line and peering down the tracks. Back and forth, back and forth they went. I finally snapped a picture of the two of them leaning out, and when I look at it today, their heads turned sideways, their wide eyes staring into the dark tunnel, I can't help thinking that the anticipation they were feeling must have been something like what the first passengers in Boston and New York were feeling on the day their subways opened.

When you spend the better part of five years on a single project, there will inevitably be a lot of people who, somewhere along the way, played a part in helping you get through it. For me, that list begins at home. My wife, Mimi Braude, not only allowed me to tackle this mountain, she embraced it eagerly with me, even though she knew it would mean a greater burden on her, from weekends alone with the kids to vacations without me to greater stress in her own job as a wonderful therapist. There were many nights when I would come home after a long day at work and find a warm dinner and hug waiting for me, even though she knew that twenty minutes later I'd be upstairs writing in the office. When the idea for this book was born, we had one child and one car, were living in a third-floor Jamaica Plain condo, and my office was a rickety Ikea desk crammed inside of a tiny, lint-filled laundry room with wet gym clothes hanging over me. A lot has changed since then. But what never changed was my wife's endless supply of support. Not a day goes by that I am not grateful for our chance encounter at a Boston Speed Dating event.

Working in journalism, as I have for my entire career, you come across writers and editors who inspire you to do more and to do better at each stop in the journey. This book began for me at *The Boston Globe* under one such editor, Marty Baron, who left to be the executive editor of *The Washington Post,* and it was finished under another, Brian McGrory, who took the helm of *The Globe* at an especially challenging time. They are different editors, but they share a passion for narrative storytelling and thorough reporting. I couldn't ask for two better role models in my career. My long friendships and working relationships with Neil Swidey, Susanne Althoff, Anne Nelson and Scott Helman at the *Boston Globe Magazine* and with Hayley Kaufman, Rebecca Ostriker, Janice Page, Anne Fitzgerald, and Sheryl Julian in the Living/Arts team mean a great deal to me. Lisa Tuite, Wanda Joseph-Rollins, and Jeremiah Manion in the *Globe* library are some of the friendliest and most helpful people I've ever encountered at the paper, and when there was a hundred-year-old photo or story that I needed, they inevitably knew where to find it.

Joe Sullivan and Dan Shaughnessy are the big dogs in *The Globe*'s unrivaled sports department, whose wisdom and camaraderie make working at the paper fun. Bennie DiNardo is a friend and colleague. His New Hampshire home during one dark and cold winter week provided me six of my most productive days of writing, even if the loose shutter slamming into the side of the house made me feel like I was living out a Stephen King novel.

Writers lean on other writers in times of frustration or simply when it's 2:00 A.M. and the eyes are blurry and Facebook or Twitter beckon. Seth Mnookin, Keith O'Brien, Jon Marcus, and Paul Rogers all received more than the occasional late-night note from me, and they were always quick to reply with words of encouragement or to read a passage. Jon Chesto, a Boston business journalist and friend, loaned me his Cape Cod cottage for a week of solitude, a generous gesture I won't forget. John Gates and the entire team at Elevate Communications helped build my Web site and are as tapped into the Boston media scene as any group. My in-laws, Eric and Judy Braude, helped out in so many ways, from babysitting duties when a night at the movies was in order to words of encouragement to an old tunnel book that proved incredibly useful.

As you get older in life you come to appreciate your closest friends. Dan O'Neill, his wife, Carina, and their two children are like family to us. My jogs with Dan were about so much more than desperately trying to stay in shape during the writing of this book. They were my release valve, a place for me to bounce ideas off him, but also to talk about anything other than subways. He never tired of hearing one more story about Henry Whitney or William Parsons or the dangers of tunnel building, and the value of a friend like that cannot be overstated.

As invaluable as the Internet was in my research, there were plenty of documents not available online that sent me into research facilities throughout Boston, New York, and Washington, D.C. The cavernous reading rooms at the Boston Public Library and New York Public

Library are two of the most architecturally beautiful spaces in the world, and they also happen to be incredibly conducive to hammering away at a keyboard. The Massachusetts Historical Society, Bostonian Society, Library of Congress, and the libraries at Columbia University, Tufts University, Harvard College, and Cooper Union all provided useful materials. Lynn Matis at the Massachusetts Transportation Library saw me so many times she set aside a separate shelf for my things. Researchers at Parsons Brinckerhoff dug up some wonderful photos, as did Carey Stumm at the New York Transit Museum.

Several living ancestors of Henry Whitney, especially Lee Sylvester and Laura Marshall, shared invaluable photos and letters, as did Frank Sprague's grandson, John Sprague. An interview I did with ninety-four-year-old Lydia Lyman Whitney, who described her grandfather Henry as "deaf as a post," but a man with "a great sense of humor" and who was "good with people," confirmed everything I'd read about him.

My literary agent, Lane Zachary, at Zachary Shuster Harmsworth, sat with me for many lunches as we brainstormed ideas until we hit upon one that seemed just right, and then was a constant source of encouragement and wisdom. And by landing with St. Martin's Press, I was fortunate to work with an editor, Michael Flamini, whose sense of humor and broad vision helped improve this book in so many ways. Everybody at St. Martin's was incredibly encouraging, and on those nights when the clock ticked past midnight, their enthusiasm for this project kept me going.

Finally, I have to thank my older brother Jordan Most and my parents, Al and Paula Most, for so much support and encouragement. While writing this book, my wife and I moved our clan from the city to the suburbs, and during the packing I stumbled upon an old envelope filled with clippings from my childhood that my mother had saved. There were silly drawings of my brother and me, and there was a term paper I'd written on "Moby Dick" that my father had bled red ink all over to help me become a better writer. Sitting with my father and brother as a young boy on our couch in Barrington, Rhode Island, devouring box scores and reading the sports columnists in *The New York Times*, feels like a long time ago, but it also feels like yesterday.

Doug Most

September 2013

AUTHOR'S NOTE

One day while researching for this book, I was sitting in a back room at the New York Public Library with cardboard boxes in front of me, the private papers of Frank Sprague. As I opened up one envelope after another and gently fingered two particularly crinkled, yellowed letters from 1884, it was difficult to not pause and appreciate how we got where we are today. One of the letters was from Sprague to another inventor of his day, Thomas Edison, explaining why he was resigning from Edison's engineering firm. The second letter was from Edison back to Sprague, accepting the resignation. The electric subway that took me to the library and the soft light that filled the room were the achievements of these two titans, and here I was holding their original words in my hands.

The number of pages that have been devoted to the Boston subway compared with the number devoted to the New York subway is about as different as the subways themselves. The New York subway system has been the subject of dozens of books; the most authoritative is Clifton Hood's *722 Miles,* and one of the most entertaining is Benson Bobrick's *Labyrinths of Iron,* which covers the New York subway in two captivating chapters. *The City Beneath Us,* from the New York Transit Museum, has some wonderful anecdotes, and the photographs tell a story all by themselves. Of course, the Pulitzer Prize–winning historical tome *Gotham* devotes various sections to the subway's development, and every page provides an invaluable nugget.

Even though Boston's subway was America's first, it has been largely ignored by historians and authors. Bradley Clarke and O. R. Cummings's *Tremont Street Subway* is a thorough and detailed work. Stephen Puleo devotes a terrific chapter to the subway in his book, *A City So Grand*. And Brian Cudahy has written several books about Boston transit that explore its evolution. One of the most complete works of reporting on Boston's subway was done by a graduate student. Asha Elizabeth Weinstein, in her 2002 dissertation for University of California, Berkeley, delved deeply into the subway debate in a four-hundred-page study titled "The Congestion Evil: Perceptions of Traffic Congestion in Boston in the 1890s and 1920s." Her meticulous footnotes proved enormously valuable. And one book that covered the subway projects in both Boston and New York in particularly detailed fashion is Charles Cheape's *Moving the Masses*.

Just as the two cities have been covered so differently, the Whitney brothers have been treated unequally by historians. No doubt because of his political and familial connections, William Whitney became the more famous of the two. His papers have been collected at the Library of Congress, and they provide insight into his political decisions and his personal life. Mark Hirsch's 1948 biography *William C. Whitney: Modern Warwick* is authoritative, comprehensive, and wonderfully written. Less comprehensive but also useful is *Whitney Father, Whitney Heiress*, by W. A. Swanberg. The early life of Henry Whitney is best captured by his family, in Josephine Whitney Duveneck's *Life on Two Levels*. But his career really only comes to life in the pages of the *Boston Daily Globe* and the city's other newspapers of the day, which covered one of Boston's most important businessmen of the nineteenth century with detail and flair.

Finally, the transit commissions in both cities deserve credit for the papers they left behind. Without their lengthy and detailed reports in the 1890s and early 1900s, there would be no official record of how decisions were made or of the debates behind those decisions. The Internet is a wonderful thing. But the public libraries in Boston and New York are two of the finest libraries in the world, and without them, and their troves of archived materials, it's frightening to imagine how much history would be lost.

NOTES

INTRODUCTION: TWO CITIES, ONE CRISIS

1 "A menace to the health of the public": "Against the Subway," *Boston Daily Globe*, March 27, 1895.

1 "living in a tomb": "Scooting Under Boston," *Boston Daily Globe*, March 29, 1891.

2 He was short, stocky, nearly deaf: Josephine Whitney Duveneck, *Life on Two Levels: An Autobiography* (Trust for Hidden Villa, 1978), 19.

1: A SECRET SUBWAY

9 Crystal Palace was as much of an attraction as the inventions inside: "Burning of the Crystal Palace," *New York Times*, October 6, 1858.

9 In 1867, its home was the Fourteenth Street armory: Clifton Hood, *722 Miles* (The Johns Hopkins University Press, 1993), 44.

9 Alfred Ely Beach was born into a prestigious family: Joseph Brennan, *Beach Pneumatic: Alfred Beach's Pneumatic Subway and the Beginnings of Rapid Transit in New York* (2004–05), 122–23; Hood, *722 Miles*, 43; Martin W. Sandler, *Secret Subway* (National Geographic Society, 2009); Benson Bobrick, *Labyrinths of Iron* (Henry Holt, 1986), 169–93.

10 the two of them paid $800: *Scientific American* Web site, Company History, http://www .scientificamerican.com/pressroom/aboutus.cfm.

11 The patent business earned Beach a fortune: Sandler, *Secret Subway*, 24.

13 That's when Abraham Brower saw an opportunity: John Anderson Miller, *Fares, Please* (Dover Publications, 1941), 1–3.

13 The vehicle, which he called *Accommodation*: Brian J. Cudahy, *Cash, Tokens and Transfers* (Fordham University Press, 1982), 8.

14   "Bedlam on wheels": *New York Herald,* October 8, 1864.

15   "This event will go down in the history of our country": New York City Transit, "Facts and Figures" (Public Affairs Department, New York City Transit Authority, 1979), 3.

16   "You must button your coat tight about you": Francois Weil, *A History of New York* (Columbia University Press, 2004), 103.

16   On the chopped-up streets, garbage and debris: Clay McShane and Joel A. Tarr, *The Horse in the City* (The Johns Hopkins University Press, 2007), 26, 121.

17   "We can travel from New York half-way to Philadelphia": Bobrick, *Labyrinths of Iron,* 171.

17   "Nothing less than a railway underneath, instead of one above": Alfred Ely Beach, "An Underground Railroad in Broadway," *Scientific American,* November 3, 1849.

18   "It's better to wait for the Devil than to make roads down into hell": Christian Wolmar, *The Subterranean Railway* (Atlantic Books, 2004), 33.

19   Rammell and Clark story: Sandler, *Secret Subway,* 31.

20   "We feel tolerably certain": *Mechanics' Magazine,* September 1864.

20   "Ladies and gentlemen": *New York Times,* September 13, 1867.

21   "swift as Aeolus (god of Breezes) and silent as Somnus": Bobrick, *Labyrinths of Iron,* 84.

21   "The most novel and attractive feature": *Scientific American,* October 19, 1867.

21   "A tube, a car, a revolving fan!": Alfred E. Beach, *The Pneumatic Dispatch* (The American News Company, 1868), 5.

22   "Passengers by a through city tube": *New York Times,* September 16, 1867.

22   William Magear "Boss" Tweed Jr. ran the most corrupt political machine in the country: *The National Cyclopaedia of American Biography*; Edwin G. Burrows and Mike Wallace, *Gotham: A History of New York City to 1898* (Oxford University Press, 1999); David Black, *The King of Fifth Avenue: The Fortunes of August Belmont* (Dial Press, 1981).

24   Devlin's clothing store: Brennan, *Beach Pneumatic,* chapter 6.

27   "As the street in which the company": *New York Times,* January 4, 1870.

27   "In reference to the ridiculous stories": *New York Times,* January 8, 1870.

27   Western Tornado: Brennan, *Beach Pneumatic,* chapter 6.

28   "The problem of tunneling Broadway": *Evening Mail,* February 27, 1870.

28   "Certainly the most novel, if not the most successful": *New York Times,* February 27, 1870.

29   One woman later described her ride as "most delightful": Brennan, *Beach Pneumatic,* chapter 6.

29   "We took our seats in the pretty car": Ibid.

31   "Next to the air we breathe": "The Great Need, a City Railroad as a City Work," an address to property holders and the people, 1873.

2: WHERE SPIRITS, THE DEVIL, AND THE DEAD LIVE

34   Deep inside the earth: Rosalind Williams, *Notes on the Underground* (MIT Press, 2008), 9–11.

34   "the first truly atrocious Hell": Ibid., 9.

35   Sticks, rocks, picks: Don Murray, *Man Against Earth* (J. P. Lippincott, 1961), 16–23.

36 It must have been a terrifying experience: Ibid., 28.

38 "We have seen you invading our soil": Neil Swidey, "New York vs. Boston: The End Game," *Boston Globe Magazine,* July 8, 2012.

38 It had to be the strangest dinner party ever thrown: Bobrick, *Labyrinths of Iron,* 65.

39 Almost from the day he was born in 1769: Richard Beamish, *Memoir of the Life of Sir Marc Isambard Brunel* (Longman, Green, Longman and Robert, 1862), 1.

39 "Having borrowed a passport": Ibid., 20.

40 "forming tunnels or drift-ways": Ibid., 159.

41 "If I see honourable and personal employment here": Ibid., 172.

41 "My affectionate wife": Ibid., 174.

41 "preparing plans for the service of the British government": Ibid., 175.

42 The Brunel shield was an amazing machine: Ibid., 219–25.

43 "The water came on in a great wave": Ibid., 246–47.

43 "The water is in!": Ibid., 261.

43 "Ball! Ball! Collins! Collins!": Ibid., 260–62.

44 "The ground was always made to the plan.": Celia Brunel, *The Brunels, Father and Son,* (Cobden-Sanderson, 1938), 69.

44 "Another wonder has been added": "Opening of the Thames Tunnel," *Court Magazine and Monthly Critic,* April 1841, 108.

44 For the opening ceremony, a "tunnel waltz" was composed: Bobrick, *Labyrinths of Iron,* 71.

45 "The majority of the visitors went the whole distance, 1200 feet": "The Thames Tunnel," *London Times,* March 27, 1841.

3: A FAMILY FOR THE AGES

46 On May 6, 1635, John Whitney and his wife: Mark D. Hirsch, *William C. Whitney: Modern Warwick* (Archon Books, 1969), 2–3.

47 James Scollay Whitney was born on May 19, 1811: John William Denehy, *A History of Brookline, Massachusetts* (Brookline Press, 1906), 121–25.

47 Not even a year after they married: Frederick Clifton Pierce, *The Descendants of John Whitney, Who Came from London, England, to Watertown, Massachusetts, in 1635* (W. B. Conkey, 1895), 514–21.

47 Shepard & Whitney established itself: From the private writings of Josephine Whitney Duveneck, Henry Whitney's youngest daughter, courtesy of the family's descendants.

48 The boy was not even ten years old: Ibid.

49 William was called Deacon: Hirsch, *Modern Warwick,* 6.

50 At Williston Academy, nobody was allowed to coast: Ibid., 9–10.

50 On July 30, 1863, speaking to his graduation class: Ibid., 17–18.

51 "The Drama closes": Ibid., 18.

51 "It was too much bother to memorize so many words": Ibid.

52 "My dear Bill": Letter from Henry Whitney to Will Whitney, from the papers of William C. Whitney (WCW), Library of Congress, May 10, 1865.

52 "If there was anything in New York": Letter from Henry Whitney to Will Whitney, from the papers of WCW, Library of Congress, June 13, 1865.

52 "His own means don't amount to much": Don MacGillivray, "Henry Melville Whitney Comes to Cape Breton: The Saga of a Gilded Age Entrepreneur," *Acadiensis: Journal of the History of the Atlantic Region,* vol. 9, no. 1, Autumn 1979, 48.

53 Edison befriended an inventor: David Kruh, *Always Something Doing: Boston's Infamous Scollay Square* (Northeastern University Press, 1989), 35.

54 "unless you are willing to go in a packed omnibus that labors and plunges": Mark Twain, *The Chicago of Europe: And Other Tales of Foreign Travel* (Sterling Publishing Co., 2009), 79.

54 "I am entirely satisfied": Letter from William Whitney to H. B. Willson, from the papers of WCW, Library of Congress, September 11, 1867.

55 During a visit to the Fifth Avenue Hotel: Hirsch, *Modern Warwick,* 36.

56 "they would fall in love with each other": Ibid.

56 "How you looked I plainly recall": Undated letter from William Whitney to Flora Payne, from the papers of WCW, Library of Congress.

56 "The carriage would undoubtedly be a vast ornament to us": Letter from Flora Payne to Will Whitney, from the papers of WCW, Library of Congress, December 1868.

57 They married at Cleveland's First Presbyterian Church: Hirsch, *Modern Warwick,* 47–48.

57 "You have got a sweet, good wife": Ibid., 48.

57 In 1871, the street railways of Boston carried 34 million passengers: "Rapid Transit Plans in Boston," *Street Railway Journal,* January 1892.

58 In the fall of 1878: From the private writings of Josephine Whitney Duveneck.

58 impressive salary of $15,000 a year: Hirsch, *Modern Warwick,* 94.

59 clean up nearly four thousand pending suits against the city: Ibid., 95.

60 A close observer of Henry Whitney's: MacGillivray, "Henry Melville Whitney Comes to Cape Breton," 48.

60 "The car that was left behind would then fall back": Prentiss Cummings, *Street Railway System of Boston* (Professional and Industrial History of Suffolk County, Massachusetts, 1894), 292.

60 He was on his way toward investing more than $800,000: Barbara J. Sproat, "Boston Studies in Urban Political Economy, Henry Whitney's Streetcar Suburb, Beacon Street, Brookline, 1870–1910," (working paper, no date, c. 1973), 4.

61 On August 9, 1886: Legislative Committee on Roads and Bridges, *Beacon Street, Its Improvement in Brookline by Connection with Commonwealth Avenue* (Chronicle Press, 1887), 3.

61 He described Olmsted as "a man who stands second to none": *Brookline, Allston-Brighton and the Renewal of Boston* (History Press, 2010), 26.

62 He gave the town 630,000 square feet of his own land: Sproat, "Boston Studies in Urban Political Economy," 6.

63 But when Oliver Payne: Hirsch, *Modern Warwick,* 145.

64 On a February morning in 1882, William Whitney was driving his carriage: Ibid., 178.

65 On Monday, November 6, 1882: Ibid.

66 "I am exceedingly anxious": Ibid.

66 "Frankly I think there is no more chance of his being nominated for governor": Edwin Hoyt, *The Whitneys: An Informal Portrait, 1635–1975* (Weybright and Talley, 1976), 133.

67 "There is nothing prettier in the world": Letter from William Whitney to Flora Whitney, from the papers of WCW, Library of Congress, May 27, 1883.

67 "Bear up, My dear, we must": Ibid., June 6, 1883.

68 "The only time [Olive] spoke when I could not understand her": W. A. Swanberg, *Whitney Father, Whitney Heiress* (Charles Scribner's Sons, 1980), 64–65.

68 He placed it inside an envelope and would hold on to it for the rest of his life: Hirsch, *Modern Warwick*, 198.

68 when he came to speak he was armed with maps, schedules, and even sample tickets: "The Story of Your Whitney Ancestors (especially Henry Melville Whitney)," from the private papers of Josephine Whitney Duveneck.

69 *The Boston Globe,* in 1887, showed just how busy Tremont Street was downtown: Louis M. Lyons, *Newspaper Story: One Hundred Years of "The Boston Globe"* (Belknap Press of Harvard University Press, 1971), 66.

69 "That the streets of Boston are and have for a long time": Reports of Proceedings of Boston City Council, 1893.

71 "I believe that this company is destined to play a very important part": George L. Austin, "Henry M. Whitney, the Builder of the West End Street Railway System of Boston," Whitney Research Group, http://wiki.whitneygen.org/wrg/index.php/Family:Whitney ,_Henry_Melville_(1839-%3F).

71 "Into whose hands will all this pass?": "West End Stock," *Boston Daily Globe,* July 14, 1887.

71 "locate, construct and maintain one or more tunnels": Acts and Resolves Passed by the General Court of Massachusetts (Secretary of the Commonwealth, 1887), 1076.

72 "If our delegation will present the name of Mr. Cleveland": *New York Herald,* July 6, 1884.

73 "Governor—Pay no attention to newspaper or other advocacy of me": Grover Cleveland papers, undated letter written from 2 West Fifty-seventh Street, from the papers of WCW, Library of Congress.

74 On a summer's day on the outskirts of downtown Boston: "High Praise for Henry M. Whitney," *Boston Daily Globe,* October 8, 1905.

75 "You'll have to step up on the platform": Ibid.

4: HISTORY MADE IN RICHMOND

78 In the spring of 1882, a skinny young American naval officer: L. R. Hamersley, *First Citizens of the Republic, An Historical Work* (New York, 1895), 141.

79 Sprague was born on July 25, 1857: William D. Middleton and William D. Middleton III, *Frank Julian Sprague: Electrical Inventor and Engineer* (Indiana University Press, 2009), 3–6.

79 "A career afloat was far from my ambition": Frank J. Sprague remarks, *Frank J. Sprague: Seventy Fifth Anniversary* (Frank J. Sprague Anniversary Committee, July 25, 1932), 29.

79 He wrote stories that he filed for *The Boston Herald* while in Asia: Middleton and Middleton, *Frank Julian Sprague,* 24.

79 Two years later, Sprague filed his first patent: Frederick Dalzell, *Engineering Invention: Frank J. Sprague and the U.S. Electrical Industry* (Cambridge: MIT Press, 2010), 49.

80 It was there, while at London's Crystal Palace, that Sprague had the meeting that would change the course of his life: Ibid., 53.

81 "I hear nothing from you as to young Sprague": Thomas Edison Collection, Online Collection, Letter from Edward Johnson to Thomas Edison, April 11, 1883.

81 "I received your favor of the 11th": Ibid., April 23, 1883.

81 "The electric light has long ceased to be a curiosity": "Electric Railways," *Electrical World,* May 5, 1883.

82 "visions of accidents, collisions and crumbling tunnels": Fred T. Jane, "The Romance of Modern London," *English Illustrated Magazine,* August 1893.

83 May 24, 1883, was a sunny day in New York City: David McCullough, *The Great Bridge* (Simon and Schuster Paperbacks, 1972), 525–40.

83 He was thinking only about the job that was waiting for him across the Hudson River: Frank J. Sprague, "Digging in 'The Mines of the Motors,'" *Transactions of the American Institute of Electrical Engineers,* vol. 53, no. 5 (May 1934), 697.

84 "since the president of the United States of America had walked dry shod to Brooklyn from New York": McCullough, *The Great Bridge,* 533.

84 To build the bridge: Ibid.

85 "I arrived home": Sprague, "Digging in 'The Mines of the Motors,'" 697.

85 "The executive department of my body was about to issue an order of ejectment": Kruh, *Always Something Doing,* 38.

85 Aside from feeling underpaid by Edison: Harold C. Passer, *The Electrical Manufacturers, 1875–1900* (Arno Press, 1972), 238–41; Middleton and Middleton, *Frank Julian Sprague,* 39–40.

85 "You will surely understand me": Sprague, letter to Edison, Papers of Frank J. Sprague, New York Public Library, April 24, 1884.

86 "Sprague, as we are about": Edison, letter to Sprague, Ibid., April 25, 1884.

86 In November 1884, with a measly budget of $100,000: Passer, *Electrical Manufacturers,* 238.

86 There, he met a younger, beautiful, dark-haired woman: Middleton and Middleton, *Frank Julian Sprague,* 44.

87 "loveliest and most charming girls": Ibid.

87 "The only true motor": *The Philadelphia Press,* September 21, 1884.

87 "The peculiar device which ought to be adopted in New York and all other cities": "Thomas A. Edison's Plans," *Boston Daily Globe,* January 27, 1886.

88 In early 1886, in a narrow alleyway between two brick buildings near the Durant Sugar Refinery: Middleton and Middleton, *Frank Julian Sprague,* 53.

89 Nervous and determined to make sure his experiment: Passer, *Electrical Manufacturers,* 242; Hammond, *Men and Volts,* 84.

91 "I have presented these facts about the present and future": "Application of Electricity to Propulsion on Elevated Railroads," By Frank J. Sprague, Read before the Society of Arts Boston, 1885, Papers of Frank J. Sprague, New York Public Library, December 10.

91 "Such roads can be built": Ibid.

91 "Dust, smoke, cinders, oil and water will disappear": Ibid.

92 The contract Richmond offered Sprague: Passer, *Electrical Manufacturers,* 243–45.

93 "laid for profit, not for permanence." Frank J. Sprague, "Lessons of the Richmond Electric Railway," *Electrical Engineer,* September 7, 1894, 272.

94 "I was for a moment doubtful of the outcome": Ibid.

94 "go to hell": Middleton and Middleton, *Frank Julian Sprague,* 76–77.

95 "playing mule": Thorburn Reid, "Some Early Traction History," *Cassier's Magazine,* vol. XVI, May–October 1899, 363.

95   Sprague's $110,000 payment was cut to $90,000: Passer, *Electrical Manufacturers*, 244.

96   "the pesky thing": "Electric Street Car," *Boston Daily Globe*, October 11, 1887.

97   "Yes, that bad portion we bought from the Cambridge railroad": Ibid.

98   A month after Whitney's successful test: Middleton and Middleton, *Frank Julian Sprague*, 77; Frank Rowsome Jr., *Trolley Car Treasury* (McGraw-Hill, 1956), 85–86.

98   "If you can get out of such a curve": Sprague, "Lessons of the Richmond Electric Railway," 273.

98   The car, after working so hard, had stalled: Allyn Tunis, "Father of the Trolley: Frank J. Sprague Made Richmond Cradle of Electric Transportation," *Richmond Times-Dispatch*, December 29, 1935.

99   "My own reputation and future career": "A Memorable Anniversary," *Evening Post: New York*, February 3, 1898.

100 And two days after that, a passenger named William A. Boswell: *Richmond Dispatch*, January 10, 1888.

100 "Don't pay a bill that you can help until after April 1st": Letter from Frank J. Sprague to Dana Greene, Papers of Frank J. Sprague, New York Public Library, 1888.

100 "I am completely overwhelmed": Dalzell, *Engineering Invention*, 87.

100 But then one winter morning a new problem greeted Sprague: Sprague, speech to the American Electric Railway Association, "The Growth of Electric Railways," *Proceedings of the American Electric Railway Association*, 1916.

101 "This is hell": Frank J. Sprague, "Electric Traction in Space of Three Dimensions," reprinted from the *Journal of American Academy of Sciences*, July 1932, 6.

102 which he would later call a "supreme moment": Frank J. Sprague, "The Electric Railway," *Century Illustrated Monthly Magazine*, May–October 1905, 519.

102 Sprague had lost more than $75,000: Middleton and Middleton, *Frank Julian Sprague*, 83.

102 "We are ready to run commercially": Letter from Sprague to Henry Whitney, Papers of Frank J. Sprague, New York Public Library, May 16, 1888.

103 "Lincoln set the negroes free! Sprague has set the mule free!": American Electric Railway Association, *Proceedings of the American Electric Railway Association* (1916), 306.

104 On a warm night in early July 1888: *Richmond Dispatch*, July 10, 1888; Sprague, "Digging in 'The Mines of Motors'"; Carlton Norris McKenney, *Rails in Richmond* (Interurban Press, 1986); Frank J. Sprague, "Growth of Electric Railways," *Electrical Engineering*, October 10, 1916, 295–304.

105 "On receiving word about midnight": Sprague, "Lessons of the Richmond Electric Railway," 272.

105 "This was an experiment that had never before been made": "Street Railway Success," *Richmond Daily Times*, July 9, 1888.

106 In 1888, there were six thousand miles of street railway systems: William J. Clark, "Electric Railways in America, From a Business Standpoint," *Cassier's Magazine*, vol. 16, 1899, 519.

5: THE BLIZZARD THAT CHANGED EVERYTHING

111 It was swallowing him up like white quicksand: Samuel Meredith Strong, *The Great Blizzard of 1888* (self-published, 1938), 83–84.

113   John Meisinger, the hardware buyer for E. Ridley and Sons: Jim Murphy, *Blizzard!* (Scholastic, 2000), 2, 12, 63–64.

113   That night, on the ninth floor of the Equitable Building: Tracee de Hahn, *The Blizzard of 1888* (Chelsea House Publishers, 2001), 11–21.

114   It started as a gentle and mild rain: Murphy, *Blizzard!*; de Hahn, *Blizzard of 1888*; Strong, *Great Blizzard of 1888*.

115   "I had the strangest of feelings": Murphy, *Blizzard!*, 9.

116   "Although I had fought the snow for more than four hours": Strong, *Great Blizzard of 1888*, 84.

117   "Jump, for God's sake, jump!": Judd Caplovich, *Blizzard! The Great Storm of '88* (Vero Publishing, 1987), 81.

118   At the New York Infant Asylum: Ibid., 118.

119   "The blizzard sale": Ibid., 128.

120   "Who will be the Moses to lead us through this wilderness of uncertainty": Allan Nevins, *Abram S. Hewitt, with Some Account of Peter Cooper* (Octagon Books, 1967), 497.

6: NEW YORK CITY'S MOSES

121   "The Father of Rapid Transit": "Board Asks to See Subway Sign Contract," *New York Times*, December 2, 1904.

121   "I won't buy them, but I'll give you materials to make them": Polly Guerin, *The Cooper-Hewitt Dynasty of New York* (History Press, 2012), 31.

122   Abram Stevens Hewitt was born in a log house forty miles north of New York City: Nevins, *Abram S. Hewitt*, 15–30.

122   "nearly blind": "Abram Stevens Hewitt," *New York Times*, November 1, 1896.

122   "It taught me for the first time that I could stand in the face of death": Ibid.

123   A cable dispatch on January 23, 1862, changed Hewitt's life: Nevins, *Abram S. Hewitt*, 201–06.

123   "I am told that you can do things which other men declare to be impossible": Ibid., 201.

124   U.S. GRANT, CAIRO. NOT TO BE SWITCHED UNDER PENALTY OF DEATH: Ibid., 204.

124   "If that is so": Ibid.

124   "No effort has been spared": Ibid.

125   "Are you Mr. Hewitt?": "Abram S. Hewitt Dead," *New York Times*, January 19, 1903.

125   "Do you suppose that if I should write on that bill": Nevins, *Abram S. Hewitt*, 205.

125   "O.K. A. Lincoln": Ibid.

126   In 1874, Hewitt changed his residence: "Abram S. Hewitt Dead," *New York Times*, January 19, 1903.

126   His first name was often misspelled in the newspapers as Abraham: Nevins, *Abram S. Hewitt*, 294.

126   "I will make no promises or confessions": Nevins, *Abram S. Hewitt*, 469.

127   "This is the end of my political career": Edmund Morris, *The Rise of Theodore Roosevelt* (Random House, 1979), 831.

128 It was a strange and unsettling time for the city: Nevins, *Abram S. Hewitt*, 480–83.

129 "Can they be closed up?": Ibid., 473.

129 It is "an absolute solution of the problem of rapid transit": Letter from Joe Meigs to Hewitt, Abram S. Hewitt Papers, Cooper Union Library, January 25, 1888.

130 "The time has come": "The Mayor's Big Scheme," *New York Times*, February 1, 1888; "The Mayor's Rapid Transit Plan," *New York Times*, February 1, 1888.

130 "imperial destiny as the greatest city in the world": "New York's Imperial Destiny," *New York Times*, February 5, 1888.

131 "Objections will be made by those who have not fully studied the subject": "The Mayor's Big Scheme," *New York Times*, February 1, 1888.

7: WILLIAM WHITNEY'S MISSED OPPORTUNITY

134 Whenever William Whitney took one of his horses out for a ride: Swanberg, *Whitney Father, Whitney Heiress*, 82.

134 "Mr. Whitney," Rainsford said: Ibid.

135 "Well," Rainsford replied to Whitney's pledge: Ibid., 83.

135 "The driver quarrels with the passengers": John Anderson Miller, *Fares, Please!* (Dover Publications, 1941), 13.

136 "a perpetual city of night": Robert Fogelson, *Downtown: Its Rise and Fall, 1880–1950* (Yale University Press, 2001), 50.

137 Walter Gore Marshall was in Greenwich Village: Walter G. Marshall, *Through America, Or Nine Months in the United States* (Sampson Low, Marston, Searle & Rivington, 1882), 24–28.

138 "Mr. Whitney had more calm, forceful efficiency than any man I ever knew": "W. C. Whitney dead after operation," *The Day*, February 3, 1904: *Life*, February 18, 1904, 158.

138 In Thomas Fortune Ryan, an aggressive Irish-American: Lewis Randolph Hamersley, *First Citizens of the Republic, An Historical Work* (L.R. Hamersley, 1906), 143.

139 Whitney and Ryan helped form the New York Cable Railway Company: Burton J. Hendrick, *The Age of Big Business* (Kessinger Publishing, 1919).

139 It was a formidable team these men created: Burton J. Hendrick, "Great American Fortunes and Their Making: Street Railway Financiers," *McClure's Magazine*, November 1907, 33.

139 "My marriage with Miss Folsom will take place": Ibid., p 306; Hirsch, *Modern Warwick*, 306.

140 On June 2, beginning at 6:30 in the evening: *New York Times*, June 3, 1886.

140 "Grover, do you take this woman": Frederick Elizur Goodrich, "The Life and Public Services of Grover Cleveland" (Winter, 1888), 491.

141 "The Secretary of the Navy has spent much more time in this city": *New York Tribune*, January 17, 1886.

141 "The system could not be perfected with crosstown lines alone": Charles W. Cheape, *Moving the Masses: Urban Public Transit in New York, Boston, and Philadelphia, 1880–1912* (Harvard University Press, 1980), 49.

143   O'Keefe's death caused so much worry: McShane and Tarr, *Horse in the City,* 153.

143   New York City could collect as much as $4.60 per horse for its manure: Ibid., 27.

143   As most New Yorkers slept early on the morning of May 27, 1887: McShane and Tarr, *The Horse in the City,* 102; "Horses Die by Hundreds," *New York Times,* May 27, 1887.

144   And it was only fourteen years old, built in 1873: McShane and Tarr, *Horse in the City,* 102–03.

146   "There is growing public sentiment": *New York Times,* May 29, 1887.

146   a new operation they called the Metropolitan Traction Company: Hirsch, *Modern Warwick,* 223.

146   served as a "holding company," the first one in the United States: Hendrick, "Great American Fortunes and Their Making: Street Railway Financiers."

147   It had been almost six years since September 4, 1882: Jill Jonnes, *Empires of Light: Edison, Tesla, Westinghouse, and the Race to Electrify the World* (Random House Digital, 2003).

147   More than fifteen hundred street lamps were alive in the city by 1886: "On This Day," *New York Times,* March 3, 1888.

149   "New York would undoubtedly lose a great deal in prestige": Burrows and Wallace, *Gotham: A History of New York City to 1898,* 1223.

149   after one o'clock in the afternoon on October 12, 1889: "Met Death in the Wires," *New York Times,* October 12, 1889.

150   "The work your Brother is doing in Boston": Letter from Peter Widener to William C. Whitney, from the papers of WCW, Library of Congress, March 4, 1889.

151   "the cable system was far superior": Cheape, *Moving the Masses,* 60.

152   "Dead Man's Curve": Ibid., 61.

153   "It must be a matter of deep thought to all of us": "City and South London Railway," *Railway Times,* November 8, 1890.

154   "Can this electric railway": "Opening of the Electric Railway," London *Times,* November 5, 1890.

8: THE ENGINEER AND THE PIANO MAKER

155   There were four gangs: "Boring for Rock," *New York Times,* June 14, 1891.

156   "About how far'll they have to go daown": Ibid.

157   At various points along Whitehall Street: Ibid.

158   For an island that stretched only seven miles long: Hood, *722 Miles,* 75–76.

159   "When I squeeze lemons, what I'm after is lemon juice": Arthur Goodrich, "William Barclay Parsons," *The World's Work* (Doubleday, Page, 1903), 3467.

159   dubbed him Reverend Parsons: Tom Malcolm, *William Barclay Parsons: A Renaissance Man of Old New York* (Parsons Brinckerhoff, 2010), 8.

160   the highest scores on record at the school: Ibid.

160   "He has never given me, an anxious, watchful parent, one single cause of complaint": Ibid., 9.

160   "Oh, but this is the part I have rebuilt": Goodrich, *World's Work,* 3468.

161 "will place him in the front rank of the profession in this city": Malcolm, *William Barclay Parsons,* 11.

162 "During these years I was engaged in various private practice": Ibid.

162 "I've had considerable experience in this subject": Letter from Parsons to Hewitt, Abram S. Hewitt Papers, Cooper-Union Library, January 16, 1888.

164 NOW FOR RAPID TRANSIT: *New York Times,* February 1, 1891.

163 anglicized into Steinway: "Steinway to Mark 160th Anniversary with Events, Celebrations," http://www.steinway.com.

165 "The question is practically narrowed down": "Now for Rapid Transit," *New York Times,* February 1, 1891.

166 "the Royal Feast of Belshazzar": Donald Dewey, *The Art of Ill Will: The Story of American Political Cartoons* (New York University Press, 2008), 35.

166 The frustration of the Steinway Commission boiled over: "More Rapid-Transit Talk," *New York Times,* October 3, 1891.

168 On January 1, 1892, a fifteen-year-old Irish girl: "Landed on Ellis Island," *New York Times,* January 2, 1892.

169 "I haven't the slightest doubt that capitalists would have eagerly sought the opportunity": "Money in Rapid Transit," *New York Times,* December 15, 1892.

170 "When this is accomplished": Ibid.

170 at eleven o'clock, the piano king and president of the Steinway commission climbed into bed: William Steinway Diary, 1861–1896, entry for December 21, 1892, http://americanhistory.si.edu/steinwaydiary/diary/?entry=12040&search=burglar.

171 The entire first floor of City Hall was packed: "Failure to Make a Sale," *New York Times,* December 30, 1892.

172 "In what respect is it defective?": Ibid.

172 "Resolved: That the bids made this day by W. Nowland Amory": Ibid.

173 "Much has been made about the objections to underground transit": "Statement of Mr. Steinway," *New York Times,* December 30, 1892.

174 "To my dismay I see I stand alone in my stand to guard the city": The Willliam Steinway Diary, 1861–1896, entry on January 14, 1893.

175 "Hello, Hewitt": Swanberg, *Whitney Father, Whitney Heiress,* 90.

177 "Empire on Wheels": Hirsch, *Modern Warwick,* 421.

179 Many New Yorkers said his hiring "was a mistake": Goodrich, *World's Work,* 3471.

179 "The devil take him": New York Transit Museum with Vivian Heller, *City Beneath Us* (W. W. Norton, 2004), 19.

180 "he doesn't know any better": Goodrich, *World's Work,* 3471.

180 "I am glad I was not older": Malcolm, *William Barclay Parsons,* 17.

9: THE RISE AND FALL OF HENRY WHITNEY

181 "We went to work vigorously on the contract": *Fifty Years of Unified Transportation in Metropolitan Boston* (Boston Elevated Railway Company, 1938), 21–22.

182 "They gave Mr. Whitney permission": Ibid., 22.

182   Pearson worked at the Medford Hillside train station: "Fred Stark Pearson: 1861–1915," *Concise Encyclopedia of Tufts University*, Fred Stark Pearson Papers, Tufts University Library, 356.

183   he offered Pearson $2,500 a year to be the chief engineer: Ibid., 380.

183   "It's got to be done": Ibid., 382.

184   "great electric monsters": Edward H. Clement, "Nineteenth Century Boston Journalism," *New England Magazine*, vol. 37, September 1907–February 1908.

185   "without having been obliged to leave the store.": Fogelson, *Downtown*, 15.

186   "Experience has shown . . . The number of passengers": Auditor's Report, West End Street Railway Company, year ending September 30, 1890.

187   The Reverend William Blaxton was living alone: Lawrence W. Kennedy, *Planning the City Upon a Hill* (University of Massachusetts Press, 1992), 12, 19.

189   On the evening of January 6, 1891, a steady stream of carriages: "Bright Lights, Bright Men, Bright Speeches," *Boston Daily Globe*, January 6, 1891.

190   In 1890, 114 million passengers rode the company's cars: Auditor's Report, West End Street Railway Company, year ending September 30, 1891.

190   "I am in my capacity as president of a transportation company": "Bright Lights, Bright Men, Bright Speeches," *Boston Daily Globe*, January 6, 1891.

191   "The city of Boston is no longer a New England town on a large scale": "Mayor Matthews, Takes the Helm at the City Hall," *Boston Globe*, January 6, 1891.

191   A traffic count on Tremont Street: *Argument of Mayor Matthews Before the Committee on Transit of the Massachusetts Legislature* (Rockwell and Churchill City Printers, 1894), 13.

192   *The New York Times* described him as a "brilliant orator": "Boston's Local Election," *New York Times*, December 8, 1890.

192   those who knew him called him Johnny Fitz: Gerard O'Neill, *Rogues and Redeemers* (Crown Publishers, 2012), 25–32.

194   A two-wheeled invention called a safety bicycle: Samuel Eliot Morison, *One Boy's Boston, 1887–1901* (Northeastern University Press, 1962), 30.

194   "From dusk": Ibid.

194   In 1871, 34 million passengers rode the street railways: Massachusetts Rapid Transit Commission, *1892 Report of the Rapid Transit Commission*, 7.

195   At its first hearing on June 25, 1891: "The Rapid Transit Problem," *Boston Daily Globe*, June 26, 1891.

196   "We intend to hear everybody": Ibid.

196   "The length of this report is greater than we had expected": Report of the Rapid Transit Commission to the Massachusetts Legislature, April 5, 1892, 103.

197   "As a piece of engineering I presume it is perfection": Ibid., 162.

197   "The well-worn list of public works": Report to the Massachusetts Legislature, Massachusetts Commission to Promote Rapid Transit for the City of Boston and Its Suburbs, April 5, 1892, 98.

198   "which shall take the greater part of the through cars": Ibid., 104.

198   "If anything is to be undertaken": Ibid., 106.

198   "Dear Sir": Letter from Nathan Matthews Jr. to William Jackson, Papers of Nathan Matthews Jr., Littauer Library, Harvard University, August 5, 1893.

199 "They were uniformly horrible": Duveneck, *Life on Two Levels*, 18.

200 He gave Josephine a strawberry-colored pony she named Merry Legs: Ibid., 16.

200 The company finished 1892 with $6.3 million in gross earnings: Auditor's Report, West End Street Railway Company, year ending September 30, 1893.

200 "The time has come when I feel that I have not the strength to manage": "Whitney Out," *Boston Daily Globe*, September 7, 1891.

201 "pleasant, personal relations": Letter from Nathan Matthews to Henry Whitney, Letters of Nathan Matthews Jr., City of Boston Archives, March 15, 1893.

202 "Construction would seriously interfere with travel and traffic": "Against the Subway," *Boston Daily Globe*, March 27, 1894.

202 Led by a jeweler named John W. Wilson: "Subway Scare: Merchants Fear Injury to Their Trade," *Boston Daily Globe*, March 26, 1894.

203 "I think that it is a very expensive method of solving that problem": "Against Subway," *Boston Daily Advertiser*, April 30, 1894.

205 On July 23, 1894, the New York Giants visited Boston: "1894 Boston Beaneaters, Schedule, Box Scores and Splits," Sports Reference LLC, http://www.baseball-reference.com/teams/BSN/1894-schedule-scores.shtml.

206 The referendum was passed: "Rapid Transit Act Accepted," *Boston Daily Globe*, July 25, 1894.

206 "I really thought a large number of people demanded an elevated road": Ibid.

206 "I don't believe in a tunnel or a subway": Theodore G. Clarke, *Beacon Hill, Back Bay, and the Building of Boston's Golden Age* (History Press, 2010), 115.

207 "The people have spoken . . . I should assume": "Rapid Transit Act Accepted," *Boston Daily Globe*, July 25, 1894.

10: BIDDING TO BUILD HISTORY

211 Beal hoisted the box up and turned it over: "Bids for First Subway Section," *Boston Daily Globe*, March 21, 1895.

213 "elbowing each other off the sidewalk into the gutter": Fogelson, *Downtown*, 16.

213 There would be eleven sections to the subway: Bradley H. Clarke and O. R. Cummings, *Tremont Street Subway: A Century of Public Service* (Boston Street Railway Association, 1997), 15.

214 "An inclined open entrance to subway in the public garden": *First Annual Report of the Boston Transit Commission, For the Year Ending August 15, 1895* (Rockwell and Church City Printers, 1895), 44.

215 J. W. Hoffman and Co. from Philadelphia bid $181,206: "Bids for First Subway Section," *Boston Daily Globe*, March 21, 1895.

216 Meehan was born in Ireland in 1840: "Looking over Ground," *Boston Daily Globe*, March 27, 1895.

217 Three days after they opened the bids: "Going Right Ahead," *Boston Daily Globe*, March 24, 1895.

218 "The mayor is too busy to attend the proceedings": "Subway Begun," *Boston Daily Globe*, March 19, 1895.

218   "Mr. Crocker of the transit commission": Ibid.
219   "I now proceed to take out the first shovelful of dirt": Ibid.

11: MEEHANVILLE

220   They called it Meehanville: "Subway Work Starts Slowly, Laborers Register at Meehan-
      ville," *Boston Daily Globe,* March 30, 1895.
221   "Do you want to pick and shovel": "Progress of the Subway," *Boston Daily Globe,* April 3,
      1895.
222   "The Italians, you see, they are not wanted": "First Pile for the Subway," *Boston Daily
      Globe,* May 3, 1895.
223   Carson came home on the largest and fastest passenger ship afloat in the 1890s: "Pride of
      City," *Boston Daily Globe,* May 26, 1895.
223   "What's the news in Boston?": Ibid.
224   in Charlestown a *Globe* reporter knocked on the front door: "It's a Humbug," *Boston
      Daily Globe,* March 31, 1895.
225   a young courier raced straight from the statehouse across the street to the Common:
      "Now for a Rush," *Boston Daily Globe,* April 30, 1895.
225   "McCarthy was buried out of sight": Ibid.
227   There were occasionally exciting moments: "Strange Finds on the Subway," *Boston Daily
      Globe,* September 25, 1895.
227   The deeper the workers went, the greater the risk: "Could Not Stand the Gases," *Boston
      Daily Globe,* June 2, 1895.
227   "What's the matter": Ibid.
229   Three plans were studied for the tunnel: *First Annual Report of the Boston Transit Com-
      mission,* 39–43.
230   S. Homer Woodbridge, a heating and ventilating engineer: Ibid., 43.
230   In mid-April, the day arrived: Ibid., 65–68.
231   "buried-alive feeling": Report to the Massachusetts Legislature, Massachusetts Com-
      mission to Promote Rapid Transit for the City of Boston and its Suburbs, April 5, 1892,
      162.
231   "I would say that there would be no danger whatever to the workmen": Annual Report of
      the Boston Transit Commission, Boston Transit Commission, 1895, 66.
231   "The dead are not allowed to rest quietly in their graves": Puleo, *A City So Grand,* 227.
231   Lydia Kimball, died October 29, 1821: Annual Report of the Boston Transit Commis-
      sion, 1895, 70.
232   A week into Green's work in late April 1895: "Bones Identified," *Boston Daily Globe,*
      April 25, 1895.
233   9,000 cubic yards were needed for the Public Garden: *First Annual Report of the Boston
      Transit Commission,* 19.
234   "So rare an opportunity for making this important improvement": Ibid., 62.
235   By early May, 130 elm trees: "Hills and Hollows," *Boston Daily Globe,* May 9, 1895.
235   2,300-pound pile driver: "Last Tomb Demolished," *Boston Daily Globe,* May 8, 1895.

235 David Keefe, a young worker from Charlestown: "Keefe's Narrow Escape," *Boston Daily Globe*, May 22, 1895.

236 Reverend Isaac J. Lansing, an odd-looking pastor with a small chin: "Infernal Hole," *Boston Daily Globe*, November 25, 1895.

237 On March 28, 1896, a large party gathered at the Hotel Thorndike: "Were in a Hole," *Boston Daily Globe*, March 28, 1896.

239 "This subway is like a ship": "Another Opening Made," *Boston Daily Globe*, July 27, 1895.

239 "Now . . . we will ascend by this ladder": "Inspecting the Subway," *Boston Daily Globe*, April 23, 1896.

240 "the finest example of concrete work to be found anywhere on the American continent": Ibid.

241 In February 1897, a gigantic new piece of equipment: "Labor and Time Saving Machine," *Boston Daily Globe*, February 15, 1897.

242 "labor and time saving machine": Ibid.

243 "I had hoped to go through with this job without injuring a man": "Keefe's Narrow Escape," *Boston Daily Globe*, May 22, 1895.

244 He dropped forty-two feet to his death: *Annual Report to the Boston Transit Commission* (Rockwell and Churchill, 1897), 40.

12: BOOM!

245 James Groake took hold of a lantern with a candle burning: *Wolf Koplan v. Boston Gas Light Company*, Defendant's Bill of Exceptions, Superior Court, Suffolk County, Massachusetts (Alfred Mudge and Son, 1900).

246 The biggest attraction besides the subway project: "Fall of Babylon," *Boston Daily Globe*, February 9, 1897.

247 Just after eight o'clock: *Wolf Koplan v. Boston Gas Light Company*; "Court Admits It," *Boston Daily Globe*, November 19, 1898.

247 two thousand leaks, or about twenty per day: *Wolf Koplan v. Boston Gas Light Company*.

247 The leather badge: "Licenses to Boston Bootblacks and Newsboys," *Boston Traveller*, March 5, 1868.

248 When Koplan got to his corner: "The Suit of Wolf Koplan, the Bootblack," *Boston Journal*, October 19, 1900.

248 The smell had been getting worse for months: "Told by Eyewitnesses," *Boston Daily Globe*, March 5, 1897.

248 responsible for killing a cat: "Piling up Facts," *Boston Daily Globe*, April 1, 1897.

248 "The subway people were to blame": Ibid.

249 When the police officer Michael Whalen first detected the smell of gas: "Many Smelled the Gas," *Boston Daily Globe*, March 5, 1897.

249 "Do you smell that?": *Wolf Koplan v. Boston Gas Light Company*.

250 "Are you the Boston Gas Light Company?": Ibid.

250 A few minutes before noon, three crowded streetcars rounded the corner: "Story of the Explosion," *Boston Daily Globe,* March 5, 1897.

251 As Wolf Koplan gave one last wipe: "The Suit of Wolf Koplan, the Bootblack," *Boston Journal,* October 19, 1900.

251 He cut his right thumb badly: "Court Admits It," *Boston Daily Globe,* November 19, 1898.

252 "The people didn't have a chance for their lives": "People in Car Had No Chance," *Boston Daily Globe,* March 5, 1897.

252 Reverend W. A. Start, the Tufts University bursar: "Six Killed, Others May Die," *Boston Daily Globe,* March 5, 1897.

253 "It certainly seems that this accident could not have occurred": "Mayor Quincy's Statement," *Boston Daily Globe,* March 5, 1897.

254 Carson wasted no time touring the tunnel: "Subway Is Not Injured," *Boston Daily Globe,* March 5, 1897.

255 "It isn't often that home news outshadows the inauguration of a new president": "Story of the Explosion," *Boston Daily Globe,* March 5, 1897.

255 On July 3, 1897, Sam Little invited a dozen reporters: "Rapid Transit Insured," *Boston Daily Globe,* July 4, 1897.

256 On August 25 the joyous mood of the city: "Derrick Toppled Over," *Boston Daily Globe,* August 26, 1897.

257 "remarkable . . . so conservative an American town": "Boston's Subway Finished," *New York Times,* August 15, 1897.

13: "FIRST CAR OFF THE EARTH!"

259 She must have been quite the sight: "First Car off the Earth!," *Boston Daily Globe,* September 1, 1897.

261 "birds were bubbling with the exuberance of morning": Ibid.

261 "It has more galleries, colonnades, piazzas, and passages than I can remember": Charles Dickens Online: The Works and Life of Charles Dickens, http://www.dickens-online.info/american-notes-page16.html.000.

263 Strapping James Reed: "Reward for Faithfulness," *Boston Daily Globe,* September 1, 1897.

264 "All aboard for the subway and Park Street": "First Car Off the Earth," *Boston Daily Globe,* September 2, 1897.

264 He announced that his name was C. W. Davis: "First Car off the Earth!" *Boston Daily Globe,* September 1, 1897.

267 A "horror of tunnels": Fogelson, *Downtown,* 57.

267 "the roaring of the ocean after a storm": Report to the Massachusetts Legislature, Massachusetts Commission to Promote Rapid Transit for the City of Boston and Its Suburbs, April 5, 1892, 155.

267 "Oh, dear, isn't it delightful": "First Car off the Earth!" *Boston Daily Globe,* September 1, 1897.

267 "What a difference there was in the ride this morning": Ibid.

268 "O, Mister Captain, stop the ship!" Ibid.

268 "Bravo, bravo": Ibid.

269 "Damn me if I'll go through this again": Ibid.

269 They were especially admiring of the subway employees: Ibid.

271 "hissed along like a brood of vipers": Ibid.

271 The turnstile was a new contraption for the times: "Novelty Over," *Boston Daily Globe*, September 3, 1897.

271 When one exceptionally overweight gentleman got stuck: "Every Car Crowded," *Boston Daily Globe*, September 2, 1897.

272 By 11:15 A.M., one office had sold 2,500 tickets: Ibid.

272 "Why can't the conductors take cash fares on the cars as before": Ibid.

272 "It's a shame to have such incompetents doing such work": "First Car off the Earth," *Boston Daily Globe*, September 1, 1897.

274 "Nearly everything went as smooth": Ibid.

274 "If a woman should fall": Ibid.

274 "Hmmm": Ibid.

274 "I think Boston is going to like it and like it a great deal": Ibid.

14: THE BRAINS, THE BUILDER, AND THE BANKER

275 "In spite of these precautions, however, the air in the tunnel is extremely offensive . . . small, badly ventilated": W. M. Barclay Parsons, "Report on Rapid Transit in Foreign Cities," 1894, 10.

277 "decidedly novel features": Ibid., 51.

277 "These motors are designed to attain a speed of fifty miles per hour": Ibid., 52.

277 "This is due largely to the confusion": Ibid., 57.

278 "the nervous and active temperament of the people": Ibid.

278 "There is a wide-spread popular idea": Ibid., 60.

278 "On [steam] locomotives": Ibid., 10.

279 "the balance of economy is in favor of electricity": Ibid., 63.

280 On March 12, 1895, fifty angry developers stampeded into a meeting: "Property Owners Object," *New York Times*, March 13, 1895.

281 "I feel that an elevated railroad would be ruinous to this property": Ibid.

281 "What character of construction other than a viaduct would you advise?": Ibid.

281 "I am prepared to act understandingly": "Great West Side Wins," *New York Times*, March 20, 1895.

282 "More than 1,800 years ago": *Report of the Board of Rapid Transit Railroad Commissioners for the City of New York* (W. P. Mitchell and Sons, 1896), 114.

283 "It means the end": "Decides Against Tunnel," *New York Times*, May 23, 1896.

283 "You must excuse me": "Mr. Parsons Not Communicative," *New York Times*, May 23, 1896.

284 "exceedingly expensive . . . It is therefore not unlikely that within a couple of years": "Boston's Subway Finished," *New York Times*, August 15, 1897.

284 "We have the worst": New York Transit Museum with Heller, *City Beneath Us*, 20.

286 "They are very similar to our Boston plans": "Subway Plans Favored," *New York Times,* October 7, 1897.

286 he drank a glass of pilsner at ten thirty before going off to bed: William Steinway Diary, entry for August 6, 1896, http://americanhistory.si.edu/steinwaydiary/diary /?entry=12040&search=burglar.

287 "I am not and will not be a presidential candidate": "So says Ex Secretary of the Navy William C. Whitney: 'I am not a candidate!'" *Boston Daily Globe,* June 10, 1895.

288 Her head slammed with a sickening thud: "Met with an Accident," *Boston Daily Globe,* February 22, 1898.

289 *The Times* projected that if the new route carried: "Profits of the Underground Road," *New York Times,* November 29, 1899.

289 one of New York's most famous lawyers, Wheeler H. Peckham: "Boston's Subway Favored," *New York Times,* October 7, 1897.

290 Even the steady rain and soggy snow falling: "Damp Day for Old New York," *New York Times,* January 1, 1898.

292 Before leaving, Parsons penned a seven-page letter: Malcolm, *William Barclay Parsons,* 19–20.

293 He offered to build the subway within three years: "All City Railways in One," *New York Times,* March 30, 1899.

293 In a statement released by his company on April 17, 1899: "Subway Bid Withdrawn," *New York Times,* April 18, 1899.

294 mountains of peanut shells, and random pieces of clothing: "City's Greeting to 1900," *New York Times,* January 2, 1900.

294 "Money is not so cheap now": "Bids for Rapid Transit," *New York Times,* January 12, 1900.

294 On Monday around eleven o'clock, January 15, 1900: "Two Rapid Transit Bids Are Received," *New York Times,* January 16, 1900.

296 "I expect to get the contract": Ibid.

297 "My Dear Mr. Orr": "Mr. Whitney to Mr. Orr," *New York Times,* January 18, 1900.

298 "Absurd!": "Mr. M'Donald Gets Rapid Transit Work," *New York Times,* January 17, 1900.

298 he enjoyed a quiet dinner and drinks at the Hotel Savoy: Ibid.

300 "Yes, I am Mr. McDonald's financial agent": "Rapid Transit Situation," *New York Times,* January 30, 1900.

300 Three weeks later, on February 24, 1900: "The Rapid Transit Contract Is Signed," *New York Times,* February 25, 1900.

300 "Here is the gentleman who gives me the privilege of signing this contract": Ibid.

301 "I am a contractor, not a railroad man": Brian Cudahy, *A Century of Subways: Celebrating 100 Years of New York's Underground Railways* (Oxford University Press, 2009), 10.

301 "I found the door closed": James Blaine Walker, *Fifty Years of Rapid Transit, 1864–1917* (Law Print, 1918), 169.

302 "I resolved to go straight to a man who was all powerful": Ibid.

302 It was a secret that Whitney took to his grave: "Crisis in Subways that Belmont Met," *New York Times,* October 2, 1913.

303 "Constructing the tunnel will be simple": "Talks of Tunnel Plans," *New York Times,* January 18, 1900.

15: PLAYING WITH DYNAMITE

304 "stood out like poppies in a dandelion field": "Edwin A. Robinson, Poet, Is Dead at 66," *New York Times,* April 6, 1935.

305 "Haven't you any water or soap in Yonkers?": "Dirty Italians Lectured," *New York Times,* March 25, 1900.

306 It was supposed to be a miserable day of rain: "Rapid Transit Tunnel Begun," *New York Times,* March 25, 1900.

307 "The completion of this undertaking": Ibid.

307 "Bravo, old man": Ibid.

308 "If your laborers shirk work like that": Bobrick, *Labyrinths of Iron,* 227.

308 Two days later, on March 26, 1900, at the corner of Bleecker and Greene streets: "Actual Work on the Big Tunnel Begun," *New York Times,* March 27, 1900.

309 A single actor named Joseph Jefferson played Rip Van Winkle more than 2,500 times: Felicia Londre and Margot Berthold, *The History of World Theater* (Continuum International Publishing Group, 1999), 213.

309 At Sherry's on Forty-fourth Street and Fifth Avenue: New York Public Library, Menus, http://menus.nypl.org/menus/13242.

310 Giant mastodon bones surfaced near Dyckman Street: New York Transit Museum with Heller, *City Beneath Us,* 19.

311 It came to be called the Bloody Pit: Carl Byron, *A Pinprick of Light* (New England Press, 1995), 1.

312 "I am no prophet": *New York World,* December 23, 2004.

312 His task was a routine and essential one: "Rapid Transit Sub-Contract Let," *New York Times,* March 24, 1900.

313 A mixture of Italians, Swedes, blacks, and Irish: "Actual Work on the Big Tunnel Begun," *New York Times,* March 27, 1900.

313 "I'm on strike": "Tunnel Strike Was Brief," *New York Times,* April 3, 1900.

316 It sat on a rock at such a steep angle: Hood, *722 Miles,* 87.

317 Ira Shaler was never the war hero like his father: "Major Ira A. Shaler Dead," *New York Times,* June 30, 1902.

318 "Run for your life!": "Death in Tunnel Dynamite Explosion," *New York Times,* January 28, 1902.

318 On the morning of January 27: Ibid.

318 "blow the whole hill to hell": "Excess of Dynamite Stored in Tunnel," *New York Times,* February 5, 1902.

319 "I thought the end of us had come": Ibid.

319 But the hotel manager, a kindly fellow named Washington L. Jacques: Ibid.

320 "I knew that something big was on hand": Ibid.

320 Two months after the fatal blast: "Cave-in and Ruin Along Park Avenue," *New York Times,* March 22, 1902.

321 "This accident. . . . was one which could not be foreseen": Ibid.

321 "Hoodoo Contractor": "Major Shaler Crushed Under Fall of Rock," *New York Times,* June 18, 1902.

322 They arrived on June 17, a few minutes before eight o'clock, and all three men walked down into the ground: Ibid.

322 "That stone doesn't look right to me": New York Transit Museum with Heller, *City Beneath Us*, 22.

323 "I think my back is broken": "Major Shaler Crushed Under Fall of Rock," *New York Times*, June 18, 1902.

323 "It was simply Major Shaler's ill fortune": Malcolm, *William Barclay Parsons*, 51.

323 Shaler's death shook Parsons: Ibid.

323 "We have the tools and machinery": "Parsons and McDonald Clash over Subway," *New York Times*, September 18, 1903.

324 "Clash?" Parsons answered: Ibid.

324 Andrew Carnegie, was awarded the bid to supply: "Sub-Contracts for Tunnel Awarded," *New York Times*, April 17, 1900.

326 The moment the Miners' Union got word: "Miners Flock to New York," *New York Times*, April 28, 1901.

327 "they are in love with life in the bowels of the earth": Ibid.

328 It was about ten thirty at night on October 24: "Death and Destruction by Subway Blast," *New York Times*, October 25, 1903; "Ten Were Killed in Subway Disaster," *New York Times*, October 26, 1903.

329 "Kyrie, eleison," or "Lord have mercy": Ibid.

329 "Sorry for you, little man": Ibid.

329 "Whether the falling in of the mass of rock was due to moisture": Ibid.

329 "a seam that could not have been detected": Malcolm, *William Barclay Parsons*, 52.

330 "The rock was weaker than any of us knew": New York Transit Museum with Heller, *City Beneath Us*, 23.

331 On New Year's Day of 1904, New York's newest mayor: "On Handcars Through Six Miles of Subway," *New York Times*, January 2, 1904.

331 On January 28, 1904, a Thursday evening, Whitney joined his secretary: "William C. Whitney Passes Away," *New York Times*, February 3, 1904.

332 eulogized Whitney in the pages of *Harper's Weekly*: "William Collins Whitney," *Harper's Weekly*, February 27, 1904.

332 Dr. Thomas Darlington, New York's commissioner for public health, wrote an essay in the Sunday *World*: Bobrick, *Labyrinths of Iron*, 232.

333 *If a fuse on the front engine burns out*: "Some Subway 'Ifs' and 'Don'ts,'" *New York Times*, October 27, 1904.

16: OCTOBER 27, 1904

335 For older New Yorkers, October 27, 1904, had a familiar feel: "Our Subway Open, 150,000 Try It; Mayor McClellan Runs the First Official Train," *New York Times*, October 28, 1904.

336 "Git a programme": Ibid.

337 "I don't want the public to pass judgment on the road": "Subway Opening Today with Simple Ceremony," *New York Times*, October 27, 1904.

337 "Presented to August Belmont by the directors": "Loving Cup to Belmont Given at Sub-way Feast," *New York Times*, October 28, 1904.

338 "The subway would not have been built if I had not taken hold of the work": Walker, *Fifty Years of Rapid Transit*, 167.

339 "When the dirt is off your shovel": Michael W. Brooks, *Subway City: Riding the Trains, Reading New York* (Rutgers University Press, 1997), 64.

339 "Without rapid transit, Greater New York": "Exercises in City Hall," *New York Times*, October 28, 1904.

339 "Mr. Mayor, Mr. Orr, and Mr. President": Ibid.

339 "I scarcely believe that their patience": Ibid.

340 "I, as mayor, in the name of the people": Ibid.

340 "Doesn't fit very well": "McClellan Motorman of First Subway Train," *New York Times*, October 28, 1904.

341 "Shall I slow her down here": Ibid.

342 "Slower, here, sloooow-er!" Ibid.

342 "Well, that was a little tiresome": Ibid.

343 In the next five hours, 111,881 passengers would pay to ride the subway: "Rush Hour Blockade Jams Subway Crowds," *New York Times*, October 29, 1904.

343 "Let 'em in": "McClellan Motorman of First Subway Train," *New York Times*, October 28, 1904.

EPILOGUE

346 In Boston, on September 3, 1897, two day after America's first subway opened: "Novelty Over," *Boston Daily Globe*, September 3, 1897.

347 F. B. Shipley stood up: "Our Subway Open, 150,000 Try It," *New York Times*, October 28, 1904.

347 And it took barely a minute of operation: "Lost Diamonds in Subway," *New York Times*, October 28, 1904.

349 Sadly for Sprague, who died on October 25: Harriet Chapman Jones Sprague, *Frank J. Sprague and the Edison Myth* (William Frederick Press, 1947).

350 A rambling letter to his daughter Laura in 1914: Letter from Henry Whitney to daughter, October 28, 1914, courtesy of Laura Marshall to author.

351 And all he left behind was $1,221.93, a $400 Dodge: "H.M. Whitney Left $1,221," *New York Times*, June 22, 1923.

351 On a bitter morning in February 1912: "Visit Old Pneumatic Tunnel," *New York Times*, February 9, 1912; Brennan, *Beach Pneumatic*; Hood, *722 Miles*, 48.

353 One count tallied 2,131 shipwrecks: Malcolm, *William Barclay Parsons*, 78.

354 On March 21, 2013, a present-day sandhog: "To Save a Man's Life, a Muddy Tug of War with the Earth Itself," *New York Times*, March 20, 2013; "Trapped Worker Rescued by FDNY Says Thanks," New York *Daily News*, April 17, 2013.

355 In New York, 1.7 billion trips: MTA Facts and Figures, http://www.mta.info/nyct/facts/ffsubway.htm; "MBTA Ridership Hits New Record," *Boston Globe*, July 31, 2012.

355   an article appeared in the *Los Angeles Times*: "L.A. to N.Y. in Half an Hour?," *Los Angeles Times*, June 11, 1972.

356   "Safe, convenient, low-cost, efficient": Robert M. Salter, "Trans-Planetary Subway Systems," The Rand Paper Series, The Rand Corporation, February 1978, 1.

BIBLIOGRAPHY

Blodgett, Geoffrey. *The Gentle Reformers: Massachusetts Democrats in the Cleveland Era.* Cambridge: Harvard University Press, 1966.

Bobrick, Benson. *Labyrinths of Iron: Subways in History, Myth, Art, Technology, and War.* New York: Henry Holt, 1981.

———. *Parsons Brinckerhoff: The First 100 Years.* New York: Van Nostrand Reinhold, 1985.

Brennan, Joseph. *Beach Pneumatic: Alfred Beach's Pneumatic Subway and the Beginnings of Rapid Transit in New York.* 2004–05. http://www.columbia.edu/~brennan/beach/.

Burrows, Edwin G., and Mike Wallace. *Gotham: A History of New York City to 1898.* New York: Oxford University Press, 1999.

Byron, Carl. *A Pinprick of Light: The Troy and Greenfield Railroad and Its Hoosac Tunnel.* Shelburne, Vt.: New England Press, 1974.

Caplovich, Judd. *Blizzard! The Great Storm of '88.* Vernon, Conn.: VeRo, 1987.

Cashman, Sean Dennis. *America in the Gilded Age: From the Death of Lincoln to the Rise of Theodore Roosevelt.* New York: New York University Press, 1984.

Cheape, Charles W. *Moving the Masses: Urban Public Transit in New York, Boston, and Philadelphia, 1880–1912.* Cambridge: Harvard University Press, 1980.

Clarke, Bradley H., and O. R. Cummings. *Tremont Street Subway: A Century of Public Service.* Boston: Boston Street Railway Association, 1997.

Clarke, Ted. *Brookline, Allston-Brighton and the Renewal of Boston.* Charleston: History Press, 2010.

Cudahy, Brian. *Cash, Tokens and Transfers: A History of Urban Mass Transit in North America.* New York: Fordham University Press, 1982.

———. *Change at Park Street Under.* Brattleboro, Vt.: Stephen Greene Press, 1972.

Dalzell, Frederick. *Engineering Invention: Frank J. Sprague and the U.S. Electrical Industry.* Cambridge: MIT Press, 2010.

De Hahn, Tracee. *The Blizzard of 1888.* Philadelphia: Chelsea House Publishers, 2001.

Duveneck, Josephine Whitney. *Life on Two Levels: An Autobiography*. Los Altos Hills, Calif.: Trust for Hidden Villa, 1978.

Fogelson, Robert. *Downtown: Its Rise and Fall, 1880–1950*. New Haven: Yale University Press, 2001.

Gies, Joseph. *Adventure Underground: The Story of the World's Greatest Tunnels*. New York: Doubleday, 1962.

Hirsch, Mark David. *William C. Whitney: Modern Warwick*. Archon Books, 1969.

Howard, Brett. *Boston: A Social History*. New York: Hawthorn Books, 1976.

Hoyt, Edwin. *The Whitneys: An Informal Portrait, 1635–1975*. New York: Weybright and Talley, 1976.

Illustrated Boston, the Metropolis of New England. New York: American Publishing and Engraving, 1889.

Katz, Wallace B. *The New York Rapid Transit Decision of 1900*. Washington, D.C.: Department of the Interior, National Park Service, n.d. http://www.nycsubway.org/wiki/The_New _York_Rapid_Transit_Decision_of_1900_(Katz).

Kay, Jane Holtz. *Lost Boston*. Boston: Houghton Mifflin, 1980.

Kennedy, Lawrence. *Planning the City Upon a Hill: Boston Since 1630*. Amherst: University of Massachusetts Press, 1992.

King, Moses. *King's Handbook of Boston*. Cambridge: Moses King, 1883.

Kruh, David. *Always Something Doing: Boston's Infamous Scollay Square*. Boston: Northeastern University Press, 1989.

Lyons, Louis. *Newspaper Story: One Hundred Years of "The Boston Globe."* Cambridge: Belknap Press of Harvard University Press, 1971.

MacGillivray, Don. "Henry Melville Whitney Comes to Cape Breton: The Saga of a Gilded Age Entrepreneur." *Acadiensis*, vol. 9, no. 1, Autumn 1979.

Malcolm, Tom. *William Barclay Parsons: A Renaissance Man of Old New York*. New York: Parsons Brinckerhoff, 2010.

McCullough, David. *The Great Bridge: The Epic Story of the Building of the Brooklyn Bridge*. New York: Simon and Schuster, 1983.

McShane, Clay, and Joel A. Tarr. *The Horse in the City: Living Machines in the Nineteenth Century*. Baltimore: The Johns Hopkins University Press, 2007.

Middleton, William D., and William D. Middleton III. *Frank Julian Sprague: Electrical Inventor and Engineer*. Bloomington: Indiana University Press, 2009.

Miller, John Anderson. *Fares, Please! A Popular History of Trolleys, Horsecars, Streetcars, Buses, Elevateds, and Subways*. New York: Dover Publications, 1941.

Morison, Samuel Eliot. *One Boy's Boston, 1887–1901*. Boston: Northeastern University Press, 1962.

Murray, Don. *Man Against Earth: The Story of Tunnels and Tunnel Builders*. Philadelphia: J. B. Lippincott, 1961.

Nevins, Allan. *Abram S. Hewitt with Some Account of Peter Cooper*. New York: Octagon Books, 1967.

New York Transit Museum with Vivian Heller. *The City Beneath Us: Building the New York Subway*. New York: W. W. Norton, 2004.

O'Neill, Gerard. *Rogues and Redeemers: When Politics Was King in Irish Boston*. New York: Crown Publishers, 2012.

Passer, Harold C. *The Electrical Manufacturers, 1875–1900*. New York: Arno Press, 1972.

Puleo, Stephen. *A City So Grand: The Rise of an American Metropolis*. Boston: Beacon Press, 2010.

Rowsome, Frank Jr. *Trolley Car Treasury: A Century of American Streetcars, Horsecars, Cable Cars, Interurbans, and Trolleys*. New York: McGraw-Hill, 1956.

Sandler, Martin. *Secret Subway: The Fascinating Tale of an Amazing Feat of Engineering*. Washington, D.C.: National Geographic Society, 2009.

Sprague, Harriet Chapman Jones. *Frank J. Sprague and the Edison Myth*. New York: William Frederick Press, 1947.

Sproat, Barbara J. *Boston: Studies in Urban Political Economy: Henry Whitney's Streetcar Suburb: Beacon Street, Brookline, 1870–1910*. Center for the Study of Metropolitan Problems, 1974.

Strong, Samuel Meredith. *The Great Blizzard of 1888*. New York: Samuel Meredith Strong, 1938.

Swanberg, W. A. *Whitney Father, Whitney Heiress*. New York: Charles Scribner's Sons, 1980.

Vrabel, Jim. *When in Boston*. Boston: Northeastern University Press, 2004.

Walker, James Blaine. *Fifty Years of Rapid Transit*. New York: Law Printing, 1918.

Warner, Sam Bass Jr. *Streetcar Suburbs: The Process of Growth in Boston, 1870–1900*. Cambridge: Harvard University Press, 1962.

Weinstein, Asha Elizabeth. "The Congestion Evil: Perceptions of Traffic Congestion in Boston in the 1890s and 1920s." PhD diss., University of California, Berkeley, 2002.

Williams, Rosalind. *Notes on the Underground: An Essay on Technology, Society and the Imagination*. Cambridge: MIT Press, 2008.

Wolmar, Christian. *The Subterranean Railway: How the London Underground Was Built and How It Changed the City Forever*. London: Atlantic Books, 2004.

INDEX